THE EXCEPTIONAL STUDENT IN THE REGULAR CLASSROOM

THE EXCEPTIONAL STUDENT IN THE REGULAR CLASSROOM

FOURTH EDITION

BILL R. GEARHEART
MEL W. WEISHAHN
CAROL J. GEARHEART

University of Northern Colorado

Merrill Publishing Company
A Bell & Howell Information Company
Columbus Toronto London Melbourne

Cover Photo: Merrill Publishing/Tom Hubbard

Published by Merrill Publishing Company
A Bell & Howell Information Company
Columbus, Ohio 43216

This book was set in Usherwood.

Administrative Editor: Vicki Knight
Developmental Editor: Amy Macionis
Production Coordinator: Linda Bayma
Art Coordinator: Pete Robison
Cover Designer: Cathy Watterson
Text Designer: Cynthia Brunk

Library of Congress Catalog Card Number: 87–61706
International Standard Book Number: 0–675–20830–0
Printed in the United States of America
1 2 3 4 5 6 7 8 9 — 92 91 90 89 88

Photo credits: All photos copyrighted by individuals or
companies listed. Anne Carlsen School, p. 218; Ben
Asen/Envision, pp. 9, 110, 185; Edgar Bernstein, pp. 308,
368; Barbara Clark, *Growing Up Gifted,* Merrill
Publishing, p. 379; Fritz Locke/Edgar Bernstein, p. 144;
Merrill Publishing, p. 172/photographs by Andy Brunk,
pp. 242, 305, Jerry Garvey, p. 43, Jean Greenwald, pp.
101, 139, Mary Hagler, pp. 32, 164, Jo Hall, p. 3, Tom
Hubbard, p. 227, Bruce Johnson, pp. 53, 89, 252, 257,
332, Lloyd Lemmermann, pp. 57, 247, 262, 353; Tom
Morton, pp. 19, 46, 188, 223, 293, 357; Harvey
Phillips/Phillips Photo Illustrators, pp. 17, 23, 151, 240,
269, 284; Phonic Ear, Inc., p. 219; Prentke Romich
Company, pp. 217, 218, 219; Charles Quinlan, p. 273;
Blair Seitz/Robert Maust Photography, p. 91; Ronald
Stewart, pp. 163, 166, 169, 171; Strix Pix/David S.
Strickler, pp. 73, 80, 123; Tom Tondee, p. 213; William
Williamson, pp. 156, 157, 158, 159, 160.

PREFACE

This fourth edition of *The Exceptional Student in the Regular Classroom* reflects a continued effort to fulfill what we believe to be a critical need. This need was great even when we wrote the first edition of this text. Public Law (PL) 94-142 had not yet been passed, and our concern was with the growing number of handicapped students in regular classrooms in school districts where students were integrated because someone believed it was the right thing to do, not because of federal mandate. In those settings, even though teachers needed information and assistance, the attitude was positive because the program was generated by interest and a belief in principle.

After the passage of PL 94-142 and the mandate to integrate handicapped students whenever possible, "mainstreaming" was implemented in a hurry, in too many cases with little motivation except to obtain federal dollars for compliance to the law. Administrators who organized such implementation often understood neither the needs of handicapped students nor the law. At times, students in critical need of a great deal of specialized support were inappropriately placed in regular classes with little or no support. When this happened, teachers were upset and confused and there was limited benefit to students. Even if the letter of the law was seemingly satisfied, the spirit and purpose was not. For some teachers and some students, those were very difficult years.

Today the situation is much improved. Though there will always be some problems when our point of focus is students with learning difficulties, what is happening in our schools is most encouraging. An increasing number of regular classroom teachers truly believe in the principle of maximum integration consistent with good educational practice, and the future seems bright. As new teachers complete their college teacher-education programs, they learn about the needs of exceptional students and expect to have them in their classes. This is where we hope this text will have its primary application. We have worked with teachers too long to believe that we might somehow, in one text, provide sufficient information and insights to make every teacher an "expert" in work with exceptional children. We have, however, tried to provide a base on which teachers might build to increase their competence and therefore become more effective in their work with students with special needs.

In this edition we have made some significant changes, in addition to updating basic information. At the suggestion of readers of the third edition, we have reorganized the content to present most of the information generally applicable across the various exceptionalities in the first part (chapters 1–4). This sets the stage for part two, in which we consider the eight exceptionalities. In each of these eight chapters, we review definitions, characteristics, and teaching strategies. In addition to considering what the regular classroom teacher should do, we outline what should be expected of the special educator and provide suggestions to maximize the effectiveness of the cooperative efforts so essential to success with students with special needs.

In our 60 years combined experience in special education we have learned from both teachers and students. We are grateful for the learning opportunities afforded us and have tried to share our knowledge with the readers of this text.

In addition to the many individuals who have provided suggestions for improvement, new teaching ideas, and the like, certain others provided more specific assistance. We would like to acknowledge these individuals, offering our sincere thanks to Cliff Baker, George Betts, LeAnn Olson, Irving Sato, Dean Tuttle, and Elaine Uhrig. Finally, we want to acknowledge the excellent assistance provided by reviewers who were contacted by our editor and were responsible to our publisher; namely, Rachel Bruno, Northern Kentucky University; Ann Carroll, University of Denver; Ralph G. Leverett, Trevecca College; Patricia M. Phipps, California State University—Chico; Thomassine Sellars, San Francisco State University; Rochelle Simms, Louisiana State University; and John Toker, Kearney State College.

We appreciate user response to our third edition, and hope that this fourth edition will merit continued acceptance. We are even more pleased to see that regular classroom teachers are accepting students with special needs as part of their classes and are teaching them with increasing skill. We want to remain a part of this effort.

Bill Gearheart
Mel Weishahn
Carol Gearheart

TO THE READER

DISCUSSIONS OF SPECIFIC EXCEPTIONALITIES

Our major interest is to assist regular classroom teachers to better understand, and thus to teach more effectively, exceptional students. The term *exceptional students* is meant to include all those whose educational needs are not effectively met through use of the usual, or "standard," curriculum; thus they may also be called *special-needs* students. They are in common practice (including most state and federal laws and regulations) identified as hearing impaired, visually impaired, gifted, mentally retarded, etc., but these labels can be misleading. They are misleading if they lead us to believe, when we use the term *hearing impaired* or *mentally retarded,* that all students with the same label share all the same characteristics. Nothing could be more inaccurate. There are certain characteristics that apply to each exceptionality (i.e., all hearing impaired students have some hearing loss), but beyond that,

each student is an individual, with unique characteristics and learning abilities. As we discuss the major characteristics associated with the various exceptionalities, it is important to remember that these are generalizations.

One other misconception is sufficiently important that we want to attempt to guard against it in advance. Because of the manner in which this text is written, we will sometimes speak of the exceptionalities in a manner that might lead the reader to think that each is always separate and discrete. This, too, is inaccurate. Even though we may discuss the exceptionalities separately, they often overlap. For example, a student with a moderate hearing loss may also be mildly mentally retarded, or an orthopedically impaired student may also have a speech impairment. For this reason, suggestions made with reference to students with one particular disability may be appropriate to students with other disabilities. We ask the reader to consider the overlapping of exceptionalities, and of educational-strategy suggestions each time a specific exceptionality is discussed.

USE OF CERTAIN TERMINOLOGY

We have attempted to use a minimum of special and/or technical terms, but our use of certain terms requires special comment. For example, we have used *mainstreaming* and *integration* interchangeably in many instances. We would rather not use the word *mainstreaming* because it has been misused and misunderstood, but it is in common use; thus we felt the need to discuss and define it. Integration of handicapped students means (to us) assisting students to become as much a part of the mainstream as possible; it im-

plies and requires concerted joint efforts on the part of regular and special educators.

"Regular classroom teachers" or "regular educators," that is, educators who are not trained special educators, are the dedicated professionals to whom our text is addressed. They are the most important agents in vitalizing the process of integration.

Finally, the terms *handicapped, handicapping conditions,* and *disabilities* are used interchangeably. You should note, however, that there is disagreement among national organizations that have been established on behalf of persons with disabilities (or handicaps, or handicapping conditions) and among our colleagues in higher education as to just how these terms should be used.

CONTENTS

PART ONE

SETTING THE STAGE AND CREATING THE CLIMATE

This part (chapters 1–4) establishes the framework for consideration of the unique educational needs of students who may be classified as having a specific handicapping condition or as being gifted/talented. Chapter 1 includes a review of the historical and philosophical bases for the education of students with special needs. Chapter 2 considers the legislation and litigation that has shaped the development of educational programs for special-needs students and discusses the size of the target population. Chapter 3 considers the principles, ideas, and techniques that promote more effective instruction for exceptional students, regardless of exceptionality. These "generic" ideas are, for the most part, time-tested and are applicable to nonhandicapped students as well as to students with special needs. Chapter 4 addresses feelings, expectancies, and interactions and how the affective component of teaching may be of unusual importance in working with exceptional students. It shows that if teachers attend to students' feelings and expectancies as expressed in personal interactions, the teaching-learning process will be more satisfying for all concerned and more effective in terms of achievement of educational objectives.

Chapters 1 and 2 are *essential* to the meaningful consideration of the rest of this text; chapters 3 and 4 include information and ideas that may apply across the span of exceptionalities, so they may be used effectively either before or after part two (chapters 5–12).

The Foundation for Education of Students with Special Needs

HISTORICAL ORIGINS OF PRESENT PROGRAMS FOR THE HANDICAPPED

THE EFFECT OF LITIGATION ON PROGRAMS FOR THE HANDICAPPED

THE SCOPE OF SPECIAL EDUCATION

A PHILOSOPHY OF EDUCATION FOR THE HANDICAPPED

- ☐ Why have many "special class programs" for the handicapped been maligned? When, and on what basis, can they be justified?

- ☐ In your opinion, which handicapping condition may likely be the most difficult to deal with in the classroom? What objective data do you have to support this opinion?

- ☐ What is the "circular effect" of legislation and litigation?

- ☐ How does your state view the gifted and talented with respect to the need for special educational programming?

- ☐ Can you develop an unambiguous, practical definition of "talented student"?

Educational programs for children with special needs have changed significantly, in some cases radically, in the past 50 years. The quality of services is generally better, and the scope is certainly greater. Comprehensive services for the handicapped are a matter of federal mandate, which the 50 states have followed for the most part. Actually, some of the more progressive states led the way, establishing a pattern that became the national norm, and states that had previously lagged behind were encouraged (some would say "dragged") into general conformity with federal leadership. As for the other end of the continuum, education of the gifted/talented, there is less national conformity and no national mandate, but there certainly are more and better programs than 10 or 20 years ago. These changes are widely recognized; we will review what has happened, why it has happened, and the general status of programs for exceptional students as we move toward the 21st century.

As the quality and quantity of programs have increased, there has been another significant change in services, especially as it relates to the handicapped. That is the matter of how, and in what setting, students receive their education. Earlier programs for the handicapped were primarily "separate programs"; that is, students were in separate classrooms or separate buildings. Now, education of the handicapped must be provided in the regular classroom, *whenever this is the most appropriate, effective setting.* This principle was established by federal law and led to the need for all teachers to know more about education of the handicapped. We want to emphasize the phrase "whenever this is the most appropriate, effective setting," because federal law does *not* require that all handicapped students remain in the regular classroom. Rather, it requires that they be educated in the most normal setting possible, given their special educational needs. Because state education agencies in all 50

states now have regulations quite similar to federal regulations, it might seem that the appropriate education of all handicapped children and youth should be an accomplished fact. This is, however, not the case. The concept is legally in place and the regulations exist, but the major determining factor in attaining the goal of appropriate education for most handicapped students is the regular classroom teacher. Regular classroom teachers must have the knowledge and skill to help handicapped students develop cognitively, emotionally, socially, and physically. More importantly, they must *believe* in the principle of education of the handicapped in the regular classroom. They must accept such students and have a genuine desire to assist them to learn in their classrooms. Experts can provide information about working with the mildly handicapped that offers a sufficient base of knowledge and skills, but only the individual teacher can make the affective decision to accept students who require these special teaching skills and techniques. We cannot with this one book make the teacher a master teacher of the handicapped, but we can provide a basic core of information on which the teacher may build the required skills. We believe that the goal of education of the handicapped in the least restrictive environment is important. We know that some handicapped students have too many special needs to be educated in the regular classroom and must have more specialized programs. But when handicapped students can be educated along with all other students, we are certain this is best. We hope that the information, ideas, insights, and concepts provided in this volume will assist the regular classroom teacher to fulfill more successfully his or her role in this very important undertaking. And we hope that we can convince those who may have doubts about their responsibility to teach special-needs students that this goal is possible, that it is consistent with the democratic philosophy of education, and that although challenging, it can provide tremendous personal satisfaction.

As educators have worked toward the goal of education of the handicapped in the least restrictive environment, certain misunderstandings and confusion have arisen. Part of our purpose is to promote understanding and reduce confusion. Thus, it is important first to discuss the word *mainstreaming,* which came into common use in the early 1970s. Unfortunately, mainstreaming has meant a variety of things to legislators, parents, and educators. To some, mainstreaming has meant the return of *all* handicapped students to the regular classroom. It may also indicate to some that no student should be served in a segregated setting. These are not acceptable concepts and are *not* consistent with the laws that have led to the emphasis on mainstreaming. The reasons for the mainstreaming emphasis are many, ranging from evidence of the lack of effectiveness of various special educational efforts (Dunn, 1968) to indications that members of various ethnic groups have been improperly placed in special education programs, a form of racial segregation. Special education classes were sometimes used as a place for any student who was thought not to fit into existing programs or who could not adjust to a particular teacher, regardless of whether the available special education program was appropriate for the student's special needs. Mainstreaming often was supported by the knowledge that many handicapped students, namely the visually impaired and the physically handicapped, had been successfully integrated for many years. This success led to an increased realization that other handicapped students could be successfully educated in regular classrooms.

If retention in the regular classroom is possible, given the student's special needs, this is where the student should be. If a separate special program is required, it should be provided. Our concept of mainstreaming is that of maximum integration in the regular class combined with concrete assistance for the regular class teacher. The role of the special educator is often that of a helping or assisting teacher, who works cooperatively by sharing unique skills and competencies with general educators and who also has a great deal to contribute to the education of handicapped students.

This chapter provides a historical account of the development of special educational services plus a statement of our philosophy of education for the handicapped. This historical account is provided so that the reader may better understand the relationship between general programs and practices on the one hand and special education on the other and the major forces that have shaped this complex, but beneficial, relationship.

We wish we could effectively discuss handicapped students, or students with special needs, without using the traditional categories of handicaps, for there is certainly some danger in causing bias or a self-fulfilling prophecy effect with the use of categorical labels. We use them, however, because from a practical point of view they remain the most efficient term of reference. We will refer to students who have learning problems as an apparent result of less-than-normal ability to hear as *deaf, hard of hearing, hearing handicapped,* or *hearing impaired,* even though some might view these as old-fashioned terms. There are other available terms, but new terms simply become new labels. We believe that although the public has some misunderstandings about deafness or hearing problems even after decades of efforts to promote better understanding, the introduction of new terms for these problems serves no useful purpose. We also persist with the idea that there is such a thing as mental retardation (mental handicap or limited intellectual ability) even though errors have been made in assessments of mental ability, particularly with children who are culturally different from the majority, middle-class population. This principle also applies to the other handicapping conditions.

The major errors that have been made with respect to categorical terminology have been errors in identification of students and/or the presumption that a particular categorical label automatically dictates a particular type of educational programming. We are making progress in correcting these very serious errors, though much remains to be accomplished.

HISTORICAL ORIGINS OF PRESENT PROGRAMS FOR THE HANDICAPPED

The history of early efforts to assist (or in some instances to eliminate) the handicapped provides a perspective for consideration of present educational efforts. This section examines the history of programs for handicapped individuals through four historical eras, as follows:

Early history—before 1800
Era of institutions—1800 to 1900
Era of public school special classes—1900 to 1960/70
Era of accelerated growth—1960 to present

These eras overlap to some extent; in many cases a new era may start in some parts of the nation or world while an older era still exists in others. All events before 1800 are considered "early history"; in much of this pre-1800 period individuals were not recognized as handicapped unless the handicap was severe. This was particularly true with respect to mental retardation, partly resulting from the lack of any type of universal educational effort. With this fact in mind, we proceed to the early history of recognition and provision for the handicapped.

Early History—Before 1800

The early history of societal involvement with the handicapped is primarily one of misunderstanding and superstition. It would seem likely that blindness, deafness, and mental retardation have existed since the beginning of the human race, and early references clearly document abandonment of handicapped infants. Roman history repeatedly refers to "fools" kept by the wealthy for entertainment. It was almost universally held that individuals who were considerably "different" from normal in appearance or behavior were possessed by demons or evil spirits.

Historical writers such as Zilboorg and Henry (1941), Pritchard (1963), and Kanner (1964) have provided comprehensive accounts of the manner in which society has related to the handicapped, mainly accounts of inhumanity that developed as a result of fear and ignorance.

In this section, origins of present-day programs for the handicapped are outlined, based on documentation found in the preceding three sources and in Gearheart and Litton (1979).

Most early records refer to handicapped or defective individuals in such a manner as to make it quite difficult to determine whether those referred to were mentally retarded, mentally ill, or perhaps deaf and unable to communicate. In many societies a father could determine whether he wanted to keep a newborn infant; if he indicated he did not, it might be thrown off a cliff, left in the wilderness, or perhaps simply left by the roadside. Such infanticide was supported by the common belief that individuals who were unusually different were possessed by demons or evil spirits and that the actions taken were not directed against the human infant but against the demon. At one time the Romans even extended this absolute rule of the father over infants to include the possibility that any female infant might be so disposed of, with general public acceptance.

There were, of course, short periods of time during which specific rulers imposed more humane practices, but the foregoing, repugnant as it may seem today, was the general practice in much of the "civilized" Western world for centuries.

The Middle Ages and the rise and further development of Christianity brought about varied effects, depending on the type of handicap, the geographic location, and the specific era. Although the idea of love and concern for others gained some headway, the handicapped were variously viewed as fools, nonhumans, or perhaps witches (witches being an obvious throwback to earlier demonology). The belief that the mentally ill or retarded were possessed by demons or evil spirits at times led to the offering of prayers or in some instances the practice of exorcism. On many occasions this exorcism was somewhat rigorous but was not nearly so final as the later treatment of witches, such as burning at the stake.

Although there were some bright spots, all the more bright for their infrequent appearance, until the 16th century the general picture was very bleak. The handicapped were not accepted as totally human and were misunderstood, mistreated, and in many cases put to death. Leading philosophers, national governments, and the organized church all shared responsibility for this attitude.

Then, slowly and with frequent backsliding, the picture began to change. During the latter part of the 16th century a Spanish monk, Pedro Ponce de León, was successful in teaching a small group of deaf pupils to speak, read, and write. This major breakthrough led to a reversal of the official position of the church that the deaf could not speak and were uneducable, a position based on the writings of Aristotle. In the fol-

lowing century an early version of fingerspelling for the deaf was developed by Juan Bonet, and in 1760 the Abbé de l'Épée opened a school for the deaf in Paris. Organized education for the deaf became a reality.

An associate of the Abbé de l'Épée became interested in the blind and by 1784 had established a school for the blind, also in Paris. This man, Valentin Huay, had also associated with such intellectuals as Voltaire and Rousseau, and after the traumatic personal experience of witnessing ten blind men being exploited for public entertainment, he vowed to improve the lot of the blind. The National Institution for Young Blind People was the result of this resolve.

Only a few years later, in 1798, an event took place near Aveyron, France, that was to lead to educational programs for the retarded. A boy of 11 or 12 years of age was found roaming "wild" in the woods. Discovered by hunters, this boy was unable to speak, bore the scars of years of encounters with wild animals, and was most animal-like in appearance. He bit and scratched all who approached, chose his food by smell, and was in nearly all respects more animal than human. This boy, eventually named Victor, was taken to Paris to be observed by students who were studying the development of primitive faculties. There, Phillipe Pinel, a renowned scientist, declared him to be an incurable idiot, but Jean Marc Gaspard Itard, who also saw him there, thought otherwise. He obtained custody of Victor and launched an involved program to civilize and educate him, hoping to make him normal. Unfortunately, though the "wild boy" showed improvement, he did not become "normal" in any sense of the word. The record of Itard's work, *The Wild Boy of Aveyron* (Itard, 1801, 1932, 1962), is an important classic in the education of the retarded.

Thus we see that educational programs for the deaf, blind, and retarded had their beginnings within less than a half a century, all in or near Paris, France. Perhaps the most fitting comment on the long era brought to a close by these new efforts is that the change, the opening of a new chapter in the history of treatment of the handicapped, was long overdue. May we never again see such a time.

Era of Institutions—1800 to 1900

The manner in which the institutional movement swept Europe and the United States is a reflection of the combination of a critical need on the part of the population of handicapped persons, an awareness of this need on the part of professionals (both physicians and educators), and changing attitudes among the general population permitting its popular acceptance.

Some of the motivations of the general public may seem less than desirable in light of accepted philosophy today. Considerable support for institutionalization seems to have come from the fact that such a practice kept these undesirable or physically unattractive persons out of the public eye and thus off the public conscience. This attitude, of course, is unacceptable today but was a vast improvement over deliberate infanticide or the use of prisons as holding centers for the handicapped.

Institutions for the handicapped were initially developed for the blind, the deaf, and the mentally retarded, with those for the blind and deaf initiated at about the same time and those for the retarded coming some 50 to 60 years later.

The first institutional programs for the handicapped were initiated in Europe, with France, Germany, Scotland, and England leading the way. By 1800, recognized programs for the blind existed in France, England, and Scotland; for the deaf, in France, Germany, Scotland, and England. Institutions specifically for the mentally retarded were not begun until 1831, when the first such program was initiated in France, but multi-

purpose institutions such as the Bicetre and Salpetriere in Paris had housed a variety of societal outcasts—the blind, senile, mentally ill, prostitutes, and mentally retarded—since the 17th century. Institutions were *the* way to provide for the handicapped throughout the 19th century; but as the century came to a close, new voices and new ideas began to be heard. For example, Alexander Graham Bell, in an address to the National Education Association in 1898, suggested that an "annex" to the public school should be formed to provide special classes for the deaf, the blind, and the mentally deficient. Then in 1902 he further urged that this "special education" should be provided so that these children would not have to leave their homes to attend institutions and that the National Education Association should actively pursue such educational provisions. As a result, the NEA officially formed a Department of Special Education, thus originating a name that remains to this day (Gearheart, 1974). These efforts by Bell and the actions of the public schools, which soon followed, ushered in a new era.

Era of Public School Special Classes—1900 to 1960/70

Educational efforts designed specifically for handicapped students had their origin before 1900, but such efforts were sporadic and met limited acceptance and success. The order of introduction of special programs in the public school was reversed as compared to that of institutional programs, with public school classes for the retarded coming before those for deaf or blind. Such classes had been attempted in New York, Cleveland, and Providence, Rhode Island before 1900; but they tended to be classes provided for "problem children" and probably included more acting-out nonretarded than retarded students. Then, early in the 20th century, several cities tried gathering groups of students who had been previously unschooled and who for the

This student would not have been in a regular classroom 50 years ago.

most part were definitely mentally retarded. Like the institutions, the schools were interested in a return to normalcy, including normal learning ability, and were for the most part unsuccessful. Later in the century, particularly after the appearance of a more adequate way to determine degree of mental retardation (Lewis Terman's revision of the Binet test of intelligence—the Stanford-Binet), classes for the more mildly retarded were started and were successful enough to warrant continuation.

Day-school classes for the visually impaired and hearing impaired were slower in starting but did not tend quite so much to the start-and-stop pattern that characterized early classes for the retarded. With institutions for the deaf and blind, the institutional setting was more truly a school, and parents

were more likely to accept and support this residential school setting. Thus there was not the kind of urgency that was felt regarding the mentally retarded.

With the enactment of compulsory school attendance laws in the early part of the century came the problems involved in providing for *all* minors, including the handicapped. It should be noted that since most states provided residential schools for the blind and deaf (the more severely mentally retarded were often institutionalized at an early age), the real problem for school officials was that of provision for the more mildly retarded.

Thus the public schools concentrated on special classes for the mildly retarded. Some of these classes included children whose problems were mostly behavioral, resulting in low academic performance, because there was no other program available. The only exceptions to this strategy were some special programs for students with visual and hearing handicaps, speech defects, or unusual physical or orthopedic problems.

Few regular classroom teachers complained when they lost to the special class those students who were experiencing serious academic problems. In fact, many teachers were tempted to send along another student or two, those without the prerequisite low IQ but with academic problems similar to those with lower intelligence. In some cases, for a variety of reasons, these ineligible students were placed in the special class, perhaps on a so-called trial placement, which sometimes lasted for years.

After about 1920, as special classes for the mentally retarded (later called the *educable mentally handicapped* to differentiate them from the *trainable mentally retarded*) continued to grow in popularity, there was similar growth in special programs for students with less than normal visual acuity (called the *visually handicapped, visually impaired,* or *partially seeing*) and classes for those with less than normal hearing (called the *deaf* or *hearing handicapped*). In addition, there were special programs for students with speech problems and often a special room for students with heart problems or orthopedic handicaps. Some classes for students whose major problems related to unacceptable or antisocial behavior were also initiated; but as often as not, if the problem was not too severe, these students were placed in the class for the retarded, and those who could not get along in this obviously special setting were expelled from school.

This section of the historical review has been called the *era of special classes,* spanning the time interval from 1900 to 1960-70. The close of this era is given a dual date because although there was a considerable increase in the use of service delivery plans

other than the special class during the 1960s, many special classes remained in 1970. By calling this the era of special classes, we do not mean that other means of serving the handicapped were not in use during this time. Many students with physical disabilities or with visual or hearing impairments were integrated with excellent success.

It must also be recognized that a "special class" may be either a full-time or part-time special class. For example, speech therapy has been conducted for years in small groups of two to four students in a totally segregated special setting, usually for periods of only 30 to 40 minutes per day, 2 or 3 days per week. Programs for the visually impaired have sometimes consisted of segregated special classes at the preschool level while students are learning special skills such as braille, but these same students may be almost totally integrated in the regular classroom from second grade on.

This first 60 to 70 years of the 20th century are properly called the *era of the special class* because the special class was the *major* means whereby handicapped students were served and because this era represented a definite evolution beyond the institutional era. This time was characterized by general educators happily sending problem students to the special class for the mentally handicapped and by special educators accepting a number of students who should not have been so placed. Toward the end of the era it became a time of contradictory and inconclusive efficacy studies as well as claims— verified in court—that special classes were sometimes dumping grounds, other times a vehicle of segregation, and in some geographic areas a convenient way to do something for culturally different or bilingual children without actually starting a bilingual program.

As the era came to a close, many had a negative feeling whenever the phrase *special class* was uttered, particularly when the reference was to a self-contained special class. The misuse of the special class is not questioned by most special educators, but the assumption that the special class is *never* the right program is just as wrong as the earlier assumption that it was *always* the right one. Our concern must be for the evaluation of individual needs, and programming must be designed to meet those needs. Any other procedure may lead to additional negative results.

Era of Accelerated Growth— 1960 to Present

The first half of the 20th century showed improvement and growth in services for the handicapped; but truly rapid growth, unparalleled in history, began in the 1960s, with the period of most concentrated growth between 1965 and 1980. The changes that took place led to increased acceptance of the handicapped as individuals, more positive attitudes on the part of educators regarding their responsibility for education of the handicapped, and actions of courts and government leaders to attempt to assure continuing, appropriate education of handicapped students. There were important individual advocates for the handicapped, and organized parent and professional groups played their roles as catalysts for this change; but it was the U.S. Congress that would provide the major impetus for this positive movement. Congressional interest was indicated not by one or two laws but by a series of legislation through which Congress as a whole indicated its support of better educational programs and services for handicapped children and youth.

The pattern through which the Congress became involved with the education of the handicapped was similar to that of Congress entering any new and unfamiliar arena. At first, legislation was limited in scope and funding. Then, as results seemed to warrant further consideration, broader laws were

passed in a sequence that culminated in Public Law 94-142: The Education for All Handicapped Children Act of 1975. Individual members of Congress and congressional committees did not, of course, achieve this entirely on their own. Various factors contributed to their actions, including the following:

1. A number of major political figures, including President Kennedy, had a personal interest in the handicapped because of handicapped individuals in their immediate families. Twenty years earlier the existence of handicapped family members might have been hidden; but increased objectivity about the handicapped, public relations efforts by major organizations concerned with the handicapped, and national concern about minority populations made it socially and politically acceptable to promote such causes.
2. Organizations such as the National Association for Retarded Children (now the National Association for Retarded Citizens) and the United Cerebral Palsy Associations had become increasingly active in the preceding years. Leading national figures, particularly those in show business, had supported their efforts and had given the cause of the handicapped unusually high national visibility.
3. Professional organizations, led by the Council for Exceptional Children (but including many more) had grown in power, recognition, and lobbying expertise.
4. Congress was venturing into new fields of involvement, and this subject appeared to be a fruitful one. Few would criticize efforts to assist the handicapped.

The end result of this continuing congressional interest, the passage in 1975 of The Education for All Handicapped Children Act, established the framework for education of the handicapped as it exists today. Although funding of some of the federal programs designed to encourage better programs for the handicapped was reduced as a result of general federal funding cutbacks starting in 1981, it appears that the intent of Congress has mostly been maintained. To a considerable extent, related legislation in the 50 states seems likely to assure continued educational programs for handicapped students. But in the midst of this success, there were questioning voices.

THE EFFECT OF LITIGATION ON PROGRAMS FOR THE HANDICAPPED

In a series of court actions, important questions were raised about special education classes and services for handicapped children and youth. This litigation began to appear in earnest in the early 1970s; and although it took many forms, it had two major thrusts. The first may be characterized as litigation that alleged that special education classes (often classes for the educable mentally retarded) lead to stigma, inadequate education, and irreparable injury. These lawsuits convinced some that special education programs as they then existed were a disservice to many students and resulted in a reduction in the numbers of students served by special education in certain parts of the nation. The second type of litigation involved students who were not served through special education but who were in serious need of such service. These suits led to the initiation of a number of new programs and the *addition* of students to special education rolls in some areas. The remainder of this section further considers the effect of litigation on special education.

The base for much of the special education-related litigation of the 1960s and 1970s was established by a U.S. Supreme Court ruling in *Brown v. Board of Education* (1954), a decision in which it was declared that separate schools for black and white students were unconstitutional. The essence of this decision was that segregation solely on the basis of race deprives minority children of equal educational opportunities, even if various tangible factors appear to be equal (Zirkel, 1978). Parents of handicapped children later sued school systems in relation to segregated facilities for their children, basing their arguments in part on *Brown v. Board of Education*. Three special education cases, *Diana v. Board of Education* (1970), *PARC v. Pennsylvania* (1972), and *Mills v. D.C. Board of Education* (1972), are considered below in some detail, and Table 1–1 provides a condensed summary of these and other selected cases that have had unusual significance for the development of educational programs for the handicapped. Such litigation started in the 1960s but reached previously unheard-of proportions in the 1970s. As noted by Ysseldyke and Algozzine in a discussion of legal regulation of special education, "Educators today are as much concerned with matters of litigation and legislation as of education" (1982, p. 212). It is certainly unfortunate that educators must spend so much time, effort, and concern on litigation and legislation.

Diana v. State Board of Education, used as a basis for similar suits, alleged that intelligence tests used for placement were culturally biased and that class placement based on these inadequate tests led to an inadequate education. In addition, this suit also claimed that as a result, the stigma of mental retardation was suffered by children who were not mentally retarded. In the *Diana* case the plaintiffs sought relief from existing practices of identification and placement. They also sought compensatory damages.

Diana v. State Board of Education was settled out of court with the following points of agreement: (1) children whose primary langauge is not English must be tested in their primary language and in English; however, "verbal" (as opposed to "performance") questions, which by their very nature are unfair to children whose primary language is not En-

TABLE 1–1. Court cases that have greatly influenced special education

Court Case	Summary of Ruling or Settlement
Brown v. Board of Education (1954)	School segregation solely on basis of race deprives children of equal educational opportunities and thus violates the equal protection clause of 14th Amendment.
Hobson v. Hansen (1967)	Tracking (ability grouping) based on standardized tests that are not relevant to many minority students violates both the due process and equal protection guarantees of the 14th Amendment.
Diana v. State Board of Education (1970)	(Settled through consent decree.) State of California agreed to change evaluation practices with respect to the language in which students are tested and to eliminate certain test items. Also agreed to develop tests designed to reflect minority cultures and to reevaluate all Mexican-American and Chinese students enrolled in EMR classes.
Pennsylvania Association for Retarded Children v. Commonwealth of Pennsylvania (1972)	(Settled through consent decree.) State must provide access to free, appropriate public education for retarded children of Pennsylvania. "Education" was redefined to include activities that the state had earlier held were not "educational." Other benefits for the retarded were also gained.
Mills v. D.C. Board of Education (1972)	Students cannot be excluded from school because they have been found to be behavior problems, emotionally disturbed, mentally retarded, etc. Students must have a hearing before exclusion or placement in a special program. *All* students have a right to an appropriate education.
Frederick L. v. Thomas (1977)	Philadelphia schools were directed to search systematically for learning disabled students. (They had claimed the existing differentiated program provided adequately for such students and that such screening was thus unnecessary.)
Stuart v. Nappi (1978)	Disciplinary expulsion may constitute denial of appropriate education. Due process procedures must be followed.
Board v. Rowley (1982)	(Settled by U.S. Supreme Court.) Amy Rowley, a deaf student with excellent speechreading skills, was provided limited instruction by a tutor for the deaf and a speech pathologist, plus amplification equipment. Amy was performing at an academic level above average for her grade and class. Her parents (also deaf) requested a qualified sign-language interpreter for all academic classes. This request was denied. Supreme Court affirmation of this decision supported comparable, appropriate education, but not necessarily maximum opportunity for each handicapped student.
Roncker v. Walters (1983)	Cost of services may be considered since spending on one handicapped student may deprive another handicapped student; however, a proper continuum of placements must be provided.

glish, cannot be used in testing such children; (2) all Mexican-American and Chinese children already enrolled in special education classes must be retested in accordance with the preceding principle; (3) every school district in the state must develop and submit to the court the school district plan for retesting and reevaluating Mexican-American and Chinese children presently in classes for the educable mentally retarded, and as a part of this plan the district must show how it will place back into regular classes those children whom this reevaluation indicates were misplaced; (4) school psychologists must develop more appropriate testing devices and measures to reflect Mexican-American culture; and (5) any school district that has a significant disparity between the percentage of Mexican-American children in regular classes and the percentage in classes for educable mentally retarded must submit an acceptable explanation for this discrepancy.

The *Diana* case is similar to many filed against the schools. Most were settled in a manner similar to that in the *Diana* case.

A second type of major litigation appeared to be going in a different direction, that of demanding more special education classes and services for the handicapped in the public schools. The following description of two cases, one in Pennsylvania and the other in Washington, DC, illustrates this effort (Gearheart & Litton, 1979, pp. 17–18). Although the first affected only the mentally retarded, the second specifically related to all handicapped and, because it was based on the U.S. Constitution, has ramifications for all areas of the United States.

Two major cases appear to have established the right of free access to public education for the school age trainable mentally retarded. The first, *The Pennsylvania Association for Retarded Children v. the Commonwealth of Pennsylvania,* questioned educational policies of the state of Pennsylvania, which led directly to practices that denied an appropriate education at public expense to retarded children of school age. This case was filed on January 7, 1971, by the Pennsylvania Association for Retarded Children on behalf of fourteen specifically named children and all other children similarly situated. This was a typical *class action* suit, filed in such a manner as to affect those fourteen children named, all others of a similar "class" now residing in the state, and all children similarly situated who will be living in Pennsylvania in the future.

Pennsylvania, like a number of other states, had compulsory school attendance laws, provided certain types of special classes for handicapped

children within the public schools, and provided residential schools for some handicapped children. But within the Pennsylvania School Code, there were two specific ways in which the trainable mentally retarded child could be excluded from public education. First, if a qualified psychologist or personnel from a mental health clinic certified that a given child could no longer profit from public school attendance, the child could be excluded. Second, because the law provided that the local board of directors could refuse to accept or retain children who had not reached the mental age of 5 years, most trainable retarded were never admitted to the public schools. Even if a child were not excluded under either of these two provisions, there was a third provision that permitted the local board to provide training outside the public schools, "if an approved plan demonstrates that it is unfeasible to form a special class."

The Pennsylvania Association for Retarded Children (PARC) set out to establish three main points in their case: (1) mentally retarded children can learn if an appropriate educational program is provided, (2) "education" must be viewed more broadly than the traditional academic program, and (3) early educational experience is essential to maximize educational potential.

After considerable testimony by the state and by a variety of "expert witnesses," the case was won by PARC. . . .

The Pennsylvania Association for Retarded Children v. Pennsylvania suit, like many that were to follow, was settled on the basis of a *consent agreement.* This is an out-of-court agreement, usually formally approved by the court. In this suit, the state was ordered to provide free public education, appropriate to the learning capabilities of retarded children, and the consent agreement provided the working framework. To make certain that the consent agreement was carried out, the court established a time schedule for implementation and appointed two "masters" to oversee the total process.

A second case, *Mills v. the Board of Education of the District of Columbia,* is of unusual significance because it applied to *all* handicapped children. To a certain extent, it established a principle that tended to lead to the inclusion of all handicapped students in future class action suits. This case, like *PARC v. Pennsylvania,* led to a court order that required the public schools to provide for handicapped students even if they did not fit the educational mold. As in the Pennsylvania case, the court appointed masters to oversee the operation. Unlike the Pennsylvania case, which resulted in a consent agreement between the parties, *Mills v. District of Columbia* case was decided through a judgment of the court and was based on a constitutional holding.

All of these cases were important. In combination, they provided the mosaic base that led to the establishment of the right of all handicapped students to a free, appropriate public education and to protection from inappropriate assessment and classification procedures. In addition, parents won the right to become totally involved in educational planning and placement of their child. These various cases, especially the *PARC* and *Mills* cases, set the stage for the passage of PL 94-142. As later amended by PL 89-773 (1978) and PL 98-199 (1983), PL 94-142 is the federal basis for education of handicapped children and youth in the nation.[1] A great deal more will be said in chapter 2 about this legislation and the structure for education it has provided. Now let us consider the children toward whom this legislative effort was directed.

THE SCOPE OF SPECIAL EDUCATION

The scope of special education differs in various areas of the United States. For all practical purposes, *special education* is defined on a state-by-state basis in relation to two factors: (1) specific legislation defining special

---

[1]PL 99-457 (1986) included additional amendments, such as mandatory education of handicapped children of ages three to five, and encouragement for early childhood intervention from birth to age two. The direct impact of these amendments on teachers in the regular class has yet to be determined. One distinct possibility is more involvement with more severely handicapped children at an earlier age.

education for purposes of special state reimbursement to those districts providing such programs or services and (2) legislation relating to mandatory education of the handicapped.

There is some national acceptance of a common definition of special education, but because education is primarily a state function, a degree of variation continues. Two national groups have, in effect, defined special education, and with the exception of gifted, talented, or creative students, there is growing agreement among the states. The two national definitions are primarily operational in nature and are provided by the Council for Exceptional Children, an organization of professionals who work with exceptional children, and by the division of the federal government that is responsible for programs for the handicapped (the Office of Special Education). These two national entities have provided definitions that are more meaningful than theoretically oriented verbalizations that find limited application in practice.

The Council for Exceptional Children has 13 divisions or affiliates, 7 of which relate to recognized categories of exceptionality. These 7 exceptionalities are (1) gifted, (2) behaviorally disordered, (3) communication disordered, (4) learning disabled, (5) mentally retarded, (6) physically handicapped, and (7) visually handicapped. Thus, in addition to the three areas of handicap having a well-established historical base, special education now includes the gifted, those with behavioral disorders and learning disabilities, and the physically handicapped. In the text, the term *handicapped* refers to all recognized categories of disability. The term *exceptional* includes all categories of disability and gifted students.

Federal agencies and offices that monitor special education programs have one major function: to be certain the dictates of federal legislation are followed. In a related subfunction, these agencies provide reports to the

Congress relative to existing services for handicapped students. These reports have used essentially the same terminology as the Council for Exceptional Children, reporting on the same categories of handicap. Thus the scope of special education—at least that part of special education related to the handicapped—has been defined in practice by these two organizations. It has been further defined in terms of types of services that may be required by handicapped students through the regulations of PL 94-142 and through state regulations. The major differences between state definitions of special education involve terminology used with respect to the various handicapping conditions; the range of students served is essentially the same. There are, however, other differences related to quality of services; differences that, one hopes, will some day be reduced in the direction of better services in all states.

We view a special education system as an integral part of the total education system, responsible for the provision of specialized or adapted programs and services and for assisting others to provide such services for exceptional children and youth. One must remember that exceptional students may be defined in a variety of ways, depending on the state in which one is involved in special educational programming.

Although specialized educational provisions for the gifted are not mandated by federal law, as is the case with the handicapped, there is a steadily growing interest in such programming in most of the nation. The classroom teacher is well advised to plan for those gifted or creative students who will sooner or later make their presence known.

The Target Populations

PL 94-142 and subsequent amendments spell out the target populations for services for the handicapped at the federal level. State laws and regulations further define these populations on a state-by-state basis, and the "targets" are the same (though given varying names in the various states). Whatever the terminology, it may be said that the intent is that *all* handicapped children and youth be provided a free, appropriate education by some agency of the state, usually through the structure of the public schools. As for the gifted/talented, most states provide some sort of statement of intent to provide services, though there is no national mandate similar to PL 94-142.

Because of the national mandate, it might seem that numbers of students served in the various states would represent the total population of handicapped students, that is, if all *must* be served and if state officials are conscientious and law abiding, the national data on students served in special education programs should represent the prevalence of handicapped students in the United States. There is, however, serious question as to whether this is the case. For example, if we examine the information provided by the states we find that one state ("A") reported only .3% of their total student population in public school programs for the mentally retarded. Another state ("B") reported 4.6% of their total student population classified as mentally retarded and receiving service. Given other information about these two states, we may conclude that it is highly unlikely than one really has 15 times more mentally retarded students per thousand students of school age than the other. It is also unlikely that state A is ignoring such a large group of students. Probably state A is classifying students differently from state B, and a variety of information gathered by various investigators over the years seems to support this conclusion.

What, then, may we conclude about the prevalence of exceptional students in our schools? Two different types of data are provided in Tables 1–2 and 1–3, reflecting two different ways we may attempt to find the

Though visually impaired, this student enjoys a wide variety of activities.

answer to this question. Table 1–2 presents information regarding prevalence as it has been traditionally presented for the past 30 or 40 years. This information is based on U.S. government agency estimates, which in turn are based on estimates provided by recognized authorities. These are reasonably good prevalence estimates, given the variable nature of the definitions of many of the exceptionalities. Table 1–2 provides information regarding the prevalence of handicapped students receiving services in the public schools as reported by the 50 states. You will note great differences between the percentages of students served in the various states under the percentage range heading in the right-hand column. The range in percentage of students served as mentally retarded (the highest percentage 15 times the lowest) is surpassed in the area of emotional disturbance, where the high-percentage state serves 30 times as many students per thousand as the low-percentage state. It is doubtful that this apparent difference reflects

TABLE 1–2. Target population of exceptional children (theoretical prevalence of exceptional children in the United States)

Exceptionality	Percentage of Population
Learning disabled	2.0–4.0
Speech handicapped	2.0–4.0
Mentally retarded	2.0–3.0
Emotionally disturbed	2.0–3.0
Hearing impaired (includes deaf)	0.5–0.7
Multihandicapped	0.5–0.7
Orthopedically and health impaired	0.4–0.6
Visually impaired (includes blind)	0.08–0.12
Gifted and talented	2.0–3.0

Note. Based on U.S. government agency estimates and estimates by recognized authorities.

TABLE 1–3. Target population of exceptional children (handicapped students receiving service in the United States)

Exceptionality	Percentage of National Public School Enrollment	Percentage Range (as reported by individual states)
Learning disabled	4.6	3.6–9.6
Speech handicapped	2.8	1.1–4.3
Mentally retarded	1.5	0.3–4.6
Emotionally disturbed	0.8	0.1–3.0
All other handicapping conditions	<0.25	
Gifted and talented	no comparable data on a national basis	

Note. Based on 1985 reports from the 50 states to the U.S. Department of Education and public school enrollment estimates from the National Education Association.

a real difference in numbers of students with significant behavior problems. We leave it to the reader to draw reasonable conclusions from the data in both tables after further study of the field of special education. These data do imply that adding together the numbers of students served under the various classifications in the 50 states does not necessarily provide highly accurate or meaningful information regarding, for example, the number of emotionally disturbed or mentally retarded students in the United States.

A PHILOSOPHY OF EDUCATION FOR THE HANDICAPPED

Although many questions may be asked about the actual number of handicapped students in our schools and whether we have established a meaningful, defensible system of classifying such students, most would agree that there *are* students who have very special needs and that we should attempt to meet those needs. Federal and state laws dictate that we provide special assistance to these

Career choices need not be limited by disabilities.

students, and we believe it important to establish some basic principles to guide our efforts as we plan and implement such assistance. The following statement of our beliefs has been developed over many years of work with the handicapped and with educators and other professionals who provide programs or services for individuals with handicapping conditions or disabilities.

We believe that all individuals in American society have the right to receive an adequate education that will permit them to develop their abilities to the fullest possible extent. We believe that if they have unique needs related to their ethnic background, earlier lack of opportunity, or other similar factors, educational programs should be modified and specialized to meet these needs. We believe that the handicapped individuals of this nation have these rights and that the public, tax-supported, educational systems of the nation must adjust and adapt existing educational programs and offerings to make this possible. We believe that educational planning should emphasize the learning

strengths and abilities of the handicapped and that labeling according to handicap should be avoided whenever possible. On the other hand, students who have hearing or visual impairments must have certain specific assistance related directly to the sensory loss; thus it is often advantageous to the students and to their educational programming to think of them as and at times call them *visually impaired* (*handicapped,* or *disabled*) or *hearing impaired.* We believe it would be a professionally unforgivable error to be so concerned about labeling that teachers would be permitted or encouraged to overlook hearing losses or other disabilities because educators are afraid to use categorical terminology such as *hearing impaired.* We believe this principle applies to all handicapping conditions.

Handicapped children and youth should be served in the regular classroom whenever possible, and additional efforts should be directed toward increasing the effectiveness of such programming. If a student must receive specialized assistance in a small, separate grouping of others with special needs, such help should be provided, but he should be kept in the normal classroom setting as much as possible. The single most important consideration in *all* planning for handicapped students is their ultimate educational, social, and physical well-being.

Certain principles closely related to this philosophy are of prime importance, including the following:

1. Early intervention is highly desirable in all cases in which the handicap is readily identifiable.
2. Minority or low socioeconomic status may present unusual problems in assessment, and special care must be taken when this may be a factor.
3. Some disabilities may be more appropriately viewed as symptoms rather than specific physical disorders and may exist at one time in life and not exist at another.
4. Even in the case of a specific, irreversible disability, the need for special educational services may vary from full-time, special class service at one time in the student's life to little or no service at another time.
5. A wide variety of services and the total spectrum of service delivery capabilities are essential.
6. Services for a broad age range, preschool through high school, are essential.
7. For some individuals, continued efforts beyond high school and extending for many years into adulthood are essential.
8. A broad, flexible assessment program is required, including provisions for initial and ongoing assessment and formal and informal evaluation.
9. Parents must be involved in both assessment and program planning. A certain amount of involvement is now required by law and regulation; in many instances, even more involvement will be

of great benefit.
10. The concept of the least restrictive environment, when properly applied, will effectively unite the skills of the regular educator and the special educator, thus providing maximum assistance to the handicapped student.

SUMMARY

Over the centuries, handicapped persons have been feared and misunderstood and in a few cases viewed as special children of God. Their treatment has included exorcism, burning as witches, and infanticide with public approval. They were permitted to be beggars or became indentured servants or court fools, but in nearly all instances their true condition was misunderstood. At best they were second-class citizens; they were not even accepted as being fully human by most of their nonhandicapped peers.

Slowly, as more scientific methods of observing and investigating human behavior developed, it became apparent that some who had been rejected in the past had many normal attributes. Deaf children learned to read and write, the blind learned through early versions of braille, and mentally ill persons were miraculously "cured." Physicians began to differentiate between the mentally ill and the mentally retarded, and special training facilities (early institutions) were established to assist the handicapped to develop whatever abilities they might have. Many of those pioneers who established the early institutions believed that they might cure most of the handicapped, but that soon proved an empty dream. Institutions became holding centers that kept the handicapped out of sight of the nonhandicapped. The more mildly handicapped, especially those whom we might today call *mildly mentally retarded, learning disabled,* or *behaviorally disordered,* were not usually institutionalized but remained on the fringes of society as village "fools" or "dummies." It soon became evident that they could not learn, thus they did not attend school. When they broke a law (that they often did not understand) they were jailed as criminals.

Soon after the start of the 20th century, public school special classes began to appear and were commonly accepted by the 1940s and 1950s. They were a significant improvement over earlier practices but were available only to those children and youth who were relatively well behaved and who fit whatever standards the local school established. Other children were not permitted in the public schools. Their only choice was the institution. Still others were eligible for neither public school programs nor institutions.

By mid-century, parents and special-education professional groups began to advocate more comprehensive services for all handicapped children. Parents organized and enlisted the aid of interested members of Congress, and soon Congress enacted legislation designed to encourage the states to provide more educational programming for the handicapped. Court decisions supported the right of all children to an appropriate educa-tion and encouraged or required that this education be provided in the most normal setting possible. The idea of education of the handicapped in the least restrictive environment took root and grew quickly. In 1975 PL 94-142 was passed, formalizing what a variety of litigation and certain, more progressive state laws had been indicating. Recognition of the educational needs of all students regardless of handicap, level of intelligence, or cost of such education, had finally arrived. With PL 94-142 came the requirement for education of the handicapped in the least restrictive environment consistent with appropriate education.

The philosophy of education for the handicapped presented at the close of this chapter is consistent with PL 94-142 and provides related principles that may be used to guide implementation of effective, appropriate, educational programs. Most handicapped students can be served effectively in the regular classroom if materials and consultative assistance are provided. All possible effort should be directed toward such participation in the regular class.

The Law and Services for Exceptional Students

PUBLIC LAW 94-142

A CONTINUUM OF EDUCATIONAL SERVICES

SERVICES PROVIDED BY SPECIAL EDUCATORS

REFERRAL, CLASSIFICATION, AND PLACEMENT

WHAT ABOUT THE GIFTED?

☐ In what way(s) are the rights of students with handicapping conditions different from the rights of nonhandicapped students? Is this difference justifiable?

☐ Does "most appropriate, least restrictive environment" mean placement in a regular classroom?

☐ Is the IEP a "contract"?

☐ How and when must parents of handicapped students be involved with placement decisions?

☐ How would you modify or rewrite PL 94-142?

☐ Can a residential school ever be a fair, viable alternative for some students?

☐ What is the regular classroom teacher's responsibility in the decision-making process regarding placement?

☐ What problems are inherent in the assessment of students who are culturally or ethnically different from majority, middle-class students? How have the courts reacted to such differences?

2

S ervices to the handicapped/disabled are a matter of mandate today; in chapter 1 we reviewed many of the reasons for this mandate. Why do we provide such services? Because we believe that all children deserve an opportunity to learn and because the law requires that such education be provided. But *how* handicapped children are to be provided their "free, appropriate public education," as required by PL 94-142, cannot be answered in a few simple sentences. Turnbull (1986), in his book-length analysis of the law and its influences on education of handicapped children and youth, considers six primary principles of special education law: (1) zero reject—the right of every child to receive an appropriate, publicly supported education; (2) nondiscriminatory evaluation—the right to an accurate, meaningful evaluation so that proper educational planning and placement may be accomplished; (3) an individualized educational program (IEP) established specifically for each student's special needs; (4) placement in the least restrictive environment that will permit an appropriate education—an opportunity to associate with nondisabled students when possible; (5) due process of law—a system that permits parents and advocates to challenge educational planning when that seems necessary; and (6) parent participation in planning and implementation of the educational program.

Turnbull's first principle—the right of every child to receive an appropriate, publicly supported education—is the basic intent of all of the laws that have led to the present status of education of the handicapped/disabled. Principles 2 to 6 provide the guidelines through which we are to accomplish the basic principle of appropriate, publicly supported education. Our focus in this book is on information and understandings that will permit the regular class teacher to teach students with handicaps/disabilities more effectively. But before discussing the various topics the regular teacher must consider to understand the legal and administrative framework, we should consider the basic law that dictated Turnbull's six principles.

PUBLIC LAW 94-142

Public Law 94-142, the Education for All Handicapped Children Act, was enacted in 1975. Public Law 98-199 was enacted in 1983. We will refer primarily to PL 94-142, although actually both PL 94-142 and PL 98-199 were amendments of an earlier law, PL 93-380 (1974). In any event, PL 94-142, in its statement-of-purpose section, indicates that it was designed to assure that

all handicapped children have available to them . . . a free appropriate public education which emphasizes special education and related services designed to meet their unique needs, to assure that the rights of handicapped children and their parents or guardians are protected, to assist states and localities to provide for the education of all handicapped children, and to assess and assure the effectiveness of efforts to educate handicapped children.

PL 94-142 specifically directs that certain handicapped children be served, including (1) the deaf, (2) the deaf-blind, (3) the hard of hearing, (4) the mentally retarded, (5) the multihandicapped, (6) the orthopedically impaired, (7) the other health impaired, (8) the seriously emotionally disturbed, (9) the learning disabled, (10) the speech impaired, and (11) the visually handicapped. The law is written so that it is clear that all special programs and services required by such handicapped students between 3 and 21 years of age should be provided. This mandate for services does not apply to children 3 to 5 years of age nor to those 18 to 21 years if such requirement is inconsistent with a state law or practice or any applicable court decree.

Services to be provided, as indicated in the rules and regulations for the act,[1] include (1) audiology, (2) counseling services, (3) early identification, (4) medical services, (5) occupational therapy, (6) parent counseling, (7) physical therapy, (8) psychological services, (9) recreation, (10) school health services, (11) social-work services, (12) speech pathology, and (13) transportation (*Federal Register,* August 23, 1977, pp. 42479–42480). This specific list of services, according to comments in the rules and regulations, was not intended to be exhaustive but was included to indicate the broad scope of services encompassed in the intent of the law.

Public Law 94-142 was passed in an attempt to correct a number of known problems in educational programs for handicapped children and youth. In an analysis of PL 94-142, Ballard and Zettel (1977) indicated four major purposes:

1. to guarantee free, appropriate education to handicapped children and youth
2. to assure that decision making with regard to special programs and services is accomplished fairly
3. to establish clear auditing and management procedures for special education programming at local, state, and national levels
4. to use federal funds to assist state and local governments in carrying out the provisions of the law.

Other authors have emphasized slightly different aspects of the law. For example, Ysseldyke and Algozzine (1982) in a discussion of legal regulation of special education indicate that four provisions of PL 94-142 deserve particular attention: (1) the provision of due

process, (2) the provision for protection in evaluation procedures, (3) the requirement of education in the least restrictive environment, and (4) the requirement that each student have an IEP.

Another principle we believe to be of equal importance is that to carry out the provisions of the law, joint planning and close, ongoing cooperation between regular and special educators is required. Just as some parents will not work with educators no matter how hard the educators try to provide opportunities for close cooperation—so, too, some special educators and regular educators find it difficult to cooperate. However, educators are public employees, are supposed to be professionals, and have a professional obligation to work together on behalf of children with special needs. Public Law 94-142 indicates that they must. To do so, they must first understand their respective roles and responsibilities. In the remainder of this chapter we will consider a number of topics critical to a successful joint relationship between regular educators and special educators—a relationship directed toward providing the best possible program for children in our schools.

The Right to Due Process of Law

PL 94-142 and related regulations detail precisely how the law must be implemented. Most of its legal requirements are the responsibility of local special education personnel or state officials, but certain aspects of the law and related regulations are quite important to the regular classroom teacher. One of the more important areas is the assurance of due process in all of the proceedings involved with identifying those students who require special educational services and with planning and implementing those services.

Before the passage of PL 94-142, due process was primarily limited to matters involving identification, evaluation, and placement.

---

[1]The rules and regulations for PL 94-142 and for all federal laws are not a part of the actual legislation. They are guidelines for implementation, spelled out after the legislation is enacted into law and usually developed with input and assistance from professionals in the field.

The law extended due process to include any matter relating to the provision of free, appropriate education and specifically provided parents the right to, and a specific procedure whereby they might, present concerns or complaints (Abeson & Zettel, 1977). Specifically, the law requires or provides for

1. notification in writing before evaluation (in language parents can understand)
2. parental consent before initiating evaluation
3. the right to an interpreter or translator when needed
4. the school district to outline all anticipated evaluation
5. the right of the parent to inspect all educational records
6. the right of the parent to obtain an independent evaluation
7. written notice when a change of placement is planned or when the district refuses to make a change in placement
8. parental consent to changes in placement
9. a specific procedure for an impartial due-process hearing in cases of disagreement, including the following:
   a. the right to a specific, timely notice of hearing
   b. limitations on who can serve as hearing officer (to prevent bias)
   c. the right of the parents to legal counsel or other representative
   d. the right to require witnesses to attend and the right to confront and cross-examine witnesses
   e. the right to present evidence
   f. the right to appeal to the state educational agency if either party is aggrieved by the results of the first hearing
   g. the right to bring civil action if either party so desires after the state educational agency review and decision

These due-process provisions are described in detail in the rules and regulations,

along with other related procedural matters. In addition, each state is required to outline its specific regulations, which must be consistent with these requirements. In actuality, the due-process hearings provide additional protection for the student in that the school district also has the right and the responsibility to appeal parental decisions that are thought to be in direct violation of the educational rights and needs of the student; however, the fact that the law provides parents these rights has received most of the attention of those commenting on this aspect of PL 94-142.

Protection in Evaluation Procedures

The various court cases that preceded the passage of PL 94-142 established the minimum basic requirements for nonbiased, meaningful evaluation procedures. The rules and regulations for PL 94-142 (*Federal Register,* 1977, pp. 42496-42497) outline the following minimum evaluation procedure requirements:

State and local educational agencies shall insure, at a minimum, that

(a) Tests and other evaluation materials:
   (1) Are provided and administered in the child's native language or other mode of communication, unless it is clearly not feasible to do so;
   (2) Have been validated for the specific purpose for which they are used; and
   (3) Are administered by trained personnel in conformance with the instructions provided by their producer.
(b) Tests and other evaluation materials include those tailored to assess specific areas of educational need and not merely those which are designed to provide a single general intelligence quotient
(c) Tests are selected and administered so as best to ensure that when a test is administered to a child with impaired sensory, manual, or speaking skills, the test results accurately reflect the child's aptitude or achievement level or whatever other factors the test pur-

ports to measure, rather than reflecting the child's impaired sensory, manual, or speaking skills (except where those skills are the factors which the test purports to measure).

(d) No single procedure is used as the sole criterion for determining an appropriate educational program for a child; and

(e) The evaluation is made by a multidisciplinary team or group of persons, including at least one teacher or other specialist with knowledge in the area of suspected disability.

(f) The child is assessed in all areas related to the suspected disability, including, where appropriate, health, vision, hearing, social and emotional status, general intelligence, academic performance, communicative status, and motor abilities. . . .

Comment. Children who have a speech impairment as their primary handicap may not need a complete battery of assessments (e.g., psychological, physical, or adaptive behavior). However, a qualified speech-language pathologist would (1) evaluate each speech impaired child using procedures that are appropriate for the diagnosis and appraisal of speech and language disorders, and (2) where necessary, make referrals for additional assessments needed to make an appropriate placement decision.

The various states have promulgated state regulations consistent with the preceding minimum requirements but more specific in many cases. These federal evaluation requirements are the base; the states have added additional detail to make their state regulations consistent in terminology with their own state laws and other regulations.

Education in the Least Restrictive Environment

Public Law 94-142 requires "that special classes, separate schooling, or other removal of handicapped children from the regular educational environment occurs only when the nature or severity of the handicap is such that education in regular classes . . . cannot be achieved satisfactorily" (p. 9), but it is important to note that the law first mandates a "free, appropriate education." The "least re-

strictive environment" must be determined for each student *on an individual basis.* What is appropriate for one student might be totally inappropriate for another. As noted by Ballard and Zettel (1977, p. 183), the requirement of the least restrictive educational environment "is not a provision for mainstreaming. In fact, the word is never used." They further note that the concept of the least restrictive environment "does not mandate that all handicapped children will be educated in the regular classroom" and that "it does not abolish any particular educational environment, for instance, educational programming in a residential setting" (p. 183). Ballard and Zettel were leading advocates for the handicapped and strongly supported the concept of the least restrictive environment, but they were well aware that by 1977 there were many misunderstandings about the least restrictive environment and the idea of mainstreaming.

Another statement on the least restrictive environment appeared as an editorial comment in the publication *Closer Look* (Parents' Campaign for Handicapped Children and Youth [PCHCY], 1978):

One of the basic principles of the new education law for handicapped children is the right of each child to be educated in the "least restrictive alternative" setting. It emphasizes the importance of learning in as normal an environment as possible. PL 94-142 makes clear that children should be removed from the mainstream of school life *only* if it really isn't possible for them to make it in regular classes (even with extra assistance). When a child *is* in a separate program, every effort should be made to provide experiences for give-and-take with non-handicapped peers.

That's the spirit—and the letter—of the law. Mainstreaming covers a wide variety of alternatives, and placement *should* be made on the basis of individual needs. For some, it means learning in a regular classroom with the help of resource teachers, or special kinds of aid. For others, it may mean spending most of their day in separate classrooms, with as much opportunity as possible

RULES AND REGULATIONS FOR PL 94-142
REGARDING LEAST RESTRICTIVE ENVIRONMENT

General

Each public agency shall insure:

That to the maximum extent appropriate, handicapped children, including children in public or private institutions or other care facilities, are educated with children who are not handicapped, and

That special classes, separate schooling or other removal of handicapped children from the regular educational environment occurs only when the nature or severity of the handicap is such that education in regular classes with the use of supplementary aids and services cannot be achieved satisfactorily.

Continuum of alternative placements

Each public agency shall insure that a continuum of alternative placements is available to meet the needs of handicapped children for special education and related services.

The continuum required under [the first paragraph] of this section must:

(1) Include the alternative placements listed in the definition of special education (instruction in regular classes, special classes, special schools, home instruction, and instruction in hospitals and institutions), and

(2) Make provision for supplementary services (such as resource room or itinerant instruction) to be provided in conjunction with regular class placement.

Placements

Each public agency shall insure that:

(a) Each handicapped child's educational placement:

(1) Is determined at least annually,

(2) Is based on his or her individualized education program, and

(3) Is as close as possible to the child's home:

(b) The various alternative placements included are available to the extent necessary to implement the individualized education program for each handicapped child;

(c) Unless a handicapped child's individualized education program requires some other arrangement, the child is educated in the school which he or she would attend if not handicapped; and

(d) In selecting the least restrictive environment, consideration is given to any potential harmful effect on the child or on the quality of services which he or she needs.

Note: Federal Register vol. 42, no. 163, 1977, p. 42497.

to participate in regular school activities. For a few, it may still be necessary to live and learn in a residential setting—but close to home, with as many contacts with the real world as possible.

These are important decisions, and they must take into account many aspects of each child's needs and levels of ability. They are not fixed, unchanging plans; they should be evaluated and revised as children develop.

Underlying the philosophy of mainstreaming is the recognition of the growth in self-esteem, social skill and awareness that takes place when handicapped and nonhandicapped children have the chance to learn, play and grow together.

We feel that this statement is unusually significant because *Closer Look* is an advocacy-oriented publication by PCHCY, an organization that is strongly dedicated to assisting parents in obtaining educational rights for their children. It has always supported the concept of maximum integration in the regular classroom but in this statement carefully explains that all students may not be able to function in the regular classroom.

The actual statement from the rules and regulations of PL 94-142 appears in the box on p. 28. In addition to the general statement about the least restrictive environment, there is a requirement that local educational agencies have available for use when needed a continuum of placements *including* special classes and special schools. The first question involves what is most appropriate. It is first a matter of meeting the student's individual, educational, and social needs. Then, if these needs can be met in any of two or three placements, the rule is to use the least restrictive setting.

To show the problems that potentially can arise from misunderstandings about the concept of the least restrictive environment, mainstreaming, and another closely related topic, the IEP, Table 2–1 outlines the more common fallacies about these topics and the facts, as we see them. We hope it is of value in clarifying both this subject and certain concerns about the IEP, which is discussed in the following section.

The Individualized Educational Program

As a result of PL 94-142, all students who are placed in special educational programs must have an IEP. To a considerable extent, the requirement for an IEP for each student is the result of unacceptable past practices in special classes for the handicapped in which different students were placed in the class but all received essentially the same educational program. The rules and regulations of PL 94-

142 in the *Federal Register* indicate that the IEP must include the following:

1. A statement of the present levels of educational performance.
2. A statement of annual goals, including short-term instructional objectives.
3. A statement of the specific educational services to be provided to this handicapped student and the extent to which such student will be able to participate in regular educational programs.
4. The projected date for initiation and anticipated duration of such services.
5. Appropriate, objective criteria and evaluation procedures and schedules for determining, on at least an annual basis, whether instructional objectives are being achieved. (*Federal Register,* vol. 42. no. 163, 1977, p. 42491)

In addition to the preceding requirements, which should be considered *minimum* requirements, many states have added others, usually developed by state education department personnel with input from special educators from local educational agencies.

Although due process is clearly an essential part of PL 94-142, there are teachers who believe that there may be "more process than is due." One of the serious concerns expressed by teachers is that procedures (particularly the development and monitoring of IEPs) take a significant amount of time and that this limits their direct instructional time with students. We certainly respect this concern, but there appear to be alternatives that may greatly facilitate the development and updating of IEPs. One such alternative is computer-assisted management (Behrmann, 1984; Bennett, 1982; Brown, 1982; Hagen, 1984; Wilson, 1981). Brown reported one such approach, Computer-Assisted Management of Educational Objectives (CAMEO), that demonstrated that IEP development and

TABLE 2–1. IEPs, mainstreaming, and the least restrictive environment—facts and fallacies

Commonly Accepted Fallacy	Fact
PL 94-142 and the principle of "mainstreaming" dictate that all handicapped students should be enrolled in the regular class for all, or at least part, of the school day.	Handicapped students should be enrolled in the regular class for as much of the school day as appropriate, given their unique needs. This may mean that they are in the regular class for all of the day, in a special class for all of the day, or anywhere on the placement continuum between these extremes.
If the parent says *no* to a proposed plan that includes some special-class programming, the school has no alternative but to retain the student in the regular class.	The parent(s) must be a part of all deliberations regarding the educational programming and may say *no* to a given plan. The school may decide to go along with the parent's stand, but when this does not work out, in certain very clear-cut cases, school officials have the responsibility to initiate an appeals procedure in which outside authorities are involved in final determinations about placement.
The IEP is a contract, and if the student does not reach the educational goals described in the IEP, the teacher and other school authorities may be liable to lawsuit for breaking or not living up to the contract.	The IEP is an educational-management plan or tool. It does require good faith efforts to achieve the goals and objectives listed in the IEP, and the parent can ask for revisions, but federal regulations specifically note that the IEP does not constitute a guarantee that the student will progress at a specified rate or achieve specific academic levels.

updating could be reduced by half, allowing teachers more time for instruction with individual students. This system employs computer technology in conjunction with a bank of several thousand skill-based objectives. The teacher uses a key-word entry system, and the computer locates and produces objectives in a letter-quality, typed IEP. This type of technology may provide a welcome time-saving solution to the work load created by IEPs, but at present there are legal proceedings underway regarding computer-designed IEPs that may be too similar (not really "individually developed") according to plaintiffs. It is perhaps too early to predict the outcome of this controversy.

The major components of the IEP (as shown in the box on p. 33) reflect the kind of information that will more often be found in this document. It is the responsibility of *special educators* to see that the legal requirements of the state are fulfilled; regular classroom teachers are not absolutely required to know the details of IEP development. On the other hand, the regular classroom teacher is involved in IEP planning meetings and certainly may be involved in implementing the IEP for any handicapped student who may be in her or his classroom. Therefore, it is prudent for all teachers at least to understand the basic requirements for and the purposes of this important management tool. A careful review of the 11 basic components of the IEP will provide a basic concept of the information actual IEPs may contain. We have seen IEPs ranging from 2 to 10 or 12 pages but

TABLE 2–1. (continued)

Commonly Accepted Fallacy	Fact
If a student does not reach the goals and objectives outlined in the IEP, the teacher will be blamed by the administration at teacher-evaluation time.	As noted above, the IEP is recognized in the federal regulations as a plan, not a contract. The local school district can establish whatever means of teacher evaluation it deems feasible, but the strong NEA stand on this issue makes such use of the IEP highly unlikely.
Mainstreaming is less costly than providing services in a special-class setting.	Mainstreaming may be either more costly or less costly than education in a special-class setting. This depends on the needs of the student under consideration. In most cases, *given the provision of proper support services,* it will cost the same or perhaps slightly more.
Mainstreaming handicapped students will detract from the educational progress of nonhandicapped students.	There is little question that many students are limited in their understanding of the extent and nature of differences between individuals in society. Through mainstreaming they may learn to better understand and appreciate human differences, while recognizing important similarities. *If* the regular classroom teacher is assisted through special materials and alternative teaching strategies, *all* students may benefit academically. If such assistance is *not* provided or if students who should be in special programs are placed in regular classes, nonhandicapped students may suffer academically.

have noted that their value is not always related to their length. It is not as much a question of length as of the nature of the information and planning provided and the degree to which the information truly reflects an *individualized* program. If assessment is planned with care, if assessment tools are appropriate and administered properly, and if assessment information and other related information are considered thoughtfully by professionals and parents, a meaningful program can be developed. The IEP form—the paper on which the IEP is recorded—provides a structured format with which to record both the basis for educational deliberations and the long-range program through which teachers plan to assist the student. The format *is* important, in that it is a reminder to

consider a variety of factors and to be as specific as possible in planning. It may also be important as a legal instrument, in case of controversy, to provide evidence concerning whether school officials have followed the requirements of the law. It is possible that some school districts are continuing to break the law (or severely bend it), but we believe there has been great improvement in IEP development since IEPs were first dictated in the mid-1970s.

Parental Involvement and Consultation

There is no major section of the regulations governing PL 94-142 separately considering parental involvement and consultation, but we believe that this is one major intent of the

Regular classroom teachers, parents, teachers of the handicapped, and others are involved in developing the IEP.

law, as is indicated by the following requirements in the rules and regulations:

1. Native language of parents must be used, with interpreter or translator provided as needed. Communications must be in native language.
2. Parents' permission is required to initiate assessment.
3. Parents must be informed about conference in which assessment results are considered.

4. Parents should be involved in the IEP meeting. Meeting time must be established far enough in advance to permit opportunity for parent to attend, and the meeting must be in convenient place at a convenient time. If parents cannot attend, the public agency must use other methods to obtain parent participation (conference phone call, etc.).
5. School records must be made available to parents.
6. Parents may ask for amendment of

MAJOR COMPONENTS OF THE INDIVIDUALIZED
EDUCATIONAL PROGRAM (IEP)

1. IEP development checklist and procedural checklist.
2. Identification and background information. Student's name, parents' names, address, telephone numbers, sex, birthdate, primary language.
3. IEP committee members. Names and functional titles of IEP committee members.
4. Assessment information. *All* information obtained by school personnel through formal or informal assessment procedures that was considered in developing the IEP; this should *always* include a definitive statement of present level of academic functioning in pertinent areas and information about nonacademic areas (e.g., social skills) if such information is in any way pertinent to targeted learning problems or concerns.
5. Other information. This may include medical information, health-history information, information from other community agencies, and historical information about past school attendance and past academic performance; when this information is included, the source must be fully documented.
6. Statement of annual goals. A statement of academic and/or social performance goals to be attained by the close of the school year and how these are to be evaluated.
7. Statement of short-term objectives. More specific objectives, indicated on monthly or quarterly basis; these must be consistent with annual goals and should include at least the following: (a) who will provide the required services, (b) where the services will be provided, (c) special materials or media required, and (d) any special information, such as reinforcers to be used.
8. Educational services provided. For example, occupational therapy or speech therapy services, resource room instruction, or instruction in special-vocational setting.
9. Educational placement recommendations. Should include setting (e.g., resource room and regular classroom), time spent in each placement (e.g., two hours each day in resource room, remainder in regular classroom), and rationale for such placement.
10. Time frame for special services. Significant dates, including at least (a) service-initiation dates (may be different dates for different services), (b) duration of services, (c) approximate dates for evaluations, and (d) approximate dates for additional conferences when applicable.
11. Signatures. IEP conference participants or IEP developers' signatures and parents' signature indicating program approval.

records they feel are inaccurate.

7. Parents may ask for independent evaluation of their child.
8. An involved, detailed procedure for appeals of educational decisions is provided by the law and must be fully explained to parents.

The intent of PL 94-142 regarding parents is clear: parents can play a significant role in the education of their children. The law and regulations guiding implementation of the law indicate rights and responsibilities. The law makes it necessary for educators to do all possible to involve parents in planning for children with special needs and thus demands increased sensitivity on the part of educators to the potential value of the parents' help. It does not mean that parents should dominate such planning. Stories about parents who attempt to do this reflect perhaps 1% or 2% of all parents of exceptional children. More often it is necessary to *encourage* parents to provide information and ideas, and it is the educators' responsibility to do this. Parents must be asked to provide information both in initial planning and in continued program evaluation. This is clearly the intent of the law, and in most instances the results have been positive, leading to a better, more effective, more appropriate program.

Cooperation and Joint Planning by Regular and Special Educators

As is the case with parental involvement and consultation, there is no major section or sub-part of the regulations that separately considers regular and special educator cooperation, but it is a major intent of the law. For example, the law requires that each state have a "Comprehensive System of Personnel Development," which includes training for both regular and special educators. The rules and regulations also provide that a "teacher" must be involved in IEP meetings. The rules further indicate that the "first choice" teacher for a child who is being considered for initial placement in special education is the child's regular teacher. Finally, and probably of most importance, the law directs that the student be in the "least restrictive" educational environment consistent with appropriate programming, which means the regular classroom for most mildly handicapped students. And it indicates that there are to be services from various special education specialists, as dictated by the student's individual needs. Therefore, the law dictates that regular and special education personnel work together for the good of the student.

Two studies point out what is believed to be true about the result of cooperation and joint planning. The first indicates that the team decision-making process does, in real life, lead to superior decision making with regard to placement decisions and educational programming for handicapped children. Pfeiffer notes, "Quite clearly, the group decision-making process facilitated a significant reduction in erroneous placement decisions" (1982, p. 69). The second study involves the degree of participation of regular education teachers in special education placement-

team decisions. The essence of the results of this study by Ysseldyke, Algozzine, and Allen (1982) was that regular classroom teachers tend either not to participate or, if they do, to participate in a superficial manner.

We may speculate that many factors known to influence the involvement of teachers in other aspects of the school will come into play here. The attitude and actions of administrators will have a considerable influence. Extra duty assignments, time provided for meetings and cooperative planning, and the general tone of cooperation in any given school will influence the involvement of teachers in all activities. Acceptance or nonacceptance on the part of special educators is another critical factor. But there is one factor under the direct control of regular class teachers that will most certainly be of considerable importance. Most individuals are more likely to participate in any given process if they feel comfortable with their information/knowledge level as it relates to that process. This is a responsibility that regular class teachers must take care of for themselves.

Advantages and Disadvantages of Mainstreaming

There are both advantages and disadvantages to what has happened in the regular classroom as a result of the concept of the least restrictive educational placement for students with handicapping conditions. Every teacher knows that an additional student with behavior problems or one requiring a good deal of additional, individualized planning and attention, means a more busy, perhaps a more trying, school day. As one teacher told us, "too much is just too much." We agree. In fact, that is why we—and the law—have never indicated that all students with handicapping conditions should be in the regular classroom. But if this concept is properly implemented, there can be benefits to nonhandicapped students, and to the teacher. We will outline just a few.

One major advantage of educating handicapped students in regular classrooms is that all students are thereby exposed to differences in individuals. They can learn not to feel sorry for the disabled, but to gain respect for and appreciation of human differences while recognizing inherent similarities. Students must be exposed to racial, ethnic, intellectual, and psychological differences if they are to reach their full personal potential.

Perhaps today's adults were disadvantaged to some extent because when they were in school they did not have the opportunity to know classmates who were handicapped or different. This disadvantage may be observed in many ways. For example, why do adults today express so many prevalent misconceptions about disabled individuals? Could it be that they had little opportunity to learn about differences in individuals? Is it that they never sat next to a braille-reading classmate or a classmate in a wheelchair? Are the less-than-desirable attitudes often reflected by today's society an indication of our lack of experience with different persons? If so, the integrated classroom may be of great benefit to *all* students.

There are also certain obvious advantages to teachers. Most evidence indicates that today's teachers are the best prepared and in general the most competent ever. The trend to include as a part of every teacher's professional preparation specific coursework and/or skills and competencies to work with handicapped students greatly increases their ability to work with handicapped students and special educators. After many years of separation, general and special educators are beginning to assume cooperative teaching roles. Each discipline has unique skills and competencies that must be shared, and both are seeking insight and specific suggestions about how best to meet the needs of all students. Regular classroom teachers now have the opportunity to provide cooperative learning experiences for themselves and their students, including those who present a special challenge.

Teachers must have challenges to grow personally and professionally. A handicapped student presents one such challenge. We have had considerable experience with regular classroom teachers who express concern when they are informed that they will have a handicapped student in their classroom. It has been very encouraging, however, to observe these same teachers grow personally and professionally and at the end of the year indicate this has been one of the most exciting and challenging experiences of their teaching career. Often such teachers ask if they may have another handicapped student the following year. What initially may be seen as a serious threat often turns into a positive growth experience. Very often the methods and instructional techniques used with a handicapped student may be used with other students, and the challenge of working with students of different abilities— intellectual, physical, or both—may keep teachers from teaching *at* students. With minimal help regular teachers may learn to serve as a facilitator to provide each student with the opportunity to reach his fullest potential.

As for those students with handicapping conditions, whose unmet needs led to present programming practices, certain questions remain as to when, how, and under what conditions the moderately and severely handicapped should be integrated with nonhandicapped students. Public Law 94-142 requires that we provide special classes and even residential settings as available alternatives, implying that some students may require such separate settings. For the most part, it is the severely handicapped, and in some cases the moderately handicapped, who require separate settings. The placement of the mildly handicapped, when appropriate assistance is provided to the classroom teacher, is a different matter.

If our purpose is to provide handicapped students with the opportunity to reach their maximum potential and to become contributing members of society, we must provide them with an *equal* educational opportunity, an opportunity to be educated with their nonhandicapped peers in the least restrictive educational environment. When this is possible and educationally appropriate, it is the best way to prepare them to live as successful adults in an integrated society.

A CONTINUUM OF EDUCATIONAL SERVICES

Federal law requires the provision of a continuum of alternative educational services. This concept predates PL 94-142 but became the accepted standard as a result of the passage of PL 94-142. This standard does not mean that all local school districts actually provide the total continuum but rather that there has been relatively rapid movement since the mid-1970s toward acceptance of this concept as a goal. This continuum is as follows:

Regular classroom teacher has primary responsibilities.

1. regular classroom with consultative assistance from special education
2. regular classroom with consultation plus special materials from special education
3. regular classroom with itinerant-teacher services from special education
4. regular classroom with resource room, resource teacher service from special education

Special education has primary responsibility.

5. special class in regular school with some integration for at least some children
6. special class in separate, special, day school
7. hospital and homebound service[2]
8. residential or boarding school

---

[2]May follow several different patterns.

In the first four plans, the student remains in a regular classroom for all or most of the school day, and his regular classroom teacher has primary responsibility for his program. In the first two plans the regular classroom teacher receives consultative assistance or special instructional materials from special education personnel, but the student is not assisted directly by special educators. In the third and fourth plans the regular classroom teacher retains primary responsibility, but special education personnel provide supportive or supplemental assistance to *both* the student and the teacher or teachers. The services provided may take place in the regular classroom but are more often provided in another area, such as the resource room.

In plan 5 the student attends the regular class part-time and a special class part-time. The amount of time spent in the regular classroom depends on the student's ability to profit from regular classroom instruction and the extent of need for special assistance. In plan 5, the student will normally spend the majority of the day in a special class and is selectively included in regular classroom activities.

In plans 6, 7 and 8 more comprehensive services are provided. Plan 6 involves service by specialized personnel in a school in which all students are receiving special assistance because of handicapping conditions. Plan 7 may involve the regular classroom teacher, and instruction may be provided through an electronic hookup with the regular classroom. Plan 8 is for students with severe problems, who require a 24-hour program.

Although we agree that placement in regular classrooms is desirable for the majority of students, there are and will be students whose needs must be met through more segregated programs. The alternative-program continuum does not assume that one type of program is better for *all* students. The basic underlying rationale is that each and every student must be considered individually. For one student, special class placement may be the least restrictive alternative, whereas another may be most effectively served in a regular classroom with a minimum of special education services. Still another student may be most appropriately served in a residential or boarding school.

The alternative educational placement continuum must be flexible. Teachers must recognize that students' needs may change over time or as a result of corrective changes (such as glasses, prostheses, or hearing aids) or educational remediation. According to PL 94-142, students must be reevaluated annually to determine whether they are able to move to another program. It is also possible that a student may make a large skip from one type of program to another. One hopes that most moves will be in the direction of less restrictive settings.

SERVICES PROVIDED BY SPECIAL EDUCATORS

What services can the regular educator expect from special educators? Though both the quality and quantity of such services will vary from state to state and from district to district, certain generalizations may be made.

Consultation will vary in type and amount and will normally relate to such factors as the nature of the handicap, degree of severity of the handicap, amount of time the student spends in the regular class, and, of course, the dictates of the IEP. One of the more highly regarded models for consultative service, often called *collaborative consultation,* appears to be effective in many cases. This strategy borrows much from psychology and leadership/management orientations, and assumes a triadic model: the consultant (in this case the special educator), the mediator (the classroom teacher), and the target learner (the student). The model is too complex for

full explanation here, but the assumption is that for effective results, all parties work together to solve problems.

For ideas from the special educator to make maximum sense for the student, there must be continuing input from the regular educator. For example, the regular teacher may have additional information that might change the consultative advice. Or the teacher may simply disagree. The reverse is also true. Parity among these two individuals must be achieved and maintained. Decision making must be mutual, based on collaborative efforts.

The type and amount of materials provided will vary greatly, but the teacher and special educator must agree on any approach requiring resource materials. For example, enlarged materials may be provided for a low-vision student, or high-interest, low-vocabulary-level reading materials for a student experiencing difficulty with the regular materials. Materials, along with ideas for use of such materials in the regular class, may be provided in any of the "continuum" 2–5 and, of course, consultation, in plans 1–5.

The *itinerant-teacher plan* (plan 3) deserves some special comment. When served by an itinerant teacher, the student is enrolled in his neighborhood school, but he and his teachers receive direct assistance from special education personnel. The itinerant-teacher plan with which most educators are familiar is that followed by public school speech specialists. This plan has also been used extensively by teachers of the visually impaired and hearing impaired.

Although the manner in which this plan is implemented varies, the itinerant or traveling teacher generally works with students on a regularly scheduled basis (two or three times a week) or whenever necessary, depending on a student's needs at a particular time. The itinerant teacher provides instruction in a designated area outside of the classroom or may meet with the student in the classroom.

The itinerant teacher may also assume a helping- or assisting-teacher role by working with a small group of students who are in need of the same remedial work as the handicapped student.

In sparsely populated areas of the country, where schools tend to be small in total enrollment, it may be difficult to justify a full-time, resource room program at one school, and because of long distances between schools, equally difficult to justify busing students to a specific school to enlarge the population of students requiring special services. In such cases the itinerant-teacher plan may be the most appropriate approach. This plan does not seem as practical as the resource room plan for students with learning disabilities, behavior problems, or limited intellectual ability, because it does not provide intensive services on a daily basis.

The *resource room plan,* that is, regular classroom placement plus resource room and resource teacher assistance (plan 4) appears to be the most used of these special education models. In this plan, the student is enrolled in a regular classroom but receives supplemental or remedial instruction in a resource room. The resource room plan differs from the itinerant-teacher plan in that the student is provided more specific assistance from the resource teacher on a regularly scheduled basis (usually daily), and there is a specific room in which he receives this assistance. The ways in which resource programs operate vary extensively. In some instances the resource teacher may serve the student on a temporary basis while using assessment techniques and planning instructional strategies to be carried out in the student's regular classroom. In this situation the student may go to the resource room for a brief period of time each day until assessment procedures have been completed and a program plan has been implemented. In most school systems, however, a placement- or program-planning committee reviews a variety of information about any student referred for possible assistance in the resource room, and programming is initiated only insofar as this committee indicates its feasibility for the student and its consistency with local school district policy. In all cases the parents must be involved in such placement-planning committee deliberations and must give express permission for resource room intervention.

The resource room teacher should have the time, the materials, and the specific training needed to find more effective ways to teach students with special needs. His or her function is dual: to initiate alternative strategies and help the student find success in the resource room and to provide suggestions to the regular classroom teacher to increase the likelihood that the student will find success in that setting.

Often the resource room teacher provides valuable unofficial assistance to various teachers, sometimes in terms of general instructional ideas but more often in relation to a specific student. This is one of the more effective functions of the resource room teacher, although in some states it must be performed unofficially because state reimbursement guidelines restrict the number of students who may be served.

In recent years some resource teachers have been providing their services in regular classrooms rather than in separate resource rooms. When the student is assisted in the regular classroom, it is assumed that transfer and maintenance are greater than when programming is provided only in a special setting.

Students often perform in a very different way or at a different level in their regular classroom as compared to a small-group situation in the resource room. By working with the students in their regular classroom, the resource room teacher may gain greater insight into their needs. In addition, the regular classroom teacher and the resource teacher may be able to share ideas and materials and establish a stronger working relationship that accepts individual teaching strategies, strengths, and weaknesses. One of the greatest gains in retaining handicapped students in regular classrooms is that general and special educators may share their unique skills and competencies rather than working in isolation, a practice that occurred for many years.

Two special class plans are shown in the continuum of services (plans 5 and 6). The first, *special class in the regular school,* is a continuation of the model that "launched" special education in the public schools many years ago. In this plan, the student usually receives most of his or her academic instruction from a special education teacher, but may receive some instruction from regular class programs. This plan should be used only when absolutely essential to the social and educational goals of the student. The second, *special class in a separate day school,* is seldom used today. This plan is designed for students who are very severely disabled or multihandicapped and need comprehensive special education services for their entire school day. Many of the students served in this plan would in years past have been placed in a residential setting and would have had little or no contact with their family or community. The special day school permits a return to home and family at the close of each day and thus moves the student in the direction of a less restrictive environment.

The program of *hospital and homebound service* does not fit into the continuum-of-services concept as easily as most of the other plans. Students with chronic conditions requiring long-term treatment in a hospital or in their homes receive special instruction from homebound-itinerant special education personnel. The nature of the educational program depends on the student's ability and level of achievement, the prognosis of the condition, and the likelihood of the student's returning to school. Some students who are hospitalized or homebound because of a short-term illness may also be served on this basis; in this instance the instruction is closely related to the programming in the regular classroom and is planned in conjunction with teachers of the classes to which the student will return. In situations in which the student requires long-term care, a two-way communication system between the student's home or the hospital and the regular classroom may be set up. This system may employ a telephone or a videophone to reduce the isolation of being at home or in a hospital. This two-way telephone or videophone system provides an opportunity for full-time educational programming and maximum interaction with other students. In many ways this hospital/homebound service may be more closely aligned with the regular classroom than plans 5 and 6, especially if the service is provided through a two-way telephone or videophone system, for it puts the student in regular, daily contact with his or her classmates. On the other hand, there is complete physical separation. Its placement on the continuum of services is debatable, but its value for students who need it is undeniable. The classroom teacher's participation in this program will vary widely from situation to situation.

Residential or boarding schools are a last resort. If other plans cannot be made to work, these must be considered. Historically, residential schools were established for students who were visually impaired, hearing impaired, emotionally disturbed, or mentally retarded because local school districts did not offer the needed services. Students may attend these programs during the 9-month school year or on a year-round basis, depending on the extent of the handicap. Because of the trend toward placing handicapped students in the least restrictive setting, these programs now tend to serve only the more seriously involved and multihandicapped. The primary purpose of schools for the visually impaired and hearing impaired is educational, whereas residential facilities for the emotionally disturbed emphasize treatment. Residential schools for the mentally retarded have a primary custodial emphasis but have more recently begun to focus on education and training goals as an important secondary emphasis. In addition to educational programming, residential facilities can also provide 24-hour comprehensive services required by some of the more severely handicapped.

REFERRAL, CLASSIFICATION, AND PLACEMENT

Identification of students who need special services is an all-important function that is more often initiated by the regular class teacher. This usually takes place after various efforts have been made to make the regular program work, with very little success. Such identification begins when a referral for further evaluation is made and concludes when a group of professionals, and the parent(s) decide on the best possible path for future efforts on behalf of the student under consideration. Many steps must be taken between these two points, and one goal—the best possible educational program for the student—must remain uppermost in the minds of all involved in this procedure. In the following sections, we will consider the major steps in this process and cautions that must be observed.

The Teacher's Responsibility to Make Referrals

There is one function that must—in most instances—be carried out by the regular class teacher. Before assessment, planning, and special programming can take place, someone must ask the question, "Does this student need special help beyond that which is normally provided in the regular classroom?" Sometimes this question comes from parents, physicians, or professionals in other community agencies, but more often than not it is the regular class teacher who first recognizes that a student needs assistance. When continued, serious efforts to modify or adapt the normal program prove ineffective, and either academic performance or interpersonal relationships are sufficiently different from those of other students in the class, a formal request for assistance should be made. This request is commonly called a referral.

Specific referral procedures vary from district to district, but there usually is a special referral form to be completed by the regular classroom teacher. In addition to the student's name, age, grade, and sex, most referral forms ask questions about (1) grade level in academic areas (usually means grade equivalent on a standardized achievement test), (2) data on behavior (e.g., interpersonal relations with other students and with teachers), (3) specific reading strengths and deficits (e.g., word-attack skills, memory for words, and ability to read orally), (4) ability (relative to others in class) in class discussion and interaction, (5) specific strengths and deficits in arithmetic/mathematics, (6) strengths and weaknesses in nonacademic areas, (7) any unusual family data that might be pertinent, and (8) a summary of any methods or approaches that have been unusually successful or total failures for the student.

Students should be formally referred when appropriate, but overreferral should be avoided if at all possible. Since parents must be contacted to gain additional information and to obtain permission for further assessment, the matter of referral must not be approached lightly. If a student is referred when there is no need, the parents may become upset, and many people will spend time and effort needlessly.

Some school districts hold an informal, preliminary review meeting to discuss the major concerns of the referring teacher, whether those concerns are academic or behavioral, before the formal referral is made. This meeting will include the classroom teacher and at least one special educator and may include the principal, counselor, and in some cases, the parents. The purpose of this meeting is to examine various factors that may have a bearing on the student's behavior or academic performance, methods or techniques tried by the teacher, and their success or failure. At this meeting the decision may be made to try other academic approaches or motivational techniques (where academic performance is the problem) or other behavior-management techniques (in the case of behavior disorder). Often the meeting will be adjourned with the understanding that the group will meet again at an established time to evaluate change. It may, however, be decided that an immediate formal referral will be made so that appropriate multidisciplinary evaluation may be initiated.

Some recommend a formal *prereferral-intervention system* based, according to its major advocates, on the principle of prevention (Graden, Casey, & Christenson, 1985, p. 379). Prereferral-intervention advocates assume that many students who might otherwise be placed within the special education framework (classified) might be served through consultative help (what they call *indirect* special education services) and thus permit special education personnel to assist more students, without those students being formally assessed and classified. In this model "resources are directed at providing intervention assistance at the point of initial referral" (Graden et al., 1985, p. 379). Using this framework, the teacher requests consultation, such consultation being accomplished in a variety of ways. In the Graden et al. description, parents are not formally included in this initial consultation, though

certainly some schools might decide they should be. After the consultation and planning of various intervention strategies, the next stage is evaluation of the results of these strategies. Following this evaluation, a conference is held to determine whether to continue the interventions, modify the interventions, or refer the child for a more formal assessment. In other words, this process is a step between the teacher's realization of a need for help and the actual, formal, special education referral. One question about a formalized preferral-intervention system, openly using the time and skills of the special educator, is that in many states the special educator cannot formally work with students except as they have been classified as eligible for and requiring special education services. This policy may seem a bit rigid, but its origins are in situations where school districts have used the services of special educators to do many things other than work on behalf of handicapped students, even though the extra funds (both state and federal) that help support their salaries are conditional on their serving only the handicapped.

Whatever the means, we would recommend that some type of additional consideration be given teacher referrals before starting a formal assessment procedure. This review should be accomplished consistent with state and federal regulations, and its purpose should be to help as many students as possible without having to classify them as "students requiring special education services." However, the use of such a system must *not* lead to denial of needed special education services for students who have such special needs. If we are not careful, this procedure could become an easy way for school administrators who want to save scarce tax dollars to do so by serving many children "just a little bit," in the name of intervention and prevention.

In cases where there is an apparent (or verified) problem with hearing or vision, or where classroom adaptations are required due to physical problems, the major question is not classification of the disability (though there may be multiple disabilities), but rather the best way to provide the most effective educational program, given the disability. The problem may be mental retardation, behavior disorder, or learning disability. If so, the matter of classification is important for purposes of effective planning for the present, for realistic future planning (on the part of both the school and parents), and of course for the various states' legal requirements relating to special financial support for programs for students with disabilities. This statement leads directly into the question of the advisability, the necessity, and perhaps even the morality, of classification.

Testing and Classification

Some have questioned the necessity of testing and classification of students, and various lawsuits have led to changes in the manner in which testing and classification take place; but they must be continued, given the education system and funding mechanisms as they exist today. H. Rutherford Turnbull III, lawyer, advocate for the handicapped, parent of a child with disabilities, and leading national authority on the law and disabilities, believes there must be "procedures to protect children from improper testing, misclassification, and inappropriate placement" (1986, p. 73). He adds that this is the major focus of current legislation. But he also indicates that "testing, classification, and placement in special education programs must be continued" (p. 72). Reasons listed by Turnbull and others include

1. to permit the planning and implementation of appropriate services
2. to provide a basis for funding to encourage more and better programming

3. to permit more accurate evaluation of the effectiveness of various types of efforts
4. to provide a focal point for advocacy efforts of parents and others
5. to provide a common denominator for professional groups
6. to provide a more meaningful basis for preventive or early intervention efforts

Misclassification, inappropriate testing and placement, and other problems must be dealt with; but ignoring the presence of a condition that can properly be classified as *mental retardation* or *hearing impairment* is certainly not the answer to assisting students who have unique problems requiring innovative educational interventions.

Although classification, according to federal guidelines, means use of traditional categories of mentally retarded, learning disabled, emotionally disturbed (or behavior disordered), and so on, there is a growing trend across the nation to use a cross-categorical or noncategorical classification system at the state level. This trend is not nonclassification, but rather classification without using traditional terminology. To receive the special funding that "fuels" special education services for children with special needs, some type of classification is required in all states. However, because it is sometimes difficult to differentiate between mental retardation and learning disabilities, especially when dealing with younger children and with mild levels of disability, these two categories and mild behavioral disorders are sometimes combined in a classification such as *educationally handicapped* or some similar terminology. Sensory disabilities (the areas of vision and hearing) and physical disabilities are likely to be classified in a more straightforward manner, since there is less chance for confusion or misclassification.

We believe that classification is justified only if it permits some educational provision

Appropriate assessment is essential and is required by PL 94-142.

and assistance that would not be provided without such classification. It is the personal hope of most special educators whom we know that many students with mild disabilities can be served in the regular class without ever needing to attend separate, special-service programs. However, the more severe the learning problem, the more likely that help from outside the classroom is needed. For these students, comprehensive, careful identification and classification procedures are essential. It is, of course, possible that some day the system we call public education will provide appropriate, individualized educational programming for all of those students we now call exceptional without the need for classification reflecting the type of exceptionality and the type and extent of specialized services required. However, until that time, it would appear that identification of such students and classi-

fication according to some established system are necessary.

After Formal Referral

What happens after formal referral is shown graphically in Figure 2–1. Most of these steps have been discussed previously in this chapter. Parents must give permission for the assessment, and they must be told their rights under due-process procedures. If they give permission (and most do, if the situation is explained properly), the various parts of the interdisciplinary assessment are completed. A staffing is held (parents must be invited, and efforts must be made to get them to attend), and it must be decided whether the student's problems result from a handicapping condition. If the decision is that they do, then a classification is agreed upon, and the matter goes to a group that must develop an IEP. Parents must be involved in the IEP

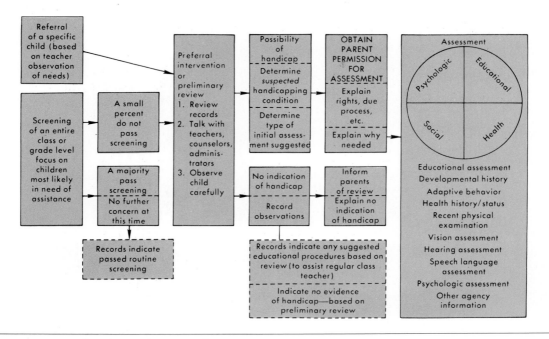

FIGURE 2–1. Referral, assessment, staffing, IEP, and placement

Note. From *Special Education for the '80s* by B. R. Gearheart, 1980, Columbus, Ohio: Merrill Publishing Co. Copyright © 1980. Reprinted by permission of the author.

development and must sign the IEP. The content of the IEP will commonly determine both the type and extent of special services provided the student and whether he or she receives any services outside of the regular class. If there is any such "outside class" placement, parents must approve of this placement. The range of possible services that should be available to meet the student's needs is the "continuum of educational services."

The Placement Decision

When a student is determined to require the more specialized program that should follow classification and the determination of special needs, a decision must be made as to where—on the continuum of services—he should receive such a program. The rule is, of course, the least restrictive placement required to meet his or her needs. But what

variables should be considered in making this decision? Logically enough, these variables include, in order of importance, the student, parents, teacher, and administration. The four variables may be detailed as follows:

Student

1. chronological age
2. type and degree of impairment or disability
3. age at onset of disability (congenital or acquired)
4. level of academic achievement
5. measured intellectual ability
6. social maturity/social skills
7. presence of multiple handicapping conditions (need for related noneducational services)
8. ambulation or mobility (particularly important when considering orthopedic and other health and visual impairment)

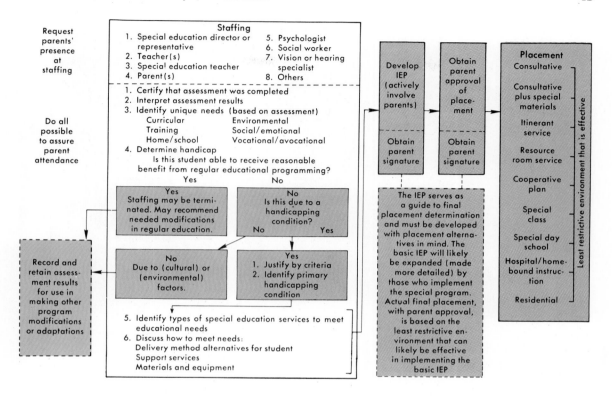

Request parents' presence at staffing

Staffing
1. Special education director or representative
2. Teacher(s)
3. Special education teacher
4. Parent(s)
5. Psychologist
6. Social worker
7. Vision or hearing specialist
8. Others

1. Certify that assessment was completed
2. Interpret assessment results
3. Identify unique needs (based on assessment)
   Curricular   Environmental
   Training   Social/emotional
   Home/school   Vocational/avocational
4. Determine handicap
   Is this student able to receive reasonable benefit from regular educational programming?
   Yes   No

Do all possible to assure parent attendance

Yes
Staffing may be terminated. May recommend needed modifications in regular education.

No
Is this due to a handicapping condition?
No   Yes

Record and retain assessment results for use in making other program modifications or adaptations

No
Due to (cultural) or (environmental) factors.

Yes
1. Justify by criteria
2. Identify primary handicapping condition

5. Identify types of special education services to meet educational needs
6. Discuss how to meet needs:
   Delivery method alternatives for student
   Support services
   Materials and equipment

Develop IEP (actively involve parents)

Obtain parent signature

Obtain parent approval of placement

Obtain parent signature

The IEP serves as a guide to final placement determination and must be developed with placement alternatives in mind. The basic IEP will likely be expanded (made more detailed) by those who implement the special program. Actual final placement, with parent approval, is based on the least restrictive environment that can likely be effective in implementing the basic IEP

Placement
Consultative
Consultative plus special materials
Itinerant service
Resource room service
Cooperative plan
Special class
Special day school
Hospital/home-bound instruction
Residential

Least restrictive environment that is effective

9. success of past and present educational program
10. speech and language ability
11. wishes of student and student's parents

Parents.   Before the passage of PL 94-142 parents were primarily passive consumers of service and had limited input in the process. They were occasionally involved in program and placement decisions, but generally the nature of their involvement was as receivers of information from professionals, for example, being told their child will be assigned to a particular room. Today, as a result of federal legislation that was a direct result of parental demands and litigation, parents have become integral and active participants in educational decision making and in monitoring their child's acquisition of essential skills. This is evidenced not only by mandatory participation in due-process procedures but also by parental involvement in the devel-

opment of the student's IEP, discussed earlier.

Teachers.   After preliminary placement determinations based on specific student characteristics have been made, the next step is to consider existing programs and services relative to the apparent needs of the student. In most cases some variation of existing programs is effective. Where this is not the case, the possibility of initiating new programs or of obtaining services by contract or by some type of tuition arrangement with another school district must be considered. There is little question that the teachers who actually contact the student have a major influence on the student's success in the regular classroom. Some teachers readily accept the challenge of serving a handicapped student in their classroom whereas others have considerable difficulty in making the adjustments necessary to be effective with these students. Among the most important variables are the following:

Can you find the student with disabilities?

1. professional preparation or in-service education concerning handicapped students (not a prerequisite but highly desirable)
2. previous experience with handicapped students (not a prerequisite but highly desirable)
3. willingness to work cooperatively with resource personnel and parents (resource personnel must be readily available)
4. willingness to accept variations in scheduling, teaching assignments, and classroom structure
5. ability to assess individual learning needs, set goals and objectives, plan and implement teaching strategies, and evaluate student progress
6. acceptance of the basic premise that *all* students have the right to the most appropriate education in the least restrictive environment

Administration. A highly important variable is the degree of administrative commitment to serve all students regardless of learning abilities or disabilities. The administrative staff from the superintendent to the principal must have a real commitment to developing the most appropriate, least restrictive alternatives. There are indications that a very high correlation exists between administrative commitment to the concept of serving handicapped students in regular classrooms and the attitudes of teachers and students. In other words, if the principal is sincerely interested in serving *all* students, this commitment has a very positive influence on the teacher's attitude toward these students. If, however, the principal's attitude toward handicapped students is essentially negative, this attitude is often also exhibited by the teachers. The commitment must go beyond a desire to merely comply with federal and state regulations and must recognize the inherent abilities and potential of all students.

We are not suggesting that most school districts use such a formal checklist when final placement decisions are made. Rather, we are suggesting that these are the kinds of factors regularly discussed in final placement conferences. All placements should be considered as tentative; that is, professionals must recognize that they are a matter of "best present judgment." When such placements prove to be ineffective, essential components of this process should be repeated and earlier plans and decisions reevaluated. There may be no such thing as an absolutely right IEP and/or placement decision.

Cultural/Ethnic Differences and Bilingualism

We have previously considered some of the problems generated by difficulties in carrying out meaningful assessment of students who are culturally, ethnically, or linguistically different from the majority, middle-class, Anglo population of the public schools. Court cases relating to misidentification of some minority students as *mentally retarded* led to some of the requirements in PL 94-142 that we have already reviewed. Though not as often discussed, reaction to this litigation may well have led to some minority children not even being considered for programs they may have needed, so as to avoid controversy.

Even if they had been properly identified, significant questions remain as to how their special programs should be organized and delivered. How similar, for example, should the educational program for a 10-year-old student of Hispanic background, whose first language was Spanish, be to that of another 10-year-old student, whose language had always been English, if both are actually "learning disabled"?

Cummins (1984), in a book-length treatment of issues in assessment and pedagogy of bilingual students in special education programs, makes the following observation: "Although research has amply documented the abuses of the past, there is a noticeable absence of empirically-supported alternative procedures for assessing and meeting the educational needs of minority students. Even the most enlightened policies that have been implemented are, at best, educated guesses as to what might be appropriate, and there is no consensus among the educated guesses of experts" (p. 17).

Expanding on this negative assessment of the situation, we would enumerate the following difficulties:

1. Given existing definitions and assessment techniques, we may identify some students as learning disabled whose problems relate more to language differences than to what most authorities call learning disabilities.
2. Given existing definitions and assessment techniques, we may identify some culturally different students as behaviorally disordered because we do not understand the cultural origins of their behavior and are not organized to deal with their needs in our schools.
3. Because of the cost and bad public relations associated with mistakes in identification and placement of culturally, ethnically, or linguistically different students in the past, school officials may decide to not search with any real diligence among the minority populations for students in need of special services.
4. Identification procedures in existing programs for the gifted/talented undoubtedly lead to "not finding" many potentially gifted/talented students among minority populations.
5. Special education programs have traditionally been viewed as a way to take care of "kids with special problems." Thus there may be a tendency to try to use special education programs as a substitute for other types of programs that should be organized for students who have special needs but are obviously not mentally retarded, learning disabled, emotionally dis-

turbed, or otherwise handicapped. This tendency is encouraged by the fact that programs for the handicapped receive substantial state funding, while many of the other programs do not.

The problems are real and, as Cummins (1984) notes, there is no consensus among the experts, even with respect to their educated guesses. It is not a lost cause, but it does mean that we must remain alert to potential mistakes, oversights, and difficulties. The regular classroom teacher will not likely be asked to solve this problem, but he or she should be fully aware of its existence and complexity.

WHAT ABOUT THE GIFTED?

This consideration of the gifted has been deliberately left to the end of the chapter not because it is less worthy of discussion, but because there is little to report. When asked, most persons in positions of educational leadership tend to agree that special education for the gifted/talented is of great importance, and it certainly can be easily justified on the basis of either the rights of gifted/talented students to maximum opportunity for self-realization or the needs of the nation for gifted leadership. However, PL 94-142 has no direct effect on programs for gifted students except when those students are also handicapped (e.g., a gifted blind student or a gifted orthopedically handicapped student). Attention given to programs for the handicapped has led parents and other advocates for the gifted to demand more recognition of the special needs of the gifted, but such demands have led to only limited action on the part of legislators and educators. There have, however, been some federal laws that have had an impact on programs for the gifted and talented. One of the most important, PL 91-230 (1970), mandated that the

U.S. Commissioner of Education study the needs of gifted and talented students of the nation and report to the Congress. As a result of this report (often called the Marland Report), additional attention was focused on the unmet needs of gifted and talented students, and important initial momentum was gained. Later federal efforts led to the development of The National/State Leadership Training Institute on the Gifted and Talented (NSLTIGT), which has played a most important role in developing training programs at the local and state level and in increasing public interest in the education of the gifted and talented.

A positive step was taken when the Office of Gifted and Talented was established in the Department of Education as a focal point for efforts on behalf of gifted and talented students. For the first time a federal office and federal employees were located in Washington with full-time responsibility to monitor and encourage programs for the gifted and talented and with some access to congressional committees. A later law, PL 95-561, provided a modest amount of federal financial assistance to local and state educational agencies and institutions of higher education to plan, develop, and improve educational programs for gifted and talented children and youth. These federal efforts were important in providing increased attention to the needs of gifted children and youth, but there are no federal legislative guarantees for the gifted that parallel the educational guarantees for the handicapped found in PL 94-142. Federal legislation for the handicapped is mandatory; federal legislation for the gifted and talented is designed to stimulate, encourage, and promote new programs and improve existing programs, but it does not approach education of the gifted and talented as an absolute right to be supported and ensured by the federal government.

Who, then, speaks for the gifted? How are their educational needs met, and who governs and monitors programs established on their behalf? The laws, regulations, and policies of the 50 states and the District of Columbia determine whether there are special programs, which students are served, the qualifications of teachers who teach the gifted and talented, how much of the state's educational resources are committed to this task, and all other related questions. Therefore there is much more variation between states as well as sometimes confusing and/or misleading information about state practices and policies.

The National/State Leadership Training Institute on the Gifted and Talented has provided a center of focus for efforts to promote more effective programs through better trained leadership in the field. Individual universities have provided unique contributions. But despite these efforts there are many areas of the nation where viable programs are not available. The special needs of gifted/talented students in those areas are apparently not recognized; or if they are recognized, they are not met. Whether gifted students in any given school district have special programs that provide for their unique educational needs appears to depend on local interest and the ability of interested persons to influence the local administration and school board. The situation is unquestionably improving, and state laws, reimbursement formulas, state consultants, and growing interest among both general and special educators have been positive factors in this growth. But the absence of federal mandates along with the apparent lack of interest or ability of state officials to monitor and enforce state mandates in some states makes it difficult to generalize beyond the following:

1. More states had legislation regarding the gifted and talented in the eighties than had such legislation in the seventies, and other states have such legislation under consideration.
2. Special reimbursement appears to be in most states a meaningful incentive but not sufficient to cause all districts to initiate special programs for the gifted and talented.
3. An increasing number of school districts are initiating programs designed to identify gifted/talented students at an early age.
4. Definitions of gifted and talented vary widely.
5. The scope and quality of programs vary widely.

This review of federal and state laws, policies, and practices with respect to programs for gifted and talented students is provided here as a status report and as a perspective in comparison to programs for the handicapped. Some school districts with no recognized, formalized programs may be providing for many of their gifted and talented students, but for the most part this is unlikely. We agree with Khatena when he states that a successful, continuing program requires the "combined commitment and press of both local initiative (including professionals, educators, and parents as well as local education agencies), and the state agency (voluntarily or, if necessary, compelled by legislation to enact financial appropriations) . . ." (1982, p. 395). Regular classroom teachers can effectively teach many gifted and talented students, but to do so they require special training and assistance from trained specialists. And there are some gifted and/or talented students who *must* have additional specialized efforts or, as with the handicapped, a significant part of their potential will not be realized. (We will not further discuss concerns and issues in education of the gifted/talented in this chapter but will provide in chapter 12 some detail regarding major issues.)

SUMMARY

Mildly handicapped students are now an accepted part of the regular classroom. Students with moderate-to-severe handicapping conditions may spend much of their school day with their nonhandicapped peers, but most will also receive other services outside the regular classroom. The extent of such outside help is a very individual matter, and federal and state regulations require that such decisions be made on an individual basis.

This chapter outlines the major provisions of PL 94-142, a federal law that mandated nationwide the integration of handicapped and nonhandicapped students with particular emphasis on (1) the right to due process of law, (2) protection in evaluation procedures, and (3) the individualized educational program (IEP). In addition, the chapter considers how the movement toward education of the handicapped in the least restrictive environment has led to more regular teacher/ special teacher consultation and cooperation, and more consultation and cooperation between teachers and parents.

This chapter also provides a number of guidelines for more successful implementation of the principle of education in the least restrictive environment and summarizes the major advantages of such programming. We firmly believe that most of the misconceptions seen today about disabled individuals can be avoided in the future if nonhandicapped and handicapped students are more closely associated as children and youth. And we believe that misconceptions and misunderstandings about handicapped persons are similar to misconceptions and misunderstandings about individuals of other racial and ethnic groups; that is, the consequences are bad for the nation and the world.

As for education of the gifted/talented, the scene is one of great variation. There has been some limited stimulation at the federal level; but with no mandate, it is up to the states and to local authorities as to whether or not they want to follow the leadership provided. Some states have good programs statewide; most states have at least a few good programs; but there are large geographic "pockets" of essentially no meaningful recognition of the unique needs of the gifted/talented. The situation is much better now than in the past, but much remains to be accomplished.

Effective Instruction

TEACHING GUIDELINES—A SEQUENTIAL
CHECKLIST

CLASSROOM DISCIPLINE—THE KEY TO
CLASSROOM CONTROL

STRUCTURE AND INSTRUCTIONAL
MANAGEMENT

THE ROLE OF TECHNOLOGY

GOOD PEDAGOGY

SECONDARY SCHOOL INSTRUCTIONAL
STRATEGIES

- [ ] What are the advantages and disadvantages of a traditionally arranged classroom compared with an informally arranged classroom?
- [ ] What are some misunderstandings about learning centers?
- [ ] How can heterogeneous groups be used effectively with low-achieving students?
- [ ] How can computers be used with students with special needs?
- [ ] How does informal assessment differ from formal assessment?
- [ ] How can you assess a student's preferred learning style, and how would you then adjust your approach to instruction?
- [ ] What are the major advantages and disadvantages of peer-tutoring programs?
- [ ] What is an "advance organizer" and how might it help students with handicapping conditions?
- [ ] How can all students profit from teacher-presentation alternatives directed at students with special needs?
- [ ] What specific strategies would you use with a secondary student who is often moody?

Some teachers want a magic "bag of tricks" to use in teaching exceptional students. Most experienced teachers know that no such bag exists, but that certain instructional and management techniques are more likely to be effective with exceptional students in the regular classroom. We will provide a number of principles, ideas, and techniques we have found to be of value and that others have recommended for use in planning for more effective instruction of exceptional students. Many of these suggestions will be applicable to exceptional students with a variety of needs. They should be supplemented with ideas more specific to certain exceptionalities (as presented in the various chapters of part two of this text) and employed in concert with suggestions provided by special education resource personnel. For the most part, these ideas are also of value in teaching nonhandicapped students, however, some would not likely be used except in situations where unusual instructional needs exist. We will initiate this consideration of instructional ideas and techniques with a review of principles considered important in teaching students with learning or behavior problems, as outlined by Wallace and Kauffman (1986).

TEACHING GUIDELINES—A SEQUENTIAL CHECKLIST

1. *Base initial teaching strategies on assessment information.* This objective means more than the use of test results obtained by a psychologist or educational diagnostician. It includes the results of careful observation, tests given by the teacher, information from school records and parents, and all other available sources. The goal is to establish an overall picture of the student, which will provide a beginning point for planning instructional strategies.

2. *State instructional goals and specific performance objectives and allocate sufficient time to carry them out.* Appropriate goals providing general parameters for instructional planning should come first. Specific instructional objectives, stated in terms of student performance, should follow. In some cases, subobjectives must be added. The purpose is to know where we are heading and to have a means to determine the extent to which we have achieved what we are trying to accomplish. This strategy is important in the education of all students but is particularly important with students with learning problems.[1]

3. *Analyze the student's performance of specific tasks to pinpoint learning problems more precisely.* Careful analysis of the manner in which a student completes learning tasks permits more precise information as to what the student can and cannot do. Error analysis provides guidance as to what must be taught next. Analysis may lead to modification of initial plans or may verify them. In any event, it is an essential step in the instructional process.

4. *Present a new set of tasks, designed to help the student overcome performance deficits.* In expanding on this step in the process, Wallace and Kauffman (1986) suggest the following: (a) organize tasks for efficient presentation, (b) be directive—tell, don't ask, (c) get student attention before attempting to start the task, (d) provide sufficient time for student

---

[1]Specific performance objectives may not be regularly used by regular educators, but the IEP may require them, and they are often essential to plan for instruction for students with special needs effectively.

response, (e) if the student does not respond, repeat and simplify the directions given, (f) cue responses (with a word, gesture, or other signal), (g) use prompts, (h) provide a model for the student to follow, (i) present only those tasks essential to the concept being taught, (j) present tasks in logical sequence, and (k) provide opportunity for practice until mastery is achieved.

5. *Provide feedback on task performance.* Such feedback should be unambiguous, immediate, and corrective (reinforce correct responses, which should reduce incorrect responses).

6. *Structure the learning environment for success.* Later sections of this chapter will provide more information on this topic.

7. *Monitor student performance and keep records of progress.* This objective would include keeping a log of teaching activities, maintaining a chart of student progress, and testing what is being taught. Though such record-keeping does take time, we believe it may *save* time, in the long run, for those one or two students who may be having significant difficulties.[2]

The preceding guidelines might be viewed as "simply common sense," but teachers have told us that such reminders of good teaching practices can be of value. At the very least these seven guidelines provide a yardstick against which teachers may measure their own teaching behavior. They provide a starting point in efforts to develop teaching competencies that will greatly increase the likelihood of success in teaching exceptional students.

---

[2]Abbreviated and adapted from *Teaching Students with Learning and Behavior Problems,* 3d ed. (pp. 126–147) by G. Wallace and J. Kauffman, 1986, Columbus, OH: Merrill Publishing Co. Used with permission.

CLASSROOM DISCIPLINE—THE KEY TO CLASSROOM CONTROL

Effective classroom control is the result of many factors, but one important aspect is what is popularly called *classroom discipline.* Most would agree that the teacher is responsible for what happens in the classroom, including both behavior and learning. The teacher should be in control of the classroom and the activities that are supposed to lead to the realization of the wide variety of learning goals that society has determined to be desirable and in the public interest. Researchers and theorists have promulgated principles and theories about how teachers can accomplish this control and thus have effective classroom discipline, and the list is long and sometimes confusing.

McDaniel has compiled a list of 10 principles he believes will provide general guidelines for teachers who want to "modify their own behaviors in ways that will yield effective group management and control" (1986, pp. 63–67). We will briefly consider McDaniel's list (which was meant for all teachers, not only those of exceptional students), and the reader will discover that many of these principles are discussed in greater depth in other parts of this text. This specific list deserves consideration because it is an excellent compilation of principles aptly described as "traditional and modern, practical and theoretical, pedagogical and psychological" (p. 63):

1. *Focusing.* This principle reminds us that if we do not have students' attention, little learning will take place. Trying to teach over the noise of students who are talking to each other or are running around the room is essentially useless. Learning activities, as selected by *the teacher,* must become the focus of attention, if learning is to be maximized.

2. *Direct instruction.* Students must be told

what they are expected to do, how to do it, and when it should be done. To *keep* students on task, consider topic interest, relevance and individual needs.

3. *Monitoring.* Monitoring means regular, planned checking to see what students are doing, and whether they need assistance or encouragement. It is student accountability, and as students learn they are accountable, classroom control is more easily achieved.

4. *Modeling.* McDaniel emphasizes modeling with respect to the teachers using a soft, low-pitched voice, and suggests that soft reprimands (for example) keep a problem more private and do not tend to encourage loud denials or protests. This point is particularly important with students who are frustrated or students, such as those with behavior disorders, with low tolerance for criticism.

5. *Cueing.* Cues, as discussed by McDaniel, are nonverbal reminders of rules or expectations. Cues may involve facial expressions, raising one's hand, pointing, clearing one's throat and so on. Some cueing is done automatically, without deliberate planning. Other cueing must be learned, and students must learn what cues mean. It is possible that some students with learning disabilities or below-average intelligence will have more difficulty with cues than the rest of the class and that some direct instruction regarding the meaning of specific nonverbal reminders will be required.

6. *Environmental control.* Controlling the classroom environment through grouping, scheduling, organization of classroom furniture, controlling noise, and the like are examples of environmental control.

7. *Low-profile intervention.* This involves intervening to prevent trouble, catching off-task behavior before it becomes a serious problem, and other, less direct kinds of intervention. This principle overlaps, and is consistent with, principles 3–5.

8. *Assertive discipline.* This principle is described and discussed in some detail in chapter 11.

9. *I-messages.* McDaniel points out that there are at least two different types of "*I*-messages." For the assertive-discipline advocate, it is a matter of indicating that "I want you to———" or some such assertive, absolutely clear message regarding the expectation of the teacher. For the humanistic-discipline advocate, the *I*-message principle suggests that the teacher communicate how the student's behavior affects the teacher. It is a matter of communication of feelings. The *I*-message principle requires the teacher to communicate clearly, in a manner consistent with the rest of his or her approach to teaching.

10. *Positive reinforcement.* This principle is much discussed in the popular press and is applicable in various realms of life. A further discussion may be found in chapter 11.

McDaniel's 10 principles provide a good starting point for the development of better classroom discipline (control) and are quite valuable as applied to teaching exceptional students. The alert reader will find various aspects of these principles woven into the fabric of much of the remainder of this text. Morsink, Soar, Soar, and Thomas indicate that "few studies have been made with handicapped students from which inferences about teacher effectiveness can be drawn" (1986, p. 34). However, they do note two: the importance of direct instruction and contingent praise for appropriate social behavior. Until the compilation of more direct research in this area, it would seem wise to use the aspects of effective instruction that seem to ap-

A short physical activity break can reduce the likelihood of disruptive behavior.

ply to most other students and be guided by continuing observation and common sense.

STRUCTURE AND INSTRUCTIONAL MANAGEMENT

Structure is quite important to effective teaching. Dictionary definitions of structure relate to the idea of putting interrelated parts together systematically, and that is certainly

what we must do to maximize educational opportunity for exceptional students. In education, structure might include scheduling, classroom organization, grouping, and other related factors. It might also include the manner in which teachers respond to students' behavior. To be structured does not mean to be inflexible. Scheduling, classroom organization, and grouping may require change, but they should be changed for specific reasons and be consistent with some sort of overall approach logic. The discussion that follows expands on this concept in certain areas of instructional management. Teachers should adopt the concept of structure and apply it regularly. When they do so, students have more security, and most teachers find more satisfaction in the teaching process.

Scheduling

A concern of many regular classroom teachers involves scheduling resource services. Students with handicapping conditions may be required to leave their regular classroom one or more times each day to receive assistance from resource or itinerant teachers, speech or language specialists, or physical or occupational therapists.

The most common problems identified by regular classroom teachers are generally related to (1) the optimum time for resource services, (2) the student's completion of work missed while in the resource program, (3) the leaving and returning of students on time, (4) the transition to and from the resource room, and (5) a lack of continuity in programming. Each of these problem areas is discussed below.

When a student attends the resource room, he obviously misses some of the activities in his regular classroom. There is generally no single best time for the student to be absent, but the advantage of receiving intensive instruction or therapy for a short time outweighs the need for continuous regular classroom attendance. Therefore the issue involves which activity should be missed. It is tempting to send the student to the resource room during noncore activities such as art, music, or physical education. This practice must be questioned, however, because these may be the activities in which the student finds his greatest success. Often the student is sent to the resource room during practice or seatwork periods, but this time also may

be crucial to the student's success in the regular classroom. The relative advantages and disadvantages of missing particular regular classroom activities must be carefully weighed, and each student's unique needs must be considered. Of course, the scheduling needs of resource personnel must also be considered. Often the decision of the optimum time to be absent from the regular classroom is "the least of several evils." Very close communication and cooperative planning between resource personnel and the regular teacher can help alleviate this problem.

The question of whether the student should be expected to complete assignments while attending resource services is related to the question of the time when the student is absent. Expecting the student to complete a missed assignment may place an unnecessary burden on a student who already has difficulty completing assignments. This problem should also be discussed with the resource teacher.

The resource teacher and the regular classroom teacher must respect each other's schedules. Once a schedule has been agreed to by the regular teacher and resource personnel, every effort must be made to send and return the student on time. If the schedule is not followed, it can be extremely frustrating to the teachers and the student. Being late in reporting to the resource room or in returning to the regular classroom can adversely affect the quality of the student's instruction. This matter may seem trivial, but 10 minutes of tardiness multiplied by 180 school days can amount to a considerable problem for both the student and his or her teachers.

The student's movement to and from the resource room should be closely supervised. Some students abuse this "free time" unless specific efforts ensure that students take only a minimum of time in moving between rooms. It is unreasonable for either teacher

**A QUICK-REFERENCE CHECKLIST—TEACHING TIPS FROM
SUCCESSFUL TEACHERS**

While not all-inclusive, the following checklist will provide a starting point for improving teaching success. The ideas are not "ranked," and the groupings might be considered arbitrary.

Teaching methodology

1. Attempt to make your classroom "psychologically safe."
2. Use objectives that are challenging but obtainable.
3. Use objectives that are individually "adjusted" for different students.
4. Consider peer teaching and small-group methodologies.
5. Make certain students know what they are to do and how to proceed.
6. Make certain students know how well they achieved their goals and objectives.
7. Emphasize the positive in providing feedback to the entire class, to small groups, and to individuals.
8. Systematically *plan* for success experiences for individual students.
9. Anticipate possible disruptive behavior and have an alternative plan.
10. Change activities as often as possible within the limits of good instructional practice.

Teacher attitude

1. Show that you are interested in students and that they "belong" in your classroom.
2. Employ "active listening": avoid judging, moralizing, or "pulling rank."
3. Treat students as individuals, not "subjects to be taught."
4. Maintain an open-door policy, before and after school.
5. Be enthusiastic; show a positive attitude.
6. Model empathy and social responsibility.

Building and maintaining interest

1. Continually attempt to show relevance to real-life settings and problems.
2. Make learning as "active" as possible; involve your students.
3. When there is a choice of several different ways to teach a given skill or subject, use the most interesting, attention-holding way.
4. At times (and within limits) be a "ham," an entertainer.
5. Encourage students to direct their own learning whenever possible.
6. To the extent practicable, give students a choice of topics and approaches.

Note. We have "collected" these tips from successful teachers over the years. Each idea has been suggested by many teachers as a factor in their personal success. These ideas do not represent a formula for success—they are just as presented, teaching tips from successful teachers.

to accompany the student; thus the student must assume this responsibility. A system of reinforcement should be used to encourage the student to be on time.

The final area of concern involves a possible discontinuity between the regular and special programs and possible disagreement about the responsibility of the resource teacher. Regular teachers may believe that resource teachers should provide tutorial help with subjects with which the student is having difficulty in their class. This may be part of their assignment, but for the most part they must devote time to highly specialized interventions directed at remediation or compensatory-skill development. This potential problem may be circumvented by close communcation between the resource and regular classroom teacher and a greater understanding of the educational objectives. Greater continuity can also be accomplished by the regular classroom teacher sending seatwork with the student to be completed during free times; however, this work must be very carefully supervised so that the student does not become caught between the two teachers and their expectations. Some teachers use "help notes" to communicate needed areas of assistance and thereby facilitate cooperation. These notes may be placed in the teacher's mailbox or hand-carried by the students. This type of communication is essential to assure needed cooperation.

Classroom Organization

Throughout this text it will be emphasized that students learn in different ways and at differing rates. Students also learn more or less effectively in different settings—some students do well in a traditionally arranged classroom (rows of desks with the teacher at the front of the room) whereas others learn more readily in an informal classroom. The arrangement of the classroom is based on many variables, including the age or grade level of the student, the subject or subjects being taught, and the teacher's philosophy and approach to instruction.

The traditional arrangement, which is not as frequently used now as in years past, has been termed a "teacher-centered environment." It emphasizes certain expected behaviors of the students and the teacher, such as lecturing, directing and questioning, listening and note taking, authoritative control, visual supervision of students, and passive use of space. It also implies that all students learn in the same way.

The informal classroom arrangement (Figure 3–1) provides a more student-centered environment that uses a variety of work areas and learning centers, a direct-instruction area, a manipulative work area, and individual study carrels, while still allowing for occasional large group instruction.

This informal arrangement allows students to move to several areas in the classroom—allowing them the freedom, within the class structure, to work independently or as a group. If a particular student is easily distracted, he may use one of the study carrels until such time as he can work more effectively in a larger group. This room also contains an area for direct teacher instruction, a listening center, a group-projects center, a quiet area, a computer terminal, and a resting area supplied with beanbag chairs or large pillows.

There may be considerable noise, movement and general activity in an informally structured classroom, and the teacher must establish clear expectations and rules governing the use of each area. The teacher should be cautious when using a more informal structure because some students with learning and/or behavior problems may need a more structured learning environment. Some teachers have experienced considerable success by introducing only one or two special areas to the classroom at a time, adding more centers as the students demonstrate the ability to complete assigned tasks and responsibilities.

No one classroom organization is appropriate for all teachers and classes. The best arrangement is one that effectively unites the unique teacher and learner characteristics with the objectives of the curriculum.

Learning Centers

Although there is considerable misunderstanding of the purpose and instructional usefulness of learning centers, they do provide an alternative to traditional instruction and can be organized to meet individual needs. The following are some misconceptions held by teachers:

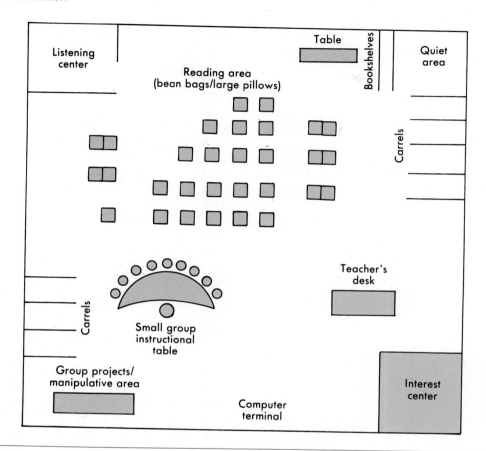

FIGURE 3-1. Informal classroom arrangement

1. They are only for "fun activities" and cannot be oriented to academic tasks.
2. The entire curriculum must be offered through learning centers.
3. Centers must be constantly changed.
4. They are not suitable for students with special needs.
5. They take a disproportionate amount of time to develop.
6. They are just for seatwork activities.

Although it is not our purpose to advocate learning centers for all teachers, we do think that many teachers do not fully understand how learning centers may be used to enhance teaching effectiveness and, ultimately, to increase the performance of their students. To fully understand the potential of learning centers, the teacher should first identify how she views her role as a teacher. If the teacher sees herself as a disseminator of information, then she will have considerable difficulty with learning centers. If, however, the teacher views herself as an orchestrator or facilitator, as one who serves as a guide and directs students' learning, then she will readily understand the advantage of an instructional alternative such as learning centers.

Learning centers may be used for skill development, independent study, reinforcement, practice, or follow-up of teacher-introduced concepts, enrichment, or substitute assignments. The following are significant advantages of learning centers:

1. They provide an alternative to pencil-and-paper seatwork.
2. They allow students to work at their own rate.
3. They provide an opportunity to learn through various modes.
4. They can provide instruction in the student's preferred learning style.
5. They allow the teacher time to work with individual students while other students are at the learning center.
6. They may help develop responsibility and self-discipline through accomplishment and success.
7. They may provide immediate self-evaluation.

As mentioned earlier, one of the most common problems associated with learning centers is the time it may take to develop them. Initially, development does take extra time and effort by the teacher, but once developed, they may be easily modified and used in subsequent years (or at the secondary level with more than one section of the same course). Some teachers seek assistance from students in setting up special-interest centers, and in some instances students with higher ability may with the teacher's guidance develop an entire center. Other teachers have had considerable success with jointly establishing and sharing centers with teachers in the same grade or content area.

There are essentially four types of learning centers:

1. *Skills center.* A skills center can include activities such as practice sheets, drill cards in mathematics, sentence completion activities, dictionary skills, and so on. The center should have an activity card that states the goal, objectives, and pretest and posttest criteria.

2. *Discovery or enrichment center.* This center might include science activities, brainteasers, or advanced mathematics activities.
3. *Listening center.* This center may provide lessons on tape, supplemental instruction in another mode, or leisure listening.
4. *Creativity center.* This center may include art, music, crafts, mathematics, or language-arts activities.

A learning center has several essential components, varying, of course, depending on its objectives and topics, the age of the students, and the teacher. Each learning center should have clearly stated objectives that structure the activities. Understandable directions should be provided that specify what should be done, where and which materials should be used, and how the work is to be evaluated. Samples of student work should be provided to give additional direction and serve as motivators. If media are to be used, instruction in their use should be provided.

The teacher should be certain to introduce the center in such a way that students fully understand the directions, how to use the media, the available activities, the materials to be used, evaluation procedures, and how materials are to be returned. A schedule should be established to inform students when it may be used and how many students may use it at one time. There must also be a record-keeping procedure so that the teacher knows who uses it, for what purpose, and how long. If the teacher carefully demonstrates the use of the center and periodically monitors its use, many problems may be avoided.

Some individuals believe that learning centers lack sufficient structure and may not provide enough direct teacher involvement to be advantageous for students with learning problems. We believe that if carefully planned and designed, learning centers can be used effectively with all students, allowing them the freedom to work at their own pace and at an appropriate skill level while learning through a variety of sensory modalities. Although there may be some disadvantages, we believe that these advantages far outweigh them.

Grouping

Students with special needs are more likely to require small-group instruction in basic academic subjects. Although most teachers, particularly in elementary school, are familiar with grouping procedures, several general practices should be considered. The following discussion briefly considers grouping by instructional level, skill-specific grouping, and heterogeneous grouping.

Grouping should always be considered temporary. Because student learning rates are not static, there should be sufficient built-in provisions to allow students to move to a higher or lower group as their needs dictate. The practice of assigning students to a group at the beginning of the school year and leaving them there for the duration of the year can impose serious educational limitations.

Grouping students by instructional level is probably the most common method, based on the desire to reduce the range of abilities by dividing the class into several small instructional groups in which the students are similar in learning ability, rate, and style. Students in these groups are generally expected to progress through learning materials at about the same rate. Although it does reduce the number of students being taught at one time, this procedure does not accommodate differing skill needs that must be addressed even in students at the same instructional level. An alternative to instructional-level grouping is skill-specific grouping.

Skill-specific grouping challenges the teacher because it takes a little longer to organize initially, but once it is organized it more directly addresses individual student needs. In a skill-specific arrangement, students are grouped on the basis of short-term objectives established after initial testing to determine the specific skills needed. The size of the groups varies depending on how many students need instruction in the specific identified skill. As the students move from initial acquisition to mastery of the skill, they move on to a more advanced skill and a different group. This arrangement also allows students the opportunity to interact with different peers throughout the year, thus they may avoid the stigma of continued placement in the low group.

With the skill-specific system, teachers develop a master list or chart of target skills; such a list may also originate from their basal material or a commercial publisher. The teacher should analyze tasks involved with a specific skill (see section on task analysis) and then provide instruction in skills to assist the student to meet the designated objective. A chart or file system that cross-references the student's name and specific skills to be developed assists the teacher to know precisely what should be taught next and which students should be placed in a particular skill group.

Instructional-level and skill-specific groupings emphasize placing students with similar abilities and skills together to form a *homogeneous* group. *Heterogeneous* grouping is another grouping procedure that may be used in certain activities, such as checking comprehension, completing social studies projects, or reviewing math. With heterogeneous grouping, students with varying abilities and skill levels are placed in the same group. The teacher may use this grouping to ask specific questons, at each student's level of comprehension, about a subject the group has studied. The teacher may ask a student with lower ability, "What was the main character's name?" and may ask a student with higher ability, "What would be another title for this story?" or "If you were the author, how would you have written the story?" Although the teacher should be careful not to confuse the student with less ability by presenting information that may interfere with learning a new concept, the use of heterogeneous grouping is an excellent way for students with learning problems to be a part of many different groups. Johnson and Johnson (1975) have described in detail the relative advantages of cooperative learning experiences and mixed-grouping procedures. (See chapter 4 for a complete discussion of cooperative learning.)

Carefully planned grouping procedures can do a great deal to maximize the teacher's effectiveness and provide specific instructional assistance to students. Each teacher must develop her own system to promote cooperative learning and enhance student performance.

THE ROLE OF TECHNOLOGY

Alcorn, in his discussion of social issues in technology (1986), suggests that technological devices are artificial devices created by the human race in an attempt to "manipulate natural law to our advantage." Thus such devices are inherently neither good or bad but may be effective or advantageous depending on how and why we use them. This concept certainly applies to the use of technology in education. The microcomputer, for example, has some useful applications with all exceptional students, handicapped or gifted, but it may be misused like, for example, the movie projector. It's not a babysitter or just for entertainment. The questions of how and why it is used remain central. In contrast, a number of other technological devices for very specific applications with the visually impaired and hearing impaired are much more likely to be used appropriately. These are discussed in more detail in chapters 5 and 6.

In citing the value of the microcomputer, Hagen notes that it can "bring speech to the nonvocal, telephone use to the deaf, grade II Braille or voice to the blind, and environmental control to the physically handicapped. It can remove the paper and pencil blockage for the learning disabled and improve the quality of life for the mentally handicapped. All of these dramatic uses of the microcomputer can be accomplished without knowing one word of programming" (1984, p. 1). We agree with Hagen's glowing account. The microcomputer is (potentially) a tremendous tool in the hands of the teacher of exceptional children and youth.

Other computer applications for handicapped people of working age promise much as they become widely available. Reports in the popular press and on television feature computer modifications that make it possible for quadriplegics to control computers through use of a mouth-held typing stick or a breath-controlled device sometimes called a "sip-and-puff" switch. An eye-tracking system developed for jet-fighter pilots measures the the reflection of light from the retina of the eye, which permits a person to look at a command on the screen, leading to the computer's execution of the command. Apple Computer has a separate Office of Special Education, and other computer manufacturers have persons who specialize in the development of computer applications for the handicapped. In fact, the federal government has at least one task force—including representatives from a number of computer companies—whose task is to *avoid* problems for the handicapped that might be created as computers become even more sophisticated in the future. (For example, on-screen visual cues that make computers more "user friendly," make them inaccessible to the blind.) There is little doubt that microcomputers hold much promise in potential applications for the handicapped and that computer manufacturers are considering the unique needs of the handicapped, attempting to make computers readily available as tools for the adult handicapped in the workplace.

But there is another side to the story of the magic of the microcomputer. It is of great value in the uses cited by Hagen, but it is misused when it becomes a substitute for real teaching. It can be of concrete value when used for drill and practice, but because of the nature of some of the existing software, it is possible for a student to "give the computer" an answer his teacher would have accepted, but which is not accepted because it is not exactly the answer which the software developer wanted. With some of the available software, especially in areas other than mathematics or spelling, synonyms for the desired answer are simply "wrong" as viewed by the computer. In a similar situation, where a teacher might have been delighted to reward an answer that is almost correct, the computer cannot do so. This situation is particularly unfortunate with handicapped students and may also be very distressing to some gifted students who may answer a question with a creative response that is more complex than the software is programmed to recognize. Unfortunately, especially with some subject material, there has been a rush to provide software quickly to meet the burgeoning demand, and the quality has been questionable. The bottom line is that teachers must carefully evaluate all software before putting it to use. What the publisher says it will do is not enough. Though it may do most of what it is supposed to do, it may also have negative side effects. These words of caution are not intended to indicate that microcomputers should not be used with exceptional students. We think they *should* be used. But they must be used with care and caution. Materials must be carefully evaluated. They may be of particular value in relieving the teacher of drill and practice and in providing at the same time high-level motivation to the student. They may be of almost miraculous

value in some applications with the hearing impaired and visually impaired. They may also have unique applications to the learning disabled. There has been considerable emphasis on becoming "computer literate," that is, learning to use the computer with some degree of skill; but unfortunately, there has been too little emphasis on evaluating materials for their effectiveness relative to specific educational goals. We will now outline the major applications of microcomputers in regular classrooms, emphasizing positive aspects and potentialities.

Behrmann (1984) categorizes microcomputer applications in special education into three broad categories:

1. Computer-assisted instruction (CAI), or direct instruction of students for such purposes as drill and practice, simulation, tutorial efforts, and so on.
2. Computer-managed instruction (CMI), including data collection, assistance in writing reports and/or IEPs, and management of school achievement data.
3. Computer-assisted management (CAM), an administrative function through which school administrators may handle statistics for resource allocation; prepare local, state, or federal reports; and track and manage personnel.

Of these three, CAI has received the most attention and, when fully developed, may hold the most promise for more effective teaching and significant time saving for teachers. Computer-managed instruction, in the form of data collection, has value and appears to be used in varying degrees. As a form of assistance in developing IEPs, it has received attention from various educational publishers, and if it can be made effective and *sufficiently individualized,* it could save a great deal of valuable educational time. Whether IEPs developed through computer programs are sufficiently individualized is still a question. Resolution by law of this

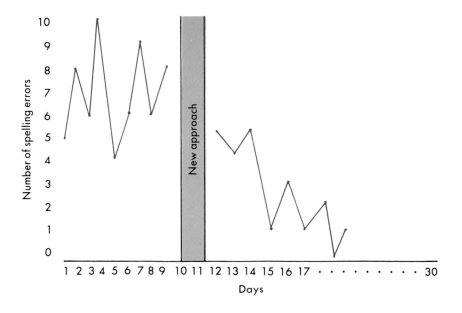

FIGURE 3–2. Student-performance recording system

question may be necessary before more is developed in this area.

Computer-assisted management (that is, using computers to manage the various types of data required for state and federal reports and for tracking and managing student and personnel demographics) appears to be in use to varying degrees in all the states. Some states have established report formats that greatly encourage such use, and some type of CAM use appears to be established practice.

Vargas, in addressing instructional-design flaws in CAI, concluded her consideration of this problem as follows: "Computers have the flexibility to teach effectively. They will do so, however, only if CAI programs adopt those features shown to be necessary for learning: a high rate of relevant responding, appropriate stimulus control, immediate feedback, and techniques of successive approximation. Until program developers heed the findings

of relevant research in instructional design, the computer revolution in education will remain just one more bright technological future waiting to begin" (1986, p. 744). We strongly agree.

GOOD PEDAGOGY

As we have observed and interacted with successful teachers, we have noted good teaching practices that appear to be particularly helpful with special-needs students. For the most part these are general practices rather than special techniques; it could be said that they are simply good pedagogy. This section considers a number of these general practices in random order, for they are not by nature sequential. To be of maximum value, these practices must be systematically integrated with other elements of the instructional process.

Measuring Student Performance

Teachers must constantly strive to provide learning and specific skill-development activities at the level required by the student, to modify instructional approaches, and to monitor the student's progress. The monitoring of this progress, however, too often culminates only with a letter grade or number recorded in the teacher's grade book. Reporting the student's progress and the assignment of grades are important responsibilities, but greater attention must be given to monitoring the student's progress on an ongoing basis. Often teachers are so involved with instruction that the student's progress is only casually or subjectively assessed. We are not advocating that teachers record hourly data for all students each day, but some ongoing monitoring system should be employed, particularly for students with unusual learning problems. Such a monitoring system can provide important information about the student's general performance and skill development and can provide direction for program modification.

The student's performance can be recorded in many ways including anecdotal records, grades, numerical values, charts, and graphs. Often teachers think they do not have time enough to use precise measurement systems. Several other approaches, however, may be used, such as enlisting the help of volunteers, parents, aides, older students in another grade (such as Future Teachers of America), peers, or the students themselves. Self-monitoring by a student can provide considerable reinforcement, meaning, and purpose to learning activities.

Figure 3–2 shows an example of a recording system teachers can use. Without such a chart the teacher might not be fully aware of the value of a new approach to instruction and practice. In this instance the chart provided feedback that assisted the teacher in evaluating a new approach. (It should be noted that a new approach might also result in *more* errors, and it woud be just as important to learn this, too).

Measurement and charting procedures are particularly helpful for students with behavior problems. (For detailed information about precise charting procedures, see Affleck, Lowenbraun, and Archer [1980] and Alberto and Troutman [1986].)

Informal Assessment

Generally teachers do not have difficulty identifying students with learning problems. Specifying the problem, however, is often more difficult because of the likelihood of overlapping problem areas. The underlying difficulty may be intellectual, social, emotional, the result of inadequate instruction, or some combination of these and other factors. By using informal assessment, the teacher can more precisely define the nature of the problem.

Three general types of informal assessment may be developed to assess academic or social behavior and vocational needs and interests: (1) informal inventories, (2) observation, and (3) interviews. The easiest informal inventory to develop and use is a checklist used to determine the student's level of functioning. The tasks may be listed in order of increasing difficulty to provide information about levels of functioning and areas of needed instruction. A checklist inventory can be developed for nearly all skills and subject areas.

A checklist can be developed through the following steps:

1. List the skills and concepts discussed in the instructor's manual or textbook.
2. Divide the list of skills into smaller lists of subskills or subtasks.
3. Sequence the subtasks in order from least to most difficult.
4. Develop statements of performance for the sequenced skills.
5. Administer a pretest to the entire class.

This pretest can provide information about which students are apparently lacking which basic skills, concepts, and prerequisite skills. This information then provides the basis for individual instructional planning.

Anecdotal records are another form of informal assessment for identifying problem areas. Anecdotal records assist teachers in clarifying the events leading to the behavioral or learning problem by providing a factual description of the event. The factual record should describe (1) the *antecedent* (the event that occurred immediately before the behavior), (2) the *behavior* (quoting the student and using action verbs), and (3) the *consequences* of the behavior. In describing the behavior, the teacher should attempt to use quantitative statements. It may not be sufficient to state, "He is always out of his seat" or "He never turns in his assignments." Preferred statements are "During a 50-minute period, he was out of his seat four times" or "During the last 3 weeks he turned in only two of the nine assignments." Anecdotal records are commonly used to describe disruptive student behavior and can assist the teacher to analyze more accurately what is actually happening. Often teachers develop anecdotal records before discussing the problem with a resource person or school counselor.

The third type of informal assessment technique is the interview, which is a useful means for learning the student's perspective. The steps in interviewing are (1) to establish rapport by being sincere and honest and showing interest; (2) to present reasons for the interview; (3) to formulate open-ended questions, avoiding questions calling for only a *yes* or *no* response; (4) to listen to the student in an accepting enviroment to gain information and insight into the problem, rather than offering suggestions or pointing out what you think is wrong; and (5) to terminate the interview with a goal or a plan of action. Preferably the plan should be estab-

lished by the student with the teacher's input, including an agreed time when student and teacher can meet again to modify or evaluate the plan.

Other types of informal assessment include work-products assessments; learning-styles inventories; informal reading inventories; and writing, spelling, and mathematics inventories. Further information concerning the administration and interpretation of such inventories may be obtained from resource teachers or content specialists such as remedial mathematics or reading teachers.

Task Analysis

Teachers often experience considerable frustration when students do not successfully complete an assigned task or assignment. To minimize such frustration and failure, it may be helpful for the teacher to divide the task into smaller steps. Each step then becomes a separate goal or objective. Many teachers routinely use this approach without thinking of it as task analysis and without actually writing the subparts—they simply do it as they plan their assignments.

Task analysis is based on the assumption that the student may not be able to accomplish a given task or assignment because of an inability to accomplish one or more of its subparts. The following nonacademic analogy roughly illustrates this concept:

A person has a flat tire on an automobile trip. Some individuals would have difficulty changing the flat tire to resume the trip. Is it sufficient to state simply that they can not change the flat tire, or is it more helpful to analyze the necessary substeps of the tire change? What is the actual problem? Is it the use of the jack, or is it a question of whether they should loosen the lug nuts on the wheel before or after using the jack? Is the problem perhaps related to the fact that the automobile is not on a level surface, or is it related to the spare tire?

The process of changing an automobile tire

could be divided into many substeps. To be able to change the tire, one must understand each of the small steps that must be taken and the order in which they must be taken. In total, these steps or tasks make up the total task of changing the tire. A lack of ability or understanding with just one of these steps may make it impossible for the person to change the tire to resume the trip.

Nearly every learning situation can be divided into as many components or subcomponents as necessary to understand the whole. Often the essential subskills can then be identified and taught, thus allowing the completion of the larger task or assignment. In more difficult situations it may be helpful for the teacher to record the subtasks.

The following list of subtasks is an example of task analysis directed to the objective of alphabetizing the following words, each of which has been placed on a separate card: *stop, ask, dinner, name, boy.*

1. The student can write the alphabet in the correct order.
2. Provided a stack of 26 flash cards, each containing a different letter of the alphabet, the student can place the cards in alphabetical order.
3. Provided a stack of 26 flash cards, each containing a word beginning with a different letter of the alphabet, the student can place the cards in alphabetical order with the help of an alphabet chart.
4. Provided a stack of 26 flash cards, each containing a word beginning with a different letter of the alphabet, the student can place the cards in alphabetical order without the help of an alphabet chart.
5. Provided a stack of 15 flash cards, each containing a different letter of the alphabet, the student can place the cards in alphabetical order with the help of an alphabet chart.
6. Provided a stack of 15 flash cards, each containing a different letter of the alpha-

bet, the student can place the cards in alphabetical order without the help of an alphabet chart.
7. Provided a stack of 15 flash cards, each containing a word beginning with a different letter of the alphabet, the student can place the cards in alphabetical order with the help of an alphabet chart.
8. Provided a stack of 15 flash cards, each containing a word beginning with a different letter of the alphabet, the student can place the cards in alphabetical order without the help of an alphabet chart.
9. The student can alphabetize the following words, each of which has been placed on a separate card: *stop, ask, dinner, name, boy.*

Task analysis may serve as a guide for decisions and help the teacher identify (1) what steps are necessary to accomplish the task, (2) where students are having difficulty with a task, (3) what should be taught next, and (4) what adaptations may assist the students with task accomplishment (Bigge, 1982).

As mentioned previously, many teachers routinely use this approach to instruction without thinking of it as task analysis. Good teachers continually use an analytic or diagnostic approach to instruction to enhance the success of both the students and teacher.

Preferred Learning Styles

Most teachers would agree that each student is unique and has individual needs, likes and dislikes, accomplishments and failures, and strengths and weaknesses. Students also have different preferred ways of learning, and although teachers generally agree that students learn in different ways, they do not always attempt to assess and accommodate these differences. Students are often expected to fit into an established pattern of learning that commonly emphasizes learning through reading and listening.

The concept of different learning styles is

not new to educators or psychologists; however, in recent years there has been renewed interest in this important area of learning. Dunn and Dunn define learning styles as "ways of identifying patterns by which individuals conceptualize information from their environment most efficiently" (1978, p. 36). Every student has a unique learning style that differs from that of his peers, and teachers need to be aware of these unique styles.

Dunn and Dunn (1978) group factors influencing the individual's learning style into four areas: (1) environmental elements, (2) the individual's emotionality, (3) socialized needs, and (4) physical needs.

Environmental elements have different effects on students in the learning environment. Noise, in this context, is important in terms of the student's ability to tolerate sounds while learning. Some students are able to block out extraneous noises, whereas others may need a quiet environment. Lighting may also affect students in different ways—some prefer a brightly lit area, whereas others prefer subdued light. Some students prefer an easy chair when tackling a difficult learning task, whereas others prefer a straight-back chair and desk. Although the teacher may not be able significantly to modify all aspects of the environment, consideration should be given to its effects. If it seems that a student's difficulty may be related to an environmental problem, attempts should be made to adapt or modify conditions as necessary.

Elements in the *emotional* realm include persistence, motivation, responsibility for learning, and need for structure. Some students need well-defined guidelines and structure, whereas others may be more creative and respond better when given considerable freedom in carrying out assignments. The teacher should recognize these elements and make adjustments to accommodate each student's unique needs.

The *sociological* dimension involves the ability of a student to learn from or with others. Some students prefer to work alone, while others may choose to work in pairs, in small groups, or with an adult. Few prefer to work in the same way all of the time. Therefore the teacher should consider varying the instructional approach to fit individual learning styles and preferences.

Elements in the *physical* dimension include the student's best time of day for active involvement and learning (early birds or night owls), mobility needs (to move or change positions), and preferred perceptual strengths. Students vary considerably in the ways in which they learn. Some students tend to learn better by listening to the teacher (auditory learners). Other students prefer to read or see the material (visual learners), and still others may learn more readily by touching and interacting with the material (tactile and kinesthetic learners). Nearly all students learn better when they are actively involved in the instructional process and are using all their senses, including whole body movements. This multisensory learning approach is preferable to a more limited sensory approach such as lecturing. If it is not practical to offer multisensory instruction, it is often advantageous to present new material through the student's strongest perceptual mode while reinforcing through the other senses. By teaching to the student's strength, the teacher can increase the student's attention, success, and achievement, whereas insisting that the student focus on his weakest perceptual mode may have the opposite effect.

The teacher can assess student learning styles by using a questionnaire. The questionnaire may be administered orally in a personal interview with one student or be given to a small group of students. The statements on the questionnaire should be short, direct, and stated as simply as possible. The

PREFERRED-LEARNING-STYLES QUESTIONNAIRE

	True	False
Environmental statements		
1. I like to have it quiet when I'm working.	☐	☐
2. I work best when there is a little noise in the classroom.	☐	☐
3. I prefer rock music in the background when I am studying.	☐	☐
4. Music of any kind makes it difficult for me to work.	☐	☐
5. I can study when people are talking.	☐	☐
6. I prefer bright light when studying.	☐	☐
7. I learn best in the morning.	☐	☐
8. I learn best in the afternoon.	☐	☐
9. I like to study while sitting in a comfortable chair.	☐	☐
Emotional and social statements		
1. I prefer to work with the teacher.	☐	☐
2. I learn best when I work alone.	☐	☐
3. I need specific rules and directions about what I should do.	☐	☐
4. I prefer to work in a small group.	☐	☐
5. I prefer to work in a traditional instructional situation.	☐	☐
6. I like to work with one friend.	☐	☐
7. I need a lot of reinforcement to complete a task.	☐	☐
8. I have a lot of difficulty completing assignments.	☐	☐

teacher may add other statements to learn the student's preferred general learning climate.

To assess the student's perceptual strengths, the teacher should observe his behaviors. Visual learners may close their eyes or look at the ceiling when they try to recall a visual image or picture. Auditory learners may subvocalize or move their lips when they are attempting to memorize information. Tactile or kinesthetic learners may use their fingers to count off items or write in the air with their fingers. The analysis of these behaviors is subjective, of course, and they may or may not indicate a preferred perceptual strength; however, such observation at least provides preliminary information on which the teacher may base continued observation and assessment.

Another informal assessment procedure

that may provide insight into students' perceptual strengths and preferred learning styles involves the presentation of three lists of words and numbers as follows:

1. Tell the students that they will be given a test to determine what kind of learner they are: visual, auditory, or tactile-kinesthetic.
2. Write a list of five to seven words on the blackboard while students are watching. Use everyday words such as *toothpaste, soap, salt, comb,* and *milk* (the number of words used depends on the age of the students).
3. Allow the students to view the list of words for approximately one minute.
4. Erase the list, then ask the students to write down the words.
5. Ask for a volunteer to repeat the list of

words. Volunteering may be an additional indication of strong visual learners.

6. Ask students to score their papers.
7. Dictate orally a different list of similar words, such as *automobiles, bicycles, birds, pencil, paper,* and *shoes.* Dictate the list a second time; neither the teacher nor students should be writing at this time. Then ask the students to write down the words.
8. Use the same process of correction as with the written presentation in steps 5 and 6.
9. Dictate a different list of words of approximately the same length and ask the students to write the words while they are being dictated. When finished dictating, ask the students to copy their list; they may look at their initial list if they wish. Next, ask them to turn their paper over and rewrite the words from memory. Follow the correction procedures as with both earlier lists.
10. Repeat all nine of the these steps using a series of numbers such as 8, 6, 4, 3, and 9 instead of words. Present the numbers visually, auditorily, and tactile-kinesthetically.

When this process has been completed, ask the students to total their scores of the word and number parts for each of the three tests. Explain to the students that there may be some relationship between their scores on the three types of tests and the way they learn. If the teacher observes definite patterns, she may want to note this observation for future planning. As mentioned previously, this is an informal method for general assessment of students' preferred learning styles and is not intended to be a precise instrument or procedure. An informal assessment such as this may provide insight into reasons why some students may perform better in some situations than in others. More

formal assessment procedures have been described by Dunn and Dunn (1978), Carbo (1983), and R. Dunn (1983).

These learning-style characteristics apply to gifted students as well as students who have learning problems. A study reported by Dunn and Price (1980, p. 35) indicated that "gifted elementary students are somewhat different from non-gifted elementary students on 6 of the 18 learning style variables." Some of the results of this study were not anticipated by the investigators—for example, the fact that such a high percentage of the gifted preferred tactile-kinesthetic to auditory learning—and although it was only a preliminary investigation, it demonstrates that teachers must consider learning styles when planning for the gifted just as with students with learning problems. In practice, since gifted students may seem to be doing very well in school, teachers are more likely to overlook learning-style considerations. This tendency, of course, is all the more reason to keep these factors in mind when dealing with any exceptional student.

Peer Tutoring

Peer tutoring is not a new concept and has been widely used with considerable success. In one-room schoolhouses in which the one teacher provided multigrade instruction, older or more able students often taught younger or less able students in certain subject areas and for specific parts of the school day. The term *peer tutoring* is here used to refer to both cross-age tutoring, in which older students provide instruction to younger children, and same-age tutoring arrangements.

Peer tutoring has many positive benefits for both students with special learning problems and students who are achieving adequately. Often regular classroom teachers say that they do not have sufficient time to provide needed instructional assistance to mildly handicapped students without ne-

Peer tutoring can be highly effective.

glecting other students in their classroom. In such cases peer tutoring can, if used properly, be a viable source of assistance to the teacher. Handicapped students may also be peer-tutors for younger children. In several programs students with lower skills have instructed younger children (Delquadri, Greenwood, Whorton, Carta, & Hall, 1986). Although there may be considerable advantage to using handicapped students as tutors—and we hope that teachers consider this method—the primary purpose of the following discussion involves the handicapped student as the recipient of peer tutoring.

Peer tutoring is most effective when the teacher introduces the new concepts to be learned and the tutor provides the necessary

review. The teacher must maintain full responsibility for the program and should carefully and continually monitor it by periodically observing sessions. Tutors must also report the learner's performance on a routine basis. Probably the most common form of peer tutoring occurs when the teacher spontaneously asks one student to help another. Such assistance may or may not be helpful; benefits are more likely to result from a carefully planned program with (1) precise instructional objectives, (2) careful selection of the tutors, (3) specific tutor training, and (4) careful pairing of the tutor and tutee.

The selection of tutors depends on the nature of the program, the subject, and the age of the students. As mentioned previously, students with mild learning problems may be tutors for younger children. According to Ehly and Larsen (1980), teachers can choose any of the following as tutors: (1) all students who volunteer, (2) students who excel in school, (3) well-behaved students who have some academic difficulties, and (4) students who meet the criteria established for the proposed program. Students selected as tutors should have good skills in listening, prompting, modeling, and reinforcing. Above all other criteria, sincerity, genuineness, and commitment are perhaps the most important.

The amount and nature of training for the tutor depend on the teacher's time, the materials available, and objectives of the tutoring program. Of course, the tutor must have demonstrated proficiency in the topics to be presented.

A teacher inexperienced in the use of a peer tutoring program may think that a considerable amount of time is required for training before implementation. This is often true, but careful planning usually results in significant benefits.

When deciding which students to place in a tutoring program, inexperienced teachers may feel that many students need extra time and instruction. Some students, however, have needs so great that they require special assistance from the teacher, an instructional aide, or special education personnel. A peer-tutoring program should not be used as a substitute for a carefully planned program delivered by a competent professional. Other students who would not be good candidates to receive peer tutoring include students with severe behavior problems or students who are aware of their academic deficiencies and might openly reject assistance from peers that would call further attention to their learning difficulties.

Pairing the tutor with the student to be tutored must be carefully considered. The requirements of the program and the specific objectives influence this decision. The final decision concerning pairing is best made by the teacher, who is well acquainted with the students and can predict how well they can cooperate. Of course, pairings are not final and should be changed as needed.

These suggestions are intended to serve not as instructions for establishing a peer tutoring program but as an overview of some of the essential components. We recommend that new teachers consult the following before beginning a peer tutoring program: Ehly and Larsen (1980); Haisley, Christine, and Andrews (1981); Allen (1976); Epstein (1978); and Harris and Aldridge (1983).

Self-Management Skills

Academic achievement appears to be closely related to self-management skills. Students with good self-management skills tend to do well in school, to persist with assignments, and to seek assistance from teachers and peers when appropriate. Many low-achieving students, however, do not have the self-management skills that are obvious prerequisites to learning. When given a task, low-achieving students tend to use their poor organizational strategies consistently regardless of whether they are effective. In other

words, they impulsively and often hurriedly complete the assignment without the prerequisite organizational skills. Students who do not possess the necessary self-management skills must be taught how to search for useful information, how to order this data, and how to organize this information for learning and retention.

An environment that encourages students to develop self-management skills generally results in greater independence, increased task completion, and ultimately greater achievement. Teachers should be alert for students who do not have needed organizational strategies and should provide specific instruction in this important area.

When assisting students who do not have self-management skills, the teacher must serve as a model, actually demonstrating the skill to the student. The teacher should talk aloud while the student watches her model the strategy. The teacher identifies a series of steps (organizational skills) through which they proceed. The student is then asked to perform the task while instructing himself aloud with assistance from the teacher. The student verbally guides himself through the steps with statements such as "First, I must do this, and then this, and this." The next step involves the student performing the task, still speaking aloud but without assistance from the teacher. In the next step the student whispers to himself the necessary tasks, and in the final step he subvocalizes the tasks.

Essential to the success of self-management skills teaching are (1) teacher modeling through talking, (2) student self-talk, (3) self-reinforcement, and (4) praise from the teacher.

Concept Analysis Skills

The ability to develop concepts, or to conceptualize, is considered the highest level of human language and thought (Johnson & Myklebust, 1967). Authorities vary in their definitions of concept development, but most agree that conceptualization includes classifying experiences into groups according to some common denominator. Writers in various education fields agree that concept development is highly important. Authorities in the areas of mental retardation and learning disabilities seem to agree that conceptualization is more difficult for students with these handicapping conditions; the same is true for students with visual and hearing impairments. The reasons for the difficulties in developing conceptual skills vary among these four areas, but it is agreed that teachers must assist handicapped students in the development of conceptual skills.

Unruh, Gilliam, and Jogi (1982) have provided some practical guidelines for assisting students to develop concept analysis skills. These guidelines should be of value in developing new concepts or broadening underdeveloped concepts.

1. Concepts used in teaching concept analysis skills should not be abstract. The concepts should be defined by specific, observable, essential characteristics. Red, circle, dog, and six are examples of concepts that meet this criteria. Each concept should have a unique set of shared essential, relevant characteristics that are not shared by other concepts presented.
2. Concepts cannot be taught through a single example. Students must use as many examples of the concepts as available when attempting an analysis. Although every instance of a concept cannot be presented, several instances or examples of the concept must be presented if it is to be analyzed successfully.
3. Each example of the concept should exhibit both essential and non-essential characteristics of that concept.
4. The essential, relevant characteristics of the concept should not be varied in positive examples (those that represent the concept). Furthermore, the non-essential, irrelevant characteristics should always be varied when negative examples are presented (those examples that do not represent the concept).

5. Both positive and negative examples of the concept should be presented to make sure the student has successfully analyzed the concept presented.[3]

Unruh, Gilliam, and Jogi (1982) suggest three steps should be followed when using these guidelines:

1. Assist the student (as necessary, considering the student's basic disabilities) to discover those characteristics that are the same in all positive examples of the concept under consideration. Discuss these common characteristics and verify that the student understands them.
2. Assist the student to discover nonessential characteristics in both the positive examples and the negative examples, which are used for contrast. Discuss and verify the student's understanding of nonessential characteristics.
3. Make certain the student is fully aware that the essential characteristics are not shared by the negative examples. A new set of examples, including both positive and negative examples, should be presented, and the student should now be able to point out which characteristics are essential to the concept and which are nonessential.

This procedure can be followed using words, pictures, or actual objects. For example, the teacher might use words to teach the concepts of verbs or plural nouns. Pictures or real objects can be used to teach the concepts of dishes, furniture, or the spatial arrangement of one thing above another. Pictures can be used to teach the concepts of transportation or helping. Many students master most concepts necessary to reach es-

[3]From "Developing Concept Analysis Skills" by D. Unruh, J. Gilliam, and A. Jogi, 1982, *Directive Teacher, 4*(2), p. 27. Copyright 1982 by National Center, Educational Media and Materials for the Handicapped, Ohio State University. Reprinted by permission.

tablished educational goals with little difficulty; however, when there is a need to teach a certain specific concept, this procedure is of value.

Consistency

When teachers are asked what factors most contribute to a successful classroom learning situation, they tend to mention qualities such as the teacher's open and honest communication, knowledge of subject matter, sincere interest in and caring about young people, enthusiasm, and consistency. The quality most frequently mentioned is *consistency.*

The teacher's behavior, clear expectations for the students, carefully planned classroom rules and procedures, and natural consequences are all closely related to consistency. It is an obvious prerequisite to consistency that the teacher be knowledgeable about the subject matter and have organized this information into a meaningful instructional plan. The teacher may be extremely capable and knowledgeable about the subject, but unless she has carefully thought out and organized this information for instruction, it may be to no avail. Unquestionably, the teacher is the single most critical influence on the classroom atmosphere, and the degree of consistency in the classroom depends on the teacher.

The establishment of clear expectations is essential to promoting a consistent classroom atmosphere. If the teacher has established certain expectations for performance and behavior, both the students and the teacher must adhere to them. Posting these expectations or writing them on the chalkboard can provide the needed continuity. One should also allow students to discuss and possibly modify these expectations so that they may feel some ownership, but when the expectations are finally established, they must be followed by everyone.

Success

It is essential in any educational program to ensure that all students meet with some success, particularly students with special learning problems, because they most likely have had considerable failure. This 'failure syndrome" must be broken through systematic counterconditioning efforts by the teacher. Careful planning to provide instruction at a level commensurate with the student's ability is of the utmost importance.

Occasionally, the student's failure may result more from instructional methods than from the student's inadequate skills; therefore the teacher should watch for opportunities to provide success experiences. The student's achieving success may be encouraged, for example, by decreasing the amount of required written work, by making certain that language or other assignments are on the student's reading level, by encouraging group projects, by allowing the student to choose among a variety of carefully planned activities, by using learning contracts, and a myriad of other techniques.

Fernald (1943) worked with students who had experienced considerable academic difficulty and systematically planned "positive reconditioning" before actually starting the remedial program. She described four conditions that are to be carefully avoided:

1. Avoid calling attention to emotionally loaded situations.
2. Avoid using methods that experience suggests are unlikely to be effective.
3. Avoid conditions that may cause embarrassment.
4. Avoid directing attention to what the student cannot do.

These principles can be applied to almost all remedial situations and are particularly important for the student who has failed many times over a period of several years.

In addition to these specific suggestions, teachers should question their teaching methods to increase the likelihood of their students meeting with success. For instance,

1. Do I emphasize and build on the student's strengths rather than weaknesses?
2. Do I ask the student to perform tasks that are clearly too difficult for him or her to perform?
3. Do I systematically plan for small increments of successful performance?
4. Do I permit my students to make mistakes?
5. Do I provide genuine feedback?
6. Do I look for positive rather than negative aspects of a student's work?
7. Do I provide a sufficient amount of assistance and encouragement to students with learning problems?
8. Do I take special opportunities to provide positive reinforcement?
9. Do I structure honest experiences of success for my students?
10. Do I identify areas of the student's interest and capitalize on them?
11. Do I allow low-achieving students to perform tasks given to high-achieving students?

Another dimension of providing success experiences is to encourage the student to assume responsibility for succeeding. Often a student who has experienced considerable failure tends to blame external factors for his difficulties. Students must be taught that they have much control over their own success or failure and that it is their responsibility to enter into learning activities believing they will be successful. Joint planning between the teacher and students can greatly assist them in understanding that they *can* achieve and be successful. Contracting, for example, gives the student the responsibility to succeed, and if the contract is realistically established with input from the teacher, it

may give the student the opportunity to assume responsibility and to achieve much-needed success. As the student achieves success, he will gain confidence and come to view himself as someone who can be successful. Nothing succeeds like success should be the motto of every teacher.

SECONDARY SCHOOL INSTRUCTIONAL STRATEGIES

In this section the reader will find discussions of study-skills instruction, a variety of instructional-presentation alternatives, grading alternatives, suggestions as to how to help students prepare for exams, and a list of student-centered problems with suggestions on how the teacher may deal with these problems so as to minimize their influence on school performance.

We believe that part of the frustration of some secondary school teachers may relate to the predominant teaching mode in many secondary school classes. It may also relate to the fact that secondary school teachers must teach many more students each day and may have much less time to really get to know any one student. If students do not possess the prerequisite skills and knowledge base and if the teacher uses, for example, only the lecture approach to instruction, both the student and the teacher will meet with failure and frustration. A student's poor attitude toward school may further complicate the situation. This dilemma may be resolved by coordinating the curriculum and the teacher's approach to instruction with the needs and learning characteristics of the student. The teacher must remain willing to analyze this difficult situation and to consider alternative ways of achieving this essential match.

Most teachers, when informed that they will have a blind student in their course, begin making plans for alternatives for this student. They accept the concepts for peer teaching, alternative learning modes (braille, taped lectures, alternative forms of responding, modifying examinations), assignment modification, different methods of presentation, and modifying evaluation procedures. If teachers are willing to make the necessary modifications for visually impaired students, they should be as willing to consider alternatives for students with other learning problems. We believe that alternatives to maximize the success of both the teacher and student must be provided if the potential of each student is to be fully realized.

In the following paragraphs, we will review several alternatives, including presentation options, student-centered problems, grading alternatives, preparation for examinations, and study-skills instruction.

Presentation Alternatives

Teachers should systematically consider alternative ways of providing meaningful instruction. The following 10 suggestions are relatively easy to implement and do not require substantial time. They effectively promote teacher enthusiasm while providing a more effective instructional environment.

Study Guides. A study guide may provide needed direction for many students with learning problems and should be of some value to all students. The guide can include statements of objectives, assignment requirements, suggested readings or media to be used, and evaluation criteria used in the course. It may provide direction regarding time lines, resources required, and peer teaching opportunities. Learning contracts can be established in combination with the guide. The study guide can be developed cooperatively by the teacher and a small group of capable students and then shared with classmates. Once developed, the study guide may be used in subsequent courses.

Topical Outlines. A topical outline is less formal than a study guide and takes less time to develop. A topical outline can be considered a condensed study guide. It provides a general flow of course content and may assist students in organizing their lecture notes. Like the study guide, a topical outline can be developed by the students.

Technical Vocabularies and Glossaries. Technical vocabularies or glossaries can be a tremendous aid for nearly all students. Effectively used, they may eliminate many of the problems resulting from students' being unable to understand the content of a lecture because they do not understand the vocabulary. This aid can be used in peer teaching and tutoring situations. Alternatively, vocabulary information can be tape recorded and made available. It may be written, typed, or recorded by students.

Advance Organizers. Advance organizers are easy to develop with a minimum of the teacher's time. An example of an advance organizer is an outline provided by the teacher of key points or topics to be learned. Another example is to read several questions to the students before presentation or independent study of the material. This method gives the students the needed direction and structure and tells them what is important.

Summaries of Concepts. The summary is an overview in one or two paragraphs of the topic to be studied. It should be provided in advance to clearly establish the importance of the concepts to be studied. Many teachers assign a section of a chapter or unit of study to a group of students and ask them to summarize their findings, sharing this summary in turn with other groups who have similarly prepared summaries. Different summaries may also be assigned to individuals who would then collectively overview the lesson.

Students who may have difficulty with detailed reading may be required only to develop a list of key words or concepts.

Media. Tape recording portions of a textbook or chapter summaries may be very helpful for students who have reading problems. A tape or multimedia presentation may also be developed to overview the course or specific units of study. Naturally, commercially available films and media can also be used. More capable individual students or a group of students may assist in the development of media presentations. School district or building media specialists are often pleased to assist in the development of media presentations.

Special Texts. Although special modified or adapted texts are generally not popular with students, some individuals may profit from their use. An abridged text is an alternative to a totally different book. Another alternative is to provide a distillation of the material in key concepts or a two- or three-page chapter synopsis. The preparation of such abstracts can be excellent training for academically advanced students in the class.

Alternative Responding. Typically students respond with written reports, oral presentations, and examination answers. Alternatives include tape-recorded responses, drawings, and the use of a peer to interpret examinations and record responses.

Modified Lectures. Many teachers have found that suspending a lecture after a specified time encourages greater independence and responsibility by students. Students may then be assigned group projects related to the topic being studied and after completing the projects may provide a report to the rest of the class.

Teacher Interest and Enthusiasm. Although this is not a presentation alternative, the teacher should demonstrate a sincere interest and enthusiasm for the topic. Nearly all teachers can recall a college professor who was extremely enthusiastic about the content of the course and whose enthusiasm spread to the students. Studies of effective teaching nearly always emphasize the instructor's knowledge and enthusiasm among the most important factors influencing student performance.

Student-centered Problems

Throughout this text it will be emphasized that many factors may contribute to a student's poor performance in school. Among the more common are educational materials, the environment, the teacher, and the peer group. At times, however, the primary problem may more closely involve the student himself. This section identifies several student-centered problem areas that may seriously interfere with performance. Among the more common problems are limited attention to tasks, negative school attitudes, minimal reading ability, poor comprehension, slow learning ability, poor spelling, poor written expressive ability, high rate of absenteeism, withdrawn or passive behavior, unusually high activity level, and failure orientation. Although these characteristics are centered on the student, we believe that the teacher can greatly reduce the effects of these behaviors and problems by offering specific alternatives to students who have these difficulties. The following suggestions are viable alternatives for the teacher.

Limited Attention to Academic Tasks. Many secondary students have a relatively short attention span, appear to be disinterested, demonstrate poor organizational ability, and fail to see the relevance of subjects. These characteristics may be related to

Some management practices do little to promote positive school attitudes.

a student's previous history of academic failure or any of a variety of causes, but the following teaching techniques may be of value:

1. Give short, sequential assignments, one at a time as they are completed.
2. Provide immediate feedback on work completed.
3. Pair the student with a peer who can stay on the task for a longer time.
4. Show the relevance of the subject to the student's own life.
5. Use high-interest materials.
6. Use outlining to divide tasks into smaller units.
7. Consider contracting with the student to provide the needed structure and reinforcement.
8. Provide systematic rewards such as free time or special-interest projects (reading, listening to tapes, photography).
9. Change activities frequently; know when to accelerate or decelerate assignments and activities.

10. Teach the student the following listening formula:
    a. Focus attention on the speaker.
    b. Ask yourself what you should be learning from the speaker.
    c. Listen carefully and attempt to relate what is being said to what you already know about the topic.
    d. Review in a way that works best for you, such as discussion with a classmate, reading, and so on.

Negative School Attitude. A negative attitude may result because the student perceives the subject matter as irrelevant, or it may be a disguise for an inability to succeed. Often students who have experienced considerable failure in school attempt to compensate for their failure through apathy or consistent noninvolvement. The following suggestions may help overcome such an attitude:

1. Provide alternative assignments. Alternate assignments should be related to the con-

tent of the course while focusing on the interests of the student. For example, if the primary assignment for a unit of study concerning the Civil War is to describe the major battle sites, a possible alternative for a student interested in automobiles or transportation might be to describe how supplies were transported to battle sites. For a student interested in music, an alternative assignment might be to describe the influence of music on the morale of soldiers during the Civil War.

2. Provide for small successes and attainable goals.
3. Teach to the personal interests of students.
4. Incorporate relevant information into instruction.
5. Find areas in which students can experience success and capitalize on them.
6. Look for areas in which students feel good about themselves, such as music, drama, or athletics, and advocate increased involvement in that area by contacting the music teacher, coach, or other teacher to generate interest, following through by reinforcing the student.
7. Arrange brief conferences with the student to listen to his problems and to communicate that you care about him.
8. Conduct an open class discussion with various students to identify why they do or do not like school. As other students mention positive aspects, the apathetic student may discover or realize he has similar interests.

Difficulty with Reading or Minimal Reading Ability.

1. Try to minimize tedious reading assignments.
2. Be certain students understand the purpose of reading assignments.
3. Divide assignments into smaller assignments.

4. Use topical outlines, advanced organizers, and glossaries.
5. Use fewer timed tests and tightly timed assignments or provide additional time.
6. Tell students in advance about an interesting part of the reading and ask them to find it.
7. Maintain a chart that shows reading progress.
8. Consider tape-recorded materials and other media presentations.
9. Provide summaries of key concepts to be read.
10. Consider peer teaching and group projects.

Poor Reading and Listening Comprehension.

1. Provide direct instruction in needed area.
2. Provide a summary before directed reading.
3. Divide assignments and tasks into smaller parts.
4. Shorten assignments.
5. Control the extent of verbal directions.
6. Alternate activities.
7. Maintain realistic performance expectations.

Slow Learning Ability.

1. Introduce a few concepts at a time.
2. Provide review frequently.
3. Provide concrete illustrations/examples whenever possible.
4. Consider peer teaching and tutoring.
5. Present new material in varied contexts.
6. Teach to student strengths.
7. Consider multisensory instruction.
8. Simplify explanations, materials, and techniques.
9. Chart students' progress or have students chart their own progress.
10. Establish short-range realistic goals.
11. Consider task analysis as an approach to instruction.

12. Try not to underestimate a student's capacity to learn—watch expectations.
13. Assess the student's work habits and teach study skills.
14. Call attention to work that is well done.

Poor Spelling.

1. Establish realistic goals.
2. Have students chart their own progress in spelling.
3. Have students keep a record or notebook of errors.
4. Encourage the use of a dictionary.
5. Emphasize whole word or visual aspects of spelling words.
6. Relate spelling as much as possible to student's personal interests.
7. Contract with the student for the mastery of common words.

Inadequate Written Expressive Ability.

1. Attempt to change the student's attitude by providing experiences that lead to success in writing.
2. Initially encourage the student's productivity—not structure, spelling, grammar, punctuation, or capitalization.
3. Provide free-writing opportunities in which students select their own topics. Ask them to write as much as they can for 10 minutes, encouraging them *not* to stop or correct.
4. Consider nonverbal and dramatic activities before writing, which are then discussed before students write about them.
5. Provide a wide range of interesting writing topics such as firsthand experiences, unusual pictures, films, or music.
6. Encourage students to keep a personal diary or journal.
7. Provide opportunities for students to record their ideas on a tape and to hear the tape played back before beginning to write.
8. Have students write captions for cartoons related to something of contemporary interest.

High Rate of Absenteeism.

1. Be willing to negotiate make-up work.
2. Reinforce good attendance with appropriate rewards.
3. When a student returns after an absence, attempt to involve him immediately in class activities.
4. Meet with students and discuss with them the reasons for their high rate of absenteeism.
5. Contact the student's parents and attempt to work closely with them.
6. Make classroom activities interesting and relevant.

Withdrawn or Passive Behavior.

1. Provide opportunities for self-expression through drama or role playing that involves aggressive or assertive roles.
2. Structure group participation to emphasize the student's strengths.
3. Reward participation in group activities or projects.
4. Try to become aware of the student's interests and develop conversations and projects around these interests.
5. Put the student in charge of special projects such as preparing lab materials, taking roll, and handing out and collecting materials.

Unusually High Activity Level.

1. Discuss with the student his needs for the release of tension and restlessness and work out appropriate outlets.
2. Allow the student to move around, sharpen his pencil, or get a drink when necessary.
3. Send the student on errands.
4. Establish short-term goals and shorten assignments.

5. Provide a change of activity to help focus the student's attention.
6. Reward accomplishments frequently and as soon as possible.
7. Build expectations gradually.
8. Be aware of tension as it is building and provide assistance or a change of pace.
9. Do not accept destructive actions.

Failure Orientation.

1. Discuss with the student what he needs to do to function well in the classroom.
2. Work out a success plan to help the student cope with his problems.
3. Be committed to continue with or change plans but not to give up.
4. Try to accept and understand the student's feelings without being overly judgmental.
5. Reinforce small successes.
6. Help the student achieve self-discipline and self-control.
7. Deal with immediate problems and mutually work out short-range plans.
8. Formulate realistic expectations.
9. Assist the student in coping with failure.

Grading Alternatives

Regular classroom teachers are faced with the difficult task of fairly evaluating the progress of all students in their classes. Teachers are often concerned about whether they should alter their established grading practices for students with special needs. We believe that if the handicapped student is appropriately placed and instruction is provided at a level commensurate with the student's ability, it is not necessary to significantly alter the usual grading practices. Certain alternatives, however, may be appropriate for all students. Several alternative approaches are discussed in the following sections.

Cumulative Point System.   All assignments are given a predetermined number of points,

and the student is offered several options for earning the points that determine the final grade. This system gives the student the responsibility to do as many assignments as he chooses. Some optional assignments may be modified to give the student with special learning problems an additional opportunity to succeed.

Contracted Alternative.   Students select the grade they want to earn and negotiate with the teacher the nature of the assignment and the expected quality of the work. This approach gives students the opportunity to select assignments with teacher guidance and generally encourages a greater commitment. The student with learning problems can be given reinforcement at structured intervals to help ensure his greater achievement and the much-needed success.

Alternative Assignments.   Giving credit for extra or alternative work related to course objectives but completed in a different format is often helpful for students with special needs. This approach gives the student with learning problems several options for completing course requirements in a manner appropriate to his unique needs.

Other Alternatives.   Several other alternatives that relate to the administration of examinations should be given serious consideration.

1. When scoring a student paper, be careful not to emphasize only negative aspects. Attempt to point out something the student did well.
2. Consider providing prompts to students who do not understand an examination. With prompts the teacher is not giving answers but is merely rephrasing the question in such a way that students better understand.
3. Accept that students make errors and provide feedback about what they did in-

correctly. Use the test as a teaching tool, not as punishment.

4. Consider giving a free grade. At the beginning of the term record an A in every student's folder or in your grade book. This procedure may have a positive effect for a student who has never received an A. It serves as a strong motivational tool, and the student may work diligently to maintain higher grades.

5. Consider giving a test more than once if you really want to know what students do or do not know and how much they have learned.

6. Consider an advance-warning system. When 3 or 4 weeks remain in the term, meet with the student and tell him what his final grade will be; if it is low, give him several alternatives to earn a higher grade.

7. Consider joint planning with the student for the relative value of course assignments. The student may want, for example, a special project to determine half his grade and only one fourth each on examinations and class participation.

8. Allow sufficient time for teacher-student discussions of evaluation alternatives and self-evaluation by the student.

Teachers should be willing to evaluate the purposes underlying their grading procedures. Grading should not be merely entering grades in a record book but should be used as a teaching tool to assist students in achieving goals and objectives.

Preparation for Examinations

In addition to not having adequate study skills, many students with learning problems do not have good skills for preparing for and taking examinations. Teachers may want to provide direction and instruction in this area with some of the following suggested methods:

1. Help students understand examination directions and terms such as *define, list, compare, contrast,* and *defend.*

2. Teach students to watch for cue words such as *never, all,* and *always.*

3. Tell students what you expect. Is the emphasis on content, organization, spelling, grammar, mechanics, or creative expression?

4. Provide students with a copy of a previous test, talk about it, and use it as a teaching tool.

5. With objective tests, encourage students to read all questions carefully and answer first those questions whose answers they know immediately. They may then consider more carefully the remaining questions.

6. With essay examinations, encourage students to outline their answers before writing.

7. Encourage students to answer all questions unless there is a penalty for incorrect answers.

8. Encourage students to write clearly and distinctly.

9. Encourage students to leave sufficient time to reread their answers, paying attention to such things as punctuation and spelling.

Some of these suggestions are not appropriate for all courses, but we believe these methods generally provide students with the assistance they need to be more successful when taking examinations.

Study Skills Instruction

Many students with learning problems do not have the study skills necessary to function effectively in the regular classroom. Teachers often refer to this inability as "confusion squared." The student does not practice time scheduling, "crams" for exams, misses class assignments, and in general is extremely

STUDY SKILLS QUESTIONNAIRE

	Almost always	Sometimes	Very seldom
1. Do you listen to directions or instructions provided in class?	☐	☐	☐
2. Do you take notes regarding assignments?	☐	☐	☐
3. Do you ask questions when you don't understand?	☐	☐	☐
4. Do you pay attention to class lectures and discussions?	☐	☐	☐
5. Do you keep up with assigned readings?	☐	☐	☐
6. Do you feel disorganized most of the time?	☐	☐	☐
7. Do you participate in class discussions?	☐	☐	☐
8. Do you find it difficult to complete assignments in class?	☐	☐	☐
9. Do you feel adequately prepared most of the time?	☐	☐	☐
10. Do you find the vocabulary too difficult?	☐	☐	☐

disorganized. In such cases the teacher should make systematic efforts to provide specific instruction in study skills. Often this important programming is provided by resource personnel, but in the absence of such service it must become a part of the regular classroom teacher's responsibilities.

Before actual instruction in study skills, it may be helpful to assess the student's skills informally and to make the student aware of and responsible for his study patterns. The teacher may construct an easily administered study-skills checklist or questionnaire like that in the box. After the student completes the questionnaire, the teacher should discuss his answers with him. The objective of this activity is to provide information to the student about his study skills and general classroom behavior so that he and the teacher can develop a plan of specific strategies to enhance his study skills. The student must understand his desirable and undesirable behaviors and must assume responsibility for his behavior.

Teachers may need to take time to teach some of the essential study skills related to their subject areas, including time scheduling, note taking, outlining, attending behavior, and specific skills related to the sub-ject. Students should be encouraged to use index cards to record their assignments, and the teacher may want to check these cards periodically to make necessary revisions. The teacher may also find it necessary to use outlines and advance organizers to give the student a structure for note taking. Additional skills to be taught may include using the dictionary and reviewing reading materials.

One of the more popular study techniques for reading assigned materials called is the SQ3R method. The steps in this procedure are as follows:

1. *Survey.* The student rapidly previews chapter introductory statements, summaries, and the first sentence in each paragraph.
2. *Question.* The student converts section or subsection titles into questions.
3. *Read.* The student rapidly reads the sections.
4. *Recite.* The student recites major points in his own words.
5. *Review.* The student writes or states the major points.

There are many approaches to assisting the student to build study skills. Those advocated by Sheinker and Sheinker (1983) emphasize teaching skimming, summarizing, note taking, and outlining. More detail on such approaches is provided in chapter 10, and further reading on this subject will lead to a great deal of information on learning-strategy instruction and metacognition. These approaches have been advocated by a number of recognized authorities, but like other ideas that seem to have a great deal of potential, their value remains to be verified in practice. In the meantime, helping students to better understand how they learn and to develop specific skills like outlining, summarizing, and skimming seems a sensible, logical approach.

SUMMARY

This chapter has included both general principles for more effective instruction and a wide range of specific ideas. Most of these ideas apply to students with learning problems, and many also apply to the gifted and talented. These suggestions and techniques are not "the answer." As we indicated at the beginning, there is no magic bag of tricks for teaching exceptional students, just as there is no magic bag of tricks for teaching students who follow more normal learning patterns. We do believe, however, that if teachers remain open to new alternatives and adaptations of the "regular" school program, all students may benefit. We feel certain that exceptional students will benefit.

In closing this chapter we would like to refer to research conducted by Samuels (1981) in which two primary variables were identified that interacted to determine the effectiveness of instructional intervention. Though his research related only to reading, we believe that it may apply more broadly to most instructional intervention.

Samuels carefully examined reading programs and compared the characteristics of successful and unsuccessful programs. Ac-

cording to Samuels, there seem to be two underlying factors that differentiate successful from unsuccessful programs. Samuels (1981, p. 236) found that to ensure successful reading programs, educators must believe (1) that "the school can have a significant impact on the academic achievement of its students" and (2) that "most children are capable of mastering the basic skills." Both assumptions emphasize that the school is responsible for educating its students.

This conclusion appears to be in direct conflict with the findings of a National Education Association (NEA) survey (1979). The survey asked teachers why students do poorly in school, and 95% of the teachers blamed students' poor achievement on the students' home environment or the students themselves. Only 1% of teachers attributed the cause to teachers, and 4% blamed the schools. According to Samuels, certain other characteristics also differentiate successful from unsuccessful programs. Successful programs employed teacher aides in direct instruction and had strong administrative leaders who provided "time for planning and carrying out decisions, securing financial support, and running interference against counterforces" (p. 38). Teachers in successful programs were committed to the project goals and devoted extensive time and energy to achieving the goals. In effect, teachers in successful programs believed that success or failure depended on what happened in the classroom and not on factors outside of school.

Samuels also reported that successful programs had clearly stated goals and objectives. They employed techniques such as task analysis and maintained a warm and friendly classroom atmosphere. They also emphasized teaching skills, sufficient practice of these skills, and the use of relevant instructional materials. Instruction was kept at a low level of complexity in a somewhat structured learning environment, and ample time was provided for instruction.

Unsuccessful programs, according to Samuels, demonstrated the bandwagon syndrome—using the newest or hottest idea—and lacked systemwide commitment. Unsuccessful programs were also more highly influenced by parental pressure or federal funding than by students' demonstrated need. Unsuccessful programs did not use time efficiently, failed to provide sufficient planning for teachers, and often involved piecemeal approaches.

We believe that the implications of this research are quite clear: teachers must be committed to their approach to instruction and must believe they can have an impact on their students. We hope that readers will understand the message communicated by Samuels's research and make an honest attempt to apply these principles in their work with students with learning problems. We further hope that some of the ideas contained in this chapter will help teachers have a real impact on students in their classes.

Feelings, Expectancies, and Interactions

THE IMPORTANCE OF GOOD PERSONAL INTERACTION

HANDICAPPED STUDENT OR HANDICAPPING SITUATION?

TEACHER EXPECTATIONS AND STUDENT BEHAVIOR

THE QUALITY OF STUDENT INTERACTION

ENHANCING INTERACTION BETWEEN HANDICAPPED STUDENTS AND THEIR PEERS

- [ ] What is the difference between a handicapped student and a handicapping situation?

- [ ] What is meant by a "student-materials" interaction? How can any potentially negative results of such interactions be reduced?

- [ ] What techniques can be used by teachers to measure their interactions with students?

- [ ] How can achievement test results affect teachers' interactions with students?

- [ ] How does the self-fulfilling prophecy work in the classroom?

- [ ] How can "teacher talk" in the teachers' lounge influence students?

- [ ] What kind of social skills should handicapped students possess to be successful in a mainstream classroom?

- [ ] To what extent do interactions between nonhandicapped and handicapped students influence the handicapped student's self-perception?

The content of chapters 1 and 2 was generally applicable to all exceptional students, and tended to be fact oriented. The content of chapter 3 was instructional-method oriented, and was applicable to many, perhaps all, exceptional children. The content of this chapter is also generally applicable (which is why it is part of this introductory section) but focuses on a different dimension of teaching. It is about feelings, expectancies, and interactions. It is certainly no *less* important than the information contained in chapters 1 to 3 and for some exceptional students it may be even *more* important. We will emphasize the necessity of positive interactions with students with handicapping conditions but the same principles also apply to the gifted/talented.

THE IMPORTANCE OF GOOD PERSONAL INTERACTION

Personal interaction is what goes on between students, between teachers, and between students and teachers in the schools. There *is* interaction; our concern is the *quality* of this interaction and its potential influence on the lives of students. Quality interaction is crucial for students with disabilities and other students with difficulties in their lives, whether or not we might call them *handicapped* or *disabled.* We introduce this chapter with a story of a high-school student who was experiencing difficulties in school and in his personal life. His story exemplifies the importance of teachers' awareness of their role in promoting good personal interaction.

A TEACHER WHO REALLY CARED

Mel, a teenage student in a midwestern state, was in many respects just like any other high-school student. He had grown up in a small, rural community of some five hundred people, where he

had enjoyed all the activities of his peers. He was active in Boy Scouts, he enjoyed hiking and swimming in the creek and particularly liked competitive athletics. He excelled in some areas of athletics and might have been called a standout athlete in his community. He definitely had promise and was well known and liked by almost everyone.

As Mel was about to enter high school, there was a family move to the city, and for the first time he had to break into a new group, namely, the boys who were involved in competitive sports. He tried to become a part of this group but was not accepted. This nonacceptance was a new experience and was devastating until he saw that there was another group that would accept him. This accepting group was a group of troublemakers whose like can be found in almost any school or community. To be accepted, all that was necessary was to do one better (or worse) than the next guy. If another member of the group fought someone 6 feet tall, you only needed to fight someone taller. If another member stole something worth $20, you had to steal something worth $30. The rules were clear and simple and acceptance was assured if you played by the rules.

Another sure way to be accepted was to become a thorn in the side of teachers, counselors, and school administrators. Even if part of the group was not enrolled in school, this type of behavior was very visible and highly respected. Mel wanted to be the best and he quickly moved in that direction, finding solid acceptance with his new friends. Drinking and street fighting became a routine part of his life and he was a regular troublemaker in school. Teachers came to know his problem behavior and most concluded that he was a loser. His records indicated his problems, and through coffee-room talk, even teachers who had not had Mel in their classes knew what to look for. Mel's school attendance became sporadic, and he was suspended at various times, permitting him to spend more time with his out-of-school friends. Mel was on his way down.

At this point in his life, Mel might have been considered "behavior-disordered." The school counselor suggested that he should think about what type of work he could do at age 16; the assumption was that he would quit school after his 16th birthday. But then an outside influence intervened. At about the same time as the possibility of

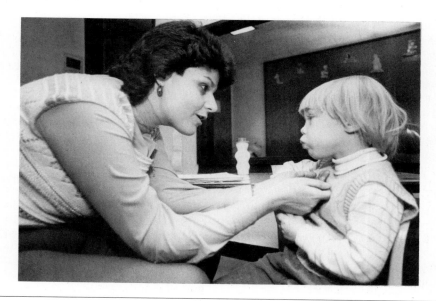

Teachers who respect students earn their respect.

quitting school became more realistic, Mel got to thinking about something he had noticed over the 18 months he had been in high school. As he walked down the halls, he noticed that one teacher (Mr. S) often had a group of students, primarily boys, gathered around him in the hall outside his classroom door. Mel was curious about what was going on. Mr. S, who taught biology, would sometimes greet Mel as he walked down the hall, and if he was not engaged in conversations with other students, would ask how Mel was doing. Mel was intrigued by this unteacherlike behavior, and would stop and talk if he was alone. He couldn't do this in front of his friends because it might be seen as fraternizing with the enemy.

Before long Mel found ways to spend more time in that group around Mr. S's door. At first he was a little uneasy, particularly when Mr. S looked him straight in the eye in a friendly, nonjudgmental manner, engaging in person-to-person conversation. Mr. S did not leave his role as a teacher, but somehow came across as a teacher who was also a friend.

Several weeks after deciding that maybe Mr. S was all right—for a teacher—Mel took something out of another student's locker just as he was entering the wing of the school that included Mr.

S's room. As he passed Mr. S, he got a look that made him wonder if his behavior had been seen. He avoided Mr. S for some time, then stopped by when no one else was there.

After a few moments of conversation, Mr. S said, "I see that you're pretty fast with your hands," at which point Mel thought, "Here it comes, he's just another teacher." But Mr. S followed quickly with, "Are you fast with your feet, too?" Before Mel could reply, he continued, "Track is going to start in a couple of weeks; are you interested in going out?" Mel wanted to go out, but athletic participation was not acceptable in his group, so he replied that as far as he was concerned, track was for sissies, and left.

In the next few days, Mel saw Mr. S a number of times, who told him he should think more about going out for track. Then he was given a handout telling when track tryouts were to be held and other such details. Mr. S didn't give up easily, and somehow Mel found himself in that wing of the school with greater frequency. Just before the day for tryouts, Mr. S said, "Why don't you come out for three days? If you don't like it, quit, but promise me you'll give it a try for three days." And Mel did try out.

Mel found success in track, which led him to

give both football and basketball a serious try. He made the team in all three sports and became a different person. His grades improved in the remainder of high school, and after graduation he entered college, in part on the strength of a track scholarship. While in college, Mel worked part-time, making deliveries for a laundry. One of his stops was a school for handicapped students. He became interested in these students and changed his major from physical education to special education in his junior year. Mel completed his undergraduate degree and became a teacher of the handicapped.

Mel continued to teach the handicapped, later completed a master's degree, and still later a doctorate in special education. Now, 30 years after a teacher took time to encourage a teenage boy to believe in himself, Mel is involved in teaching teachers. He regularly emphasizes the importance of advocacy for students, along with the importance of teaching basic skills and content in the subject areas. He maintains that "good personal interaction is what teaching is all about."[1]

Unfortunately, the experience of the authors has been that not all teachers are like Mr. S in the preceding vignette. Let's take a look at the other side of the coin.

THE POOR SCHOLAR'S SOLILOQUY[2]

No, I'm not very good in school. This is my second year in the seventh grade and I'm bigger and taller than the other kids. They like me alright though even if I don't say much in the classroom because outside I can tell them how to do a lot of things. They tag me around and that sort of makes up for what goes on in school.

I don't know why the teachers don't like me. They never have very much. Seems like they don't think you know anything unless you can name the book it comes out of. I've got a lot of books in my room at home—books like *Popular Science Mechanical Encyclopedia,* and the Sears' and Ward's catalogues—but I don't very often just sit down and read them through like they make us do in school. I use my books when I want to find something out, like whenever Mom buys anything secondhand I look it up in Sears' or Ward's first and tell her if she's getting stung or not. I can use the index in a hurry.

In school though we've got to learn whatever is in the book and I just can't memorize the stuff. Last year I stayed after school every night for two weeks trying to learn the names of the Presidents. Of course, I knew some of them like Washington and Jefferson and Lincoln, but there must have been thirty altogether, and I never did get them straight.

I'm not too sorry though because the kids who learned the Presidents had to turn right around and learn all the Vice Presidents. I am taking the seventh grade over but our teacher this year isn't so interested in the names of the Presidents. She has us trying to learn the names of all the great American inventors.

I guess I just can't remember names in history. Anyway, this year I've been trying to learn about trucks because my uncle owns three and he says I can drive one when I'm sixteen. I already know the horsepower and number of forward and backward speeds of 26 American trucks, some of them Diesels and I can spot each make a long way off. It's funny how that Diesel works. I started to tell my teacher all about it last Wednesday in science class when the pump we were using to make a vacuum in a bell jar got hot but she said she didn't see what a Diesel engine had to do with our experiment on air pressure so I just kept still. The kids seemed interested though. I took four of them around to my uncle's garage after school and we saw the mechanic, Gus, tear a big truck Diesel down. Boy, does he know his stuff!

I'm not very good in geography either. They call it economic geography this year. We've been studying the imports and exports of Chile all week, but I couldn't tell you what they are. Maybe the reason is I had to miss school yesterday because

---

[1] "Mel," in this vignette, is Dr. Mel Weishahn, one of the authors of this text. He is sorry today for all the problems he caused his parents but will be forever grateful for Mr. S, a teacher who cared. He believes that student advocacy, *really caring,* is of prime importance for all teachers.

[2] From "The Poor Scholar's Soliloquy," 1944, *Childhood Education, 20,* pp. 219–220. Copyright 1944 by the Association for Childhood Education International. Reprinted by permission.

my uncle took me and his big trailer truck down state about 200 miles and we brought almost 10 tons of stock to the Chicago market.

He had told me where we were going, and I had to figure out the highways to take and also the mileage. He didn't do anything but drive and turn where I told him to. Was that fun! I sat with a map in my lap and told him to turn south, or south-east or some other direction. We made 7 stops, and drove over 500 miles round trip. I'm figuring now what his oil cost and also the wear and tear on the truck—he calls it depreciation—so we'll know how much we made.

I even write out all the bills and send letters to the farmers about what their pigs and beef cattle brought at the stockyards. I only made three mistakes in 17 letters last time, my aunt said, all commas. She's been through high school and reads them over. I wish I could write school themes that way. The last one I had to write was on "What a Daffodil Thinks of Spring," and I just couldn't get going.

I don't do very well in school arithmetic either. Seems I just can't keep my mind on the problems. We had one the other day like this:

"If a 57 ft. telephone pole falls across a cement highway so that 17 3/5 feet extend from one side and 14 9/17 feet from the other, how wide is the highway?"

That seemed to me like an awfully silly way to get the width of a highway. I didn't even try to answer it because it didn't say whether the pole had fallen straight across or not.

Even in shop I don't get very good grades. All of us kids made a broom holder and a bookend this term and mine were sloppy. I just couldn't get interested. Mom doesn't use a broom anymore with her new vacuum cleaner, and all our books are in a bookcase with glass doors in the parlor. Anyway I wanted to make an end gate for my uncle's trailer, but the shop teacher said that meant using metal and wood both, and I'd have to learn how to work with wood first. I didn't see why, but I kept still, and made a tie rack at school and the tail gate after school at my uncle's garage. He said I saved him ten dollars.

Civics is hard for me, too. I've been staying after school trying to learn the "Articles of Confederation" for almost a week, because the teacher said we couldn't be good citizens unless we did. I really tried because I want to be a good citizen. I did hate to stay after school, because a bunch of us boys from the south end of town have been cleaning up the old lot across from Taylor's Machine Shop to make a playground out of it for the little kids from the Methodist home. I made the jungle gym from old pipe, and the guys made me Grand Mogul to keep the playground going. We raised enough money collecting scrap this month to build a wire fence clear around the lot.

Dad says I can quit school when I am fifteen and I am sort of anxious to because there are a lot of things I want to learn how to do, and as my uncle says, I'm not getting any younger.

I TAUGHT THEM ALL[3]

Naomi J. White

I have taught in high school for ten years. During that time I have given assignments, among others, to a murderer, an evangelist, a pugilist, a thief, and an imbecile.

The murderer was a quiet little boy who sat on the front seat and regarded me with pale blue eyes; the evangelist, easily the most popular boy in school, had the lead in the junior play; the pugilist lounged by the window and let loose at intervals a raucous laugh that startled even the geraniums; the thief was a gay-hearted Lothario with a song on his lips; and the imbecile, a soft-eyed little animal seeking the shadows.

The murderer awaits death in the state penitentiary; the evangelist has lain a year now in the village churchyard; the pugilist lost an eye in a brawl in Hong Kong; the thief, by standing on tiptoe, can see the windows of my room from the county jail; and the once gentle-eyed little moron beats his head against a padded wall in the state asylum.

All of these pupils once sat in my room, sat and looked at me gravely across worn brown desks. I must have been a great help to these pupils—I taught them the rhyming scheme of the Elizabethan sonnet and how to diagram a complex sentence.

[3]From "I Taught Them All" by Naomi J. White, 1937, *The Clearing House, 12*, pp. 151, 192. Copyright 1937 by The Clearing House. Reprinted by permission.

ABOUT SCHOOL[4]

This poem was handed to a high-school English teacher the day before the writer committed suicide.

He always wanted to explain things,
    but no one cared.
So he drew.

Sometimes he would just draw
    and it wasn't anything.
He wanted to carve it in stone
    or write it in the sky
    and the things inside him that needed saying.

And it was after that he drew the picture.
It was a beautiful picture.
He kept it under his pillow
    and would let no one see it.
And he would look at it every night
    and think about it.
And it was all of him and he loved it.

When he started school he brought it with him.
Not to show anyone, but just to have it with him
    like a friend.

It was funny about school.
He sat in a square brown desk
    like all the other square brown desks
    and he thought it would be red.
And his room was a square brown room
    like all the other rooms.
And it was tight and close. And stiff.

He hated to hold the pencil and chalk,
    with his arm stiff and his feet flat on the floor,
    stiff,
    with the teacher watching and watching.

The teacher came and spoke to him.
She told him to wear a tie like all the other boys.
He said he didn't like them
    and she said it didn't matter.
After that he drew. And he drew all yellow
    and it was the way he felt about morning.
And it was beautiful.

The teacher came and smiled at him.
"What's this?" she said.
"Why don't you draw something
    like Ken's drawing?

Isn't it beautiful?"
After that his mother bought him a tie
    and he always drew airplanes and rockets
    like everyone else.

And he threw the old picture away.
And when he lay out alone looking at the sky,
    it was big and blue, and all of everything,
    but he wasn't anymore.

He was square and brown inside
    and his hands were stiff.
And he was like everyone else.
All the things inside him that needed saying
    didn't need it anymore.

It had stopped pushing. It was crushed.
Stiff.
Like everything else.

PAIN IN SCHOOL IS having an indifferent teacher[5]

My unhappy experience was when I was—well—just last year. I worked on a project for about two weeks 'cause my parents didn't think I was doing enough extra projects for school. So, they wanted me to do one. So I did it. Then, when I brought it to school (these were the last few days) my teacher told me that—well—she didn't really tell me—but she didn't pay very much attention to my project. I made a map. And it just sat in the back of the room for a few days and I finally brought it home. I never got a grade on it, or anything.

PAIN IN SCHOOL IS learning to feel embarrassed

While in the second grade a question was asked and I raised my hand with much anticipation be-

[4]Original source unknown.

[5]From *Pain and Joy in School* by E. Schultz, C. Heuchert, and S. Stampf, 1973, Champaign, IL.: Research Press. Copyright 1973 by Research Press. Used with permission.

cause I knew the answer and I was the only one who had any idea of the correct answer.

I was wrong and the teacher proceeded to tell me how dumb I was to think that I could do better than her more well-versed students. This tirade went on for about ten minutes while she told me to go to the head of the class and talk about why I had made such a "stupid" answer. At the end of this she told me my zipper was down which gave me much more embarrassment.

PAIN IN SCHOOL IS traveling a lonely road with a hurt that takes many years to heal

"I am sure you will be better off in the service. The service can teach you a trade. Maybe you can finish high school while in the service."

Seventeen years old and my world had just completely collapsed around me. I had just been told by my counselor that I would be better off in the service than in school.

He was polite, very sympathetic but he was still saying "Sorry, boy, you are too dumb for school!" Even today I would like to tell him to stick his advice in his ear! My work in school had not been good, but I felt much of that was due to the fact that I did more playing than studying.

When I left school that day I wondered what I would tell my parents. What could I tell myself? How could I fight a gnawing, cancerous emotion of worthlessness? I wondered how I could face my buddies. I remember having an overwhelming urge to run, to hide, to get away. But, where does a seventeen-year-old boy hide? The only hiding place I could find was the service. That day, I enlisted in the Navy before I went home. There was only one paper to be signed before I left for the service, that was a parental permission paper for men under eighteen years of age—they signed!

The hurt I felt that day almost twelve years ago has actually helped me today. When I am working with a boy who is called stupid, can't read, maybe he feels like he isn't worth much. I can go a little further than just sympathizing with him, I can feel what he feels. . . .

Some refer to such feeling as sensitivity. Call it what you will, but I can simply tell my students to "move over, brother, you have company. I've been down this road before once by myself. It's a lonely road, let me travel with you."

CIPHER IN THE SNOW[6]

Jean E. Mizer

It started with tragedy on a biting cold February morning. I was driving behind the Milford Corners bus as I did most snowy mornings on my way to school. It veered and stopped short at the hotel, which it had no business doing, and I was annoyed as I had to come to an unexpected stop. A boy lurched out of the bus, reeled, stumbled, and collapsed on the snowbank at the curb. The bus driver and I reached him at the same moment. His thin, hollow face was white even against the snow.

"He's dead," the driver whispered.

It didn't register for a minute. I glanced quickly at the scared young faces staring down at us from the school bus. "A doctor! Quick! I'll phone from the hotel . . ."

"No use. I tell you he's dead." The driver looked down at the boy's still form. "He never even said he felt bad," he muttered, "just tapped me on the shoulder and said, real quiet, 'I'm sorry. I have to get off at the hotel.' That's all. Polite and apologizing like."

At school, the giggling, shuffling morning noise quieted as the news went down the halls. I passed a huddle of girls. "Who was it? Who dropped dead on the way to school?" I head one of them half-whisper.

"Don't know his name; some kid from Milford Corners," was the reply.

It was like that in the faculty room and the principal's office. "I'd appreciate your going to tell the parents," the principal told me. "They haven't a phone and, anyway, somebody from school should go there in person. I'll cover your classes."

"Why me?" I asked. "Wouldn't it be better if you did it?"

"I didn't know the boy," the principal admitted levelly. "And in the last year's sophomore personalities column I note that you were listed as his favorite teacher."

I drove through the snow and cold down the bad canyon road to the Evans place and thought about the boy, Cliff Evans. His favorite teacher! I thought. He hasn't spoken two words to me in two

[6]From "Cipher in the Snow" by Jean Mizer, 1964, *N.E.A. Journal, 53,* pp 8–10. Copyright 1964 by the N.E.A. Journal. Reprinted by permission.

years! I could see him in my mind's eye all right, sitting back there in the last seat in my afternoon literature class. "Cliff Evans," I muttered to myself, "a boy who never talked." I thought a minute. "A boy who never smiled. I never saw him smile once."

The big ranch kitchen was clean and warm. I blurted out my news somehow. Mrs. Evans reached blindly toward a chair. "He never said anything about bein' ailing."

His stepfather snorted. "He ain't said nothing about anything since I moved in here."

Mrs. Evans pushed a pan back off the stove and began to untie her apron. "Now hold on," her husband snapped. "I got to have breakfast before I go to town. Nothing we can do now anyway. If Cliff hadn't been so dumb, he'd have told us he didn't feel good."

After school I sat in the office and stared bleakly at the records spread out before me. I was to close the file and write the obituary for the school paper. The almost bare sheets mocked the effort. Cliff Evans, white, never legally adopted by stepfather, five young half-brothers and sisters. These meager strands of information and the list of D grades were all the records had to offer.

Cliff Evans had silently come in the school door in the mornings and gone out of the school door in the evenings, and that was all. He had never belonged to a club. He had never played on a team. He had never held an office. As far as I could tell, he had never done one happy, noisy kid thing. He had never been anybody at all.

How do you go about making a boy into a zero? The grade-school records showed me. The first and second grade teachers' annotations read "sweet, shy child"; "timid but eager." Then the third grade note had opened the attack. Some teacher had written in a good, firm hand, "Cliff won't talk. Uncooperative, Slow learner." The other academic sheep had followed with: "dull"; "slow-witted"; "low (IQ)." They became correct. The boy's IQ score in the ninth grade had been listed at 83. But his IQ in the third grade had been 106. The score didn't go under 100 until the seventh grade. Even shy, timid, sweet children have resilience. It takes time to break them.

I stomped to the typewriter and wrote a savage report, pointing out what education had done to Cliff Evans. I slapped a copy on the principal's

desk and another in the sad, dog-eared file. I banged the typewriter and slammed the file and crashed the door shut, but I didn't feel much better. A little boy kept walking after me, a little boy with a peaked, pale face; a skinny body in faded jeans, and big eyes that had looked and searched for a long time and then had become veiled.

I could guess how many times he'd been chosen last to play sides in a game, how many whispered child conversations had excluded him, how many times he hadn't been asked. I could see and hear the faces and voices that said over and over, "You're a nothing, Cliff Evans."

A child is a believing creature. Cliff undoubtedly believed them. Suddenly it seemed clear to me: when finally there was nothing left at all for Cliff Evans, he collapsed on a snowbank and went away. The doctor might list "heart failure" as the cause of death, but that wouldn't change my mind.

We couldn't find ten students in the school who had known Cliff well enough to attend the funeral as his friends. So the student body officers and a committee from the junior class went as a group to the church, being politely sad. I attended the services with them, and sat through it with a lump of cold lead in my chest and a big resolve growing through me.

I've never forgotten Cliff Evans nor that resolve. He has been my challenge year after year, class after class. I look up and down for veiled eyes and bodies slumped into a seat in an alien world, "Look, kids," I say silently, "I may not do anything else for you this year, but not one of you is going to come out of here a nobody. I'll work or fight to the bitter end doing battle with society and the school board, but I don't want to have one of you coming out of here thinking himself a zero."

Most of the time—not always, but most of the time—I've succeeded.

We believe that all teachers who work with young people should devise some system for recalling the *absolutely profound influence* they have on their students. Teachers have the potential to greatly enhance or seriously limit their students' feelings of self-worth, achievement, and behavior. After reading the last vignette, "Cipher in the Snow," a teacher we know placed a drawing of a large zero under the glass cover of her desk, to be clearly visible every school day, and pledged that each day it would remind her of her influence so that none of her students would be a "zero" in her class.

Teachers must recognize that all students need to be acknowledged as individuals in their own right and to know that significant others in their lives care about what they do and how they feel. It is easy to become trapped in a learning atmosphere that is primarily mechanical, that emphasizes achievement, test scores, and rules and regulations. We fully appreciate the tremendous demands on today's teachers, but a perspective that recognizes the worth of every individual is essential to the achievement of basic educational goals. It will be emphasized throughout this text that the teacher is the single most important factor in the successful mainstreaming of handicapped students. There is little question that teachers have a profound influence on students' behavior and achievement. We want to encourage every teacher to be aware of this influence and to make certain that it is a *positive* influence.

The importance of interaction between teachers and students will be emphasized by reviewing several studies that have demonstrated the influence of teachers' expectations on students' behavior, achievement, and feelings of self-worth. This chapter also provides a review of ways in which these interactions can be assessed through formal and informal instruments. Students' interactions are discussed, and techniques and materials to enhance positive interactions are described. The conclusion of this chapter presents vignettes and anecdotes reflecting the importance of positive interactions. We admit in advance that we are deliberately attempting a "hard sell" of the importance of positive interactions between teachers and

students. We believe that in this area, this is the only tenable position to take. We further believe that those who accept this idea will be better teachers and happier persons for having made this decision.

HANDICAPPED STUDENT OR HANDICAPPING SITUATION?

Problems with specific students (perhaps only one or two in any given teacher's classroom) are a major factor in teacher dissatisfaction. Such problems are one reason teachers leave the teaching profession. These problems are *real* and cannot be ignored or forgotten. But what about the source of the problems?

Sometimes the problem *is* Jimmy Smith or Mary Jones. The problem is attributable directly to a given student. At other times the problem has multiple sources, and they are difficult to isolate and identify.

Handicapped students have certain limitations imposed *as a result of their handicap.* By the very nature of the condition, the teacher can predict the need for certain modifications or adaptations of curriculum, materials, teaching strategies, or a combination of these factors. A student with impaired vision, for example, must have modified materials to participate fully in regular classrooms. Hearing impaired students need adapted approaches and the specialized services of support personnel, and students with orthopedic or other health impairments may need to have architectural barriers removed and some special equipment provided if they are to be educated in regular classrooms. Because of the limitations imposed by handicapping conditions, the condition itself necessitates modifications or adaptations.

With another group of students, teachers cannot clearly establish the reason for school difficulties, and it is not educationally sound to assume that in every case internal factors are the major cause. In many cases the

FIGURE 4–1. Ingredients of a handicapping situation.

failure or difficulty is the result of a number of interacting, external factors. When such is the case, the problem may be considered *a handicapping situation,* to emphasize the interaction between the student and factors that prove to be a handicap for him or her.

If a student is having difficulty in reading or math, for example, or is withdrawn or acts out in class, the teacher must consider a number of variables that may be influencing the student's poor achievement or unusual behavior. These variables include (1) the student, (2) the materials being used, (3) the environment, (4) the teacher or teachers, and (5) the student's peers. The influence of these variables is depicted in Figure 4–1.

Although the student may be the primary cause of the problem, more commonly the interaction of several factors is what produces a handicapping situation. To determine if this is so, the teacher must learn to analyze the interaction among various factors.

Student-Materials Interaction

The appropriateness of educational materials may greatly influence a student's achievement or behavior. Although this influence may seem obvious, often not enough time and effort are given to observation, planning, and evaluation of educational materials. Often, for example, the reading materials required for a particular subject may not be appropriate to the actual reading level of the

student; the student may be "required" to read a text or some other material that is far beyond his skill level. Teachers should administer an informal reading inventory to determine whether the student has sufficient skills to successfully read the assigned material. The readability of material being used may also be assessed. Studies have indicated that intermediate texts for 3rd to 6th grades may have a readability level anywhere from 2nd to 10th grades. When the readability level of a particular textbook is far beyond the instructional reading level, it is not safe to assume that the problem is exclusively with the student, for such a case may be a handicapping situation for the student. There is also evidence that students have preferred learning styles—auditory, visual, tactile, and kinesthetic—and that if assessment is made of the preferred learning channel or style and materials are matched to this preferred channel, the student's learning rate and achievement can be increased.

Student-Environment Interaction

The influence of poor student-environment interaction is exemplified by a student who is highly distracted by a noisy or visually distracting classroom. As a result, this student may not be able to attend to the task or assignment. Most students can filter out these distractions, but some cannot. For example, the last time you studied for an examination, did you seek out an area free of auditory distractions (such as a quiet corner of the library) or were you able to listen to hard rock and sit at a table with your friends who were laughing and having a good time? Some individuals have little or no difficulty studying among considerable distractions, whereas others prefer a relatively quiet atmosphere. If you prefer an environment that is free of distractions but were unable to get away from them and as a result did poorly on the examination, who or what should be blamed? In this instance you might feel that you could not concentrate because there were so many distractions and that as a result you did poorly. This situation is similar to that of a student who is distracted by extraneous visual or auditory signals in the classroom environment. In such cases is it safe to assume that the problem lies within the student? In all likelihood it is not; the difficulty undoubtedly involves a handicapping situation and the interaction between the student and environmental factors.

The five-point interaction matrix (Figure 4–1) should be considered when the teacher analyzes the needs of any student. It is not safe to assume that the failure of a student is primarily the fault of the student. Rather, it may result from a handicapping situation related to inadequacies in the environment, educational materials, instructional techniques, or interactional patterns in the classroom. This situation may be particularly true with a student who is exhibiting only mild problems and for whom there is no known reason for the difficulty. Teachers should objectively consider which factors are contributing to a particular student's difficulty and make the necessary adjustments to correct the situation.

The discussion so far has focused on the interaction between the student and his educational materials and educational environment. The remaining two factors, teacher-student and student-student interaction, are the focus of the remainder of this chapter.

Student-Student Interaction

Probably all teachers understand that some of any student's difficulties will be the result of interaction with peers. In fact, many teachers will label a student's difficulty as "problems with peers." In some cases such difficulties can be reduced by changing seating, by some specific program of behavior management, or simply by modifying the teacher's attitude. Student-environment interaction, discussed earlier, can be the key to reducing negative interaction between students. Later sections of this chapter provide more detail about the teacher's role in student-student interaction and how to assess the quality of such interaction, but the point is that interaction with peers, *combined* with other factors, may provide the best possible explanation of the problems under consideration and provide a meaningful basis for intervention.

Teacher-Student Interaction

There is little question that teachers have a profound influence on students' behavior, achievement, and feelings of self-worth. The way in which the teacher interacts with a student can either seriously impede or greatly facilitate the student's success in school. This interaction should be considered with all students but has even more implications for students who are not achieving or who are apathetic, nonconforming, acting out in the classroom, or identified as handicapped.

The nature and quality of the interaction between the teacher and student can be strongly influenced by the teacher's expectations. The teacher's expectations may be too low, expecting only minimal achievement or little acceptable behavior or too high, pressuring the student to achieve beyond his capabilities, resulting in discouragement, behavior problems, or failure. Expectations are not in themselves bad if teachers are willing to modify an initial expectation as a result of additional information and experience. However, this adjustment of expectancies does not always occur. Some teachers form inappropriate initial expectancies and do not change them even when they obtain disconfirming information. To some extent we all form expectations on the basis of preconceived information or as a result of initial interactions, but we must maintain a *flexible attitude* concerning these expectations and be willing to change them.

The concern about teachers' expectancies or biases is that they may become self-fulfilling prophecies, in which case the expected behavior is enacted by both the teacher and the student. If a teacher expects a particular behavior from a student, she may observe and react only to initially expected behaviors, and as a result the student may fulfill his role. The following anecdote illustrates this principle.

A discussion among teachers in the teachers' lounge centered on the unacceptable, disruptive behavior of a number of children from the Jones family. Teachers who had previously taught students from this family said that they *all* were troublemakers and in general were the most disruptive members of their classes. As a result of this discussion, Mr. Carlson, the sixth grade teacher, had a preconceived notion about the behavior of Jimmy Jones, a new arrival in his classroom. Mr. Carlson was ready and waiting for disruptive behavior from Jimmy. Whenever Jimmy was the least bit disruptive (even though his behavior was not significantly different from other students), Mr. Carlson saw his prophecy as fulfilled: "I knew Jimmy was going to be a problem, and I'm going to stop it before it gets started." Mr. Carlson was so certain that he would observe disruptive behavior that he interpreted minor problems as disruptive. If this situation continued, it is possible that Jimmy might also fulfill his prophecy—by becoming disruptive.

In this illustration the prophecy was initiated by a conversation in the teachers' lounge, but expectations concerning a particular student may also be influenced by information contained in a student's cumulative file that was taken from related nonschool experience with the family or acquired in many other ways. In faculty lounges, however, information is often shared in an unguarded and sometimes unprofessional manner. Although we acknowledge that in the majority of teachers' lounges the discussions are professional and in the best interests of students, there are times when discussion of a particular student can be demeaning and damaging. Frequently the discussion concerns poorly achieving students or extreme behavior problems. Teachers must vent their feelings, of course, and often the teachers' lounge is the most logical place to do so, but teachers should consider the influence such discussions may have on other teachers and the ultimate effect on the students being discussed.

In one particular teachers' lounge where this had become a serious problem, the faculty decided to post a readily observable sign: IF IT'S NOT GOOD DON'T BOTHER! When asked what the sign meant, they were quick to say, "If you don't have something positive to say about students (or any other matter), don't say it. If it is necessary to discuss a particular student, attempt to do so outside of the teachers' lounge." This concern may seem a trivial matter compared with other problems in schools, but we believe that often teachers' attitudes and interactions with students are influenced by teachers' lounge talk.

TEACHER EXPECTATIONS AND STUDENT BEHAVIOR

Student behavior includes both social behavior (interactions with teachers and other students) and academic achievement. Acceptable, appropriate student behavior/achievement is a major educational goal. But teachers should remember the common

Realistic expectations and individualization are essential to successful mainstreaming.

phrase, "what you see is what you get," and substitute *expect* for *see.* To a considerable extent, what teachers expect *is* what they get, at least within the limitations of the students' actual abilities. This process has been demonstrated over and over again both in studies cited in the literature of educational research and in many classrooms on a daily basis.

The classic research study on teacher expectations was conducted by Rosenthal and Jacobson (1968). The main purpose of the Rosenthal-Jacobson study was to determine if teachers' favorable expectations could be responsible for significant IQ test score gains of students. A group-administered test (with which the students were unfamiliar) was given to all students who would be returning to one elementary school the next fall. The test, the Harvard Test of Inflected Acquisition,

was interpreted as being a test that would predict with near absolute certainty the students who would show an "academic spurt" or demonstrate "late blooming." The test in actuality was Flanagan's Test of General Ability (1960) and yielded scores in verbal ability and reasoning and a total IQ score. On completion of the testing, 20% of the students selected to participate in the study were randomly assigned to an experimental group, and were labeled "bloomers." Teachers were given a list of the children in their classrooms who might exhibit marked intellectual growth. From this information the teachers erroneously assumed that the other children (those who were not identified) did not have the potential for marked intellectual growth.

The findings of this study indicated a significant expectancy advantage in favor of the students who were identified as "late bloomers." In other words, the students who were identified as most likely to show an "academic spurt" did spurt as evidenced by mean gains in total IQ measurements.

This study has been considerably debated and is not unanimously accepted by professionals (Jose & Cody, 1971; Kester & Letchworth, 1972; Mendels & Flanders, 1973). Numerous other studies have examined the influence of teacher-student interaction, however, and they have established that teachers' expectations do have the potential to impede or facilitate students' achievement and behavior (Brophy, 1983; Dusek, 1985; Dusek & Joseph, 1983; Harris & Rosenthal, 1985; Hersh & Walker, 1983).

An interesting experience concerning the effects of intelligence-test data on achievement was recently shared with us. Although this experience cannot be scientifically documented, it provides an interesting dramatization of the self-fulfilling prophecy.

The setting was a large urban junior high school. In an attempt to establish a sense of community and to increase the interaction of students to a level that might be expected in a smaller school, several "pods" were established. Approximately 100 students were assigned to a pod, with roughly four homerooms in each pod. By design, the pod was established to serve as a school within the larger school.

Several weeks after school began, teachers received a random listing of students assigned to their pod. Preceding each student's name was an assigned number, with numbers ranging from 50 to 150. It was assumed by some teachers that the numbers were the results of group intelligence tests, and accordingly, many teachers established groups on the basis of the number.

After several weeks it was learned that the numbers were not IQ test results but locker numbers. The ironic side effect was that the students with high locker numbers tended to be doing very well in their classes and teachers highly valued their interactions; students with relatively low locker numbers were not doing as well.

This may seem an extreme example of the influence of student data wherever or however it may be obtained, but it does further illustrate our concern. In all fairness, however, we must say that further investigation of this real-life situation revealed that a number of teachers were quick to question the "IQs" on the student listing. Our concern is for the potentially damaging effect of those teachers who could not objectively observe and evaluate their students even after several weeks.

Teachers' expectancies can definitely influence student behavior. As mentioned previously, students who are viewed negatively by their teachers and others tend to behave inappropriately. This inappropriate behavior may promote negative self-evaluation and further negative evaluations by others. There is further evidence that students with poor self-concepts may actually attempt to avoid academic situations (McCandless, 1973). In addition to behaving in accordance with their negative self-image, these students most likely perform poorly, thereby reinforcing both the negative self-concept and the teacher's continued negative expectancy.

The teacher's responsibility is clear. Teachers must do all possible to improve a student's self-concept, to provide assignments that will permit success, to expect acceptable behavior, and to increase the chances that good behavior will take place. Obviously successful teachers work towards these goals, especially with learners with special needs.

"Handicapped" Students

When a teacher refers a student for further evaluation, and that student is eventually classified as handicapped, we would hope that the teacher will have learned a good deal about the student's strengths as well as his weaknesses. Objectivity should overcome possible tendencies to expect too little and thus begin the self-fulfilling prophecy cycle. However, when the student arrives in the teacher's class precertified or prelabeled as having problems, the teacher may respond with lower expectations. Students identified and labeled *handicapped* may be stereotyped on the basis of the teacher's preconceived attitude or experience with handicapped individuals. Although the stereotype may reflect either positive or negative behavior and expectations, it generally reflects a negative attitude about a population as a whole. Once the student has been labeled, there seems to be a generalized influence on teachers' views of the student. The labels *mentally retarded, emotionally disturbed,* and *learning disabled* often have a very negative connotation and may result in the teacher having a significantly lower level of expectation.

In a series of related studies, teachers were shown videotapes of children labeled *learning disabled* or *mentally retarded,* or "unlabeled". The results indicated that teachers had lower expectations for labeled students than for unlabeled students with *identical* behaviors (Coleman & Gilliam, 1983; Foster, Algozzine, & Ysseldyke, 1980; Minner, 1982; Simpson, 1981; Taylor, Smiley, & Ziegler, 1983).

The influence of the label on the student is obvious; the student may play the role of a person who fails. Just as success breeds more success, failure and negative thinking are powerful forces for continued failure. The following situation is an example of how a label may become a self-fulfilling prophecy for a student:

One of the authors recently observed a classroom for emotionally disturbed students from the ages of 8 to 13 years. The teacher was having considerable difficulty with one student that morning. When asked to line up outside the classroom, the student blatantly refused. After several requests the teacher asked the observer to assist, thinking that perhaps a different person might have a positive effect. The observer simply asked the student to line up and said that his teacher had some very exciting activities planned and that the sooner he lined up the sooner he would be allowed to participate in these activities. The student looked up at the observer and replied, "Sir, I can't be expected to line up." When asked why, the student replied, "Sir, I can't be expected to line up because *I am emotionally disturbed.*"

As discussed previously, a student may play the role of someone who is "slow" if he is expected to fail. Likewise, if a student is expected to act strangely or in a disturbing way, he may play the role of someone who is disturbed. In this instance the label was used by the student to justify unusual behavior; the label became a self-fulfilling prophecy.

Another effect of labeling is that it is often difficult to remove the label. Just as removing a paper label from a jar may be a difficult and tedious job, and often part of the label remains, so removing a label from a student is also very difficult and some of the label often stays with the student.

Achievement-Test Results and "Tracking"

There is considerable evidence that achievement-test scores may negatively influence teachers' expectations. Beez (1972) found that teachers who expected high performance from students tried to teach more, and teachers expecting low performance tended to teach less. He demonstrated this tendency by randomly assigning a group of students to high- and low-achievement groups by using falsified achievement scores. At the end of the term teachers were asked to rate the students using a five-point scale, with five being high and one being low, in the following areas: social competency, achievement, and intellectual ability. Average teacher ratings indicated that the "high" groups were significantly higher in all three areas. One can only wonder how the "low" group might have fared if those students had been given the falsified, high achievement scores.

Two related studies (Beez, 1970; Rubovits & Maehr, 1971) conducted in tutoring settings reported that teachers' expectations were influenced by student data. In these studies students enrolled in teacher-preparation programs served as tutors for students who were identified as being high or low achievers. The tutors were provided with falsified psychological information that would predict the students' high or low performance. The results indicated that the tutors attempted to teach more to the students for whom they had high expectations and less to those identified as having lower potential, when in fact the groups did not differ in performance potential. These studies also noted that the tutors interacted more negatively with students in the low group.

Good (1970) indicated that teachers interact more often with high-achieving than with low-achieving students and that their interactions with high achievers are more facilitative and positive than with low achievers. Other studies have indicated that students of different achievement levels are exposed to different verbal interactions. Students in lower groups receive less praise and more negative comments or criticisms than their classmates in higher groups (Morrison & McIntyre, 1969).

Another result of low achievement scores may be some sort of grouping, or "tracking," based on inferred ability. Although an important, historic court case relating to the Washington, DC schools, *Hobson v. Hanson* (1967), rejected the school district's claims that tracking was beneficial to all and ordered it to end the practice, some versions of tracking remain today. (In *Hobson v. Hansen,* the court concluded that tests used to make the track placements reflected economic and social backgrounds, not ability, and resulted in de facto segregation of black children.) Ability/achievement-level grouping is intended to promote more homogeneity and thus permit more effective instruction. Though this practice may be a viable and necessary approach to providing instruction at the students' level, caution must be exercised in its use. Grouping must be flexible and based on the instructional level of the particular subject being studied. A given student may be placed in the low reading group but belong in a high group in another subject. A general problem related to grouping is a type of "spread phenomenon." The student is placed either in a high group for all activities regardless of the achievement level in that subject or all low groups on the basis of achievement in one particular subject area. Teachers must make every effort to maintain considerable flexibility when grouping students for instructional purposes.

Racial or Ethnic Minority Group Membership

Membership in racial or ethnic minority groups may contribute to lowered teacher expectations. It may also lead to different patterns of personal interaction and differences in both the quantity and the quality of verbal interaction. Although much greater awareness of these factors has undoubtedly developed in the past 20 to 30 years, there is a continued likelihood that such differences in attitude, interaction, and expectation may exist on the part of some teachers. Earlier studies indicated that white students might be held in higher esteem than black students by white teachers (Leacock, 1969) and that the quantity and quality of verbal interaction is influenced in a negative direction by minority group membership (Jackson & Cosca, 1974). More recent studies have led to similar results (Dusek & Joseph, 1983; Sorenson & Hallinan, 1984). As indicated earlier in this discussion, regardless of studies and statistics, the teacher's responsibility is clear. Students must be recognized as worthy individuals, and all possible effort must be expended to make each student an integral part of the class, with status equal to that of all other students.

Other Characteristics

A number of other student characteristics lead to negative attitudes, lower expectations, and less desirable interactions. Among the more common are sex, speech and language characteristics, physical attractiveness, and personality (Brophy, 1983; Dusek, 1985; Guttman & Bar-Tai, 1982; Harris & Rosenthal, 1985; Levine & Wang, 1983; Rosenthal & Rubin, 1978; Smith, 1980).

The crucial factor is whether the teacher firmly believes that students with a particular characteristic are in fact less able to complete assigned tasks. Often these expectations stem from preconceived notions or misinformation rather than from actual experience. For instance, if the teacher firmly believes that girls tend to be higher achievers than boys in language arts and are more capable in general than boys, the teacher's male students most likely receive greater criticism, are given less praise, and experience greater rates of failure.

The first step in attempting to avoid this type of situation is for the teacher to recognize that his or her preconceived attitudes and expectations can significantly influence a student's behavior, achievement, and feelings of self-worth. As mentioned previously, expectations in and of themselves are natural and are neither good nor bad. We all form opinions of individuals with whom we interact. The expectation may not be of any significant consequence unless it becomes a self-fulfilling prophecy, when expectations become the cause of the student's behavior. Some school faculties have addressed this concern by conducting in-service meetings or open discussions concerning students' characteristics that may negatively influence teachers' expectations. In this way teachers recognize that their feelings are not unique and that their colleagues share similar feelings. Often a student characteristic identified by a colleague seems quite trivial or humorous, although it is very real to the teacher identifying it. By sharing their feelings teachers may come to realize how absurd some feelings about student characteristics can be. Teachers may then share ways in which they have overcome such feelings.

One other type of interaction between teachers and students must be considered—the interaction between teachers and physically impaired students (visually impaired, hearing impaired, orthopedic and other health impaired) who are being educated in regular classrooms. The interaction with these students may be the opposite of that discussed in the preceding paragraphs. Rather than rejective interactions, the teachers may demonstrate a pitying or oversolicitous attitude toward the student. This attitude is revealed by such comments as "Isn't it wonderful that a blind student can do so well!" or "I think, because she's in a wheelchair, she deserves a B." Although it may be difficult to criticize this type of comment, teachers must be made aware of the inherent dangers of such an attitude. This type of attitude and interaction may defeat the very purpose of regular classroom placement. To set the student up as someone so special that he becomes the class pet may do a serious disservice to that student. Teachers must be aware of the influence of their attitudes, be they negative, pitying, or positive.

We have only briefly discussed the nature of teachers' expectations and the specific characteristics of students that appear to influence the interaction between teachers and students. It is imperative that teachers recognize the *profound influence* they have on students' behavior and achievement and that they also recognize the factors that contribute to negative interactions.

Brophy and Good (1974) identified several specific behaviors by teachers that may communicate low expectations to students:

1. waiting less time for lows (low-achieving students) to answer
2. staying with lows in failure situations (persisting in such a manner as to call attention to failure)
3. rewarding inappropriate behavior or lows (praising marginal or inaccurate responses)
4. criticizing lows more frequently than highs
5. praising lows less frequently than highs
6. not giving feedback to responses of lows
7. paying less attention to lows
8. calling on lows less often
9. differing interaction patterns with highs and lows
10. seating lows farther away
11. demanding less from lows

By recognizing these variables, teachers may begin to understand the basis of their perceptions and consider modifying their interactions (if such modification is needed) by maintaining a flexible and open attitude about all students.

Monitoring and Evaluating Interaction

The influence of teachers' expectations on students' behavior and achievement appears to be well established. Educators must go beyond the mere identification of attitudes and expectancies, however, and make specific efforts to attempt to change their biases. The first step in changing their expectations is to analyze their interactions with their students.

Teachers can assess their interactions in a number of ways. Some methods are informal and do not require specific instruments or a great deal of training, and others are the product of research studies and provide very specific information concerning interactions. The following sections consider both types of analyses.

Informal Techniques. The number and variety of available informal techniques are limited only by individual ingenuity, but certain types of approaches appear to be in fairly common use. These common techniques are described here, but teachers are encouraged to modify these informal procedures to fit their individual needs. Such modification is not acceptable with standardized or formal techniques.[7]

Time Analysis. The time-analysis technique can provide information concerning the teacher's interaction with students. The following checklist and set of directions is an example of this technique:

1 Students	2 How is time spent?	3 Pleasurable or nonpleasurable?
most time 1. 2. 3. 4. 5.		
least time 1. 2. 3. 4. 5.		

---

[7]Our thanks to Clifford Baker, who provided a number of informal techniques presented in this discussion.

Column 1. List the five students in the class with whom the most time is spent. List five with whom the least time is spent.

Column 2. Identify what is done with the child during that time—how is the time spent?

Sample Key
XH = extra academic help
BM = behavior management
 L = listening to the student
 T = talking to the student
PL = playing with the student

Column 3. Write a *P* if the time spent is pleasurable and *NP* if it is nonpleasurable.

Analyze the Results. The following questions should be answered:
1. At what kinds of activities do you spend most of your time?
2. Is most of your time spent with these 10 students pleasurable?
3. What is different about the students with whom you spend the most time?
4. Do the students with whom you spend more time need you more?
5. What is the difference between the students with whom the time is pleasurable and the students with whom the time is nonpleasurable?

The teacher may add any number of questions to increase the time-analysis findings, depending on the specific purpose of the analysis.

The time-analysis technique is simple to use and interpret and can provide considerable information concerning how the teacher spends time and the nature of the interactions.

Teacher-made Checklists. The teacher may develop a checklist to fit almost any situation. The items on the checklist can involve the teacher's interaction through verbal or nonverbal behavior or general classroom procedures. Such checklists seem to be very popular with teachers, and therefore we provide two examples (see boxes). One is for elementary students, and the other is more appropriate in a secondary classroom. These

INTERACTION CHECKLIST (ELEMENTARY)

	Always 3	Seldom 2	Never 1
1. I can get extra help from the teacher when I need it.	☐	☐	☐
2. The teacher praises me when I do well.	☐	☐	☐
3. The teacher smiles when I do something well.	☐	☐	☐
4. The teacher listens attentively.	☐	☐	☐
5. The teacher accepts me as an individual.	☐	☐	☐
6. The teacher encourages me to try something new.	☐	☐	☐
7. The teacher respects the feelings of others.	☐	☐	☐
8. My work is usually good enough.	☐	☐	☐
9. I am called on when I raise my hand.	☐	☐	☐
10. The same students always get praised by the teacher.	☐	☐	☐
11. The teacher grades fairly.	☐	☐	☐
12. The teacher smiles and enjoys teaching.	☐	☐	☐
13. I have learned to do things from this teacher.	☐	☐	☐
14. When something is too hard, my teacher makes it easier for me.	☐	☐	☐
15. My teacher is polite and courteous.	☐	☐	☐
16. I like my teacher.	☐	☐	☐

INTERACTION CHECKLIST (SECONDARY)

The teacher

	Always 5	Sometimes 4	Often 3	Seldom 2	Never 1
1. is genuinely interested in me	☐	☐	☐	☐	☐
2. respects the feelings of others	☐	☐	☐	☐	☐
3. grades fairly	☐	☐	☐	☐	☐
4. identifies what he or she considers important	☐	☐	☐	☐	☐
5. is enthusiastic about teaching	☐	☐	☐	☐	☐
6. smiles often and enjoys teaching	☐	☐	☐	☐	☐
7. helps me develop skills in understanding myself	☐	☐	☐	☐	☐
8. is honest and fair	☐	☐	☐	☐	☐
9. helps me develop skills in communicating	☐	☐	☐	☐	☐
10. encourages and provides time for individual help	☐	☐	☐	☐	☐
11. is pleasant and has a sense of humor	☐	☐	☐	☐	☐
12. has "pets" and spends most time with them	☐	☐	☐	☐	☐
13. encourages and provides time for questions and discussion	☐	☐	☐	☐	☐
14. respects my ideas and concerns	☐	☐	☐	☐	☐
15. helps me develop skills in making decisions	☐	☐	☐	☐	☐
16. helps me develop skills in using time wisely	☐	☐	☐	☐	☐

are merely examples, and teachers are encouraged to modify the lists or add statements of particular interest or concern to them.

Students should not be asked to sign their names, since this may inhibit their openness and sincerity. The teacher should analyze the results by averaging the responses and plotting the averages to get a picture of teacher interactions. Checklists may be administered several times during the year to measure changes that have occurred.

Peer-Teacher Observer. A trusted colleague can come into the classroom and observe the teacher in action. The colleague should keep running notes on the teacher's interactions during a period of several days. Often it is very helpful if the observing teacher has a checklist or an indication of specific behaviors to be recorded; otherwise at the end of the period only very general comments may be shared. The teachers may later change roles if this is agreeable to both.

Videotape. The teacher may arrange to have her teaching videotaped. She should view the videotape alone, noticing how she interacts with different students. Next, if desired, the teacher can also view and discuss the videotape with a colleague. It may be necessary to tape several sessions so that typical patterns of behavior and interaction are recorded rather than "showmanship" on the part of the teacher or students. It may be helpful to arrange for a series of taping sessions, for example, once every two or three months. Nearly every school district has videotaping equipment, and local instructional media personnel may be able to assist with the taping.

Role Playing. Another procedure that is particularly appropriate with elementary students is role playing. Young children are very honest and open and are quick to role-play

typical classroom situations. For role playing to be most effective, it is advisable for the regular teacher to switch classes with another teacher so that the students are not inhibited by their own teacher's presence. The students may be asked to act out the roles of a good teacher and a poor teacher. Other role questions include the following:

1. How does your teacher act when he is happy or sad?
2. How does your teacher look and what does he say when interrupted?
3. How does your teacher look and what does he say when asked to repeat the directions for an assignment?
4. How does your teacher look and what does he say when you make a mistake?
5. How does your teacher look and what does he say when you misbehave?
6. How does your teacher look and what does he say when you do something well?

Teachers may add other situations about which they are most interested in obtaining feedback. The role playing may be taped on a video or audio recorder so that the teacher receives a firsthand evaluation. Again, it may be helpful for the teacher to exchange classes with a colleague so that the students will not be inhibited by their own teacher's presence. Although the initiation of such role playing may require different introduction and presentation at the elementary level than at the secondary level, it works at both levels with just a little innovation by the teacher.

Formal Techniques. Formal teacher-student observational systems may provide a more reliable, descriptive picture of teacher-student interaction than informal systems, thus some teachers prefer to use formal techniques. There are several widely recognized techniques, with those developed by Galloway (1968) and Flanders (1965) among the most used. Other formal observational systems have been reported by Fink and Semmel (1971) and Soar, Soar, and Ragosta (1971). Any of these systems may prove to be of value in gathering data about teacher-student interaction to provide a basis for further planning and decision making.

Changing Teachers' Expectations

Teachers are generally willing to change their inappropriate interactions and teaching behavior once they are made aware of them. Brophy and Good (1974) suggest that a deliberate and tactful strategy should be used to help teachers with this important area, using the following steps: (1) collection of specific data, (2) identification of explicit problems from the data, (3) identification of students with whom the teacher is interacting positively, (4) encouraging teachers to explain differences in their behavior, (5) suggesting changes in teachers' behavior to reach an agreement about explicit treatment behaviors, and (6) re-observation of teachers in the classrooms.

Dworkin (1979) provided teachers with specific strategies based on the student's demonstrated successful performance. The program involved a demonstration of teaching techniques, selection of curricular priorities, and planning sessions with the teacher. Central to this study was the assumption that the success of students is related to the teacher's satisfaction expressed to the low-achieving students. The purpose of the study was to examine changes that occur in the teacher's satisfaction as a result of the specific strategies. The results demonstrated that this satisfaction can be changed from negative to positive. The implication of this research is that teachers can bring about positive changes by working through the student's strengths and that by demonstrating positive performance, they become committed to applying these strategies. It is assumed that once the teacher observes a student's progress, this observation can significantly influence the teacher's expecta-

tions and behavior toward the low-achieving student. The initial step in changing expectations from negative to positive is for teachers to recognize that they have differing expectations and that if they are sincerely motivated to change their interactive style, there are instruments and procedures to assist them in making the change. They must begin, however, with self-examination and analysis of all the variables that might contribute to a particular student's success or failure.

THE QUALITY OF STUDENT INTERACTION

Students with handicapping conditions are placed in (or remain in) the regular classroom in the belief that such placement will lead to a variety of positive results. In addition to teacher-student interaction, discussed in the previous section, there is continuous student-student interaction. If physical placement in the regular classroom is to lead to the desired results, there must be *positive* interaction, and several authorities believe that without active teacher efforts, the results may more likely be negative interaction and rejection.

In a discussion of factors contributing to the development of successful mainstreaming, Salend (1984) outlines five major categories of factors that contribute to success. Two of these five factors are preparing handicapped students and preparing nonhandicapped students. As part of an extensive review of both research and opinion regarding factors contributing to the chances of effective mainstreaming, Salend notes that nonhandicapped students can facilitate the mainstreaming process through positive interaction and can "aid their handicapped peers' adjustment and ability to function in the mainstream by serving as role models, peer tutors, and friends and by providing assistance to physically disabled and sensory impaired students" (1984, p. 411). However,

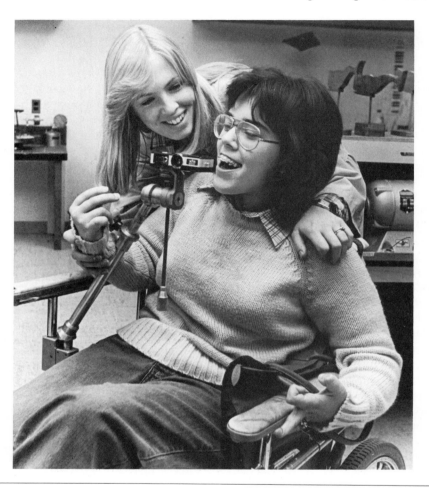

Teachers are the key to quality student interaction.

he cautions that their contributions may be negatively affected by their attitudes toward the handicapped.

Johnson and Johnson (1978, p. 152) provided a thought-provoking description of the least restrictive environment: "Mainstreaming is defined as providing an appropriate educational opportunity for all handicapped students in the least restrictive alternative, based on individualized educational programming and aimed at providing handicapped students with *access to and constructive interaction with nonhandicapped peers.*"

They extend their definition by stating, "It is when handicapped students are liked, accepted, and chosen as friends that mainstreaming becomes a positive influence on the lives of both handicapped and normal progress students."

Positive, constructive interaction between handicapped students and their nonhandicapped peers depends on the interaction of three groups of individuals: the handicapped, the nonhandicapped, and their teachers. Members of each group bring to the interactive setting (the school) their attitudes, experiences, and motivations. Students may at times prove to be an effective, positive force for improvement of the quality of interaction, but for the most part it is the teacher who must provide the positive, proactive impetus. Salend (1984) suggests that all possible effort must be expended, before students are mainstreamed, to increase the social skills of the handicapped, and that teachers should employ specific strategies to promote positive attitudes (toward the handicapped) on the part of nonhandicapped students. Whatever process or strategy is used—films, books, or discussions—the first requirement is that the teacher accept the handicapped student as a unique and valued individual. Various researchers have established that such teacher acceptance can be attained through appropriate teacher education (Donaldson, 1980; Idol-Maestas, 1981; Salend & Johns, 1983; Tymitz-Wolf, 1982). One of the authors' major goals is to encourage such acceptance.

Measuring Handicapped Students' Status

For several years researchers have attempted to measure the social development and interaction of nonhandicapped and handicapped students (Asher & Taylor, 1982; Bruininks, Rynders, & Gross, 1974; Bryan, 1974; Goodman, Gottlieb, & Harrison, 1972; Iano, Ayers, Heller, McGettigan, & Walker, 1974; Sheare, 1978; Siperstein, Bopp, & Bak, 1978; Strain, 1982). Many of these studies have indicated that the sociometric status of handicapped students was lower than that of their nonhandicapped peers. Among the reasons for the lower status of handicapped students are nonhandicapped students' (1) lack of opportunity to interact with handicapped individuals, (2) inexperience in working cooperatively with handicapped persons, (3) insufficient information concerning the potential of handicapped students, (4) negative or predetermined values and attitudes, and (5) lack of opportunity to question, clarify,

and discuss their beliefs and attitudes. Another possible reason for the relatively low status may be related to the type of sociometric instrument used. In the following paragraphs, we will provide a review of three major types of sociometric assessment.

The most commonly used sociometric technique is the peer-nomination method, which requires students to name classmates who fit a particular criterion (e.g., "In working on a project I would like to work with ———") (Cartledge & Milburn, 1986). A student's score is the total number of nominations received from classmates. An example of the nomination method, with specific directions for administration and scoring, is as follows:

Name:

In working on a project I would like to work with
1. _____
2. _____
3. _____

During breaks I would like to be with
1. _____
2. _____
3. _____

I would like to sit next to
1. _____
2. _____
3. _____

I would not like to work with
1. _____
2. _____
3. _____

The directions for administration of this nomination questionnaire are as follows:

1. The teacher explains to the class, "Today I am going to ask you to indicate on your paper the name of a classmate with whom you would like to share certain activities. We all work better when we have the opportunity to work with someone we get along with well. I am gathering this information to find out who in this class would

work well together. I hope you will be completely honest. No other student will know whom you have chosen."

2. Hand out preference forms with questions similar to those indicated.
3. Give the following instructions:
   a. At the top of this form, write the names of three classmates you would like to work with in school if you had a free choice.
   b. Write in the middle of your paper the names of three classmates that you would like to be with during breaks. You may write down any or all of the three names used previously.
   c. Next write the names of three classmates you would like to sit near in school if you had a free choice. You may write any or all of the names previously used.
   d. At the bottom of this form write the names of classmates with whom you would not like to work.

After the students have made their choices, the teacher can add up the results. Any reasonable status categories may be used to determine the sociometric status of any specific student, for example,

Star. One who was chosen 14 or more times by his classmates.
Above average. One who received from 9 to 13 choices.
Below average. One who was chosen between 3 and 8 times.
Neglected. One who was chosen fewer than 3 times.

These numbers are based on an average classroom enrollment of between 28 and 35 and should be changed proportionately depending on the size of the class. The use of both positive and negative nomination criteria generally permit more accurate status distinction.

A second method, the rating-scale technique, can also be used to measure the sociometric status of students. With this procedure, students are provided a list or classroom roster and are asked to rate each classmate on a numerical scale according to a particular criterion. A student's score on the rating scale is the average of all ratings from classmates. The criterion may be the degree to which students would like to play or work with each classmate. They may rate their classmates on a scale from 1 (wouldn't like to) to 5 (would much like to) scale. For ease of administration, the teacher can simply prepare a class roster with the range of numerical values printed next to each name, such that students can circle their rating scores.

One advantage of the rating-scale technique over the nominating method is that evaluations are obtained for all students in the class rather than for only those students nominated by others. This factor is important because handicapped students may not otherwise be chosen on a positive nomination measure.

A third method of sociometric assessment is the paired-comparison technique. With this technique, students are presented one at a time with all possible pairings of classmates and must choose the most preferred peer for each pairing. Each student obtains a score that reflects the total number of times he is selected by classmates. Although regularly mentioned in summaries of sociometric measurements, this method has one serious drawback. It takes a great deal of time in preparation and administration. For example, Vaughn and Langlois (1983) report that it took 20 to 30 hours to complete this procedure in a class of 40 preschool children.

There are many ways to obtain sociometric data and various measures to assess different dimensions of social status. The nomination method measures friendship, and the rating scale can be used to obtain information about general acceptance. Sociometric assessment should be supported by other information, such as behavioral observations and teachers' ratings, to have maximum value. Certain potential limitations of sociometric measures should be noted. For example, preference for same-sex and same-race peers, recent negative experiences, and other similar factors may lead to results reflecting influences either beyond the control of the teacher, or temporary and that are not an appropriate target for long-term, concerted efforts on the part of the teacher. Like any other measure, sociometric information must be considered as only one part of the total picture.

The use of sociometric information should not stop with the assignment of sociometric status but should be meaningfully extended. For example, it may be helpful to determine the number of mutual choices (two students who chose each other). It may also be of interest to determine whether a handicapped student was chosen in academic or social areas. The teacher should devise her own method of analysis for her situation.

Sociometric data is not the only way to analyze classroom interaction; most teachers are keenly aware of social interactions in their classroom. Naturally they should be aware of their role as a model and of how they are interacting with "different" students. At times, however, even though the teacher's interactions with handicapped students are very positive, nonhandicapped students do not reflect an accepting, empathic, and objective attitude toward handicapped students. In this instance the teacher should make a conscious effort to structure cooperative learning experiences and systematic efforts to provide experiences and open discussion.

ENHANCING INTERACTION BETWEEN HANDICAPPED STUDENTS AND THEIR PEERS

Information concerning the effects of mainstreaming on the attitudes of nonhandicapped students is contradictory and confusing. Several studies have demonstrated that the placement of handicapped students in a regular classroom may result in greater prejudice, stereotyping, and rejection (Goodman, Gottlieb, & Harrison, 1972; Gottlieb & Budoff, 1973; Gottlieb, Cohen, & Goldstein, 1974; Iano et al., 1974; Panda & Bartel, 1972). But there is also evidence that the placement of handicapped students in regular classrooms may postively influence the attitudes of their nonhandicapped peers (Esposito & Reed, 1986; Sheare, 1978; Wechsler, Suarez, & McFadden, 1975).

Based on this contradictory evidence, it is quite clear that if the handicapped student's status is low and if his interaction with peers is not positive, the teacher must make specific efforts to modify this situation. This improvement may be gained in three general ways: (1) by structuring a cooperative learning atmosphere; (2) by providing detailed information and awareness of the potential of all persons; and (3) by providing students with the opportunity to discuss, question, and clarify their beliefs and attitudes about handicapped persons. The following sections consider ways in which teachers may use these specific approaches.

Group-Learning Structures

Cooperative learning situations stress the interaction of all students. If properly planned and implemented, they promote positive group interaction. It is believed that competitive or individualistically structured classrooms provide little opportunity for nonhandicapped students to interact and work cooperatively with their handicapped peers, and so fail to deal with stereotyping, prejudice, and lack of positive interaction. The use of cooperative learning methods involves primarily a change in the interpersonal reward structure of the classroom from a competitive to a cooperative arrangement. It is also believed that in a cooperatively structured classroom, the handicapped student may come to view himself as an achiever. There are several research-based, practical, cooperative learning structures: the teams-games-tournament approach (DeVries & Slavin, 1978), the jigsaw approach (Aronson, 1978), the student teams achievement divisions approach (Slavin, 1978) the small-group teaching approach (Sharon & Sharon, 1976), and the cooperative learning approach (Johnson, Johnson, Nelson, & Read, 1978). In addition to research-based cooperative structures, rap sessions and buddy systems are other widely used approaches.

Teams-Games-Tournament. The teams-games-tournament structure involves four or five students being assigned to a team to maximize heterogeneity of ability levels, sex, and race. Following an instructional presentation by the teacher, the student groups are assigned worksheets covering academic material similar to that for the weekly tournament. Teammates study and quiz each other to be certain all members are prepared. Students are then assigned to three-person "tournament tables." The highest three students in past tournaments are assigned to Table 1, the next three to Table 2, and so on. Questions are asked during the tournament about the material presented by the teacher and studied by the teams. Each student's score is added to an overall team score, thereby allowing all students an opportunity to contribute to their team's score.

Jigsaw. The jigsaw approach also assigns students to heterogeneous teams. Learning material is divided into several sections according to the number of team members. Each student is responsible for studying one section with members of other teams with similar sections. After they have studied thoroughly, they return to their teams and teach their respective sections. On completion of their study, each team member is quizzed on all aspects of the unit. With the jigsaw approach, the grading or scoring procedure is different from that of the team-

games-tournament approach in that the quiz scores contribute to individual rather than group grades. Group members are rewarded for their contribution because each member assists other team members in the learning of the various sections. Slavin (1978) has developed a modification of the jigsaw approach that emphasizes team scores rather than individual scores.

Student Teams Achievement Divisions. Like the teams-games-tournament and jigsaw approaches, this approach also uses four or five heterogeneously grouped students. The primary difference is that the games and tournaments are replaced by 15-minute quizzes that students take after studying with their teams. The quiz scores are converted into team scores, which serve to create "achievement divisions." Achievement divisions are formed with six students in each division, and their performance is compared with past quiz scores. With this procedure, the students' scores are compared with those of students of similar ability. Students in each division do not interact with other groups and are not aware of other division assignments. A "bumping" procedure is used to change weekly division assignments and to maintain equality. This approach to cooperative learning allows equal opportunity for contributions to the team score.

Small-Group Teaching. Small-group teaching is similar to the other cooperative arrangements except that it is relatively low in group reward interdependence. In this approach learning is accomplished through group inquiry, discussion, and information gathering by students. Students choose subtopics provided by the teacher and then divide in small groups of two to six members. If needed, the groups may further subdivide the group assignment into individual responsibilities. After completing their respective assignments, they prepare for the entire class a group presentation that is evaluated by other students and the teacher. This procedure promotes a high degree of task interdependence because of students' assignments to special tasks within the group.

Cooperative Learning. Johnson et al. (1978) describe the following steps in setting up a heterogeneous, cooperative grouping process:

1. The teacher specifies the instructional objectives in such a way that all group members will master the spelling assignment.
2. The groups' size is determined. With low-achieving or younger students, two or three per group may be best; with older students, four may be preferable.
3. Students are assigned to groups on the basis of a pretest. Generally, one high-achieving student, two average students, and one low-achieving student should form the group.
4. The classroom is arranged such that group members are close together and different groups are some distance from each other.
5. Each group is given appropriate instructional materials.
6. The teacher explains the task and the expected, cooperative goal structure. It is important that each student understand the task. The teacher should also specify a group goal (completion of the assignment) and the criterion for success (90% correct). The criterion may be based on the combined score of all group members.
7. All group members are taught the following skills: helping, tutoring, teaching, and sharing. The teacher should be certain to observe the group's interaction and intervene if necessary.
8. Evaluation should be based on the group products. If a low-achieving student is having considerable difficulty, the teacher

may need to modify the student's responsibility by using improvement scores, assigning less material, or using different material.

Rap Sessions. Rap sessions may be held to bring students together to discuss such things as the nature of a handicap, the degree of a handicap, how a handicap affects learning, levels of realistic expectation, prognosis, and cause of the handicap. The type of handicap and how comfortable the teacher and handicapped student feel about the topic should be considered when determining who is included in the rap session. For some reason, people often have more negative feelings about intellectual handicaps than about physical handicaps. Generally it is a good idea to include the student with a physical impairment (hearing, vision, or health impairment) in the rap session, but occasionally it may be best to discuss the problems in an open manner without the handicapped student present. These sessions may be handled by the resource teacher or the regular classroom teacher or both.

If the rap session is handled properly, it can do much to increase nonhandicapped students' understanding of a handicapped student and to enhance interaction between students. The success of the rap session, of course, depends on the type of handicap, age of the students, and whether the teacher has developed a classroom climate that allows open and honest discussion of problems. It may be a good idea to talk with the handicapped student and his parents before the rap session. Rap sessions may do more harm than good if not handled properly. Informal rap sessions may be helpful but should not take the place of planned, systematic efforts to provide specific information.

Buddy System. The most important factor to consider when selecting a buddy for a handicapped student is the compatibility of the two students. This situation must be handled very carefully, and the teacher must observe closely to be certain the handicapped student is gaining independence. The wrong buddy could lead to increased dependence. The buddy's responsibilities usually depend on the particular type of handicap—auditory, visual, health-related, intellectual, or emotional. The buddy or helper may be rotated every few weeks so that one student is not burdened with the responsibility.

Our consideration of group learning strategies in the preceding sections provides a brief overview of such programs. It is of great value, when properly implemented, and there is a solid research base indicating that cooperative learning has consistent, positive influences on interethnic relationships and on mutual concern among all students (Slavin, 1980).

Thus far most of our suggestions emphasize interaction and cooperative working relationships—approaches believed to greatly facilitate interaction among all students. Some evidence, however, indicates that contact alone does not necessarily result in a positive attitude change. This research indicates that students also need specific information and that with specific information and awareness of the potential of handicapped persons, nonhandicapped students will have significant changes in attitudes (Cleary,1976; Gronberg, 1983; Prillaman, 1981; and Scheffers, 1977). In the next several sections we will review ways in which teachers can provide specific information to assist nonhandicapped students better understand the abilities of handicapped individuals.

Understanding Handicapped Students

Reading Books About Handicapped Persons. Many films and trade books are available about handicapped persons. Some are stories about animals that are handicapped, whereas others involve the adjustment of handicapped children and adults. Films can be shown in class and the reading materials placed on a reading shelf or in the library; students can be encouraged to read these materials. Generally, these materials provide significant insight into the problems of the disabled and the feelings handicapped persons have about themselves. The viewing of a film or a report on one of the books could serve as a starting point for the previously mentioned rap sessions or for short in-service sessions.

In-Service Sessions. Brief in-service sessions are most appropriate for students with physical disabilities. If the handicapped student uses special equipment (braille typewriter, hearing aid, or wheelchair, for example), the other students may not understand its use and purpose. In an in-service session the student can explain the use of and actually demonstrate how the various equipment operates. Often the other students' curiosity and lack of understanding about the special equipment may distract them from their own work. Once the special equipment is demonstrated and its use explained, this distraction is usually alleviated.

For example, a visually impaired student can demonstrate magnification devices and explain their value and use. He may also explain the rationale for using a regular typewriter or the use of braille or large-type materials. Other types of aids and appliances, such as tape recorders, tape players, talking-book machines, arithmetic aids, and embossed or enlarged maps, may also be demonstrated. Units of study on the eye or ear may be presented by the regular classroom teacher or special education resource teacher in cooperation with the visually or hearing impaired student.

The age of the handicapped student and his willingness to participate are factors the teacher should consider when planning the in-service session. If the student is unwilling, perhaps the special education teacher (vision specialist or hearing specialist) may conduct the in-service session. Regardless of who participates, the session must be handled very carefully so that the student is not made to seem too "special." If the presentation implies that the handicapped student is someone "super" or someone to feel sorry for, the very purpose of the session may be defeated.

Panel of Disabled Individuals. Many teachers have had considerable success by inviting a guest speaker who is disabled or a panel of disabled persons to share their life experiences. Such presentations should emphasize ways the disabled individuals modify or adapt to everyday living situations. They may also discuss their interests, hobbies, and work experiences. Students should be encouraged to ask questions of the guests. It is important that the teacher invites a disabled person who will assist in the development of positive attitudes.

Special Materials. The third general way to provide nonhandicapped students with an opportunity to discuss, question, and clarify their beliefs and values is the use of specially designed materials to stimulate discussion as well as values education and clarification materials.

Special materials have been developed to assist nonhandicapped students better to understand and accept the differences and similarities of their handicapped classmates. These materials are similar to values education and clarification approaches but have been designed specifically to provide information about handicapped individuals and to promote positive attitudinal changes.

It appears that attitudes of the general public toward the handicapped are slowly changing in a positive direction. Although some mass-media efforts such as telethons and other fund-raising projects continue to emphasize the significant differences of the handicapped, many others have brought to public attention the fact that handicapped persons are first of all individuals; differences are acknowledged while the inherent similarities in the general needs of all people are recognized.

Because people's attitudes, beliefs, and behaviors toward differences are based on values learned from important others, such as family members, or from meaningful experiences, it seems imperative that the school curriculum provide such information and experience. Nonhandicapped students should have the opportunity to participate in simulations of handicapping conditions, discussions, interviews, and presentations by handicapped adults and students, and to preview films, filmstrips, and other media about handicapped persons.

Teachers should provide specific information concerning "differences" between handicapped and nonhandicapped students, and this content should be an integral part of every student's education. It is clear that we must provide the conditions to enable students to work toward satisfying their basic needs. One such basic need is an interaction or socializing experience that begins with carefully designed instruction to assist students in relating to others in their environment.

Teaching Social Skills

Throughout this chapter we have attempted to emphasize that feelings, expectancies, and interactions are of prime importance to successful mainstreaming. The teacher must play a major role in encouraging positive interactions and must attempt to hold to optimistic expectancies but at the same time be realistic in expectations of students with handicapping conditions. However, handicapped students must also bear their share of the responsibility. What is the arena in which they may most likely be deficient? A host of researchers, authors, and observers indicate that it might be the arena of social skills (Asher & Hymel, 1981; Asher, Oden, & Gottman, 1981; Gresham, 1982).

In a commonsense definition of social skills, Cartledge and Milburn indicate them to be "socially acceptable learned behaviors that enable the person to interact with others in ways that elicit positive responses and assist in avoiding negative responses from them" (1986, p. 7). Important social behaviors include greeting others, sharing, asking for assistance when needed, initiating conversations, giving compliments, following game and classroom rules, being able to talk about such things as current movies and television shows, having a sense of humor, helping classmates, and knowing current slang words. Unacceptable social behaviors include not responding to peer social initiations, misinterpreting the approach behaviors of peers, and entering games of group activities uninvited.

Since many handicapped students do not have the social skills necessary to interact positively with their peers, it seems imperative that teachers assess their levels of social skills and begin remediation of deficits. Training in social skills may occur before and after placement in the regular classroom. Gresham (1982) categorized social-skills training under three major headings: manipulation of antecedents, manipulation of consequences, and modeling. The *manipulation of antecedents* involves having nonhandicapped students initiate social interactions with statements such as "Come with me," "Let's play a game," and "Come on." By design, these initiations establish the occasion for increased interaction. Other examples of antecedent manipulation are sociodrama techniques and cooperative games.

The most often used social-skills training approach is the *manipulation of consequences*. This approach involves having the teacher socially reinforce the handicapped student when the student interacts or cooperates with his nonhandicapped peers. This procedure is also used to reinforce nonhandicapped students when they are interacting or working positively with the handicapped student.

The third general approach used to teach social skills is *modeling*. Modeling can be used in film or live formats. With film or videotape presentations the student observes students modeling desirable social behaviors. The most practical approach for regular classroom teachers appears to be live modeling, in which the student observes models in natural environments.

Cartledge and Milburn (1986) believe that instruction in social skills "involves many of the same procedures as teaching academic concepts; that is, the exposure of the child to a model of imitation, eliciting an imitative response, providing feedback about the correctness of the response, and structuring opportunities for practice (p. 115)." Regular classroom teachers should consult with special education resource personnel for assistance with specific approaches, but awareness of these principles will assist the teacher to be involved in informal instruction throughout the school day.

For teachers interested in continued study in this area, we suggest the various social-skills curricula described by Cartledge and Milburn (1986); Goldstein, Sprafkin, Gershaw, and Klein (1980); Jackson, Jackson, and Monroe (1983); Milburn and Cartledge (1976); and Stephens (1978).

SUMMARY

In this chapter, we emphasized the teacher's role in the success of students with handicapping conditions. Teaching methods are important, but the interaction between exceptional students, their peers, instructional materials, and the teacher are also important. Teachers should closely examine their feelings and expectations to be certain that they contribute to student success. Sometimes a problem situation in the classroom can be clearly identified as originating with a student, but more often such problems result from the interaction between the student, his peers, the teaching materials, the classroom environment, and the teacher.

We reviewed specific strategies to measure the teacher's interaction with students and some research demonstrating that most teachers are willing and able to modify their interactions with students if provided with a procedure to do so. We considered the influence of student-student interaction, along with specific suggestions to measure this interaction. The final section provided intervention techniques for increasing understanding and interaction between handicapped students and their nonhandicapped peers.

Many methods and techniques are of value in promoting the positive feelings and reactions that are so important to both handicapped and nonhandicapped students. We have tried to suggest some of these strategies in this chapter, but these are only a starting point. The motivation for positive relationships must come from *within* the teacher. When it does, the feeling will spread throughout the class and sometimes even to adjoining classrooms. (Try it; you'll like it!)

We introduced this chapter with the story of Mr. S, a teacher who cared. It is our conviction that if more teachers cared, the process of mainstreaming would be more effective, and all concerned would benefit.

PART TWO
TEACHING EXCEPTIONAL STUDENTS

P art Two, the final eight chapters of this text, is designed to provide basic information about students who may be considered according to eight different "classifications." These classifications are *hearing impaired, visually impaired, orthopedically/health impaired, speech/language disordered, mentally retarded, learning disabled, behaviorally disordered,* and *gifted/talented.* As will be explained in the various chapters, some of these classifications are at times nebulous, and some, like *orthopedically/health impaired,* include multiple conditions and/or

disabilities. Nevertheless, these classifications are described in federal and state laws and regulations and thus provide the least confusing way to communicate information about exceptional students enrolled in regular classrooms. The hearing impaired and visually impaired are considered first, as they were the first, historically, to be recognized and provided some type of modified educational programming. The gifted/talented, presented last, actually receive "last consideration" in many school districts, due to a variety of factors, especially legal mandates and fiscal factors.

Teaching Students Who Are Hearing Impaired

NATURE OF HEARING IMPAIRMENT

IDENTIFICATION OF STUDENTS WITH IMPAIRED HEARING

PROCEDURES FOR REFERRAL

REGULAR CLASSROOM PLACEMENT

SUGGESTIONS FOR THE REGULAR CLASSROOM TEACHER

SPECIALIZED INSTRUCTION AND ASSISTANCE FROM RESOURCE OR ITINERANT TEACHERS

- ☐ Why may it be difficult to identify a young student with a mild hearing impairment?
- ☐ How may behavior be an indicator of possible hearing impairment?
- ☐ What student characteristics enhance a successful mainstream experience for the hearing impaired student?
- ☐ Is it necessary that the regular classroom teacher know how to "sign"?
- ☐ What modifications and adaptations are necessary to provide a successful experience for the hearing impaired student?
- ☐ How can the regular classroom teacher determine if the hearing impaired student's hearing aid is working properly?
- ☐ Is it a help or a hindrance to exaggerate gestures when communicating with hearing impaired students?
- ☐ Why do hearing impaired students less frequently interact with hearing students?
- ☐ What are the major modes of communication for the hearing impaired?

A teacher read the following question to an eighth grade student as part of a test. "Which is larger, Turkey or Greece?" To the student it sounded like "Which is larger, turkey or geese?" This normally very bright student, who lived on a farm, thought the question was strange for a history exam but answered, "It depends on how old they are."

Later the teacher asked the student to read the question and her response. As soon as she saw the question, the student realized the mistake. But determined to "tough it out," she somewhat sarcastically read the question but did not answer it. The teacher waited, then impatiently asked, "Well, which is larger, Turkey or Greece?" to which the student responded equally impatiently, "Well, if you don't know, I'm not going to tell you."

This student had learned a valuable lesson for covering her hearing loss. If teachers are angry, they shout; and if they shout, they can be heard (Ritter, 1986).

Listening is an important learning tool from the time a child is born. An infant learns to discriminate between loud and soft, high and low, and disturbing and pleasant sounds. He also learns to determine the direction, distance, and meaning of sounds. He analyzes the human voice and differentiates his own babbling and crying from the sounds of others. Sometime between the ages of 12 and 24 months, as a result of his previous language experiences, he begins to learn to speak and to develop his own language skills. Obviously, if the child has a hearing impairment, his speech and language development may be delayed. Underdeveloped speech and language skills are the greatest limitation imposed by a hearing impairment. The student's delayed speech and language influence his ability to develop communication skills, such as reading, writing, listening, and speaking. As a result, these skills develop at a slower rate than those of the normally hearing child. The hearing impaired student has the most difficulty in the language-arts areas, such as reading, spelling, and writing, because of their relationship to speech and language development. The extent of difficulty depends on the student's language level or command of the language, degree of hearing loss, and age at the onset of loss.

The student may have no trouble understanding concepts, but he may have difficulty learning the label or language used to describe concepts. For example, the concept of buoyancy may be understood by the student, but he may have difficulty in writing, saying, or spelling the word *buoyancy.* He may have much less difficulty with science, math, or other non-language-arts programs. Math, with the exception of story problems, is conceptual in nature. Science may also be thought of as conceptual rather than primarily related to the language arts. In contrast, the reading process involves associating meaning with sounds and written symbols. A hearing impairment that delays language development seriously limits the association between sounds and written symbols; therefore, reading may be an area of considerable difficulty for these students, particularly for the young child who is in the process of acquiring reading skills. He *can* learn to read; however, a very well-planned program must be offered—a program that reflects close cooperation between the regular teacher and the special education resource or itinerant teacher. Although language development is very important to success in school, the hearing impaired student is able to learn and profit from instruction in the regular classroom.

In addition to academic difficulties that may result from a hearing loss, two other limitations may be imposed by impaired hearing. The first limitation may be characterized by inability to hear music. Some such limitations cannot be overcome but must be compensated for in a manner that is acceptable to the individual. A second limitation may be imposed by society. Such societal limitations, characterized by negative or demeaning interactions with others, such as parents, teachers, siblings, and friends, may lead to self-imposed social limitations and restrictions. Teachers may play an important role in reducing this type of limitation.

In instances where a hearing impairment has been identified, the regular classroom teacher can use a number of methods and techniques that may be beneficial to the hearing impaired student. To better understand these methods and techniques, various other aspects of programs for the hearing impaired are considered here as they are administered in the public schools.

NATURE OF HEARING IMPAIRMENT

Types of Hearing Impairment

There are two major types of hearing impairment, and different degrees of hearing loss are associated with these two types. One type of hearing impairment affects the loudness or intensity with which a person hears speech. This type of loss, known as a *conductive* hearing loss, is caused by interference with the transmission of sound from the outer to the inner ear. The interference may be caused by some type of blockage, such as a foreign object, or by a malformation. If detected early, some types of conductive losses are correctable by surgery. The student with this type of loss generally can profit from the use of a hearing aid because the aid magnifies sounds at all frequency levels. The other type of loss, a *sensorineural* loss, affects the frequency, intelligibility, and clarity of the sounds the person hears. A sensorineural loss is associated with damage to the sensory end-organ or a dysfunction of the auditory nerve. This type of hearing loss is not as amenable as a conductive loss to correction by use of a hearing aid because

the problem is related to nerve damage. No matter how much the sound is amplified, the nerve damage prevents the sound from reaching the hearing area of the brain.

An analogy to a radio roughly illustrates the two types of hearing loss. By turning the volume down, we can simulate what it is like to have a hearing loss affecting the loudness with which we hear sounds. If we can hear the sounds, we can understand them; they are not distorted. This is similar to a conductive loss. The tuning dial, which controls the frequency of signals, illustrates sensorineural loss. If the radio is not tuned in correctly, the sounds are not clear and are difficult to understand. Often words are not complete. The sentence "He sat at his desk" may sound like "e a a iz de."

Measurement of Hearing

An instrument known as a pure-tone audiometer is used to measure hearing acuity (sharpness or acuteness of sensory discrimination). An audiometer produces sounds at varying intensities (loudness) and frequencies (pitch). An *audiologist,* when administering an audiometric examination, systematically presents a series of carefully calibrated tones that vary in loudness and pitch. The results are charted on a graph called an *audiogram,* which provides an indication of the person's ability to hear each tone at each of the presented frequencies. The *audiometric evaluation* assists in determining the extent and type of hearing loss so that the proper remedial or medical steps may be taken.

The unit of measurement used to express the intensity of sound is the *decibel* (dB), and the freqency is expressed in *hertz* (Hz). If an individual has a hearing loss, it is indicated in decibels; the more significant the loss, the larger the number value. For example, a 60-dB loss is a greater loss than a 25-dB loss. In addition to information concerning the extent of the loss in decibels, it may be helpful to have information concerning the frequency

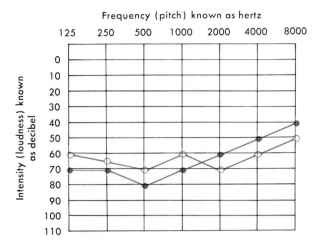

FIGURE 5–1. Audiogram (○, right ear; ●, left ear)

at which the loss occurs. The audiogram in Figure 5–1 indicates a severe hearing loss in an 11-year-old student. Numbers on the left side of the audiogram indicate the decibels (dB), or loudness of sound. The zero indicates the degree of loudness necessary for an average person to hear sound, and the other numbers indicate increasing loudness of sound. The lines on the audiogram indicate the degree of hearing loss in each ear at the various frequencies.

The following common environmental sounds expressed in intensity (decibels) may be of assistance in understanding the nature of hearing loss.

Decibels	Sounds
0	threshold of hearing
20	very quiet conversation
40	outdoor minimum sound level in a city
60	average restaurant sounds or normal conversation
80	loud radio or phonograph music in a home
100	riveting machine or air hammer at 30 feet
140	threshold of pain

The numbers across the top of the au-

diogram indicate the frequency in hertz of the sounds. The sounds that are most critical for the interpretation of speech (speech range) fall between 500 and 2000 Hz.

The portion of an audiogram shown in Figure 5–2 represents the sounds of speech at the various frequencies. As shown in this figure, many of the voiceless (f, th, s) speech sounds are in the higher ranges. If a student has a high-frequency (2000–4000 level) loss, he would miss those sounds when spoken, and since much of speech is imitation, he may leave these sounds out of his speech.

Severity of Hearing Impairment

Often, attempts to systematically classify hearing acuity in relation to actual hearing efficiency or functional ability do not account for a number of outside factors such as motivation, intelligence, social maturity, and family background. These variables may have a definite influence on the individual's functional ability. Two individuals with the same measured hearing loss do not necessarily have the same type and/or degree of difficulty in academic or social settings.

One type of classification emphasizes how the student might react to language instruc-

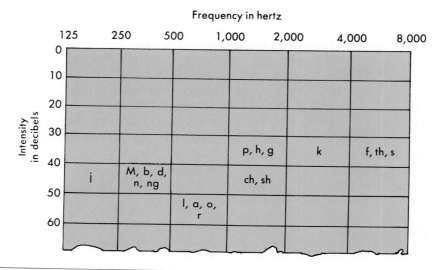

Frequency in hertz

FIGURE 5–2. Sounds of speech at various frequencies

tion based on the age of onset of the hearing loss. If the hearing loss occurs at birth or at an early age before speech and language are developed, it is classified as congenital, or prelingual, deafness. If the loss occurs after the development of speech and language, it is classified as acquired, or postlingual, deafness. These definitions emphasize language acquisition, how the student will learn language most effectively.

Although it is difficult to classify degrees of hearing impairment on the basis of severity, it is necessary to have a classification system that provides some insight into the degree of loss and the potential implications. The following system is quite commonly used by educators:

mild	27–40 dB
moderate	41–55 dB
moderately severe	56–70 dB
severe	71–90 dB
profound	91 + dB

Mild: 27–40 dB. A person who has a hearing loss between 27 and 40 dB has a mild hearing loss and is likely to have difficulty with faint or distant speech. Students with mild losses may need favorable seating; may benefit from speechreading, vocabulary, or language instruction, or a combination of these; and may need speech therapy.

Moderate: 41–55 dB. A hearing loss in the 41–55 dB range is usually classified as moderate. This individual most likely can understand conversational speech at a distance of three to five feet. The student probably needs a hearing aid, auditory training, speechreading, favorable seating, speech conversation, and speech therapy. The extent of services provided by the resource or itinerant specialist may vary considerably, depending on the student's actual achievement in the regular classroom.

Moderately Severe: 56–70 dB. The individual with a moderately severe hearing impairment has a hearing loss in the 56–70 dB range. For the student with a moderately severe loss, conversation must be loud to be understood. The student's speech is probably defective, and he may have a limited vocabulary. This student may have difficulty in group and classroom discussion, can use all the services usually provided students with mild and moderate losses, and, in addition, requires specific assistance from the resource or itinerant teacher in the language-arts areas.

Severe: 71–90 dB. A person who has a hearing loss between 71 and 90 dB has a severe loss and may not be able to hear a loud voice beyond a distance of 1 to 2 feet. The student may be able to distinguish some environmental sounds and has difficulty with consonant sounds but not necessarily vowels. He needs all the services required by hearing impaired students with less severe losses and many of the techniques used with deaf students.

Profound: 91+ dB. Individuals with a hearing loss of more than 91 dB have a profound impairment. Although this individual may be able to hear some loud sounds, he probably does not rely on hearing as the primary learning channel. This student likely needs all the previously mentioned services and possibly more intensive services from the resource or itinerant teacher of the hearing impaired. The profoundly hearing impaired student requires special assistance with emphasis on speech, auditory training, and language; however, he may be attending regular classes on a part-time basis or attend classes that do not require a significant emphasis on language skills.

Considerable caution must be exercised in using this classification system, because students with nearly identical losses may function differently. In addition to using caution with classification systems, educators must also exercise care in predetermining the extent of special education services needed in relation to the degree of loss. Experts in this field do not agree on the relative importance of various degrees of loss. In any individual case, a variety of other information must be

carefully considered. Characteristics of need may include defective speech with substitutions, omissions, or distortions; reading problems; immature language patterns; a lower level of abstraction; and perhaps lower interpersonal relationships (Marsh, Price, & Smith, 1983). Some students with severe losses may be readily served in regular classrooms, whereas a student with a moderate loss may need extensive special education services for the majority of his school day.

IDENTIFICATION OF STUDENTS WITH IMPAIRED HEARING

Although not always recognized by the regular classroom teacher, a particular student's learning or behavior problems might result from a hearing loss. The teacher could misjudge the student as being mentally retarded or emotionally disturbed or as having some type of specific learning disability. In other instances the teacher *may* feel the student's problems are caused by some failure in the teacher's methods. Until the teacher recognizes that the student's problem may be the result of a hearing loss, she could waste a great deal of time on fruitless remedial measures. Therefore, it is very important for the regular classroom teacher to be aware of some common behaviors that indicate a hearing loss. The following are the most common behaviors and medical symptoms that *may* indicate a hearing loss.

Behavioral Indications

Lack of Attention. One such behavior is an apparent lack of attention. If the student does not pay attention, it is possible that he cannot hear what is being said. Another possibility may be that the student hears sounds but they are so distorted that it is difficult to understand. Consequently, he tunes them out or does not make the effort to attend to them. Occasionally, the opposite behavior is observed. The student may be abnormally attentive—always paying close attention in an attempt to determine what is happening in the classroom. Although this is less frequently seen than inattentive behaviors, it does occur.

Lack of Speech Development. Immature, unusual, or distorted speech may be the result of a hearing loss. If speech is distorted, it may be an indication of the way the student is hearing—in a distorted manner.

Difficulty in Following Directions. An unusual amount of difficulty in following oral directions is another possible indicator of hearing impairment. The student who has little difficulty with written directions and considerable difficulty with oral directions may have a hearing loss. Also, if a student often loses his place in oral reading assignments, it could be that he has difficulty hearing what the others are reading. Another indication might be that the student asks the teacher and others to speak louder. Some students with mild losses may give inappropriate answers to questions, and this too may be an indication of a hearing impairment.

Best Work in Small Groups. If the student seems to do his best work in small groups or in a relatively quiet working area, this may be an indication of a hearing loss. Greater success with tasks assigned by the teacher at a relatively close distance or in an uncluttered auditory area (as compared with tasks assigned at a distance or in a noisy situation) may also be an indication.

Dependence on Classmates for Instructions. Another indication of which the teacher should be aware is the student who watches classmates to see what they are doing before he or she starts working. The student may not have fully heard or understood the directions given and may be looking for a cue from classmates or teacher.

Turning or Cocking of Head. A behavior that may indicate the student has a hearing loss is an unusual amount of cocking the head to one side. The student may need to turn one ear toward the speaker to hear more adequately. In addition, the student with a hearing loss may make frequent requests for repetitions.

Acting Out, Stubborn, Shy, or Withdrawn Behavior. Have you ever tried to listen to a speaker who was talking so softly you had difficulty hearing? You could see his lips move but were unable to hear what was being said. Remembering that frustrating experience may help the teacher understand why a student with a hearing loss may be stubborn, disobedient, shy, or withdrawn. If the student is unable to hear, personality and behavior problems may arise. He may compensate for his inability to hear by acting out in the classroom. Other hearing impaired students may compensate by withdrawing, acting stubborn, or being shy.

Use of Gestures. Although rare, some students with hearing loss may rely on gestures to communicate when speech would be more effective. This may be more common with younger children because they have not developed the necessary language and communication skills.

Disparity Between Expected and Actual Achievement. A possible indication of a hearing loss is a disparity between expected and actual achievement. Obviously, there may be many reasons for a student not achieving in a manner consistent with his ability, but the teacher should be aware that one of the reasons may be a hearing loss.

Reluctance to Participate in Oral Activities. A less extreme behavior sometimes characteristic of the hearing impaired student is a reluctance to participate in oral activities. Another possible identifying characteristic of the student with a hearing loss is an apparent lack of a sense of humor. The student who often fails to laugh at a joke may not be hearing the joke.

Medical Indications

So far, we have been concerned only with behavior that may indicate that a student has a hearing loss. There are also medical indications of a hearing loss that should not be ignored by the teacher. These include frequent earaches, fluid running from the ears, frequent colds or sore throats, and recurring tonsillitis.

It is advisable to be aware also of students with allergies. An allergy can produce swollen tissue in the nose and ear areas, leading to faulty hearing. Signs to watch for include dark circles under the eyes, red eyes, frequent sneezing, and a chronic runny nose. These physical characteristics must be brought to the attention of the school nurse and the parents, who should be urged to contact their physcian. Teachers should also be aware of otitis media, an inflammation of the middle ear that, without treatment, can cause a conductive hearing loss. This condition is particularly common among children with hearing problems.

Early detection is of vital importance. It has been estimated that 1 out of 10 persons in the United States has a hearing loss and it affects more people than cancer, tuberculosis, blindness, multiple sclerosis, and kidney disease combined (House Ear Institute, 1985).

PROCEDURES FOR REFERRAL

Should the teacher suspect a hearing loss, she must compile a list of the specific behaviors noted and refer the student immediately to the school nurse, speech specialist, or audiologist. Any of these professionals will conduct a preliminary screening;

and if the results indicate the need, the student will be referred to an otologist (a physician who specializes in diseases of the ear).

It is essential that the teacher monitor the referral process. Occasionally, for a variety of reasons, action is extremely slow or no action is taken. In such an unfortunate situation, the classroom teacher may have to ask pertinent questions to determine the status of the referral.

A referral does not automatically mean that a hearing loss is present. For example, let us assume the teacher observes some behavior that makes, her suspect that a student has a hearing loss. The teacher refers the student to the nurse, speech therapist, or audiologist, who concludes that a hearing loss is present. The student is then referred through the parents to an expert for a more extensive examination. The otologist may find an accumulation of wax or some other obstruction in the ears, infected tonsils or adenoids, or some other abnormality that may be medically corrected. In this instance hearing can be restored and the student returned to school without any educational modifications or adaptations. However, many referrals do not result in medical correction, and as a result, a hearing aid may be recommended. Now what happens to the student? Should he be placed in a special class, or continue in his regular class? If the student is to be retained in a regular classroom, in which classroom should he be retained? These are some of the questions considered in the staffing procedure.

REGULAR CLASSROOM PLACEMENT

The following are some advantages for hearing impaired students offered by regular classroom placement:

1. An opportunity to continue relationships with hearing classmates, which reinforces the feeling that he is more like than not

like other students. He will maintain or gain a feeling of belonging.

2. An exposure to a greater variety of language styles.

3. The necessity of keeping speech and language patterns at an intelligible level. Often when hearing impaired students are grouped together in the same class, they do not develop or maintain a high level of speech and language. A regular classroom also provides normal, age-appropriate speech, language, and other social models.

4. The necessity of establishing a wider variety of communication techniques. The hearing impaired student may have to modify his communication skills if he is not understood by his classmates. This may necessitate a reexamination of his communication skills.

5. An opportunity for the student to compete academically with hearing classmates. The academic pace is faster, and general achievement-level expectations are raised. However, in the interests of professional objectivity, we must note that this may be the major reason why some students *cannot* participate with success in the regular classroom.

6. Preparation to function in a hearing world. All individuals interacting with a hearing impaired student must remember that the ultimate objective is for the hearing impaired student to function as independently as possible in a hearing society.

Another advantage of regular classroom placement, although not related only to the hearing impaired, is that hearing students have an opportunity to become acquainted with someone who is different. This must be seen very positively, particularly today when many students may not have sufficient opportunity to mix with children of different ethnic backgrounds or races or with disabled students. We believe that most individuals benefit from the opportunity to meet and associate with individuals who are different from themselves.

Placement and/or retention of the hearing impaired student in the regular class works very well for some students and is essentially unsuccessful for others. As noted in the preceding paragraphs, we believe that retention in the regular classroom is the best procedure, *if it is effective in meeting prescribed educational goals.* One of the more important factors is the attitude and readiness of the regular classroom teacher; and his or her willingness to work cooperatively with resource personnel. Other factors to be considered include quality of lighting in the room, the teacher's rate of speech and type of voice, the visibility of the teacher's lip movements and of visual aids used. These and other factors must be carefully considered because they are important in facilitating the speech and language of hearing impaired students. A variety of interrelated factors are at work when a program for a hearing impaired student is planned.

Placement Considerations

The following student characteristics are not criteria for placement, but they are normally discussed in the staffing procedure:

1. the ability to exchange ideas through spoken, written, and read language (including expressive and receptive auditory-oral communication skills)

2. social and emotional maturity near equal to that of the other students in the classroom, as well as minimal disparity between listening age and academic skills

3. the ability to profit from large group instruction when new information is presented

4. independence, self-confidence, and determination to succeed

5. a chronological age close to that of the regular class students (McCartney, 1984)

In addition to the characteristics of the student, other factors such as the availability of sound amplification, presence of support staff for monitoring placement, counseling or remediation if necessary, acceptance and understanding level of the teacher, the degree to which the other students are capable of extending consideration and respect, and the desire of the parents to have their child in the regular classroom must be considered before such placement is made.

The previously mentioned factors relate to the child, parents, and other students. An additional factor to be considered is the working relationship between the regular class teachers and resource or itinerant personnel. They must establish and maintain a working relationship that enhances the education of the hearing impaired student. The regular class teacher must feel free to ask without reservation for assistance whenever needed. The resource teacher must be allowed to observe in the regular classroom at any time, not in a judgmental manner but as a helper. If the working relationship between the regular classroom teachers and the resource teacher is one of mutual respect and understanding, recognizing that there are no authoritative experts and that neither is self-sufficient, they will be well on the way to the critical factor: open communication for the benefit of the student.

SUGGESTIONS FOR THE REGULAR CLASSROOM TEACHER

The student with impaired hearing may be served in the regular classroom with a number of specific modifications and adaptations. These modifications and adaptations are essentially alternative teaching strategies and do not require substantial teacher time or classroom adjustment. In fact, most of the alternative strategies are based on common sense and may facilitate the education of all students.

Obtaining Complete Information About the Student

Complete information should be obtained before taking a hearing impaired student into the class; be certain that there is sufficient information concerning (1) the nature of the loss, (2) the amount of residual hearing, and (3) how the student communicates. A few brief private sessions with the student should be arranged so that a comfortable relationship and communication process can be established. Because the speech of a hearing impaired student may be defective, these sessions may familiarize the teacher with the student's unique speech patterns. The teacher may also find it very helpful to discuss the student's speech needs with the speech specialist or special education resource person. Most of this information concerning the student can be obtained from the special education resource personnel in the school or school district.

The resource teacher, by nature of her professional preparation and experience, generally has a very good understanding of medical aspects of the impairment, audiology, and speech therapy. She may serve as the liaison between these disciplines and the regular teacher, may interpret the exact nature of the hearing loss in relation to medical and audiological evaluations and provide specific suggestions related to the unique characteristics of hearing efficiency for a particular student. It is hoped that information concerning the individual's functional ability would be emphasized rather than medical or quantitative information. In addition, the resource teacher may interpret the student's development of language and its influence on learning. In general, resource personnel can provide considerable information and serve as a liaison between ancillary personnel and the regular classroom teacher.

Another valuable source of information is the parents of the hearing impaired student.

Several brief conferences with the parents, both before actual placement and on an ongoing basis thereafter, can provide considerable information about the hearing impaired student. The information, support, and participation of the parents as active partners in their child's educational program is known to be a primary determinant of successful mainstreaming programs (Marsh et al., 1983).

Preteach-Teach-Postteach Strategy

The preteach-teach-postteach strategy assumes that the itinerant or resource teacher and the regular class teacher have a cooperative, mutually respectful working relationship. The regular classroom teacher informs the resource teacher of the lesson or concepts to be taught, and it is presented to the hearing impaired student first in a one-to-one or small-group setting. The student then attends the regular classroom, and the unit of study is taught by the regular classroom teacher. After the class, the regular classroom teacher reports to the resource or itinerant teacher by means of a short note, checklist, or personal discussion indicating problems or areas of concern that may need to be retaught in the one-to-one or small-group setting. Ultimately, it is anticipated that the preteaching and postteaching phases may be shortened and possibly eliminated except where the regular classroom teacher or the student specifically request it (Reynolds & Birch, 1982).

Classmates as Helpers

The use of a "listening helper" or "buddy" can be of considerable assistance to the hearing impaired student. This peer may sit next to the hearing impaired student to ensure his turning to the correct page or taking notes or for other appropriate assistance in areas such as adjusting to a new class or school or participating in activities such as physical education. The buddy may clarify something the

teacher has said by repeating it while facing the hearing impaired student or by writing it down.

At the upper elementary and secondary levels the listening helper or buddy may assist in note taking by simply making a carbon copy of his notes. This allows the hearing impaired student to concentrate fully on what the teacher is saying.

The listening helper or buddy may be rotated weekly or monthly, or a few classmates may volunteer for an extended period of time. Some caution must be exercised so that the helper or buddy provides assistance only when needed; otherwise, the very purpose of the integrated educational experience may be defeated. If the helper provides assistance when it is not necessary, the hearing impaired student may become overly dependent on his classmates—a dependency that must be carefully avoided. A more detailed discussion of the use of peers as teachers and tutors is provided in chapter 3.

Hearing Aids

A hearing aid is not a complicated piece of equipment. The aid helps compensate for the hearing loss by amplifying sound. It cannot replace the natural ability of the ear, and the student who wears an aid should not be expected to hear normally. Limitations in the use of an aid may be imposed by damage to the ear, by the nature of speech sounds, or by the hearing aid itself. Misunderstandings of what a hearing aid can do are very common. Many individuals believe, for example, that a hearing aid is like eyeglasses: you simply put them on and you will see—or hear—better. This is not true.

There are basically three parts to a hearing aid: a *microphone,* which picks up sound and converts the sounds to electrical impulses; the *amplifier,* which makes the sounds louder by increasing the electrical impulses; and a *speaker* or *receiver,* which reconverts the electrical signals back into sound and directs them to the ear mold.

There are many types of hearing aids, but they are generally classified on the basis of where they are worn. The first type is a body aid, which is strapped to the body with a wire connecting to the ear mold. These sturdy, compact aids are generally worn by young children; often the controls are on the young child's back so that he will not play with the controls. The second type, an ear-level aid, may be mounted in eyeglasses, fit behind the ear, or fit entirely in the ear. An aid is also classified as *monaural* (one ear) or *binaural* (both ears).

Occasionally a hearing aid may squeal and annoy the hearing impaired student and classmates. This squeal may be caused by an improper fitting of the ear mold or by the mold being incorrectly placed in the ear.

Auditory Trainers. A conventional hearing aid amplifies all sounds including background noises, and this often poses a serious problem. The background or environmental sounds may mask or cover up what the teacher is saying. One way to accommodate this problem is the use of an auditory trainer.

Some hearing impaired students in regular classrooms can profit from using an auditory trainer. An auditory trainer is similar to a hearing aid and has the same basic three parts, but in addition the teacher wears a microphone around the neck that sends his voice directly to the student wearing the auditory trainer. When the teacher speaks, his voice is received by the student as if the teacher were standing right next to the student's ear. The trainer can be adjusted to eliminate most background sound except for the teacher's voice. Some types of auditory trainers use a wireless microphone that transmits an FM radio signal to a combination hearing aid–FM receiver, bypassing environmental sounds and bringing the desired sound directly to the ear.

Increasing Hearing Students' Understanding of Hearing Aids. Often hearing students are curious about how the hearing aid works. In cooperation with resource and itinerant personnel, parents, and the hearing impaired student, the teacher may present information about the operation of the hearing aid. A brief unit of study may also be conducted on the structure and function of the ear and the basic principles of acoustics. Hearing students can be given the opportunity to actually listen to a hearing aid or auditory trainer. A stethoscope may be used so that they do not have to put the ear mold in their ears. This experience may provide a greater understanding of the functioning of, and problems associated with, amplification devices. A detailed discussion of similar procedures to provide greater understanding for nonhandicapped students may be found in chapter 4.

Care and Maintenance of Hearing Aids. Even though the parents or the student have examined the hearing aid prior to coming to school, the aid may not adequately function in school. There are several things the teacher can check if the student seems not to be hearing well because of a malfunction in the hearing aid. Although it is not the primary responsibility of the regular classroom teacher to troubleshoot hearing aid problems, it is helpful to be aware of a few minor factors that may cause malfunctions so that the resource teacher or the parents can be alerted. The following suggestions are related to hearing aid malfunctions:

1. Make sure the battery is not dead.
2. Determine if the battery is installed properly, with the positive and negative terminals in the proper position.
3. Check the cord to see if it is worn or broken or if the receiver is cracked.
4. Be sure the plug-in points are not loose. Check both the hearing aid and the receiver.

5. Check the ear mold to make sure it is not obstructed by wax and that it is inserted properly. As indicated previously, an improperly fitted ear mold can cause irritation and feedback (squeaky sounds). Possibly the student is outgrowing the aid and the parents and/or resource or itinerant personnel should be informed.
6. Keep a fresh battery at school (changed at least monthly, even though it may not have been used) so that the child does not have to go without his hearing aid on the day the battery goes dead. Often the resource or itinerant teacher has an extra supply of batteries and can assist in determining whether other problems might exist.

The regular teacher should be aware of some additional considerations with respect to the proper care and maintenance of hearing aids.

1. Do not allow the hearing aid to get wet.
2. Serious damage may result from leaving the hearing aid in extremely hot or cold places.
3. Always turn the aid off before removing it from the ear. Removing the aid without turning it off causes a squeal. Whenever the aid is taken off, it should be placed in a safe, soft box.
4. If the student repeatedly removes the aid, this may be an indication that the aid is not working correctly or does not fit properly and causes the student some discomfort. Naturally, if this occurs, the teacher should contact the resource or itinerant teacher.
5. Do not allow the student to wear the hearing aid microphone too close to the receiver, or the aid will make unusual noises. If the student has a unilateral loss (one ear), the receiver should be worn on the side opposite the hearing aid.
6. Do not take the aid apart to attempt to

repair it. This should be done by a hearing aid dealer.

Assessing Hearing Aid Effectiveness. The resource or itinerant teacher can assist in evaluating many aspects of hearing aid problems and hearing aid effectiveness. She can routinely check all aspects of hearing aid operation by checking and replacing worn-out batteries and in general troubleshooting any other problems. Many resource teachers obtain a tester for use in the building or make arrangements for assistance from a local hearing aid dealer.

A more important role of the resource teacher is to assess hearing aid effectiveness in the classroom situation, particularly if the student has just recently been fitted with an aid. The teacher can appraise the effectiveness of the aid by evaluating changes in the way the student handles everyday situations. She should look very carefully for (1) changes in social interactions, (2) changes in voice quality and articulation, (3) increased language skills, (4) reactions to sound and amplification, and (5) increased educational achievement. In addition, the resource teacher should observe whether the student is turning the volume down or completely turning it off; these actions may be an indication of an improperly fitted aid. Systematic longitudinal evaluation of a student's hearing aid effectiveness is an important role of the special education resource teacher. Routine procedures should be established to provide hearing aid maintenance.

Facilitating Speechreading
Most hearing impaired students have some remaining or residual hearing, and special efforts must be made to facilitate speechreading because the student may not hear all the sounds in his environment. The student must learn to closely observe lips, facial gestures, body gestures, and other environmental clues to fully understand what

his teacher and classmates are saying. The following steps should be taken by the regular teacher:

1. Allow the student to sit where he can make the most of what he hears and sees; sometimes a younger child needs guidance in this area. Remember, the hearing impaired student listens with his eyes as well as his ears. The student should be within 5–10 feet of the speaker. Do not, however, have the student sit so close that he constantly has to look up. To aid the student in becoming a more proficient speechreader, change the seating arrangement from time to time to give him practice in watching different speakers in the classroom from different positions. Seating arrangements may depend on the classroom organization. If the class is small, arranging the desks in a semicircle and seating the hearing impaired student on the end facilitates speechreading. In a lecture situation, placing the student near the front of the room and off to one side allows him to readily read the speech of classmates and teachers. Seating arrangements must remain flexible to ensure that the student can observe and participate in class activities. The teacher should observe the student to notice whether he seems to be straining or missing important concepts; if so, modification in the seating arrangement may be necessary. It may also be helpful to ask the student periodically if he would like to move.

2. Seating should be arranged so that the student does not have to look into a light source. Do not stand in front of windows, for this makes speechreading very difficult. Do not stand in a dark area or an area where there may be shadows. Generally, speechreading is easier when the light source is behind the student.

3. Try to face the group when speaking, and when members of the class are speaking encourage them to face the hearing impaired student. Many of us frequently turn our back to the class and talk when writing on the board. The teacher should stay in one place as much as possible when giving oral examinations or while lecturing so that when the student looks up the teacher is in the same general location. Some teachers have found it helpful to reserve several seats for the hearing impaired student, with one as his "homebase." Oral examinations requiring a written response may also cause considerable difficulty for the hearing impaired student. If the student is writing a response while the teacher is giving the next item, the student may miss several items. Overhead projections and transparencies work extremely well in such cases for all students, and visual aids in general are very effective with the hearing impaired student.

4. Call attention to visual aspects of a particular concept to be learned. Phonetic analysis, as an example, may not be helpful. Generally, instruction that emphasizes visual clues is preferred.

5. Do not exaggerate your gestures, for exaggerated gestures may cause considerable confusion. Use gestures as usual, but keep hands and any objects away from the face whenever possible. Beards and mustaches as well sometimes distract attention from the lips or make them difficult to see.

6. Provide a good pattern of speech for the student; distinct articulation is more helpful to the hearing impaired student than speaking louder. Speech patterns should not, however, be exaggerated.

7. Ask questions of the student occasionally to make certain he is following the discussion. When presenting a new word or asking a question, repeat it if it

is not understood the first time, speaking directly at the student. If he seems to miss the term or request, rephrase what was originally said and ask him a question; for example, "This is a stapler—how could you use a stapler?" or "Who would use a stapler often?"

8. Certain words are not easily understood through speechreading; therefore, encourage the student to ask questions or have statements repeated if he does not understand.

9. When isolated words are presented, as in spelling lessons, the words should be used in context. Spelling tests may also be given by providing the contextual words of the sentence on a sheet of paper and replacing the spelling word with a blank space. With this method the student has the necessary contextual clues. Remember, many words appear alike on the lips and sound alike, for example, *beet* and *bead*. Other examples are *meal* and *peal, safe* and *save,* and *pie* and *buy.*

10. When presenting new vocabulary words, present the multiple meanings for these words; some words have more than five meanings. This can be very difficult for the hearing impaired student because his vocabulary may not be sufficient to understand the multiple meanings.

11. Chewing movements should be avoided as much as possible. If students are allowed to chew gum, this may make speech reading very difficult, since hearing impaired students may not be able to differentiate between chewing and speech.

12. When referring to an object in the room, it may be beneficial to point to it, walk over to it and touch it, or actually manipulate the object. This may put the object into the context of the discussion and support what is being discussed. When the teacher is speaking directly to the student or calling for the student's attention, it may be helpful to call the student's name or speak directly to him. In nearly all instances, instruction that combines both visual and auditory cues is more effective with the hearing impaired.

13. The hearing impaired student should not be seated close to audiovisual equipment that has fan or motor noise.

14. If the teacher uses pictures with verbal presentations, she should initially describe the material and then show the illustration. This allows the student to focus on one major stimulus at a time.

Facilitating Desirable Speech Habits

An essential component of educational programming for the hearing impaired student is speech training. The student's ability to monitor his language may be seriously limited by his hearing impairment, thereby limiting his expressive language abilities.

Often the speech therapist working with the student has clearly established goals and objectives related to the student's speech patterns and general articulation. The regular classroom teacher plays an important role in facilitating good speech habits. Reinforcement of therapy goals and objectives in the student's classroom is essential if the needed carryover and maintenance in everyday situations are to be expected. The following suggestions may facilitate such carryover and maintenance.

1. Encourage the student to use the dictionary to aid in pronunciation of difficult words. This practice naturally depends on the age and reading level of the student.

2. Encourage the student to participate in oral discussions and expect him to use complete sentences when speaking. Be careful, however, not to "emotionally load" the situation. If proper speech is insisted on and the student is demeaned in front of the entire class for incorrect usage or incomplete sentences, the student may be discouraged from participating in any

oral discussion. Be careful not to nag the student. Often the correction of a mispronounced word may be accomplished by a brief conference at the end of the period or day. Some teachers have had success with keeping a list of words with which the student has had difficulty and then giving them to the student with the correct pronunciation without comment. The student should also be encouraged to participate in conversation, reading, storytelling, and creative dramatics.

3. Don't be afraid to talk with the student about the hearing loss. The hearing impaired need to be told when they are speaking too loudly or too softly. Since the hearing impaired student may not be able to monitor his own speech sounds, the teacher can do a great deal to keep the student from developing dull or expressionless speech habits by speaking with him honestly and openly.

4. Praise and encourage the student when he has correctly pronounced a previously difficult word. The child needs a great deal of encouragement and success if he is to accomplish this very difficult task.

5. Provide a relaxed language environment. The more relaxed and casual the speech and language styles of the teachers and students, the better the opportunity for language acquisition.

Demonstration Teaching

Special educators have traditionally served their students in what might be termed pull-out programs. That is, they pull the students out of the classroom and work with them in a special resource room. This practice, although it may be necessary in some instances, is totally unnecessary and even undesirable in other situations.

If teachers are fully to appreciate the potential of integration or mainstreaming, general educators should attempt to involve special educators in regular classrooms wherever possible. This practice can greatly facilitate the communication between special and general educators and overcome many of the misunderstandings between them. The expertise held by both professions can be shared in the most meaningful way through the actual teaching of students. Special educators can increase their knowledge concerning large-group instruction and the limitations imposed in modifying and adapting materials, curricula, and teaching strategies. Regular classroom teachers can increase their competency in working with the hearing impaired student by observing the resource person work with large and small groups. At times, the resource teacher could assume an aide or tutor role not only with the hearing impaired student but also with small groups of students who are having problems with a difficult concept or assignment. This is not a new concept; some resource teachers have been assuming a helping or assisting role with regular teachers for some time. Unfortunately, the number of such teachers has not been significantly large.

The resource teacher may also demonstrate a particular teaching strategy. For example, if the resource teacher has asked the regular teacher to use an overhead projector to teach a science or social-studies lesson, it would be desirable for the resource teacher actually to demonstrate the use of the projector by teaching the lesson. It is also possible for the resource teacher to assist in teaching a unit on the anatomy and physiology of the ear or a unit on hearing as one of the senses to acquaint all students with the nature of a hearing loss. The resource teacher may actually conduct or assist in conducting short in-service sessions with the students concerning the nature of a hearing loss, the benefits of a hearing aid, or any other topics that may be of interest to the hearing students.

Facilitating Social Interaction

One criterion by which the success of the mainstreaming process may be judged is the extent to which the handicapped student is

For students with hearing impairments, pictures are an aid to vocabulary development.

accepted, chosen as a friend, and liked by other students (Cartwright, Cartwright, & Ward, 1984). There are indications that the social interaction between hearing and hearing impaired students is much less than that among hearing students (Schlesinger, 1985). It seems that such research tends to place responsibility for increased and positive interaction on the hearing impaired student. Part of the poor interaction may be attributed to the lack of communication skills of the hearing impaired student or to insufficient social skills, such as the ability to initiate and continue conversations or discuss playground or after-school activities. Other factors may include the teachers, the environment, and the hearing students.

Teachers. When the regular classroom teacher maintains a supportive climate within the classroom, it is possible for some hearing impaired students to become dependent on the teacher for positive and rewarding social interactions (Kretschmer & Kretschmer, 1978; Schlesinger, 1985). Teachers must be aware of their influence and the

possibility that they may be fostering an overdependence. They should recognize that this overdependence may in fact be negatively influencing the attitudes of the hearing students and limiting the interaction between the hearing and hearing impaired students. Teachers should encourage and develop procedures to enhance this interaction. Resource or itinerant personnel may have specific suggestions that would assist in this area.

Environment. The physical and instructional environment of the classroom is another factor that may discourage interaction among students. The teacher may want to change seating arrangements periodically to enhance interaction between hearing and hearing impaired students.

Hearing Students. If the objective is to increase interaction with hearing students, then systems must be developed to foster and enhance this interaction. As mentioned previously, educators may too quickly assume that the problems lie exclusively with the hearing impaired student. Quite logically, if there appears to be a breakdown, part of the problem could rest with the hearing students. As a result, specific efforts must be initiated to assist them in better understanding hearing impaired students. Perhaps the self-fulfilling prophecy is at work here not only for the hearing impaired but for the hearing students as well. Students may think, "I don't relate to ——— because I don't know how—so I guess I can't," and it becomes a self-perpetuating circle involving all of the students.

Intervention. Interaction of hearing impaired students with other students in the regular class is an agreed-upon goal; however, there is somewhat less agreement regarding whether this interaction and communication is more positive if the hearing impaired students use oral or total communication methods (Schwartz, 1984; Morsink, 1984). It is the responsibility of the regular classroom teacher to design specific interventions to facilitate communication and interaction by assisting the hearing students to become more proficient at communication skills.

Media and Equipment

Audiovisual equipment and personnel can be of particular value to the teacher who has a student with a hearing impairment in the class. Overhead projectors can greatly enhance the achievement of the hearing impaired student. As the teacher lectures, she may put important notes or key vocabulary words and phrases on the overhead projector. An overhead projector allows the teacher to maintain eye contact with students while writing on the projector. When using slides or films, the teacher should be certain there is sufficient light to enable the hearing impaired student to see faces clearly as the narrator or teacher makes comments. In general, supplementary diagrams and pictures

should be used as often as possible. Often the complete narrative script to a filmstrip or audiotape accompanies the materials and, if available, should be given to the hearing impaired student.

Many educational films have been captioned so that they can be used by the hearing impaired student in the regular classroom. More than a thousand such films are available on a loan basis, free of charge.[1] This collection contains films on subjects ranging from *accounting* to *occupations* to *zoo animals*. Also available are well-presented guides that may accompany these excellent films. The resource or itinerant teacher of the hearing impaired may provide the teacher with a detailed listing of available materials. The use of these modified and adapted instructional materials does not interfere with the education of normally hearing students but in fact facilitates their achievement as well.

Methods of Communication

The development of language and communication skills is the primary emphasis of educational programming for hearing impaired students. There has been considerable controversy concerning the most effective and efficient method of communication for these students. Three methods have been advocated: (1) the manual method, (2) the oral method, and (3) total communication. Each of these methods is briefly discussed in the paragraphs that follow.

Manual Communication. American Sign Language (AMESLAN) is a set of gestures representing words or concepts (Figure 5–3). It is generally used by the adult deaf population and has been called the *mother tongue*. Fingerspelling or manual alphabet is another form of manual communication. In fingerspelling, various finger positions represent

[1]Captioned Films for the Deaf Distribution Center, 5034 Wisconsin Ave. NW, Washington, DC 20016.

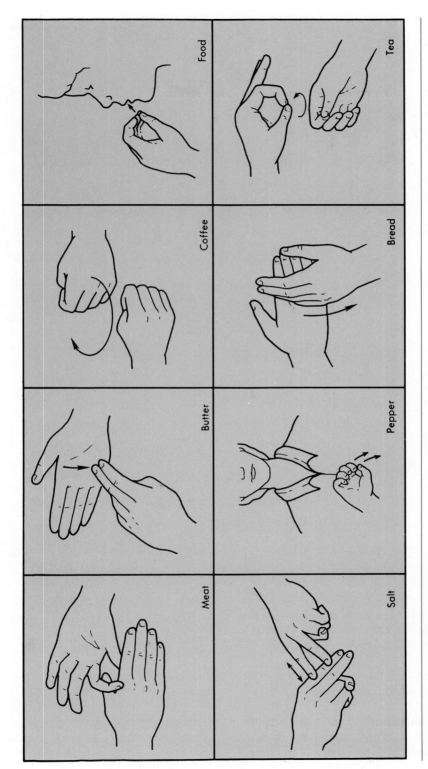

FIGURE 5–3. American Sign Language

141

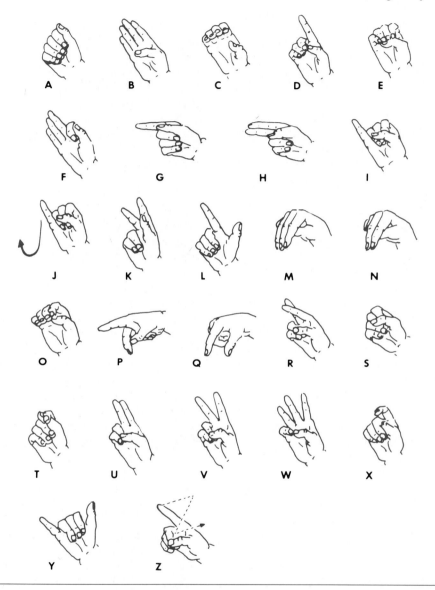

FIGURE 5—4. Manual alphabet used by the deaf of North America

Note. Courtesy American Foundation for the Blind, New York.

individual letters of the alphabet that are used to spell out words (Figure 5—4).

Oral Communication. The oral-aural method of communication makes use of oral and auditory training and speechreading. This method encourages the use of residual hearing while the presentation of material emphasizes the student's visual and auditory attention. Of course, use of amplification is stressed. The oral method emphasizes speechreading and oral speech as the primary means of communication. Gestures and other movements are generally not used other than those ordinarily used by hearing individuals to supplement conversation.

Cued Speech. Cued speech is used to augment oral programs, especially speechreading. It includes eight hand shapes in four specific positions, to represent phonetic elements that are not readily visible (Cartwright, Cartwright, & Ward, 1984; Schwartz, 1984). The cued speech system was deliberately designed in such a way that it could not be used as an independent or total form of communication (Quigley & Paul, 1984).

Total Communication. A third approach, called total communication, combines the manual and oral-aural methods according to the abilities, interests, and needs of the hearing impaired student. The total communication method teaches the student to become skillful in speechreading and oral speech. Signing and the manual alphabet are both used, the information conveyed by signs being supplemented by the manual alphabet when necessary, as for proper names.

Because of differences between sign languages and English, there has been a proliferation of methods that purport to code English in sign. The most common methods are Seeing Essential English (Anthony, 1971), Signed English (Bornstein, 1974), and Signing Exact English (Gustason, Pfetzing, Zawolkow, & Norris, 1972).

There exists some controversy between advocates of AMESLAN and advocates of coding English in sign. The main point in dispute is whether it is more effective to use AMESLAN as a *primary* tool for teaching students with hearing impairments and subsequently teach English (reading and writing) as a second language, or to bypass the necessity of learning two languages in favor of one coded-English system or a combination of coded-English systems. If the latter

procedure is followed, the student can use one form of English for signing, reading, and writing.

Although manually coded English systems in some form are widely used in the United States (Quigley & Paul, 1984) and AMESLAN was for a time about the only form of sign language used, there still is only "limited information on the educational effectiveness of the various communication forms" (p. 231).

Previewing New Materials or Assignments Before Class

Whenever possible, the teacher should briefly discuss topics with the hearing impaired student before the actual class presentation. This goal may be accomplished by providing the student with an outline of the material to be discussed. Communicating with resource or itinerant teachers and employing the preteach-teach-postteach strategy should be given consideration. Allowing the hearing impaired student to preread assignments is very helpful. Another possibility worthy of consideration is to provide on the board or a piece of paper a list of key vocabulary words that deal with the new material. When giving an assignment, write it on the board in addition to giving it orally. The student's listening helper may check to see that he has the correct assignment.

Awareness of Student Fatigue

Hearing impaired students may fatigue more easily than other students, and teachers should be aware of this potential problem. Such fatigue may be particularly noticeable in young children near the end of the day, but this is a factor for all hearing impaired students. This fatigue should not be interpreted as boredom, disinterest, or lack of motivation. The fatigue results in part from the continuous strain of speechreading, the use of residual hearing, and the constant watching required to keep up with various speakers while participating in classroom ac-

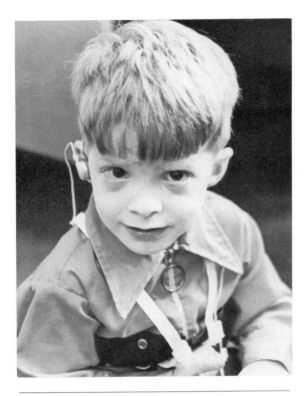

To maintain this degree of attention, teachers must be very aware of the fatigue factor.

tivities. It may be helpful to vary the daily schedule so that the student is not required to attend to academic subjects for an extended period of time. Shorten lesson periods or alternate written and oral work with rest periods. However, the student should be expected to complete all assignments. The teacher should also be aware that the hearing impaired student may hear better on some days than on others. Some students may experience tinnitus (hearing noises within the head), which may result in nervousness or irritability.

Interpreter-Tutors

Students enrolled in a total communication program may use interpreter-tutors to assist them in their regular classroom. The interpreter-tutor is usually located just outside

the direct line of sight from the student to the teacher, slightly facing the student, thereby allowing the student to directly speechread the teacher or the interpreter.

The interpreter repeats what the teacher is saying through signs, fingerspelling, and nonvocalized speech. He or she may paraphrase or modify what the teacher is saying if the student is not familiar with the words or concepts being used. Interpreter-tutors are not teachers but must be experts in total communication. They must pass a proficiency examination and may have to be certified in some states.

Using an interpreter is a new experience for many teachers. Initially it seems very unusual to both the teacher and the hearing students. In fact, for the first several days or until such time that the hearing students become comfortable, they may be seriously distracted by the signs, gestures, and expressions of the interpreter.

The following general suggestions may be helpful when using an interpreter:[2]

1. Be aware that you and the interpreter may have to adjust and modify the pace of instruction periodically. Occasionally the interpreter may ask you to stop momentarily, repeat, or slow down. Teamwork between the teacher and interpreter is vital to the student.
2. Be certain there is good lighting wherever the interpreter stands.
3. In using demonstration and visual aids, allow extra time for students to see what is being demonstrated as well as to see what is being said. With hearing students the teacher can turn her back to the class and simultaneously elaborate a point as she demonstrates. With deaf students this is not possible, since the deaf student must turn his attention from the inter-

[2]Adapted from *Guidelines for Interpreting for the Hearing Impaired,* (p. 3), 1982, Greeley, Colorado: Office of Resources for the Disabled, University of Northern Colorado.

preter to the chalkboard to see what the teacher is demonstrating and then turn back again so he will not miss the explanation. The best solution to this problem is first to be more explanatory as new points are put on the board and second to pause while maintaining eye contact with the students.

4. When using an overhead projector, slides, videotapes, or films, it is sometimes necessary either to reduce the lighting or to turn off the lights completely in the classroom. In such situations it is important to provide a small lamp or spotlight to focus on the interpreter while discussion or explanation takes place.

5. Because sign language does not contain signs for every word in the English language, the interpreter must fingerspell special vocabulary using the manual alphabet. The interpreter may also be asked by the hearing impaired student to pause and define the term. It is most helpful to write special vocabulary on the board or give a list to the interpreter before class so that neither the interpreter nor the student misunderstands the concept.

6. Question-and-answer periods may pose problems. If the student is unable to vocalize his question, he must sign the question to the interpreter and the interpreter then vocalizes the question to the teacher.

7. The interpreter cannot interpret more than one speaker at a time. During discussions, remind the other students to speak one at a time.

8. To establish rapport, speak directly to the hearing impaired student, not to the interpreter.

Some caution must be exercised to avoid a dependency relationship between the interpreter-tutor and the student: the interpreter-tutor is used only when necessary.

Students who do not have good speech-reading skills and thus might not be able to participate in the regular classroom may be able to do so with the assistance of an interpreter-tutor. It is imperative that every method that may help a student make maximum progress be fully investigated.

Hearing Students and Communication

As mentioned earlier in this chapter, hearing students often do not understand the nature of a hearing impairment or how a hearing aid functions. Brief in-service sessions may be held to explain the exact nature of a hearing loss and how a hearing aid functions. The resource or itinerant teacher, speech specialist, and audiologist are valuable persons to involve when such activities are being planned.

Although many hearing students who have hearing impaired classmates will learn some of the signs or the manual alphabet, it may be helpful to provide instruction to the hearing students systematically. Unless such instruction is provided, the hearing students often express considerable frustration when attempting to communicate with their hearing impaired classmates. Instruction in signing may be offered occasionally after school or during special Saturday-morning programs. Such an elective course may be offered on an ongoing basis and may initially be taught by resource or itinerant teachers or in cooperation with the hearing impaired students. Hearing students who have gained proficiency may also be encouraged to share in the instruction or serve as teaching assistants or peer tutors. There is little question that efforts to assist hearing students to understand and communicate better with their hearing impaired classmates can greatly facilitate interaction. In addition to hearing students learning sign language, many regular classroom teachers also learn how to sign.

These suggestions to regular classroom teachers are certainly not all-inclusive, but they do represent the areas of greatest concern. It would be helpful to review and discuss them with the resource or itinerant teacher periodically. The classroom teacher's ingenuity and creativity in modifying and adapting curriculum, materials, and teaching strategies can make the experience successful for everyone.

The most important consideration, above all other suggestions or techniques, is the attitude of the teacher. The teacher is the single most important variable. The teacher must be understanding but not pitying and should treat the hearing impaired student as nearly as possible like any other student in the classroom, being fair and truthful, not lenient, in reporting his or her progress. The handicapped student should be treated as a student who is able, who is an individual, and who, incidentally, has impaired hearing.

SPECIALIZED INSTRUCTION AND ASSISTANCE FROM RESOURCE OR ITINERANT TEACHERS

There are a number of special skills that should be routinely provided by resource personnel. The specific skills vary depending on the grade level of the students. At the primary level, the resource teacher may have responsibility for reading instruction or may supplement the material presented in the student's regular class. The reading material used by the resource teacher may be the same as that used in the regular class, except that the resource teacher spends considerably more time on comprehension, questioning, and related language activities. At the intermediate level, the resource teacher probably supplements regular classroom instruction by emphasizing phonetic and comprehension skills or by introducing new vocabulary words before their introduction in class. Hearing impaired students may need to be taught currently "in" words that are popular with their classmates.

In addition to supplemental instruction,

the resource teacher may work on a number of other areas, such as individual and small-group auditory training, vocabulary development, comprehension, questioning, speechreading, and speech correction.

In some instances, the resource or itinerant teacher is an integral part of routine classroom activities and has specific instructional responsibilities to hearing students with instructional needs similar to those of the hearing impaired. In other settings the resource or itinerant teacher may employ a preteach-teach-postteach strategy.

The exact nature of the resource teacher's role depends on the age or grade level of the students, the number of students, and the extent of hearing impairment. Generally, the role involves tutoring or supplemental instruction, the introduction of new materials or skills, and instruction in highly specialized skills related to hearing impairment.

The resource teacher may assist the regular teacher in modifying or adapting materials for the hearing impaired student. For example, the resource teacher may provide outlines or vocabulary lists that are about to be introduced into the regular classroom. Often the regular teacher does not have time to modify materials, and this service can be a tremendous help. If neither the regular teacher nor the resource teacher has the necessary time, volunteers or teacher aides may be most helpful in this area.

If activities are planned far enough in advance, often the resource teacher may obtain captioned films, slide-tape presentations, or other tangible teaching materials to be used by the regular teacher.

Depending on the geographical area to be served (one or more schools), resource or itinerant teachers may be responsible for the in-service education of regular classroom teachers in one or several buildings. Often the resource or itinerant teacher is called on to acquaint a building staff with the rationale underlying integrated placement of the hearing impaired. The nature of the in-service session may be quite general and relate only to the philosophy of integrated education, or it may be specifically related to techniques for modifying and adapting curriculum, materials, and teaching strategies.

Although it is not necessary for regular teachers to know the manual alphabet, they often are interested in learning it. In this instance the resource or itinerant teacher may conduct in-service programs for teachers and/or students or arrange for classes to be taught by another person. (For a more detailed discussion concerning the provision of specific information to nonhandicapped students, see chapter 3.)

Another role often assumed by the resource teacher is to provide selected journal articles, readings, or topics of special interest in relation to a particular student's problem or to specific teaching techniques. The orientation and in-service efforts of the resource personnel are an ongoing responsibility that must be taken seriously. How the resource personnel sell themselves, the program, and the hearing impaired students has a tremendous influence on the effectiveness of the program.

The resource teacher, due to his or her specialized preparation and experience, may assist regular teachers in counseling the hearing impaired student and the student's parents. This counseling may relate to routine academic matters, such as parent-teacher conferences, or to specific problems imposed by a hearing impairment, such as interpersonal relationships, language and speech problems, or vocational interests.

The resource teacher assists in planning and implementing work-study, vocational education, and vocational-rehabilitation services for hearing impaired students in secondary schools. The resource or itinerant teacher may be responsible for actually initiating these services or may contact others who will initiate them.

As mentioned previously, the role and responsibility of resource personnel vary considerably. The key to successful resource services is communication between the regular teachers and the resource personnel.

SUMMARY

Most students with impaired hearing are educated in the regular classroom. Younger students and students with severe and profound losses require greater amounts of special education service during their early school years and may attend regular classes on a more limited basis. After they have acquired the necessary skills, they will attend regular classrooms for increasing amounts of time, but many will need some supportive assistance from special education resource or itinerant personnel during their entire school career.

Increased success in the regular classroom may be attributed to many factors. Part of this success is due to early detection, and the provision of early services to parents. Another factor is better coordination with other community agencies. Improvement in hearing aids and the increased use of auditory trainers and devices have contributed to the increase in the number of students who can successfully participate in regular programs. In addition, the development of captioned films and other media has had a very positive influence on the education of the hearing impaired. Tutor-interpreters are being used with increasing commonness and are assisting these students a great deal. Efforts to assist hearing students to better understand their hearing impaired classmates also greatly facilitate their interaction and understanding. As a large number of hearing impaired students are integrated into regular classrooms and as professionals continue to analyze and share information and expertise about these students more effectively, mainstreaming may reach its fullest potential for these students.

In this chapter we have reviewed the nature of hearing impairments, the limitations imposed by such impairments, identification procedures, and methods of referral. We discussed alternative teaching strategies to be considered by the regular classroom teacher, including specific suggestions to facilitate the education of hearing impaired students. In addition, we provided specific suggestions to assist hearing students and reviewed the nature of the specialized instruction. The key to successful programming for these students is a cooperative, working arrangement between regular classroom teachers, parents, and special education personnel. Students with impaired hearing must experience a variety of language styles and must establish communication techniques that will work in the settings they will encounter in adult life. Those with more severe losses must receive continued support from special education personnel to assist them in maintaining intelligible speech and language. Students with mild impairments may function quite satisfactorily with a minimum of special assistance if the regular classroom teacher plays an effective, appropriate role in the educational process. Perhaps the most important benefit of the regular class setting is the opportunity for the hearing impaired student to maintain relationships with hearing individuals—to be a part of the hearing world.

Teaching Students Who Are Visually Impaired

MEASUREMENT AND CLASSIFICATION OF VISION

IDENTIFICATION OF THE VISUALLY IMPAIRED

COMMON TYPES OF VISUAL IMPAIRMENT

EDUCATIONAL PROGRAMMING

CONTINUUM OF SERVICES

SUGGESTIONS FOR THE REGULAR CLASSROOM TEACHER

SPECIALIZED INSTRUCTION AND ASSISTANCE FROM RESOURCE OR ITINERANT TEACHERS

- ☐ Should a student with very thick-lensed glasses be considered visually impaired?

- ☐ What are the observable signs and behaviors that may indicate impaired vision?

- ☐ How do you think common environmental scenes could appear to someone with cataracts, glaucoma, or a detached retina?

- ☐ What types of electronic devices are available to assist the visually impaired with reading?

- ☐ What type of lighting is required for low-vision students?

- ☐ If you were required to provide travel assistance to a visually impaired person, would you know how to do it?

- ☐ How do visually impaired students take notes?

- ☐ Should a regular classroom teacher learn braille if a blind student is placed in her class?

- ☐ What type of assistance may you expect from a resource or itinerant teacher?

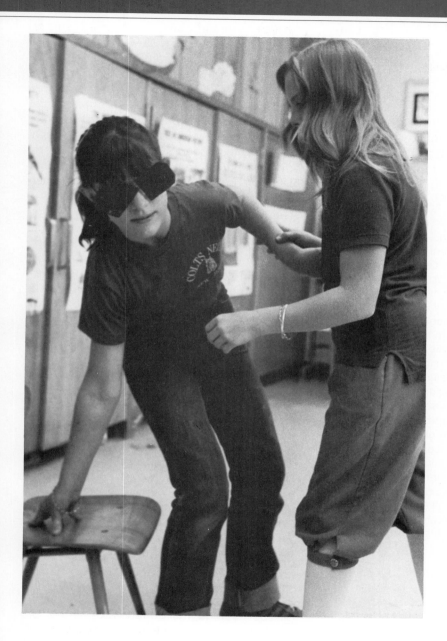

The "least restrictive environment" concept is relatively new to most of the categorical areas of exceptionality in special education, but students with impaired vision have been mainstreamed since the early 1900s. In fact, pioneer authorities in the vision field advocated mainstreaming long before the turn of the century. Dr. Samuel Gridley Howe, in 1866, made the following statement about mainstreaming in general and its specific application to the visually impaired:

All great establishments in the nature of boarding schools, where sexes must be separated; where there must be boarding in common, and sleeping in congregate dormitories; where there must be routine, and formality, and restraint, and repression of individuality; where the charms and refining influences of the true family relation cannot be had—all such institutions are unnatural, undesirable, and very liable to abuse. We should have as few of them as possible, and those few should be kept as small as possible. . . .

. . . With a view to lessening all differences between blind and seeing children, I would have the blind attend the common schools in all cases where it is feasible (depend upon it, one of the future reforms in the education of the blind will be to send blind children to the common schools, to be taught with common children in all those branches not absolutely requiring visible illustrations, as spelling, pronunciation, grammar, arithmetic, vocal music and the like). We shall avail ourselves of the special institutions less and the common schools more. (quoted in Irwin, 1955, p. 128)

As a result of this early emphasis on education in the "common schools," many of the service delivery systems used today with other handicapping conditions were modeled after successful programs for the visually impaired.

Students with impaired vision cannot readily use the same educational materials as other students, and if they do, they receive information at a slower rate, as with recorded materials, braille, large print, magnification devices, or reading machines. As a result of limited access and the slower rate, the primary features of programming for the visually impaired are related to modification and adaptation of educational materials. A related problem for students with impaired vision involves concept development. A concept is often developed and unified through our visual experiences and lends meaning to our perceptions and experiences. For example, the concepts of space, color, and other abstractions may present some difficulty for visually impaired students, since they do not have visual referents to unify the concept. Because of the potential problem in concept development, program emphasis must be placed on concrete experiences and on providing input to the other sensory channels like hearing, taste, and smell. The visual channel should be used when appropriate.

MEASUREMENT AND CLASSIFICATION OF VISION

A person is usually regarded as legally blind who has central visual acuity of 20/200 or less in the better eye after correction or who has a field of vision no more than 20 degrees in diameter (Hatfield, 1975; Vaughn & Asbury, 1977).

Ratios such as 20/20, 20/70, and 20/200 are used to express visual acuity. The first number is the distance in feet at which the test is made. The second number is the size of symbols or letters on the Snellen chart, expressed in terms of the distance at which a person with normal vision can comfortably read them. For example, if at 20 feet an individual can read the 20-foot-size symbol or letter on the chart, the measured acuity is 20/20, or normal vision; if an individual can read only the symbol representing the 70-foot-size letter or larger on the Snellen chart, distance visual acuity is indicated as 20/70; if only the largest, the 200-foot-size letter, then the individual's measured distance visual acuity is 20/200. An individual's distance visual acuity is indicated by these figures, but they do not provide information concerning near-point vision (the ability to see at close distances, as in reading). Not only do these definitions exclude information about near-point vision, but there is also a considerable variance among individuals with the same measured acuity. For example, two students may have 20/200 measured acuity, but one may be able to read printed material whereas the other may have to read braille.

The Keystone Telebinocular device may be used to assess near-distance vision, and depth perception, factors that also affect the student's ability to use vision effectively. A complete evaluation of functional vision will include near vision, far vision, depth perception, and color discrimination (McLoughlin & Lewis, 1986).

Barraga (1983) noted "a gradual trend to use *blind* and *low vision* to differentiate the population and to use *visually handicapped* as a generic term to refer to the entire population" (p. 21). Using this classification system, the blind student is one whose vision is unreliable and who finds it necessary to rely on other senses for functional purposes. Blind students cannot use print, even with maximum magnification; they must use braille. "The low-vision person is one whose corrected vision is lower than normal but who does have significant usable vision" (Faye, 1976, p. 85). If a student can perform visual tasks, but does so with reduced precision and endurance and at reduced speeds, he would likely be considered a low-vision person. Usually, the low-vision student cannot perform certain detailed tasks, but if there is significant usable vision, the classification should be *low vision* rather than *blind*.

The visually impaired student may be considered in terms of medical, legal, educational, or functional definitions, but our emphasis here involves educational and functional ability. For our purposes the visually impaired student may be defined as one whose vision is limited to such an extent that he may require educational modifications and adaptations. If the student can read printed material in either enlarged print or standard print with the use of special magnification devices, he is classified as having low vision or as being a print reader. Students whose visual impairment is so severe that they must use materials other than print (such as braille and taped materials) are classified as *educationally blind* or as *braille readers*.

The remainder of this chapter considers a number of major concerns, including (1) identification of the visually impaired, (2) common types of visual impairments, (3) educational programming, (4) the continuum of services required for the visually impaired, (5) suggestions to regular classroom teachers, and (6) specialized instruction and assistance from resource or itinerant teachers.

IDENTIFICATION OF THE VISUALLY IMPAIRED

Students with severe visual impairments are usually easily identified before enrollment in school. There are, however, some students whose impaired vision has gone undetected for many years. The student's impairment may be detected by routine visual screening during the primary grades, or it may not be detected until the student is in the fourth or fifth grade, when subject matter requires extensive visual work like reading and map study. This delay in identification may be attributed to the nature of academic tasks required up to this level or to poor vision-screening procedures during the student's early elementary years. Many screening programs are carelessly conducted; the procedures may be inaccurate or not carried out on a routine basis. In addition, tests for near-point vision (ability to read at 12–16 inches) are required by only a very few states. Most screening programs are concerned with the student's distance vision (ability to see at 20 feet). Although vision-screening procedures are improving, it must be recognized that these procedures, at best, are only a screening process and do not identify all students with impaired vision.

When the problems associated with vision-screening procedures are considered, the role of the regular classroom teacher in identifying students with vision problems cannot be overemphasized. The teacher has the opportunity to observe the student in a variety of settings and under a variety of conditions and may be in the best position to identify visual difficulties. Therefore, it may be helpful for the regular classroom teacher to be aware of behaviors and observable signs that could indicate a visual problem.

Behavioral Indications

Rubbing Eyes. One behavior that may be an indication of a vision problem is eye rubbing. The rubbing may be observed in excessive amounts or during close visual work.

Shutting or Covering One Eye. A student who is having difficulty seeing may close one eye or tilt or thrust the head forward.

Light Sensitivity. Some students with an undetected vision problem may demonstrate unusual sensitivity to bright or even normal light.

Difficulty with Reading. An unusual amount of difficulty with reading or other work requiring close use of the eyes is another possible indicator of visual impairment. The student who has little difficulty with oral or spoken directions or tasks but experiences difficulty with visual work may have a vision loss.

Losing Place During Reading. The student who has a tendency to lose his place in a sentence or page while reading may have a vision problem. The teacher should carefully observe to see if he is demonstrating a mechanical reading problem or one related to a possible visual defect.

Unusual Facial Expressions and Behaviors. The student who demonstrates an unusual amount of squinting, blinking, frowning, or facial distortion while reading or doing other close work should be observed and possibly referred for further examination.

Achievement Disparity. A possible indication of a visual loss is a disparity between expected and actual achievement. Obviously, there may be many reasons for a student not achieving in a manner consistent with his ability, but the teacher should be aware that one of the reasons may be a visual loss.

Eye Discomfort. The student who complains of burning, itching, or scratchiness of the eyes may be experiencing a vision problem and should be referred to the school nurse for closer examination.

Holding Reading Material at an Inappropriate Distance. A behavior that may indicate a student has a visual problem is holding reading material too close or too far or frequently changing the distance from near to far or far to near.

Discomfort Following Close Visual Work. The student who complains of pains or aches in the eye, headaches, dizziness, or nausea following close visual work may need corrective glasses.

Difficulty with Distance Vision. Students who experience difficulty in seeing distant objects or who tend to avoid gross motor activities may have a visual loss. These students may have a strong preference for reading or other academic tasks rather than playground or gross motor activities.

Blurred or Double Vision. The student who complains of blurred or double vision should be referred for a visual examination as soon as possible.

Reversals. A tendency to reverse letters, syllables, or words may be an indication of impaired vision.

Letter Confusion. A student who confuses letters of similar shape (*o* and *a, c* and *e, n* and *m, h* and *n, f* and *t*) may have impaired vision.

Poor Spacing. Poor spacing in writing and difficulty in "staying on the line" may be an indication of visual impairment.

Observable Signs

To this point we have been concerned only with behaviors that may indicate that a student has a visual impairment. There are also several observable indications of a visual problem that should not be overlooked by the teacher. These include red eyelids, crusts on lids among the eyelashes, recurring styes or swollen lids, watering eyes or discharges, crossed eyes or eyes that do not appear to be straight, pupils of uneven size, eyes that move excessively, and drooping eyelids.

Referral

If any of these behaviors or signs is observed in a student, he or she should be referred immediately to the school nurse, principal, or the individual responsible for vision testing. Additional tests might be conducted to determine whether the student should be referred to an eye specialist for a more extensive evaluation. After some determination is made concerning needed services, the teacher may have to serve as the catalyst or advocate to ensure that the recommenda-

tions are not lost in a file somewhere and that the needed services are provided.

Teachers may find it helpful to have information concerning the role and capabilities of the various eye specialists in the community in order to make the necessary referral or to provide information to parents. Occasionally, the classroom teacher may need to confer with one of these specialists; therefore, a brief description is provided here:

Ophthalmologist. A medical doctor who specializes in the diagnosis and treatment of diseases of the eye. This physician is also licensed to prescribe glasses.

Optometrist. A highly trained person who specializes in eye problems but does not possess a medical degree. This individual is licensed to measure visual function and prescribe and fit glasses. If disease is suspected, a referral will be made to an ophthalmologist.

Optician. A craftsman who makes glasses and fills the prescriptions of ophthalmologists and optometrists.

Orthoptist. A nonmedical technician who directs prescribed exercises or training to correct eye-muscle imbalances and generally works under the direction of an ophthalmologist.

COMMON TYPES OF VISUAL IMPAIRMENT

There are many types of eye problems that may result in reduced visual acuity, restricted field of vision, or disease of the eye. The most common visual defects in students are astigmatism, myopia (nearsightedness), and hyperopia (farsightedness). These defects are called refractive errors and can usually be corrected by lenses. Among the more common conditions that result in reduced field of vision, blind spots, or blurring of vision are glaucoma, cataract, retinal detachment, retinitis pigmentosa, macular degeneration, corneal pathologic conditions, and diabetic retinopathy.

Figures 6–1 to 6–9 depict the most common visual problems. Figure 6–1 shows a typical street scene as seen by someone with 20/20 visual acuity. The remaining figures represent the same scene as it might appear to persons afflicted with various types of serious vision problems. Below each representation is a brief description of the condition and its effect on what the individual may or may not see. These figures are only illustrative of the various conditions and should not be interpreted as the actual acuity because there may be considerable variance in any of the conditions represented.

The teacher should obtain as complete information as possible concerning the nature of the student's eye condition, its effects on learning, needed lighting characteristics, and travel limitations.

EDUCATIONAL PROGRAMMING

As mentioned previously, the placement of students with other handicapping conditions is a relatively recent trend, but students with vision impairments have been mainstreamed into regular classrooms for more than half a century. Early professionals recognized that students with visual impairments could be educated with their sighted peers with only minor modifications and adaptations and that the limitations imposed by a visual disability did not require a special curriculum.

Materials must be provided in different media or in modified or adapted form so that the student can learn through sensory channels other than vision. For example, if the student is not able to read material in printed form, the material would be provided through the tactile (touch) or auditory channels. If the student can read printed material

FIGURE 6–1. Normal vision.

FIGURE 6—2. Myopia (nearsightedness): Vision is clear when looking at near objects but blurred at far distances.

FIGURE 6—3. Hyperopia (farsightedness): Vision is blurred when looking at near objects but clear when looking at a distance.

FIGURE 6—4. Glaucoma: Loss of peripheral vision while retaining most of the central vision.

FIGURE 6—5. Cataract: Diminished acuity caused by a density or opacity of the lens. The field of vision is not affected, and there are no significant blind spots. There is an overall haziness (denser in some spots), particularly in glaring light conditions.

FIGURE 6—6. Retinal detachment: A hole or tear in the retina (back of eye) that allows fluid to lift the retina from its normal position. This results in a field defect, seen as a dark shadow. It may be in the upper portion or lower part as illustrated.

FIGURE 6—7. Retinitis pigmentosa: A form of tunnel vision. Generally only a small area of central vision remains.

FIGURE 6—8. Macular degeneration: A breakdown of a central part of the retina that results in the area of decreased central vision called a blind spot or scotoma. Peripheral vision remains unaffected.

FIGURE 6—9. Corneal pathological condition: The image may be distorted or clouded so that clear detail is not discernible. Field of vision is normal.

but only with considerable difficulty, the material may be enlarged or the student may use magnification devices or reading machines. The primary nature of special education services for visually impaired students is related to the modification and adaptation of educational materials.

Blind and low-vision students follow the same curriculum as their peers but do need additional "plus factors." The student studies reading, math, and social studies, but in addition he may need braille instruction, orientation and mobility (travel) training, typewriting, and training in the use of an abacus. Generally, plus factors, or compensatory skills, are taught by the resource or itinerant teacher and are not a responsibility of the regular classroom teacher.

CONTINUUM OF SERVICES

There is a very definite need for a full continuum of services for students with impaired vision. The following variables should be considered when placement options are being studied: (1) age, (2) achievement level, (3) intelligence, (4) presence of multiple handicapping conditions, (5) emotional stability, (6) nature and extent of eye condition, (7) wishes of students and parents and (8) recommendations of staffing team. Naturally, each student should be considered individually, but there are some general placement considerations that should be taken into account. For example, there seems to be a relationship among the age of the student, the nature and extent of the visual impairment, the student's level of achievement, and the amount of direct, special education service and instruction needed. If the child is a young braille reader (ages five to nine), resource or itinerant assistance is needed on a routinely scheduled daily basis to provide the needed instruction in braille reading and other areas requiring the specialized services of the resource or itinerant teacher. During the child's early education, he may spend 1 to 1½ hours each day with his resource or itinerant teacher. When the child has developed braille-reading skills (Figure 6–10)

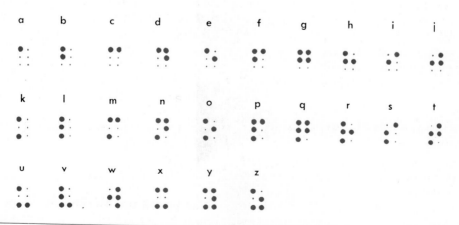

FIGURE 6–10. Braille alphabet. Each letter is represented by a pattern of raised dots within a six-dot cell. Additional combinations include letter sequence, numbers, punctuation, and words.

and a familiarity with all the necessary tangible apparatus, he or she may attend the regular classroom for increasing amounts of time. If the student is able to read printed materials with or without an aid, it is not necessary to spend as much time with the resource or itinerant teacher. The student at the secondary level may also require specific instruction from resource or itinerant personnel, but this student's needs are not the same as those described for younger students. The special teacher may be doing more counseling relevant to the student's adjustment to secondary school life, orientation, and mobility training, and use of advanced technological equipment.

SUGGESTIONS FOR THE REGULAR CLASSROOM TEACHER

The suggestions that follow may be used for the student who is either a braille reader or a print reader, because many of the techniques and modifications are the same for both groups. The suggestions fall into six categories: (1) adapted educational materials and equipment, (2) optical aids and magnification devices, (3) educational environment, (4) orientation and mobility, (5) alternative teaching strategies and adaptations, and (6) general considerations. Although some suggestions are loosely categorized here, this grouping allows easier conceptualization of the range and types of modifications.

Adapted Educational Materials and Equipment

As mentioned previously, the primary nature of educational programming for the visually impaired involves the modification and adaptation of educational materials. Most of these materials are available from private agencies at no cost to the student. Over the many years of service to the visually impaired, an extensive array of very helpful materials has been developed.

It is not practical to review all of the adapted materials and special equipment available for students with impaired vision, for there are several hundred different types. Most of these materials are directed at increasing the student's learning through sensory channels other than vision.

The following paragraphs provide a brief description of the most commonly used materials and equipment. It is important that regular classroom teachers have a basic understanding of the various kinds of tangible apparatus to ensure their proper use and thus maximize their value to the student.

Braillewriter, Slate, and Stylus. A braillewriter is a six-key (corresponding to the six dots in the braille cell) machine that is manually operated and types braille. The slate is a metal frame with openings the size of the braille dots; the stylus is a pointed object used to emboss the dots. The slate and stylus can be carried in a pocket and are often used to take notes.

Raised-Line Drawing Board. The raised-line drawing board is a board covered with rubber. A piece of acetate is placed on the board and a pen or pointed object is used to "raise" the drawings so that they may be felt by the student. It may also be used by the teacher to draw geometric shapes, script letters, or diagrams.

Raised-Line Paper. Special raised-line paper allows the visually impaired student to write script on a raised line, and it may be used to draw a graph.

Cassette Tape Recorders. Tape recorders may be used to take notes, formulate compositions, listen to recorded texts, or record assignments.

Taking notes with slate and stylus.

Talking Book and Other Recorded Programs. Records or tapes recorded specifically for individuals who cannot use print as their primary means of reading are provided by the Library of Congress. A wide variety of textbooks and leisure reading is offered on disks and cassettes.

Variable-Speed Attachments. Variable-speed attachments can be used to vary the speed at which the student listens to a tape, allowing him to listen to the material at a slower or a faster rate (speeding up the tape results in a higher pitch).

Portable Braille Recorder. A portable braille recorder may be interfaced with a computer that will convert braille to standard print and vice-versa.

Speech Compressors. A speech compressor is a modified tape recorder in which the pause between each recorded word is electronically removed, thereby compressing the material and speeding up the listening process without changing the pitch.

Optacon (Optical to Tactual Converter). The Optacon is an instrument that scans printed material electronically and raises the print feature so that it may be read tactually by the visually impaired. The reader places a hand-held scanner over the print material while placing the index finger of the opposite hand over the raised configuration.

Talking Calculator. A talking calculator is an electronic calculator that presents results visually and auditorily.

Closed-Circuit Television. A closed-circuit television is a system that enlarges printed material on a television screen and can be adjusted to either black on white or white on black. The Perkins Videoscope is an example of such a closed-circuit system.

Kurzweil Reading Machine. The Kurzweil Reading Machine, a computer-based device, provides direct access to typed or printed material by converting it to synthetic speech. The speed and tone can be controlled, and the machine can also spell a word letter by letter.

Echo Commander. The Echo Commander is a device that may be attached to the Apple II, II+, or IIe computer. It will convert the visual representation to speech. There is provision for headphone listening, the addition of a second speaker for stereo, and for attachment to a tape recorder.

Often students who have some remaining vision can use a number of optical aids. These aids may be used at all times or for specified tasks. Magnifiers that can be mounted on the student's desk, held by hand, or head mounted are frequently prescribed by low-vision clinics. These students may also use monoculars (telescopic aids for one eye) that may be mounted on glasses or held in the hand. With the monocular, the student may view the chalkboard, classroom demonstrations, or other distant objects.

The following list of additional visual aids represents the types available from various sources:

A. geography aids
    1. braille atlases

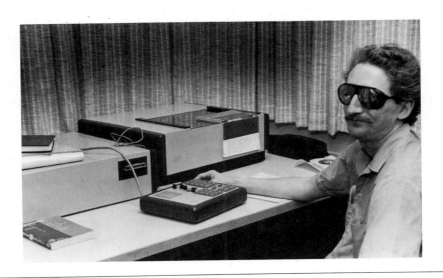

The Kurzweil print translator is one example of the advances in technology that provide assistance to persons with vision impairments.

2. molded plastic, dissected and un-dissected relief maps
3. relief globes
4. landform model (a set of three-dimensional tactile maps illustrating 40 geographic concepts)

B. mathematical aids
1. abacus
2. raised clockfaces
3. geometric area and volume aids
4. wire forms for matched planes and volumes
5. braille rulers
6. talking calculators

C. writing aids
1. raised-line checkbooks
2. signature guide
3. longhand-writing kit
4. script letter-sheets and boards

D. miscellaneous aids
1. audible goal locators, which can be used as a goal, base, or object locator or a warning device
2. special braille or large-type answer sheets
3. science-measurement kits (containing such items as thermometers, spring balances, gram weights, and gravity specimens)
4. sports-field kit (raised drawings of various sports' playing fields or courts)
5. simple-machine kits, including working models of simple machines like pulleys and levers, including plane, wheel, and axle
6. children's games, such as Rook, Rack-O, Scrabble, bingo, cards, checkers, and Parcheesi
7. adapted sports equipment (like audible balls)
8. braille clocks, wristwatches, and timers

Occasionally some students may be self-conscious of their need for special equipment and may be reluctant to use it. The teacher's openness and understanding can do a great deal to assist the student and classmates in appreciating the benefits and need for the special equipment.

The American Printing House for the Blind has a very extensive offering of adapted materials and educational equipment. In addition, the American Foundation for the Blind has an *Aids and Appliances Catalog* from which materials may be ordered. Several other agencies also have special materials available.

It is generally not the responsibility of the regular classroom teacher to obtain materials unless a resource or itinerant teacher is not available. The resource or itinerant teacher is familiar with all the agencies that provide adapted materials and equipment and how to obtain them. In the event that needed materials are not available from any of the agencies, the resource or itinerant teacher will have to reproduce these materials or arrange for them to be prepared. For example, a particular reading text may not be available in modified form because it has been published only recently. After all agencies have been queried, the resource or itinerant teacher may have the text reproduced in large type, tape-recorded, or transcribed into braille.

In addition to textbooks and special adapted materials available from an agency, there is always a need for teacher-made materials used on a day-to-day basis, such as teacher-made tests, work sheets, and special games or activities. These must be reproduced in the desired format by the resource or itinerant teacher or by specially trained aides because it is essential that the student's materials be the same as his or her peers'. Advanced planning and a special communication system must be implemented with the resource or itinerant teacher to provide an explanation of the nature of the needed materials and allow sufficient time for their reproduction. This is usually accomplished by leaving the desired materials in the resource or itinerant teacher's mailbox, establishing a routine conference with the resource or itinerant teacher, or sending the material with the student when he meets with the resource or itinerant teacher.

Occasionally the regular classroom teacher may have to modify needed materials. For example, if mimeographed materials are being prepared for class distribution, it may be necessary to darken the letters or figures with a felt-tipped pen so that they can be seen more easily by the partially seeing student. Materials duplicated in purple usually cause considerable difficulty for the visually impaired; black stencils may provide the desired contrast. Yellow acetate placed over

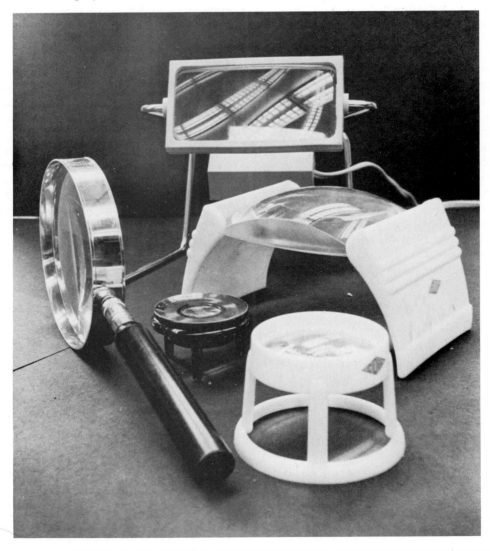

A variety of magnification devices may be used by students with visual impairments.

the printed page tends to darken the print itself as well as provide greater contrast. It may also be of value to consider preparing handout materials in primary or enlarged type for all students.

Educational Environment

Although these are not a major concern, several environmental or classroom modifications can facilitate the education of students with impaired vision. Preferred or open seating allows the student to sit wherever he or she is most comfortable. When the teacher is using the chalkboard, when a movie or filmstrip is being shown, or when the teacher is demonstrating a particular concept using tangible materials, the student should be allowed to select the best visual location.

The student's seating should be arranged for the best possible lighting conditions, but this does not mean that all students with low vision should be in bright or highly lighted areas. Some visual impairments require no special lighting, whereas others require lower levels of illumination. The resource or itinerant teacher or the report from the student's eye specialist should be of particular value in this matter.

The teacher should not stand with his back to a bright light source such as a window because the student would then be looking directly into the light. Writing on a chalkboard where there is considerable glare should also be avoided. When a demonstration is given, the student with low vision should be encouraged to stand near the teacher or actually assist in the demonstration. It may also be helpful to allow the student to handle the demonstration materials before or after the demonstration.

Before the actual placement in the regular classroom, a formal orientation procedure should be conducted. The resource or itinerant teacher or orientation and mobility specialist can provide additional guidance in structuring this learning experience. Initially,

the student should be familiarized with the general layout of the classroom, including being given guided and unguided opportunities to explore. Certain landmarks within the classroom should be established, such as (1) the student's desk, (2) the teacher's desk, (3) cabinets or bookshelves, (4) storage areas for paper and general classroom materials, (5) wastebasket, (6) bulletin boards and chalkboards, (7) windows, (8) special interest centers, (9) doorways and bathrooms, and (10) other classroom equipment.

After the student is oriented to the classroom and the general school building, other surrounding areas may be introduced, such as school offices, gymnasium, cafeteria, auditorium, restrooms, recreation areas, locker rooms, and any other areas that might be used by the student. Often, orientation to the school building and surrounding areas is taught formally by the orientation and mobility specialist or resource or itinerant teacher.

Teachers who have visually impaired students in their class are sometimes reluctant to change the classroom seating or position of desks, tables, and other items because they are afraid the student may become disoriented or sustain an injury. The physical arrangement of the room should be changed as often as normally necessary, but the low-vision student must be oriented to the changes. This should take only a few minutes of formal orientation and a few minutes of independent exploring by the student, followed by a brief question-and-answer session concerning the new arrangement. Other students in the class can be of some assistance by directing the visually impaired students through the new arrangement or describing it to them.

Safety while traveling independently in the classroom can be a problem if classroom doors and upper cabinet doors are not completely open or closed. Often the visually impaired student may think the classroom door is open, because of auditory and other cues, to find it only partially open. Keeping the door completely open or closed is difficult to accomplish with 30 other students in the classroom, but it should be attempted.

The noise level of the classroom should be kept reasonably low, since the visually impaired student must depend on his auditory skills for much of his or her educational program. Braille-reading students need open space and shelves at the side of the room, since braille materials are very large and bulky, and they may need room for their braillewriter, typewriter, books, and other materials.

Orientation and Mobility

The ability of a visually impaired student to move about independently is one of the most important factors in his total educational program. Programming efforts should be directed toward academic and social development, but if the area of travel is neglected, the student may be denied the opportunity to move freely and independently in his school and community. In view of the relative importance of independent travel, an overview of the nature of training, the major modes of mobility, and the role of the regular classroom teacher is presented in the sections that follow.[1]

The concepts of orientation and mobility are interrelated because mobility cannot be achieved unless the individual is oriented. *Orientation* refers to an individual's use of his other senses to establish his position and relationship to objects in his environment. *Mobility* refers to the individual's movement from one point in the environment to another. In other words, mobility is getting from point *A* to point *B,* whereas orientation involves the individual knowing his location, the location of his objective, and the most efficient way to reach the objective.

The regular classroom teacher is not responsible for formal training in orientation and mobility. This training is very specialized and should be conducted by an orientation and mobility specialist or, in the case of precane orientation and mobility, a resource or itinerant teacher whose background includes specific preparation in this area. It is important, however, that the regular classroom teacher understand the nature of the training and the major methods or modes of travel. The five modes of travel used by the visually impaired are (1) the sighted guide, (2) cane travel, (3) the dog guide, (4) the electronic travel aid, and (5) independent travel. The sections that follow briefly describe these modes, followed by a review of general protective techniques.

Sighted Guide. One of the most common techniques taught is the use of a *sighted guide.* It involves the visually impaired student grasping the guide's arm just above the elbow, with fingers on the inside and thumb on the outside, and assuming a position approximately a half step behind the guide. The grip is just firm enough to maintain contact. The guide's arm is positioned next to his body. In effect, the visually impaired person is "reading" the sighted individual's arm or elbow, and any movement of the guide's body and arm is detected by the student. By following approximately a half step behind, the student knows when the guide is stepping up or down and turning left or right, and this position provides the necessary reaction time. When ascending or descending stairs, the guide should approach the stairs at a right angle and pause at the first step. The student can locate the beginning of the step with his foot and negotiate the stairway, remaining one step behind the sighted guide. The guide's arm position indicates when the landing or end of the staircase is reached.

The classmates of the visually impaired student can readily be taught how to serve as a sighted guide. Additional methods related

[1]Special acknowledgment is due David Kappan, associate professor of special education, University of Northern Colorado, for his critical evaluation and assistance in the development of the section on orientation and mobility.

Students may learn to serve as sighted guides.

to the efficient use of this technique would be taught by the resource or itinerant teacher or orientation and mobility specialist.

Cane Travel. Use of a cane is a common systematic method of travel. The age at which a student is introduced to the cane and provided formal training in its use depends on the student's maturity, need for more independent travel, and physical and mental ability. Generally, the first attempt to provide orientation and mobility training is made when the child enters school, although training could begin sooner.

There are several types of canes, but the most common are made of aluminum or fiberglass and are approximately half an inch in diameter. The tip of the cane is usually made of steel or nylon. The length of the cane is individually prescribed by the orientation and mobility specialist and is determined by the user's height, length of stride, and comfort.

Cane travel is taught on a one-to-one basis by a highly specialized instructor. It initially involves fundamentals in restricted areas, and later training is applied in outdoor situations such as residential and business districts. Extensive training is conducted in crossing streets, utilizing public transportation, and dealing with complex navigational situations.

Dog Guide. The third mode of travel uses the dog guide. Generally a dog guide is not recommended until the student is at least 16 years old. Before this age the student may not have the maturity to handle a dog properly or the need for more independent travel. Often young visually impaired students want to obtain a dog guide as a pet or companion though not necessarily for independence in traveling. For obvious reasons the dog guide should be considered not a pet but rather a partner in achieving independent travel. Contrary to popular opinion, only a relatively small percentage of the visually impaired use dog guides. Specific information concerning dog guide agencies, such as cost and nature of training, may be provided by either the resource or itinerant teacher or the orientation and mobility specialist. It is essential that the potential dog guide user investigate the individual program offering dog guide training to ensure that the highest standards are offered.

Electronic Travel Aid. The electronic travel aid is the fourth mode of travel used by the visually impaired. A number of devices are available; most are used as a supplement to another method of travel. Although it is encouraging to see research being conducted in this most important area, it does not seem that any one device will meet the needs of all individuals. Some of the devices enhance auditory feedback, some detect obstacles, others enable the individual to walk in a straight line, and still others are directed at revealing the specific location of obstacles in the environment. The four most commonly used electronic travel aids are briefly described.

The Mowat Sensor is a small hand-held device that uses a high-frequency sound to detect obstacles within an elliptical beam. If an object is present, the entire sensor vibrates, and the vibration rate increases as the visually impaired person approaches the object. The sensor operates on a rechargeable battery and is small enough to be carried in a purse or coat pocket.

The Sonicguide™ emits a high-frequency sound with detection echoes converted into audible stereophonic signals. It provides information about the distance, position, and surface charcteristics of objects within the visually impaired person's travel path and immediate environment. The electronic system for the unit is built into special eyeglasses fitted for the individual user.

The Laser Cane emits invisible light beams that strike an object and are reflected back to the receiving unit of the cane. A sound or tone is emitted to warn the person of objects or dropoffs. In addition to the auditory feedback, a vibrating unit felt by the user's finger signals obstructions ahead. The three beams include upper, lower, and mid-range signals to provide basic protection for the user's entire body.

The Russell Pathsounder is a chest-mounted device that emits an ultrasonic signal. When an object is located, the device offers auditory feedback and/or tactile signals. It provides protection for the upper body and has possible value for the hearing impaired blind child.

Numerous hours of instruction by an orientation and mobility instructor are prerequisite to the successful use of these de-vices. Additional information concerning these and other electronic travel aids may be obtained by contacting an orientation and mobility specialist.

The type of mobility aid or device to be used, whether it be cane, dog, or electronic aid, is totally an individual matter and should be given very careful consideration by the student, his parents, and others after extensive thought and planning in cooperation with the resource or itinerant teacher or orientation and mobility specialist.

Independent Travel. The fifth mode of travel is independent, that is, with no aid. Generally, after a student with low vision has become familiar with the environment he or she is able to move about without aid, for in-

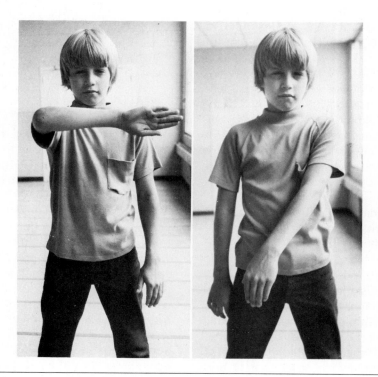

FIGURE 6–11. Use of hand and forearm for protection while traveling independently.

stance, in the classroom, short distances in the school building, to the bus, and perhaps in the school yard.

Protective Techniques. A number of protective techniques may be used by the visually impaired student while traveling independently with or without the use of other aids. These protective techniques are routinely taught to young children and are normally used only in familiar areas. They may be used in combination with the cane or an electronic aid for additional protection. Three of the basic techniques taught by the resource or itinerant teacher or orientation and mobility specialist are as follows:

1. *Upper hand and forearm technique.* For protection in familiar settings, the student may extend his arm in front of his body at shoulder height and parallel to the floor, with his palm outward (Figure 6–11).
2. *Lower hand and forearm technique.* When protecting the lower body, the student extends his arm down and forward toward the midline of the body with the palm of his hand facing him. The student may use the upper hand and forearm together with the lower hand and forearm to give both upper and lower body protection.
3. *Trailing technique.* Trailing enables the student to maintain orientation, determine his or her position in space, locate specific objects, and secure a parallel line of travel. The student positions himself a comfortable distance from the surface to be trailed, extends his arm forward at hip level, and establishes contact with this surface with the outside of the little finger. He can then walk along the object using his hand to maintain contact and detect information (Figure 6–12).

FIGURE 6–12. Trailing.

Integrating Special Services

It is highly desirable that the regular classroom teacher be aware of the nature of training provided by special education personnel so that she can reinforce concepts and specific techniques being taught. The teacher is generally able to observe the child in a variety of settings, under a variety of conditions, and at different times of the day, as well as being able to provide information to special education personnel concerning the transfer and maintenance of a desired concept or skill. Often a student may be able to demonstrate efficiency with a particular skill when working with the resource or itinerant teacher but be unable to transfer this skill when he returns to his classroom.

The teacher should be as specific as possible when giving directions to the student. For example, do not say to the child, "Go down to Mr. Jones's office, which is about halfway down corridor number three." Instead, provide very specific directions such as, "Go to Mr. Jones's office, which is on the right side of corridor number three, two doors past the water fountain." Directions in the classroom should also be specific. It is not sufficient to say, "Your science project is on the shelf in the back of the room." Instead, you might say, "Your science project is on the shelf in the back of the room, three feet to the left of the sink, at the back of the shelf."

All the students should be acquainted with the proper procedures used in serving as a sighted guide. The resource or itinerant teacher or orientation and mobility specialist may want to attend or actually conduct this type of brief in-service session. The students may want to wear blindfolds to gain a better understanding of traveling without sight. Some caution should be exercised here so that the students do not develop a pitying attitude but rather an objective understanding of travel techniques used by the visually impaired.

Alternative Teaching Strategies and Adaptations

It is generally not necessary for the regular classroom teacher to significantly change teaching strategies to accommodate a visually impaired student. However, it may be helpful to consider a few suggestions that have been found to be effective.

Concrete Materials. Whenever possible, instruction should be initiated at a concrete level. It should start with concrete materials, moving more to the abstract as the student develops the concept. The use of manipulative, tangible, or auditory materials is preferred to totally verbal instructions or lessons. "Hands-on" learning should be em-

phasized as much as possible, and the student may need repeated contact with the objects. Although a model of an object may be necessary, the real object or situation is much preferred. For example, if a science lesson is concerned with simple pulleys, an actual pulley should be provided if possible. The resource or itinerant teacher is a valuable asset in this area and may be able to assist in obtaining the actual object or may make a model similar to the one needed.

Physical Education. Lessons in physical education or gross motor activities should be demonstrated by physically moving the student through the activity. For example, if a particular tumbling routine is being taught, the instructor may want to actually move the student through the correct movements rather than merely explain the process. (See chapter 7 for a discussion of specific techniques for modifying physical education.)

"Hands-on" Learning. "Learning by doing" and "teaching by unifying experiences" are certainly not new concepts to regular classroom teachers. These concepts, however, are particularly important to the student with impaired vision because he or she may not have the same experiential background as other students of the same age. Whenever possible, the student with low vision should be allowed to actually experience physical exploration rather than having the process explained verbally. Closely related is the need to unify or integrate experiences and concepts as often as possible. A young child may not be able to relate one isolated concept to another because of a lack of any previous experience with the particular concept.

Chalkboard. When writing on the chalkboard, the teacher should be certain to explain verbally the concept or actual writing being presented. In general, any highly visual instructions or lessons should be supplemented with verbal explanation. This can become routine with a little effort and practice. Some teachers have found it helpful to give the visually impaired student a copy of the notes written on the board. To be certain that the best possible dark-light contrast is provided, be certain the chalkboard is as clean as possible. Allow the low-vision student to move as close to the chalkboard as necessary to see it comfortably.

Fatigue. The student who has low vision may become fatigued if tasks involving close visual examination are required for long periods of time. It may be helpful to vary activities as much as possible, as by alternating listening activities, close visual activities, and motor activities. The student should be encouraged whenever possible to take short breaks from activities requiring prolonged periods of visual work.

Media. If a filmstrip being used has subtitles, ask another student to read the titles aloud to the entire class. When a film is used, another student may summarize the key visual concepts or very briefly provide a running visual narrative.

Extra Time. The student with low vision may need extra time to complete assignments and examinations. Allowing time-and-a-half is usually adequate. The work may be completed in the resource room or library or at home. If the student understands the concepts being presented, it may be a good idea to shorten the assignments.

Tactile Activities. For the approximately 20% of visually impaired students who are blind, art activities should emphasize the tactile sense. Use activities such as clay modeling, finger painting, weaving, paper sculpture, and collage whenever possible. It is important that the student have the experience of carrying out the process involved in an art project; the end product should be deemphasized. By completing the process, in whatever medium, the student can achieve the same objectives as peers.

Field Trips. When going on a field trip to a museum or other exhibit, you may want to inform the staff that one of your students is visually impaired. Often they will allow the visually impaired student to go beyond museum barriers to tactilely examine some of the exhibits.

Note Taking. At the secondary level, note taking and submitting assignments are often course requirements. Visually impaired students naturally should meet these requirements, but the way they do so may be different. Visually impaired students may use a slate and stylus, braillewriter, cassette tape player, or, if they have low vision, a pen. After recording the lecture, they may transcribe their notes into braille and finally type them to be handed in to the teacher. Some teachers allow the student to provide a modified recording of their notes.

Raising Hands. If the students are expected to raise their hands to gain recognition or respond, the visually impaired student should be expected to do the same. Since the visually impaired student may not be able to see classmates raising their hands to respond, the teacher may need to provide specific instructions on hand-raising procedures.

Test Taking. Testing procedures may have to be modified for the visually impaired. Reading braille or large type takes considerably longer than reading standard print, and it may be necessary either to extend the amount of time for completion of the test or to reduce the number of test items. The student should not be penalized if he cannot finish the test because of the tools he is using. Of course, this modification depends on whether the purpose of the test is speed or power; if the purpose is speed, the visually impaired student may have considerable difficulty. The administration of the test may also have to be modified; for example, it may be necessary to (1) administer the test orally, (2) tape the test in advance and have the student record or type his answers, or (3) send the test home with the student and have the parent read the test while the student types or braillewrites his answers. If the examination is to be taped, the reader should state the total number and type of questions, the value assigned to each item, and time limitations. The examination should be read slowly and clearly. Sometimes the student can braillewrite his responses and give them to the resource or itinerant teacher, who in turn writes in the student's responses and returns the test to the regular teacher. Some students require few or no modifications and are able to take the test with the other students. Achievement tests administered at the beginning and end of the school year, because of their relative importance and the amount of time needed to complete them, may have to be administered by the resource or itinerant teacher or an aide. The regular teacher should be certain to consult with the resource or itinerant teacher in advance to consider these and other options for testing.

Knowing Braille. Teachers often express considerable concern when informed that they will have a braille-reading student in their classroom. Actually, it is not necessary for the teacher to learn braille because the resource or itinerant teacher will write or print whatever the student has written directly above the braille dots. As mentioned previously, if the student completes an assignment and turns it in to the regular teacher, the teacher should forward it to the resource or itinerant teacher, who writes in the student's responses and returns it to the regular teacher. At the upper elementary, middle-school, and secondary levels, the student may complete his assignment on a conventional typewriter.

General Considerations

When speaking to the student, a normal-volume voice should be used unless distance warrants otherwise. The visually impaired are often frustrated because most people raise their voices beyond what is necessary. When speaking to the student during class discussion, the teacher should be certain to use the student's name because the student may not know that the teacher is looking at him. The same approach is also helpful when the teacher enters a room: the teacher should address the student by name and identify herself to let him know who had entered.[2] Similarly, if the student enters a room where the teacher is alone, the teacher should indicate her presence either by speaking directly or by some other auditory clue.

If the student drops an object, allow sufficient time for him to recover the item without help. Assistance may be provided, if necessary, in the form of verbal guidance, but the student should be encouraged to pick the item up himself.

When handing the student an object, such as a book, the teacher or other students should lightly touch the student's hand with the object so that the student can know its location. It can be frustrating and embarrassing to grope around in an attempt to locate the object.

Unless the eye specialist has indicated that the student should not use his vision, every

---

[2]Once it becomes clear that a student recognizes the teacher's voice, the teacher should *not* identify himself but simply address the student by name. Visually impaired students may pride themselves on such voice recognition, and teachers should recognize this skill by not continuing the self-identification.

effort must be made to increase the student's visual efficiency. If the visually impaired student has some residual vision, encourage him to use it to the fullest extent possible. It is not unusual for a student's measured visual acuity to remain the same over a period of years while his visual performance actually increases.

There are several misconceptions concerning low-vision students' use of remaining or residual vision. As indicated above, they should be encouraged to use their vision—using it to the fullest will *not* cause it to decrease. Holding a book close to the eyes or reading in dim light will not further damage their eyesight. In fact, some students may require dim light to read more comfortably. Be certain to consult with the resource or itinerant teacher for further information concerning reading, postural, and lighting requirements.

Somewhat related to this matter is the use of low-vision or optical aids (such as magnifiers and special glasses). Students who use these aids should be encouraged to use them whenever appropriate. The regular classroom teacher should observe whether the device seems to be helpful, how often it is used, and under what conditions it is beneficial. Frequent visual fatigue may be an indication of the need for larger-print materials or reevaluation of the efficiency of the visual aid being used. Generally, the length of time a student can use special aids can be determined only after careful observation in the classroom. Some students may perform well during a low-vision examination but tire in the classroom after several hours of close visual work. Naturally, this information should be shared with the resource or itinerant teacher, who in turn may share this information with the student's physician or low-vision-aids specialist.

Students with impaired vision often develop poor postural habits. This may result from poor muscle tone, the student's lack of knowledge about preferred head or shoulder position, or continual close examination of printed material. Some system of gentle reminders should be established to assist the student in developing better postural habits. Students who are partially sighted may spend a great deal of time bent over with their head only a few inches from their desk. This position can obviously result in poor posture and considerable fatigue. The student should be provided with some means of raising the book to a comfortable reading position. An easel or bookrest enables the student to rest on his forearms while leaning forward only a few inches. The resource or itinerant teacher can provide specific suggestions concerning postural training and adaptation for reading efficiency and comfort.

Established standards for grading or discipline should not be altered for the visually impaired student. When an assignment has been given or a classroom rule established, the visually impaired student should be expected to adhere to the same procedures as the other students. If the teacher employs a double standard, one for the class and another for the visually impaired student, the other students will be quick to recognize the difference and may resent the visually impaired student. This resentment may have an adverse effect on their interpersonal relationships; the other students may identify the visually impaired student as the "teacher's pet" and subsequently reject him.

The student with impaired vision may not be able to see the teacher's facial expressions when he has completed an assigned task successfully or a look of displeasure when he has not. Physical contact, verbal feedback, or a pat on the back or a touch on the arm may be necessary. Of course, the teacher should praise the student only when the job has been well done, not just because it was done by a visually impaired student.

A "buddy" may be assigned by the teacher to assist the visually impaired student with, for example, highly visual assignments, orientation to a new school building, physical education activities, and fire drills. The use of a "buddy system" is a desirable approach to peer teaching or assistance regardless of whether there is a disabled student in the classroom.

Students with impaired vision often demonstrate unusual mannerisms, such as rocking, head movements, eye pressing, or hand waving. These mannerisms tend to occur when the student is tense or nervous or listening intently. Although the student is usually unaware of these unusual behaviors, they tend to make the student look very different to other students, and efforts should be made to discourage their occurrence. A systematic plan worked out jointly with the resource or itinerant teacher should be used to discourage these behaviors.

The teacher should watch for gaps in the information of the visually impaired student. These gaps may become evident when the teacher is presenting new information and everything seems to be going well until at some point the visually impaired student seems to be puzzled or confused. As the teacher attempts to clarify the problem, it becomes apparent that the information being presented has no meaning to the visually impaired student. Further questioning may reveal that there is a gap in the student's experiential or conceptual background of the particular subject or topic being presented. As indicated previously, concept formation is a significant problem for the visually impaired, and every effort should be made to bridge these gaps with a sequentially planned program. It is best not to assume that the student has the same reference points and experiential background as his sighted classmates. This problem is not unique to the visually impaired but has been frequently observed with hearing impaired students and other students whose information background may be delayed or different.

The resource or itinerant teacher can be of great assistance in providing the needed compensatory skills in this area.

The regular teacher should reinforce concepts taught by the resource or itinerant teacher, orientation and mobility specialist, or any other personnel working with the student. Communication among disciplines is essential if the needed transfer is to occur in every possible situation. One individual in the school environment may be emphasizing particular skills (such as using a magnification device, traveling independently, or typing), and another, being unaware of these efforts, misses the opportunity to reinforce and ensure transfer and maintenance. The importance of close communication with the parents of the visually impaired student cannot be overemphasized. Every effort should be made to work cooperatively with the parents to obtain information about the student and to work in concert with the family.

The needs for independence, freedom of movement, and play are as important for the student with impaired vision as for his sighted classmates. More than 100 years ago, Samuel Gridley Howe, a noted educator of the visually impaired, offered the following general rules in working with these children (quoted in Buell, 1950):

Never check the actions of the child; follow him, and watch him to prevent any serious accidents, but do not interfere unnecessarily; do not even remove obstacles which he would learn to avoid by tumbling over them a few times. Teach him to jump rope, to swing weights, to raise his body by his arms, and to mingle, as far as possible, in the rough sports of the older boys. Do not be apprehensive of his safety. If you should see him clambering in the branches of a tree be assured he is less likely to fall than if he had perfect vision. Do not too much regard bumps on the forehead, rough scratches, or bloody noses; even these may have their good influences. At the worst, they affect only the bark, and do not injure the system like the rust of inaction.

It is quite natural for a teacher who has not had previous experience with the visually impaired or with any handicapped students to be somewhat overprotective and to be concerned that these students might injure themselves on playground equipment or in traveling around the school building. However, every effort should be made *not* to underestimate their capabilities. The teacher's responsibility to the student with impaired vision is the same as for other students—to assist him in developing socially, emotionally, physically, morally, and intellectually.

SPECIALIZED INSTRUCTION AND ASSISTANCE FROM RESOURCE OR ITINERANT TEACHERS

The amount and nature of specialized assistance from special educators varies from school district to school district and at times within a single district. The exact nature of assistance from special education resource or itinerant personnel depends on the following factors:

1. Geographic distance to be traveled between schools. Some teachers are responsible for only one school, whereas others may have responsibilities extending to two or three schools. In some rural areas the resource or itinerant teacher may travel to several communities.
2. Number of students and teachers to be served.
3. Age of students; generally, the younger the student, the more need for direct service.
4. The number of braille readers and print readers. This can vary extensively; generally, the braille-reading student requires considerably more direct services.
5. Availability of orientation and mobility instruction. If an orientation and mobility specialist is not available, the resource or itinerant teacher may be responsible for this instruction.

6. Availability of paid or volunteer braille transcribers, large-print typists, and tape transcribers.
7. Availability of adapted and special materials. In states in which an instructional materials center for the visually impaired is available, the acquisition and distribution of educational materials can be greatly facilitated.

Resource or itinerant teachers generally provide services on the basis of direct or indirect service. Direct service involves working directly with the visually impaired student on a one-to-one basis or in small groups. Indirect service involves working with individuals other than the student, such as the child's teacher, administrators, medical personnel, and parents. The extent to which the resource or itinerant teacher works directly with the student depends on the preceding variables. Most resource or itinerant personnel provide both direct and indirect services.

Although it is sometimes difficult to clearly establish that one type of service is direct and another indirect, the following discussion of specific responsibilities is based on these categories.

Direct Service to Students

Additional compensatory skills, such as listening skills, use of the stylus and slate, and the braillewriter are also taught by the special education specialist. If academic lags are *directly attributable* to the vision deficit, these are remediated by special education personnel. Additional compensatory skills are also taught by special education persons.

Specialized Instruction in Reading. The resource or itinerant teacher provides the needed instruction in braille reading and braillewriting, the use of slate and stylus, and reading devices like Optacon or the Kurzweil Reading Machine. The amount of time required for instruction in these special skills depends on the age of the student. More time is required for a younger braille-reading student because he is developing these specialized skills during his elementary school years, whereas the student at the secondary level may have already developed these skills. Braille instruction should be provided on a daily basis for the first three years of the student's education or until he develops the necessary competency. After the student is relatively proficient at braille reading and braillewriting, it may not be necessary for the resource or itinerant teacher to work with the student on a daily basis.

If a student is a print reader, the amount of instruction is usually not as great as for a braillereader. However, if the student uses low-vision aids (magnification devices or special reading machines), it may be necessary to provide specific instruction in their use.

Instruction in Listening Skills. It has been estimated that nearly one-half of our time in communication is spent in listening activities and that approximately two-thirds of a student's school day is spent in activities related to listening. Since listening is one of the most significant avenues of learning for the visually impaired student, he must rely on the auditory channel more than the sighted classmates. As a result, systematic instruction in listening activities must be provided and incorporated into regular classroom instruction as much as possible. Instruction in listening should include a variety of listening situations, such as environmental situations, formal presentations, informal conversations, and audio reading of talking books and tape-recorded materials.

Instruction in Techniques of Daily Living. Functioning effectively as a responsible and contributing member of society requires more than just being able to complete required academic tasks such as reading and writing. Often a visually impaired individual does not know how to carry out all the activities of independent living, such as personal grooming, housecleaning, cooking and serving food, and home repair. These specific activities of daily living must be part of the visually impaired student's school curriculum. Many of these activities could be provided in a home economics course at the secondary level, but often the home economics teacher is not familiar with the ways in which these activities should be modified or adapted or with the special equipment available. Often these techniques are taught after school, in the evening, or in Saturday programs, but in the event they are not offered at these times, they may have to be provided during school hours by the resource or itinerant teacher independently or in cooperation with others.

Instruction in Orientation and Mobility. The extent to which the resource or itinerant teacher is responsible for direct instruction in orientation and mobility depends on whether an orientation and mobility specialist is available and whether the teacher is also certified as an orientation and mobility specialist. If available, the specialist is responsible for formal instruction; if not, the resource or itinerant teacher may assume some of this responsibility.

In addition, the resource or itinerant teacher is responsible for familiarizing or orienting the student to a new classroom or school building and supplementing the instruction of the orientation and mobility specialist. Throughout the student's education program, orientation and mobility training should be systematically provided.

Student and Parent Counseling. Many resource or itinerant teachers assume responsibility for student and parent counseling and for seeking appropriate professional counseling when needed. These teachers may work with the student for several years, whereas the student's regular teachers may be in close contact with the student for only one year. Resource and itinerant teachers are acquainted with the unique problems imposed by impaired vision and their relationship to adjustment and social and emotional growth. They may also be in the best position to discuss personal problems, interests, and projected vocational plans.

Although the primary responsibility for reporting student progress rests with the regular classroom teacher, the resource or itinerant teacher should attend parent-teacher conferences to report the student's progress in special areas. Often it is necessary for the resource or itinerant teacher to meet separately with the student's parents to interpret special programming efforts or other special problems that may be related to the student's visual impairment.

Instruction in the Use of Adapted or Special Equipment and Aids. Specialized instruction in the use of equipment and aids like tape recorders, tape players, speech compressors, Optacon, talking calculators, closed-circuit television, and talking-book machines is necessary for the visually impaired. Instruction in the use of special mathematical computation devices like the abacus and talking calculator and special maps is required. Generally, instruction in the use of this equipment is introduced as the need arises rather than systematically scheduled as with braille instruction.

Development of Visual Efficiency. Through systematic instruction the visual efficiency of a low-vision student can be increased. Special techniques and materials to determine the amount of visual efficiency and specific techniques to increase visual ability are available. Constant visual stimulation provided through a sequentially planned program can increase the visual efficiency of many students. This instruction should be provided by the resource or itinerant teacher on a routine basis. The resource or itinerant teacher may also observe the student in the regular classroom to determine if the student is using his vision as much as possible.

Instruction in Writing. Instruction in handwriting for a partially seeing student should be initiated at the same time as it is introduced to his sighted classmates. It may be necessary, however, for the resource or itinerant teacher to provide supplemental assistance in this area. The braille-reading student must gain proficiency at handwriting so that he can sign his own name and make brief notations. Special handwriting aids and instruction are necessary to achieve this skill.

Typing—with an electric typewriter if available—is routinely taught to visually impaired students. Since their handwriting may be difficult to read and braille writing can be read only by a few individuals, typing can be a boost to their written communication skills. Instruction is generally initiated at about the fourth-grade level. Often, typing is taught to the student along with spelling assignments because there is considerable repetition in both subject areas. As the student increases his typing proficiency, he can complete more and more assignments with the aid of the typewriter. The adapted approach to instruction is known as "touch typing" and employs a special system that does not require vision. Naturally, accuracy is emphasized rather than speed, since it is difficult for the student to check his work. Instruction in this area is usually continuous throughout the student's upper elementary and secondary school years.

Supplementary or Introductory Instructions. Because it may take longer for the student to complete an assignment or because the assignment may be highly visual, it is often necessary for the resource or itinerant teacher to supplement the instruction of the regular classroom teacher. For example, if the process of "carrying" in mathematical addition is being introduced, the resource or itinerant teacher may want to introduce the use of a special mathematics aid that would be of assistance or may want to supplement the regular classroom teacher's instruction by using a special "mental mathematics" technique.

Often the resource or itinerant teacher may want to introduce a particular concept before its introduction in the regular classroom. For example, a unit on the solar system may have considerably more meaning to the visually impaired student if the resource or itinerant teacher provides a model of the solar system and introduces the unit to the student first. In physical education it is often necessary to orient the student to special equipment, games, and activities before the physical education period so that the student acquires a basic understanding of the concept and so that the physical education instructor does not have to take a disproportionate amount of time to introduce the concept to the class.

Indirect Services

Services other than those that involve face-to-face contact with the student are considered indirect services. As mentioned previously, a number of variables determine the nature and extent of indirect services provided. The following discussion provides an overview of indirect services that might be provided by special education personnel.

Preparation of Materials. If the needed educational material is not available from any agency in the desired format and all sources have been queried, it may be necessary to have a transcriber-reproducer prepare the material. The resource or itinerant teacher serves as the liaison between the classroom teacher and the transcriber-reproducer to ensure that the material is in the needed format and that it is completed in sufficient time.

Many day-to-day materials such as teacher-made tests, work sheets, and special

projects obviously would not be available from outside agencies; therefore, it would be the responsibility of the resource or itinerant teacher to have these materials prepared or prepare them herself. The type of material needed may be quite varied, ranging from a teacher-made mathematics test to a geologic-survey map of the country.

Often it is not practical or possible to have a text brailled on relatively short notice or for use only once. In this event, the resource or itinerant teacher can assist in arranging for the material to be read aloud by another person. The use of "readers" is a technique used frequently for secondary school students, and if used properly, it can be a tremendous advantage to the visually impaired student.

Acquisition of Materials. The acquisition of educational materials such as braille or enlarged type texts, tapes, and tangible apparatus is one of the primary responsibilities of the resource or itinerant teacher. These materials must duplicate the content of the materials being used by the other students and must be obtained in the shortest possible time. There are several well-established procedures used by the resource or itinerant teacher to obtain the needed material in the needed format without duplication of efforts. These procedures involve checking national and state agencies and volunteer groups before the actual transcription or production of the desired material.

Conducting In-Service Sessions. The resource or itinerant teacher may be responsible for the in-service education of regular teachers and administrators. She may be expected to acquaint a building staff with the rationale underlying integrated placement of the visually impaired student if the staff has not had previous experience with these students. The nature of the in-service education may be quite general and relate only to the philosophy of integrated education. In other instances it may be directed at a small group of teachers who will have the student in their classes and would specifically relate to techniques for modifying and adapting materials or teaching strategies.

The resource or itinerant teacher may conduct short in-service sessions with a group of students to acquaint them with the nature of impaired vision to ready them for a visually impaired classmate. At other times, student in-service sessions may relate to the special materials and techniques that are to be used.

Another in-service role often assumed by the resource or itinerant teacher is to provide select journal articles, readings, or films for regular classroom teachers. These readings or materials are directed at providing the needed competencies to work more effectively with the visually impaired student.

Assuming Responsibility for Coordination of Outside Services. The resource or itinerant teacher often assumes responsibility for providing and coordinating many other services needed in addition to classroom activities. The resource or itinerant teacher may coordinate orientation and mobility services or therapeutic recreation and leisure activities. She may also assist in planning and implementing work-study or vocational education programs. In general, the resource or itinerant teacher's role is one of student advocacy—providing all needed services and programs necessary for the student's complete educational and social development.

Assisting in Adapting or Modifying Activities. The resource or itinerant teacher may assist the physical education, art, music, home economics, or industrial arts teacher in adapting or modifying a particular lesson or activity. If the resource or itinerant teacher has established a routine and ongoing communication system with all teachers, it is relatively easy to anticipate an activity that may need modification or adaptation. The resource or itinerant teacher may offer specific suggestions on how to change the activity in such a way that the visually impaired student can meet the objective of the lesson. Sometimes it is desirable for the resource or itinerant teacher to actually attend the activity to assist the student or his teacher.

Interpreting Medical Information. Often, the resource or itinerant teacher is expected to serve as a liaison between medical personnel and the regular classroom teachers. She may be asked to interpret medical reports and to explain the nature of the eye condition and the limitations imposed by it. In addition, the resource or itinerant teacher must share information concerning seating arrangements, lighting requirements, and levels of visual expectation for the partially seeing student. She may also be asked to evaluate the suitability of materials to be used, particularly in the areas of clarity of pictures, type size, spacing, and margins.

In addition to the specific types of indirect services already mentioned, there is, of course, the ongoing role of consultation with the regular classroom teacher. This includes monitoring the progress of the student with visual impairments, additional vision assessments that may indicate a change in the type of aids used, modifications in the student's program and provision of general support to the regular classroom teacher.

SUMMARY

Students with impaired vision were the "original" mainstreamed students; they were the pioneers who demonstrated that students with handicaps/disabilities can receive their education along with nonhandicapped students. This chapter highlights the degree to which educational content for the visually impaired can remain essentially the same as for all other students. What is required are modifications and adaptations in the classroom environment, and in the way materials are presented.

At an early age, a blind child must learn braille, along with certain compensatory skills, but these are usually taught by special education personnel. In this chapter we have provided detailed suggestions for modifications and adaptations that may be made by the classroom teacher, but would caution that care must be exercised so that the visually impaired student does not become the "teacher's pet." When this happens, due to attempts to provide very special attention, the purpose of an integrated program is defeated. Like the hearing impaired, the student with visual impairments must be prepared to live in a world where most others do not have his or her handicap/disability.

In many respects, the visually impaired student is easier to teach in the regular classroom than any other type of handicapped student, for she is likely to do well academically and may cause few if any management problems with regard to behavior. On the other hand, there are indications that educators in the past have focused too much on academic behavior to the detriment of teaching techniques of daily living; the regular classroom teacher, along with the parents, must play a major role in this area. The visually impaired student must deliberately be treated more like a normal person and less like a handicapped one in all possible classroom interactions. This may be the major challenge to the regular classroom teacher when planning the best possible program for the visually impaired.

Teaching Students Who Are Orthopedically or Health Impaired

ORTHOPEDIC IMPAIRMENTS

HEALTH IMPAIRMENTS

ADAPTING PHYSICAL EDUCATION

PURPOSE, CARE, AND MAINTENANCE OF BRACES, CRUTCHES, AND WHEELCHAIRS

SPECIAL EQUIPMENT

- [ ] What educational modifications are necessary for a student with an amputation?
- [ ] What are the duties and responsibilities of occupational and physical therapists?
- [ ] Should students with asthma be allowed to participate in physical education?
- [ ] What should the teacher do if a student has a grand mal seizure or an insulin reaction?
- [ ] What is the relationship between strep throat and heart conditions?
- [ ] Are the educational rights of students with AIDS "protected" in any manner by PL 94-142?
- [ ] What are some ways that a nonverbal or seriously physically disabled student can communicate with others?

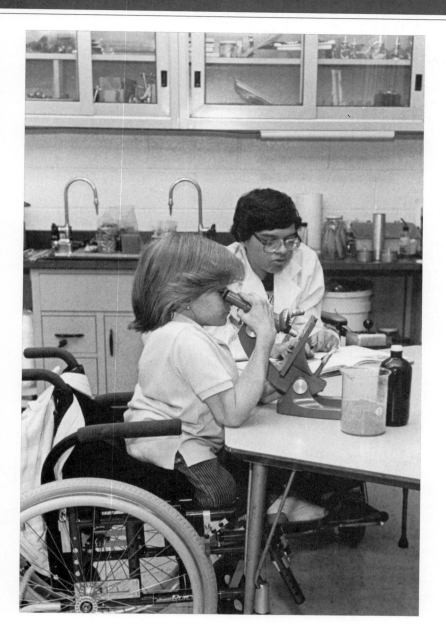

Students with disabilities included in the general term *physically impaired* may have no outward physical indicators. That is, by visual observation, there may be no signs to tell the teacher this student might require classroom modification. *Physically disabled* makes some think first of persons in wheelchairs or using crutches or wearing braces. There is, however, another group of students who receive services under the broad category of *physical impairments* that have no easily recognizable handicaps. PL 94-142 divides the extremely heterogeneous group of physically impaired into two broad categories: *orthopedically impaired* and *other health impaired.* We will use the same terminology.

This chapter is divided into five major sections. The first is concerned with orthopedic impairments, which are related primarily to disorders of the joints, skeleton, and muscles. The second part reviews the most common health impairments: allergies, asthma, diabetes, heart disorders, hemophilia, sickle-cell anemia, cystic fibrosis, and acquired immune deficiency syndrome (AIDS). The final sections provide information concerning general modification and adaptations for both orthopedically impaired and health impaired students.

As mentioned above, this is one of the most heterogeneous categories in special education. Students grouped in this broad category range from the cerebral palsied (a condition commonly associated with secondary or multiply handicapping conditions) to students with asthma, handicapped as a result of an accident, or born without a limb. One student may have limited use of his arms but have good use of his legs, another may have use of all extremities but have considerable difficulty breathing, and another may be generally weak because of a progressive condition. One may be completely mobile in the classroom, another mobile with the use of crutches, and still another con-

fined to a wheelchair. In the following sections a number of suggestions are made concerning specific conditions. There are, however, some general areas that should first be considered.

The primary focus of programming for students with orthopedic and health impairments is the modification and, as much as possible, elimination of physical barriers. The phrase "least restrictive environment" in PL 94-142 is primarily concerned with the appropriate placement of handicapped students. This term has special meaning when applied to students with orthopedic and health impairments. The least restrictive environment for these students involves appropriate academic placement but means additionally that the physical environment of the building and classroom should be given careful consideration.

Many important variables must be considered when educators are faced with placement decisions for these students. Several interrelated factors should be given serious consideration, however, before such students are placed in the regular classroom. Of course, the willingness and ability of the regular classroom teacher to accept and make changes for these students are of the utmost concern. The availability of support and ancillary personnel (resource teachers and therapists) is another factor to be considered. If the student needs daily therapy and must be bused to receive such service, provision must be made. Support from and a close working relationship with parents are essential elements for the success of a mainstreaming program. The degree of acceptance and positive interaction with nonhandicapped classmates is also very important. For a complete discussion of methods and techniques to enhance understanding and interaction, see chapter 4. Specific student variables that should be considered are (1) modes of communication, (2) stamina level, (3) intellectual ability, (4) achievement level, (5) personality, (6) relative independence in ambulation and mobility, (7) ability to profit from large-group instruction, and (8) the student's personal interest, motivation, and commitment to being served in a regular classroom setting. These variables are not intended to be used as criteria for placement or success in a regular classroom but are provided as general guidelines for professionals in making placement decisions.

If it is recommended that the student be placed in a regular classroom, the resource or itinerant teacher begins specific planning to determine the best possible school and teachers and arranges for transportation and therapeutic services.

The mere presence or placement of a handicapped student in the classroom and accomplishment of assigned academic tasks may represent only a small part of the individual's total educational need. Independent ambulation is an important factor in the student's total development, possibly more important to the student than many of the academic challenges presented in the classroom. Movement is essential not only for the obvious reasons of maintaining and improving motor function but also for facilitation of important psychosocial interactions. The teacher should be aware of the effects that the lack of movement has on the student and his interaction with peers. The school and classroom should be arranged to enable student movement to all areas. Independent ambulation must be given priority if the student is to be allowed an equal opportunity to grow socially, educationally, and emotionally.

Because of the diversity of problems presented by this population, a complete continuum of educational services must be offered, ranging from full-time special class placement for the multiply handicapped or severely physically disabled to full-time regular class placement for those able to function and achieve in that environment. Children temporarily disabled by infectious diseases or accidents may receive hospital or homebound instruction.

The primary goal or direction of educational services should be the inclusion of these students in regular classrooms wherever possible. Today it is possible for more children to be educated in regular classes than in years past because of the reduction of architectural barriers, as required by the Rehabilitation Act of 1973 (Section 504). School buildings built around the turn of the century were typically multilevel buildings with many stairs and second-story entrances, whereas today's schools are generally one-level structures, much more accessible or adaptable for the student with limited mobility. However, even more modern schools often require modifications. Some modifications include bathroom stalls made wider and deeper, sinks and water fountains lowered to enable individuals in wheelchairs to use them, classroom doors widened to accommodate wheelchairs, and blackboards lowered and hinged to allow someone in a wheelchair to write comfortably.

There are many variables contributing to the number of physically disabled students who attend regular classes. Advanced medical and technological procedures may lessen the degree of disability. For example, children born with congenital heart defects may have these corrected surgically and live without serious restrictions. This was not possible in the past. Similarly, changes in treatment procedures for conditions such as asthma, diabetes, and heart defects allow students more complete participation in normal activities. Students may be fitted with artificial limbs at an early age; congenital defects such as clubfoot may be corrected earlier, also allowing fuller participation in nearly all endeavors.

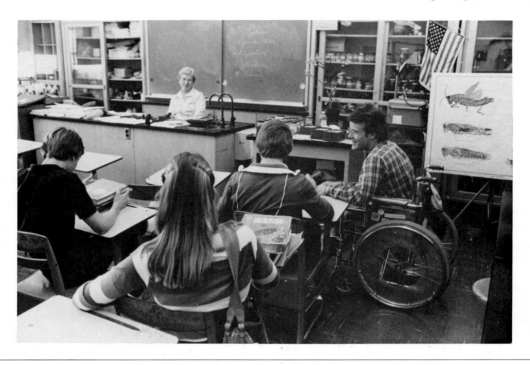

Advanced science is no problem for these students.

The information on disabilities and related adaptations that follows is presented on the basis of medically derived or defined conditions. Although there are disadvantages to discussing a condition on the basis of medical diagnosis rather than educational implications, it is hoped that through this approach, teachers will seek specific suggestions concerning educational procedures on the basis of a particular disability. For example, if a student has epilepsy, teachers are encouraged to seek information concerning the nature of the condition, the treatment procedures, educational implications, and the unique management techniques that must be employed.

More than two hundred possible conditions are included in this category; however, we discuss here only the conditions most commonly found in regular classrooms. This chapter is presented in a different format from other chapters in that educational implications are summarized after the discussion of each condition rather than at the end of the chapter.

ORTHOPEDIC IMPAIRMENTS

This section is concerned with the most commonly found serious orthopedic impairments. The conditions discussed in the following sections are (1) amputation, (2) arthritis, (3) cerebral palsy, (4) spina bifida, (5) muscular dystrophy, (6) scoliosis, (7) hip disorders, and (8) osteogenesis imperfecta. In each case, following a brief description of the nature of the condition, an overview of the treatment procedures and educational implications is provided.

Amputation

Nature of Condition. A missing limb may be a congenital condition, or the limb may have been amputated as a result of trauma, disease, or infection. In nearly all instances the student will have been fitted with an artificial arm or leg (prosthesis). Generally the student with a congenital condition is fitted with the prosthesis very early and will have adapted to it by the time he begins school. The prosthesis may be made of wood, metal, or plastic. Plastic materials are being used more commonly today because of their light weight; this factor may influence the student's functioning.

Educational Implications. Students with a prosthesis are usually able to function at nearly normal capacity and require very little educational modification. The extent of modification, however, depends on the age of the student, the site of the amputation (the higher on the extremity, the more severe), and the child's adjustment to the disability.

The regular classroom teacher should be aware of several factors to ensure the best educational programming. The following suggestions should be considered:

1. Because of growth, a student's prosthesis rarely fits for more than a year. As a result, the teacher must be certain the student is using the prosthesis effectively and that it fits properly. The student visits the prosthetist for routine adjustments and fitting.
2. The teacher should have general information, particularly for a younger student, concerning the basic mechanics, proper fitting, and maintenance of the prosthesis. This information may be obtained from the student, the student's parents, the resource or itinerant teacher, or a prosthetist. If the student feels comfortable in discussing his prosthesis, it would be of great social and psychological value for him to explain its function to the entire class. Of course, this depends on the age of the other students and the extent to which the student has adjusted to the amputation.
3. The height of the student's working surface (such as a desk or table for a student with an upper extremity prosthesis) should be adjusted so that it does not interfere with the function of the prosthesis. With young children a rim around the table or desk top may be helpful to prevent pencils or crayons from rolling off the working surface.
4. Students with a lower extremity prosthesis may need extra time to get to their classes and, if traveling a long distance or over a rough terrain, may need a wheelchair.
5. Proper exercise is very important for the child, particularly in the joints around the amputation. Physical education activities and games may be adapted or individualized to ensure maximum fitness and exercise. One commonly reads or hears about individuals with amputations who not only participate but excel in competitive athletic events. Many individuals with lower extremity amputations participate and compete successfully in activities such as bowling, snow skiing and waterskiing, golf, and even football.
6. Postural habits must be carefully observed to ensure that the student does not develop spinal curvatures such as scoliosis, a lateral curvature of the spine resulting in a C-shaped curve. The student may develop habits such as using only one side of his body, causing postural problems. Postural problems can limit his body mechanics and general functioning. If the student has a lower extremity amputation, the teacher must

observe to see that unusual gait or ambulation problems do not develop.

7. Proper hygienic principles must be exercised in the care of the stump. It should be kept clean and allowed to air for brief periods. Although these practices are typically conducted at home, the teacher should be aware of this need.

8. Some students with amputations may use modified or adapted equipment such as pencil holders, page turners, or other reading and writing aids. Many of these materials are available from commercial sources; others may be easily adapted or made by the teacher. The resource or itinerant teacher may be of assistance in modifying materials and equipment.

9. Curricular modifications may also be necessary. For example, typing may be taught using a one-handed method with very little modification. In general, typing may be a preferred means of communication for the student with an amputation because it may save time and requires less energy. The resource or itinerant teacher should have information concerning this kind of material. The occupational therapist is a valuable resource person and should be consulted when questions arise. The occupational therapist can assist in modifying equipment and materials and can plan and initiate activites that facilitate maximum functioning for the student. Amputations in children are generally not as troublesome as they are in adults because children are more tolerant and adaptable. They generally can participate in regular classrooms very successfully with only minor modifications and adaptations.

Arthritis

Nature of Condition. Although arthritis is a condition that primarily occurs in adults, it can begin at any age. The most common form of arthritis in students is called *juvenile rheumatoid arthritis.* It may have a very sudden onset, or it may be a slow, gradual disease, with quite variable effects and complications. In some instances it may last only a few weeks or months and not seriously limit the student. In other cases it may be a chronic condition that continues throughout the student's life, becoming worse as time goes on. Rheumatoid arthritis attacks the joints of the body and may involve many organs, such as the heart, liver, and spleen. There may be a skin rash, inflammation of the eyes, retardation of growth, and swelling and pain in the fingers, wrists, elbows, knees, hips, and feet. As the disease progresses, the joints may stiffen, making movement very difficult and painful. *Osteoarthritis,* or the wear-and-tear type of arthritis, is generally confined to one joint and does not affect the whole body.

Treatment Procedures. There are no cures for rheumatoid arthritis, only ways to control the inflammation and secondary effects. The majority of students with this condition will be free of active disease after a period of about 10 years. The major aim of treatment is to allow the student to live as normally as possible. Many times students with arthritis become "care-cripples." In other words, they are overprotected and not allowed to participate fully in the activities of home or school. Juvenile arthritis is self-limiting, and the student ordinarily uses good sense in determining whether he should participate in an activity.

Treatment procedures are generally highly individualized because no two cases are exactly alike. Because of the variance among patients and their individual response to drugs, the drugs prescribed by the physician may be different in each case. Generally, aspirin is the single most effective drug used in the treatment of arthritis because it reduces pain and inflammation of the joints and is among the safest drugs on the market. Usually, large amounts are prescribed on a routine basis, and dosage must be continued even after the swelling and pain have subsided. Special exercises may be prescribed, involving putting the joints through a full range of motion to prevent joint deformity and loss of strength in the muscles. Heat treatments may also be prescribed to enable joints to move more smoothly and with less pain. Heat treatments take a variety of forms and may be carried out at home or in a clinic. Surgical procedures are also used to prevent and correct deformity caused by this disease. For some children, splints, braces, or plaster casts are prescribed to subdue inflammation and protect the joint or joints from becoming frozen.

Educational Implications. The educational modifications necessary for the student with juvenile arthritis depend on his age, severity of condition, independent travel ability, and range of motion in the arms, hands, and fingers. This student probably does not need special curricular methods or materials in the academic areas. If the joints in the upper extremities are severely involved, however, the student may need writing aids, adapted paper, or special pencils. The Arthritis Foundation publishes an illustrated "Self-Help Manual for Arthritis Patients" that describes aids and devices that may be helpful.[1] It is likely that this student has the most difficulty with walking because the knees, ankles, and hips may be more involved than the upper body, and as he walks he may experience considerable pain. As a result, it may be well to consider somewhat limited movement for many of these students. However, some students may experience increased joint stiffness during prolonged immobility and may need to get up and walk to relieve the discomfort. Some students may need an individualized physical education program or a program carried out by a physical therapist, whereas others may need very little modification in their physical education program. Changes in mood or temperament are common for these students and may be related to the amount of pain. The teacher and school counselor can be very helpful in helping the student cope with the frustration, anger, and pain.

Teachers should watch for any changes in vision, because eye disease is commonly associated with rheumatoid arthritis. Inflammation of the iris (iridocyclitis) is a serious condition and may be found in association with some forms of juvenile rheumatoid arthritis. In particular, pain in the eyes or light sensitivity may indicate the need to be seen by an ophthalmologist. It is generally recommended that the student be checked for changes in vision at least every 6 to 9 months.

There is some evidence that psychological and environmental factors may influence the manifestations of the disease and its ultimate conclusions; however, they are not causes of arthritis (Hanson, 1983). Teachers need not modify academic and social standards but simply be aware of the general emotional climate and its possible effects on the student.

The teacher should be aware of other implications for the arthritic student. For example, the student may miss a considerable amount of school when he has attacks. Faulty posture habits should be avoided, since good body alignment and posture are important in reducing the effects of arthritis. Activities such as extensive and prolonged writing may need to be avoided because they may be painful for the student. It may also be necessary to give the student extra time to get to and from classrooms and extra time for completing assignments.

The student must learn to live with arthritis and accept the limitations imposed by it.

---

[1]Arthritis Foundation, 3400 Peachtree Rd. N.E., Atlanta, GA 30326.

An understanding teacher can do a great deal to assist the student in developing this acceptance.

Cerebral Palsy

Nature of Condition.   Cerebral palsy is not a progressive disease but a group of conditions that may seriously limit motor coordination. Of the serious crippling conditions, cerebral palsy is the most common. Several years ago, polio was the number one crippling condition among children; today, cerebral palsy is more common. Cerebral palsy is most commonly present at birth, but it may be acquired anytime as the result of a head injury or an infectious disease. It is characterized by varying degrees of disturbance of voluntary movements resulting from brain injury. Because of the brain injury, the majority of these students have multiple handicapping conditions, such as mental retardation, hearing impairment, visual difficulties, language disorders, and speech problems. Depending on the severity of this condition some students with cerebral palsy attend special schools or special classes that provide the comprehensive educational and therapeutic services needed. There are, however, a number of students with mild or moderate cerebral palsy who may attend regular classes for part or all of their school day.

The two most common types of cerebral palsy are *spastic* and *athetoid*. Spastic cerebral palsy is characterized by jerky or explosive motions when the student initiates a voluntary movement. For example, in a severe type, if the student is asked to draw a line from one point to another he may demonstrate erratic or jerky movements such as this:

The student with athetosis also has difficulty with voluntary movements, but controlling the movement in the desired direction is an added problem. In other words, this child demonstrates extra or purposeless movements. In drawing a line from one point to another, he may have considerable uncontrolled movement, such as this:

Cerebral palsy and other conditions may be classified on the basis of limb involvement (topographical classification) as follows:

1. *Monoplegia.* One limb
2. *Hemiplegia.* Both limbs on same side of body
3. *Paraplegia.* Lower limbs only
4. *Diplegia.* Major involvement in lower limbs and minor involvement in upper limbs
5. *Triplegia.* Three limbs, usually one upper limb and both lower limbs
6. *Quadraplegia.* All four limbs

This classification is generally specified in the diagnostic information and in the student's school records.

Educational Implications.   The degree of involvement and severity of the condition may vary considerably; therefore a full continuum of educational services is needed. The severity dictates where the student would best be served, but the emphasis should be placed on providing as normal an educational environment as possible. Wherever practicable, students with cerebral palsy should attend regular classes with their nondisabled peers. Classroom modifications vary according to the individual needs of the student. Some need no modifications, whereas others may need some minor or major adjustments.

Often an interdisciplinary approach is required in the care and treatment of the cerebral palsied. It may be necessary for some students to be served on a routine and continued basis by a physical, occupational, or speech therapist or a combination of these. If these therapies are initiated early, they may not be needed as frequently during the upper elementary and secondary school years. Therapy sessions may be attended during the school day or after school hours.

The physical therapist is primarily concerned with the lower extremities and with posture, movements, and the prevention of contractures (permanent muscle shortening because of lack of neurostimulation and muscle use). The physical therapist is trained to evaluate the physical development, ability, and movement of the student. The physical therapist works under the direction of a physician in carrying out a precise program. Nonetheless, it is necessary for the regular classroom teacher to have a basic understanding of treatment procedures so that he or she may reinforce desirable movements and postural habits.

The occupational therapist is primarily concerned with the upper extremities and with activities such as buttoning, tying shoes, eating, and all of the routine activities required in daily living. Many of these routine activities may be seriously limited for the cerebral palsied student because of the lack of muscle coordination. It is important that the regular classroom teacher have information concerning the skills being taught so that she may reinforce them in the classroom. Often, the occupational therapist may assist in modifying and adapting educational materials to be used by the cerebral palsied student. In the past there has often been a distinction between physical and occupational therapists, with the physical therapist concerned with lower extremities and large muscles and the occupational therapist concerned with the upper extremities and small muscles. This role differentiation is not as distinct now, and many therapists share responsibilities or delineate them according to student needs. The services offered by the

speech therapist also need to be reinforced by the teacher to ensure carry over and maintenance of desired speech habits.

Before the student's actual placement in a regular classroom, it is helpful for the regular classroom teacher to obtain as much information as possible about the student from parents, resource and itinerant teachers, and therapists. It is helpful to obtain specific information concerning methods of communication, therapy needs and schedule, reading or writing aids used, ambulation devices used, and any other significant needs. If time permits, actual observation of therapy sessions and a few brief meetings with the student would be most beneficial.

If the student with cerebral palsy is placed in the proper educational program, it should not be necessary to offer the student a curriculum different from that of his or her peers; however, it may be necessary to modify or adapt materials and equipment so that the student may participate more fully in classroom activities. The extent of the necessary modifications varies considerably. For example, some students have limited use of their hands and arms but have no difficulty getting around. As a result of the variance between individuals, it is difficult to offer specific suggestions. The following list of materials and equipment provides examples of ways that modifications may be made:

1. Pencil holders made of clay, Styrofoam balls, or plastic golf balls may be helpful for students with fine-motor coordination difficulties.
2. Adapted typewriters may be useful for students with fine-motor coordination difficulties or students with very weak muscles. Electric typewriters are generally preferred; a keyboard guard placed over the keys may be necessary for some students. A pencil, rather than the fingers, may be used to strike the keys if the condition is very serious.

Hand calculators may be used in arithmetic computation if the student has considerable difficulty writing.

3. Some students may have conditions so severe that communication is seriously limited. These students may have average-to-high intellectual ability but because of poor motor coordination have considerable difficulty with speech. For these students, alternative communication systems may be necessary.

4. Positioning the student so that most of the body is supported may reduce uncoordinated movements, thus allowing him to concentrate on only one or two parts of his body.

5. Page turners are useful for students with limited arm use. The turner may be attached to the head, elbow, or hand. A rubber "thumb" such as those used by office workers may also make page turning easier.

6. Weights (such as a small sandbag or barbells) placed on the wrist or hand can be used to eliminate random or uncontrolled movements. Cursive writing may be easier than manuscript writing for some students with cerebral palsy.

7. Book holders that can be adjusted to any angle may be helpful for some students.

8. The desk or table should be at such a height that the feet firmly touch the floor and forearms rest on the working surface. Occasionally, the trunk of the body may need to be stabilized by straps or a harness arrangement.

9. Paper holders may be necessary for students who have the use of only one arm or very limited use of both arms. A clipboard to hold the paper in position may be fastened to the desk, or a piece of unbleached muslin cloth may be attached to the desk and sprayed with a nonskid fluid. It may be necessary to tape down the paper while the student is writing on it; a large rubber band may also be used to hold the paper down.

10. A lip or rim around the table or desk may prevent pencils and other items from rolling off.

11. Some materials originally designed for use by the blind, such as talking books and cassette recorders, are helpful for students who have difficulty turning pages or balancing a book.

12. Stand-up tables are necessary for many students with cerebral palsy. Since a considerable amount of time is spent sitting, provisions should be made to allow those students to stand for parts of the school day. Standing is often required to prevent muscle contractures, provide proper circulation, and maintain desired postural habits. Since standing unaided may be difficult, a stand-up table may be purchased or built inexpensively to provide the needed support while the student is standing. An individual stand-up table should normally include a tray for a work area approximately two feet square. The table should have a base of the same size so that it does not easily tip over. The height of the table can be changed by raising or lowering the foot platform.

Spina Bifida

Nature of Condition. Spina bifida is a serious birth defect in which the bones of the spine fail to close during the twelfth week of fetal development. As a result, a cyst or sack is present in the area of the lower back when the child is born (Figure 7–1). This protrusion is generally surgically treated during the child's first 24–48 hours of life. The extent of the disability resulting from this condition varies enormously. Some have little or no disability, whereas others have varying degrees of paralysis of the legs and incontinence (lack of bowel and bladder control). In

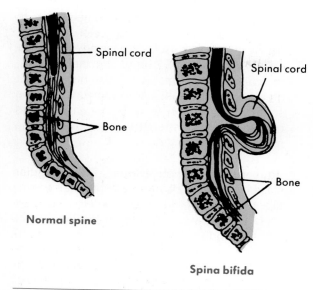

FIGURE 7–1. Spina bifida

needs, but younger children may need some assistance from a classroom aide, volunteer, parent, or resource or itinerant teacher.

Educational Implications. It is important for the teacher to work closely with medical personnel and especially the school nurse to ensure proper health care. The teacher must also maintain a close working relationship with physical and occupational therapists to meet the student's ambulation needs and activities of daily living. Last, but certainly not least, the teacher should discuss the student's special needs and problems with the parents. The teacher should be aware of the symptoms of urinary infection: increased temperature, flushed skin, and excessive perspiration. The parents or the school nurse should be contacted if any of these symptoms occurs. Infections can generally be avoided with proper care, but in the event of infection the student may have to be hospitalized, necessitating absence from school. Frequent urological, neurosurgical, and orthopedic consultations and procedures are also commonly required, necessitating careful planning between parents, resource and itinerant teachers, and regular teachers. A flexible scheduling procedure providing specific times for toileting needs should be implemented.

Teachers should be aware of problems associated with the lack of sensation in the legs. The lack of sensation can lead to skin or pressure sores. The teacher should also be watchful for injuries of which the student may not be aware because of the lack of sensation. Problems imposed by wearing braces or using a wheelchair should also be considered. It may be necessary to reposition the student or ask him to sit up straight during the school day to prevent pressure sores, postural problems, and muscle contractures.

If not handled properly, the psychosocial limitations imposed by this condition can be very serious. This may seem a trivial matter

addition to the degrees of paralysis and incontinence, the child may have impaired autonomic nervous system functioning (absence of perspiration) and absence of sensation below the level of the spinal defect. In some respects this condition is similar to other crippling conditions that cause degrees of paralysis in the legs, but it is complicated by the lack of bowel and bladder control. Because of the deficiency of nerve fibers, the student may not be able to tell when his bladder is full. The bladder may overflow, and the student may not be aware of the situation until he sees the wetness through his outer clothing. There is a threat of infection from residual urine in the bladder, and the student may also have difficulty with bowel control.

Surgical procedures can assist in accommodating this condition, or artificial devices may be worn to collect the urine. The student may also regulate his fluid intake and adhere to a systematic voiding schedule. Generally, the student is able to take care of toileting but is a very real concern expressed by many spina-bifida students. The student may bear the brunt of others' laughter or joking because of odor or accidental urination. The teacher should also be aware that factors such as excitement or spicy foods can cause a problem and should allow the student to leave the classroom suddenly if an "accident" occurs.

The problems imposed by poor ambulation skills must be taken into consideration by therapists and teachers. However, this factor would not be any more significant for the student with spina bifida than for the student with cerebral palsy or any other major orthopedic impairment.

Inasmuch as the student with spina bifida has good use of his upper body, arms, and hands, the educational modifications necessary are minimal. These children can profit from regular classroom attendance and instruction with only minor modifications and adaptations.

Muscular Dystrophy

Nature of Condition. Muscular dystrophy is a progressive condition in which the muscles are replaced by a fatty tissue. Although there are several types, the most common and most serious type, *Duchenne's disease,* occurs in children. Duchenne's disease, or childhood muscular dystrophy, is a generally fatal disease characterized by a slow deterioration of the voluntary muscles ending in a complete state of helplessness.

The onset of the disease generally occurs between the child's first and sixth year and rarely occurs after the first decade of life. Early signs of the condition include a tendency to fall easily, clumsiness in walking, difficulty in climbing stairs, and difficulting in rising from the floor. There is a steady progressive decline in the child's ability to walk. The child falls more frequently and eventually needs crutches to move about. As he

continues to lose strength it is necessary to move from crutches to a wheelchair. Later, nearly all large muscles are involved and the child is bedridden. During the later stages, the child may be unable to raise his arms, sit erect, or hold his head up. Fortunately, the small muscles of the hands and fingers maintain some strength even during the most advanced stages.

Educational Implications. The regular classroom offers obvious educational advantages as compared to a special school or class for the student with muscular dystrophy. In addition to the educational advantages, there are many recreational and social factors involved in regular school attendance. During the early stages of muscular dystrophy, very few modifications and adaptations are necessary, but as the condition progresses there is need for some modifications. Eventually, the student may not be able to attend any educational program and requires homebound instruction; however, every effort should be made to maintain the student with muscular dystrophy in regular classrooms as long as possible.

Muscular dystrophy imposes a contradiction in attitude. On the one hand, it is known that it is generally fatal, and on the other, we ask the student, parents, teachers, and others to carry on as though the student were going to live a rich and full life. This apparent contradiction must be dealt with. Guidance and counseling services can do a great deal to accommodate the acceptance of this conflict. There is little question that if the child and parents are to accept this contradiction, ongoing counseling must be offered. Counseling programs should be conducted in cooperation with the student's parents, brothers and sisters, therapists, teachers and physicians. Counseling will center around issues of acceptance of the condition, how best to utilize the time available, preparation for the inevitability of death, and related matters.

Because of variations in age of onset, speed of deterioration, and other readiness factors, all counseling must be individualized. There are currently nearly two hundred clinics throughout the United States sponsored by the Muscular Dystrophy Association of America. These clinics provide no-cost services such as counseling, physical therapy, medical management, diagnostic services, and follow-up care.

It is important that the student attend adapted physical education classes and maintain a balance among diet, activity, and rest, since there is a tendency for the child to become overweight. The child should be encouraged to participate as fully as possible in recreational and physical activities. Although the effects of the condition cannot be stopped by physical activity, there is some indication that such activity may assist in delaying some of the debilitating effects. Some caution must be exercised, however, because the student may become very easily fatigued. He should be allowed intermittent periods of rest as needed.

Several studies have been conducted to determine whether mental retardation is associated with muscular dystrophy. There have been no indications that there is a greater incidence of mental retardation in students with muscular dystrophy than in the population as a whole. A large number of research studies have also attempted to identify particular personality characteristics that might be associated with muscular dystrophy. Although some researchers have found personality patterns unique to these students, others have not been able to do so; therefore it is reasonable to assume that differences in personality may be attributed to something other than the muscular dystrophy. If there is no mental retardation or particular personality configuration that may be associated with muscular dystrophy, then achievement and adjustment in school should be similar to that of other students.

Perhaps the most important role of the teacher is to stimulate these students academically, recreationally, and socially as much as possible and to expect as nearly as possible the same of these students as of others.

The next three sections provide a brief overview of additional physical impairments found in school-age children. Although these conditions do not impose as serious limitations as cerebral palsy, muscular dystrophy, or spina bifida, they warrant consideration because teachers need information about these relatively common conditions.

Scoliosis

Nature of Condition. Scoliosis means lateral (side-to-side) curvature of the spine (Figure 7–2). The normal spine has several curvatures in a front-to-back direction but no curvature from side to side. The most common type of scoliosis, *idiopathic* (cause unknown), is most commonly but not exclusively found in young adolescent girls. The second most common form, *paralytic,* is often associated with conditions such as cerebral palsy, spina bifida, muscular dystrophy, or poliomyelitis that are the result of loss or impairment of motor function.

Scoliosis screening programs are effective and are usually conducted as part of physical education programming or by the school nurse. Teachers should watch for a difference in shoulder height, differing contours of the normal flanks, or a hump when the child bends over (Figure 7–3). If a curvature is suspected, the teacher should inform the school nurse or family so that further testing may be conducted.

Educational Implications. Since there are strong hereditary tendencies for scoliosis, teachers should be alert to signs of the condition in siblings of the student with scoliosis.

FIGURE 7–2. Scoliosis

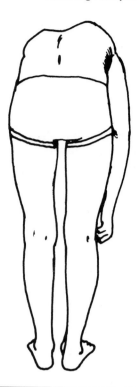

FIGURE 7–3. Appearance of scoliosis when individual bends forward

The student with scoliosis should be expected to participate in all routine activities, including physical education.

Students with other orthopedic impairments may have a more severe form of scoliosis. Often a brace such as the Milwaukee or Boston brace is used for passive correction—causing the person to assume a preferred posture. These students often wear the braces full-time; the brace is expected to prevent the progression of the curvature. In very severe cases, surgery may be recommended.

Teachers should be particularly watchful for an improperly sized wheelchair, which may result in the student's leaning to one side, thus making the condition worse. If a student is wearing a brace, the teacher should also watch for an improper fit causing discomfort, pain, or pressure sores. As indicated previously, the student with scoliosis can be expected to participate in all school activities. A teacher in doubt should consult with the parents or medical specialist.

Special care must be taken so that the treatment of the student with scoliosis does not become more of a disability than the condition itself.

Hip Disorders

Nature of Condition. The two most commonly found hip disorders in school-age children are *congenital dislocation of the hip* and *Legg-Perthes disease.* Congenital dislocation of the hip occurs as a result of an abnormally formed hip joint. The hip may be completely dislocated, partially dislocated, or generally unstable. Medical intervention is initiated at a very early age by gentle reduction of the misalignment and maintenance in the realigned position through the use of casts or splints. In more severe cases, surgery may be required to release tightened tendons in the hip area.

Generally, the child with a congenital hip problem has had the condition diagnosed and treated before entering school. In some cases, however, it is not diagnosed until after the child enters school.

Like congenital dislocation of the hip, Legg-Perthes disease is a temporary problem that can be corrected by bracing, casting, or surgery. It is a condition of unknown origin and results from a disruption of the blood supply in the head of the long bone of the thigh (the femur). The lack of blood supply to the growth center of the femur causes disintegration and flattening of the femoral head at the hip joint.

Legg-Perthes disease is more common among males than females and is seen during the elementary school years (3 to 11 years of age). Treatment is directed at reducing weight-bearing pressure on the head of the femur, allowing for bone restoration. The child may be involved with an extensive treatment period as long as two years. In some cases surgery may be required to reshape the hip socket or the head of the femur.

Educational Implications. Close communication between teachers and parents is essential in cases of prolonged hospitalization. Hospital and homebound instruction

FIGURE 7–4. Hip abduction orthosis

Note. From *Atlas of Orthotics* (p. 93) by American Academy of Orthopedic Surgeons, 1975, St. Louis: C. V. Mosby. Adapted by permission.

may be necessary to ensure that when the student returns to his regular classroom, he will not be significantly behind classmates.

During treatment, the student's legs are usually placed in a position spread wide apart and maintained in this position by a cast, brace, or splint (Figure 7–4). After the cast, brace, or splint is removed, the student may progressively bear weight on his legs. Occasionally these students may use a creeper (a low platform on wheels, similar to what an automobile mechanic uses to work underneath an automobile) for a period of time. Naturally, the student should avoid physical activities that would put weight-bearing stress on the affected hip. Other than this consideration, there need not be any significant modifications or adaptations for the student with Legg-Perthes disease.

Osteogenesis Imperfecta

Nature of Condition. Osteogenesis imperfecta, commonly called brittle bones, is a defect in the development of bone structure. Because of this structural weakness, the bones break very easily. In addition, the affected individual often has deformity, dwarfism, and hearing loss. During the child's early years, it may be necessary for him to live in a protective environment to minimize breaks and fractures.

Educational Implications. Students with the less severe type of osteogensis imperfecta should be encouraged to attend regular classes. Since their intellectual ability is within the normal range, they may attend regular classes with only minor modifications. Naturally, they should be excluded from participation in all activities that might result in bone fractures. Braces and crutches may be used for support, and some students use wheelchairs to provide a more protective environment—to decrease falls and bumps.

Other students should be asked to exercise caution when playing with these children because routine falls or bumps can mean a serious fracture. Every effort must be made to maintain this student in the regular classroom to maximize the social and educational benefits of interaction with normal peers.

HEALTH IMPAIRMENTS

The next sections review the most common health impairments found in school-age children: allergies, asthma, diabetes, epilepsy, heart disorders, hemophilia, sickle-cell anemia, cystic fibrosis, and AIDS.

Allergies

Nature of Condition. An allergy is an adverse sensitivity or intolerance to a specific substance that may not be a ·problem to other individuals. When an allergic student comes in contact with the substance to which he is sensitive, he develops a reaction, or irritation. The reaction may take many forms, such as sneezing, watering eyes, runny nose, tiredness, itching, or a rash. The student may react to a number of different substances. Among the most common are inhalants (pollen, smoke, dust, and perfumes, for example), foods (eggs, chocolate, wheat, pork, strawberries, nuts and citrus fruits), infectious agents (bacteria and fungi, for example), substances that come in contact with the skin (poison ivy, poison sumac, fur, leather, animal hair, and dyes, for example), and drugs (vaccines, serums, and antibiotics).

Treatment Procedures. The first step is to determine the cause of the allergy. The physician may prescribe medication for temporary relief, but generally he carefully examines the student's medical history, home surroundings, eating habits, and so on to determine the allergens to which the student is sensitive. He may conduct specific allergy tests such as skin tests on the arm or back to determine substances to which the child reacts. He may also suggest a series of shots to desensitize the student to a particular substance. The student with allergies can participate fully in nearly all educational programs. The teacher may, however, assist in indentifying the specific sensitivity, particularly if the student seems to have more difficulty when at school. If an alleregic reaction is suspected, this should be reported to the parents or school nurse, since treatment can do a great deal to ease the effects of the condition. In addition, students with allergies tend to develop asthma, and this should be avoided if at all possible.

Educational Implications. Some students may miss school because of their condition, particularly during early fall or in the spring when ragweed pollen levels are highest. It is the teacher's responsibility to make certain the student completes missed assignments. It may also be necessary to provide additional instruction or establish a peer teaching arrangement.

Although this varies among individuals, some students with allergies fatigue more easily than other students when participating in physical activities. As a result, they may withdraw during recess or physical education while their classmates continue. This behavior must be observed very carefully, since withdrawal may have serious social and emotional results. Because physical fitness is an important component of treatment, the teacher may assist by modifying or adapting the activity so that the student is encouraged to participate as much as possible. The teacher should also carefully observe to see if there is any change in the student's condition as a result of activity and report this information to the parents or physician. The student must learn how to live with the limitations caused by allergies and develop a life-style that allows him a maximum amount of freedom.

Asthma

Nature of Condition. Asthma usually results from an allergic state that causes an obstruction of the bronchial tubes or the lungs or both. When sensitivity flares into an attack, an excessive amount of mucus is produced and there is a spasm of the bronchial musculature. As a result, breathing becomes difficult, and the student may lose his color, wheeze, and perspire excessively. The attack may last for minutes, hours, or days.

Asthma attacks may be frightening experiences because of the labored breathing and other behaviors. The attack may be brought on by a specific sensitivity to an allergen or by excessive physical activity. Asthma attacks can cause emotional stress for the student and those around who observe the attack. The arousal of these emotional factors may intensify the frequency and severity of asthma symptoms. The disease and emotional climate are so interrelated that they affect one another (Kraemer & Bierman, 1983).

Treatment Procedures. Treatment procedures are similar to those for allergic individuals. Adrenaline administered by injection or by inhalation usually gives relief for brief periods; however, since asthma is a chronic condition, long-term treatment procedures must be employed.

Educational Implications. Students with asthma should be treated as normally as possible. Caution must be exercised to avoid overprotection from routine classroom activities. If care is not practiced, the student may become an asthmatic or emotional cripple. The teacher should be aware of the factors that precipitate an asthma attack and have information concerning the proper course of action should an attack occur.

Although the severity of each student's asthmatic condition is different and there are unique care and treatment procedures for each, there are some general factors that should be considered by the teacher. Mild attacks can sometimes be controlled by asking the student to sit down and breath easily. Medical personnel occasionally recommend drinking warm water as a way of stopping a mild attack. During an attack the student may be more comfortable in a standing or sitting position rather than lying down. The teacher should encourage the student to sit forward in a chair, with hands on knees and shoulders forward, while breathing through the mouth.

Students may have to take medicine during school hours to keep mild asthma from becoming severe. If a pressurized aerosol is used, the teacher, after careful consultation with parents, should closely monitor its use to be certain it is not overused.[2]

If a specific food being offered in a classroom party is an allergen, the teacher should check with the parents to see if a substitute may be used. It is also recommended that classmates be helped to understand this condition to avoid ridicule that would only add to the problem.

Management of students with asthma should include attention to psychological factors that may aggravate the condition. The teacher should also be aware of possible side effects or behavioral changes that may be related to prescribed drugs being used by the student. Teachers are in a unique position to observe the student during a variety of activities throughout the school day. They can provide a positive learning atmosphere, an atmosphere that promotes growth, acceptance, and independence. Information provided by the teacher may be very helpful to parents or the physician in determining subsequent treatment procedures.

For students who experience asthma attacks during periods of exercise, some general guidelines may be considered. Warm-up periods are helpful, as are short periods of moderate exercise. Certain types of exercise, such as gymnastics, wrestling, and swimming, are usually less likely to produce asthma attacks (Richards, 1986). Short sprints are also less likely to produce attacks than prolonged running. In addition, exercise in warm, humid conditions is generally less likely to induce attacks than that done in cold, dry air outdoors. With appropriate management (for example, medications taken prior to strenuous exercise), students may effectively compete in activities such as basketball, soccer, or track (Kraemer & Bierman, 1983). It is essential that the teacher check with parents or the physician to determine specifically what the student can and cannot do.

Diabetes

Nature of Condition. Diabetes is a metabolic disorder wherein the individual's body is unable to utilize and properly store sugar. This condition is a result of the inability of the pancreas to produce a sufficient amount of the hormone *insulin*.

Although diabetes is most commonly seen in adults, it does occur in school-age children and can become a serious problem if the proper treatment procedures are not adhered to. Symptoms indicative of diabetes of which

---

[2]Most school districts have a policy concerning the administration of medication to students. Some districts insist that teachers not administer medication in any form but allow the teacher to inform the student when it is time to take the medication. Other districts require that the physician write a prescription that allows the teacher to administer the medication. Still other districts require the teacher to send the student to the school nurse. In a few schools there is no policy governing the administration of medication to students. It is the teacher's responsibility to determine the school district's policy and procedure in this matter.

classroom teachers should be aware are unusually frequent urination, abnormal thirst, extreme hunger, changes in weight (generally a rapid loss), drowsiness, general weakness, possible visual disturbances, and skin infections like boils or itching. If a student shows any of these symptoms, the school nurse and the student's parents should be contacted as soon as possible. Prompt medical diagnosis and treatment are essential in the care of the diabetic student.

Treatment Procedures. If diabetes is diagnosed, treatment procedures probably involve daily injections of insulin, adherence to a rather strict diet to maintain the correct sugar level, and a balance between exercise and rest. Generally, students with diabetes have a normal childhood and adolescence and can do almost everything their peers do except fill up on sweets, and they must maintain a balance between exercise and rest.

To most of us, daily injections seem a serious problem, but to the student with diabetes they become a very routine matter. The injections are generally administered at home and become as routine as other hygienic practices such as bathing or brushing teeth. Often the student and his parents attend a clinic that teaches them how to manage daily activities such as injections, diet, exercise, care of the feet (this can be a definite problem because of poor circulation), and the changes in life-style that are necessary to accommodate the condition. As a result of these clinics, the student knows a great deal about his condition and how to manage it.

Educational Implications. The classroom teacher should be aware of several potential problems, such as an insulin reaction (hypoglycemia) and diabetic coma. An insulin reaction may result from anything that increases the metabolic rate, such as too much

exercise, too much insulin, too little food, or nervous tension. It may occur anytime during the day but most often before meals or after strenuous exercise. For instance, an insulin reaction may occur if the student refuses to finish his breakfast; the usual dose of insulin may become unbalanced by the reduced food intake. Emotional tension about school or personal problems may have variable effects. Occasionally, tension may cause the blood sugar level to fall below normal, resulting in an insulin reaction.

The insulin reaction may follow a typical pattern for each individual, and therefore it is important to consult with the student or his parents to determine what these signs may be. Often, general irritability may be the first sign. One student may be despondent and cry readily, whereas another may be exuberant or belligerent. The student may be hungry, perspire excessively, tremble, be unable to concentrate, and complain of being dizzy. These symptoms vary in duration and often disappear after the student is provided with a sugar cube, soft drink, candy, raisins, fruit juice with sugar, or any other carbohydrate. Generally the symptoms will disappear after 10–15 minutes. If they do not, the student's parents or physicians should be called.

The opposite of an insulin reaction is a diabetic coma. Although fairly rare, it does occur and can be serious if not treated immediately. A diabetic coma is the result of failure to take insulin, an illness, or neglect of proper diet. In this instance the student has too much sugar and must have an injection as soon as possible. Generally the coma is slow in onset, and the following symptoms may be observed: thirst, frequent urination, flushed face, labored breathing, nausea, and vomiting. These symptoms should be reported to the parents, school nurse, or student's physician as soon as possible. Treatment involves rest, injection of insulin, and possible hospitalization.

Table 7–1 provides a summary of the indicators, causes, and appropriate actions in cases of diabetic coma and insulin reaction. If in doubt over the symptom, administer sugar, since the body's reaction to an excess of sugar is slower and can be corrected later. However, the body's reaction to too much insulin is sudden and dangerous (Kleinberg, 1982; Winter, 1983). Specific instructions from the physician always take precedence over any such generalized instructions, but these guidelines may be of value until you consult with the physician or school nurse.

Several additional factors should be considered:

1. Check with the student's parents to see if the student should have a midmorning snack. If so, help him or her be as incon-

spicuous as possible about it. It may also be advisable to schedule the student for an early lunch period.
2. Very active or strenuous physical activities should be avoided immediately before lunch. Since the goal in the management of diabetes is to maintain a balance among insulin, food intake, and energy expenditure, it might be well to encourage the student to establish an exericse routine at the same time each day.
3. Keep candy, raisins, or sugar handy in case the student needs them.
4. Be certain to inform special or substitute teachers that there is a student in the class with diabetes, and record in writing what they should do in case of an insulin reaction or diabetic coma. This suggestion is relevant not only in the case of the stu-

TABLE 7–1. Summary of observable signs, causes, and actions to take for diabetic reaction and insulin reaction

	Insulin Reaction (Rapid Onset)	Diabetic Coma (Slow Onset)
Observable signs	facial pallor hunger impaired vision irritability excessive sweating personality change headache faintness trembling forceful heartbeat	excessive thirst abdominal pains repeated urination loss of appetite nausea or vomiting general aches weakness
Causes	reduced intake of food delayed meals abnormal amount of exercise too much insulin	infections fever emotional stress failure to follow diet too little insulin

What to do	call the parents, doctor, or
	  school nurse
	provide sugar or other food with
	  sugar, e.g., orange juice,
	  candy, sweetened soft drink
		call the parents, doctor, or
		  school nurse immediately
		allow student to lie down
		keep student warm
		provide fluids without sugar

dent with diabetes but for all health impairments.

5. Encourage the parents to have their child's vision routinely checked because many individuals with diabetes develop retinal problems.

6. Allow the student the flexibility to use the restroom whenever necessary because students with diabetes may need to urinate more frequently. Inform the parents if there is a sudden increase in use of the restroom or the drinking fountain because it may be an indication of the need for medical attention.

7. The teacher, with full permission of the student and parents, may want to present a unit of study concerning endocrine function and energy and their relationship to sugar consumption and nutrition.

8. Above all else, do not panic about having a student with diabetes; proceed calmly with the necessary steps if he has an insulin reaction or goes into a coma. The vast majority of the time he can be treated like any other student in the class.

Students with diabetes should be expected to participate in all normal school activities unless specific restrictions have been advised by the physician. The student must learn to live with the condition and to accept the limitations imposed by it. He must develop a life-style that will allow the greatest possible freedom and still maintain the necessary balance among diet, rest and activity, and medication.

Epilepsy

Nature of Condition. Epilepsy is not a disease in itself but is a sign or a symptom of some underlying disorder in the nervous system.

Convulsions, or seizures, are the main symptoms in all types of epilepsy. The seizures occur when there are excessive electrical discharges in nerve cells of the brain. When this happens, the brain cannot function properly for a short time and loses control over muscles, consciousness, senses, and thoughts. The loss of these functions is only temporary, and the brain cells work properly between seizures.

Epilepsy is actually quite common, with many cases of petit mal seizures never recognized and reported. Estimates of occurrence range from 1 of every 50, to 1 of every 500 children, depending on the criteria established for the study. The most common types of seizures are (1) *grand mal seizures* (also known as generalized convulsive or major motor seizures), (2) *petit mal* or *absence seizures,* and (3) *psychomotor seizures* (also known as temporal lobes or complex partial seizures).

Grand Mal Seizures. Grand mal seizures are the most alarming to school personnel and other students. When a grand mal seizure occurs, the individual loses consciousness, collapses, and has general convulsive movements. The student may shout or produce a gurgling sound, and saliva may escape from the lips. The muscles first become rigid or stiff, and then there are jerky movements of the arms and legs. The individual may bite his tongue or lose control of his bladder. Breathing is often labored and at times seems to have stopped completely. The student may have a bluish or pale complexion. The seizure may last for several minutes, and afterwards the individual may be confused or drowsy. He does not recall what happened or what was said to him during the seizure, and he may be very tired and want to sleep for a short time.

What to Do If a Student Has a Grand Mal Seizure. There are many misconceptions concerning epilepsy, including the presumption of mental retardation, brain injury, or insanity. But there is even more misinformation about what should be done when an individual has a grand mal seizure. A grand mal seizure can be a frightening experience for the teacher unless she is well prepared and knows exactly what to do. The Epilepsy Foundation of America suggests the following steps in the event of a grand mal seizure:

1. Remain calm. Students tend to assume the same emotional reaction as their teacher. The seizure itself is painless to the student.
2. Do not try to restrain the student. Nothing can be done to stop a seizure once it has begun. It must run its course.
3. Help the student lie down, and put something under his head.
4. Clear the area around the student so that he does not injure himself on hard, sharp, or hot objects. Try not to interfere with his movements in any way.
5. Remove glasses and loosen tight clothing.
6. Do not force anything between teeth. Under no circumstances should a hard object such as a spoon, pen, or pencil be put in his mouth; more harm may result from such an action than from doing nothing. Do not put fingers into the mouth.
7. After the seizure, turn his head to one side for the release of saliva.
8. Do not offer the student anything to drink until he is fully awake.
9. It is not generally necessary to call a physician unless the attack is immediately followed by another major seizure or unless the seizure lasts more than 10 minutes.
10. When the seizure is over, let the student rest if he needs to.
11. The student's parents should be informed of the seizure.

Petit Mal Seizures. Petit mal seizures are generally short in duration, lasting from 3 to 30 seconds. They are most common in chil-

dren and can occur between 50 and 200 times a day if untreated. Often this student may be accused of being a daydreamer because he loses contact with what is happening in the classroom during the seizure. The student may become pale, may stare into space, his eyelids may twitch, or he may demonstrate slightly jerky movements. After the seizure the student continues with activities almost as though nothing had happened because he is probably not aware that he had a seizure. Petit mal seizures have a tendency to disappear before or near puberty but may be replaced by other types such as grand mal.

One of the most significant problems of petit mal seizure behavior is that it often goes undiagnosed. Teachers can play an important role in identification and should watch for a number of signs that indicate petit mal and that might otherwise elude detection for some time. Repeated occurrences of two or more of the following signs may indicate the presence of this form of epilepsy: (1) head dropping, (2) daydreaming or lack of attentiveness, (3) slight jerky movements of arms or shoulders (ticlike movements), (4) eyes rolling upward or twitching, (5) a seeming inability to hear complete sentences or directions, and (6) dropping things frequently. If any combination of these signs is observed, be certain that the school nurse and the student's parents are contacted to ensure that a proper medical examination is obtained. Once diagnosed, petit mal seizures are almost always quickly brought under control with medication.

Psychomotor (Temporal-Lobe or Partial-Complex) Seizures. Psychomotor seizures are the most complex because they affect not only the motor system but also mental processes. The seizure may last from a few minutes to several hours. Behavior during the seizure varies from person to person, but for any individual generally the same behavior regularly occurs during each seizure. During the seizure the student may chew or smack his lips or appear to be confused. In some instances the individual may carry out purposeless activities such as rubbing his arms or legs, may walk, or may pick at or take off clothing, or he may demonstrate a sudden arrest of activity along with staring. Although this is uncommon, some individuals may experience fear, anger, or rage. After the seizure they usually do not remember what happened and want to sleep. If the teacher observes any of these behaviors, she should be certain that the school nurse and student's parents are contacted.

Educational Implications. All of the three most common types of seizures can cause severe educational problems. Grand mal epilepsy is probably the most serious because of the possibility of bodily injury and because it is so widely misunderstood. Petit mal seizures can seriously limit the student's achievement because he misses the material being covered during a seizure and because he may be labeled a behavior problem. Although psychomotor seizures are relatively uncommon in children, they too impose serious limitations on school achievement and adjustment. All three types are serious, and minor modifications and adjustments may need to be made to accommodate the student with any of these conditions.

Special curricular modifications are not necessary for students with epilepsy. Their academic program and materials are the same. Several factors, however, should be considered by the teacher. The extent to which a student's seizures are controlled determines the extent to which the following factors and suggestions should be considered. If the seizures have been controlled for several years, it is not necessary to make many special provisions. If the seizures are not well controlled or if epilepsy has only recently been diagnosed, however, many of these factors have importance.

1. If a seizure occurs, the teacher may turn the incident into a learning experience for the entire class. Explain what a seizure is, that it is not contagious, and that it is nothing to be afraid of. Teach the class understanding of the student—not pity—so that his classmates continue to accept him as "one of the gang." After the seizure and a short rest, the student can generally carry on routinely. The way in which the teacher and the students react to the seizure is very important. If the teacher overreacts, it can have a very negative effect on the student with epilepsy and on other students in the class. However, if the teacher has prepared and informed the students concerning what to do in the event of a seizure, a potentially traumatic and upsetting experience can be a routine matter.

   There is some controversy concerning whether a student's previous history of seizure behavior should be discussed with the class before a seizure occurs in the class. It is possible that seizure may never occur in class. On the other hand, if students are informed of the nature of this condition and other similar conditions as a part of their general education, it may reduce the stigma of epilepsy and provide helpful information for everyday living.

2. The teacher may want to discuss the condition with the student and the student's parents to obtain more complete information concerning how the student feels about the condition, the extent of seizure control, and any individual aspects that need to be considered.

3. If the student takes medication for the control of seizures during the day, the teacher should participate by seeing that he or she gets it. The teacher may also be asked to carefully observe and record the student's reactions to the medication. Occasionally the anticonvulsant drugs used to control epilepsy produce side effects like lethargy or irritability. Such ef-

fects should be brought to the attention of the parents and/or physician because they may indicate the need for a reduction in dose or a change to another drug.

4. The teacher should not lower the level of expectation or set up protective devices that would single out the student with epilepsy. This attitude must be avoided if the student is to develop a feeling of self-worth and a healthy personality.
5. The teacher should inform special or substitute teachers that there is a student in the class with epilepsy and should record in writing what to do in the event of a seizure.
6. School personnel, including other teachers, should be educated about the nature of epilepsy and procedures to be employed in the event of a seizure.
7. In general, a student with a seizure disorder should participate in school sports or games with as few exceptions as possible. When the physician so indicates, sports that in the past were routinely denied to students with epilepsy, such as football, karate, or boxing, are allowed. Swimming is certainly allowed; however, it is recommended that the student not swim alone. The teacher must consult the parents and physician to determine if there are any activities that must be specifically avoided.
8. The teacher should obtain information from state and national agencies concerned with epilepsy. Free information is available from the Epilepsy Foundation of America.[3] Materials from a national agency such as the Epilepsy Foundation can familiarize the class with procedures that should be employed in the event of

a seizure. Students can be assigned specific responsibilities so that care of the student with epilepsy becomes a routine matter. If the class is prepared for a seizure, it should not be a disturbing experience.

The greatest limitation imposed by epilepsy is not the condition itself but rather the misinformation, antiquated attitudes, and, in many cases, consistent rejection in a society that fears what it does not understand.

Heart Disorders

Nature of Condition. There are two major types of heart disorders in children: *congenital* and *acquired.* Congenital heart disease may be the result of maternal rubella (German measles), chromosomal aberrations (such as Down syndrome), or structural abnormalities including holes in the walls of the heart chambers and problems related to the flow of blood or valves. The most common acquired heart disorder in children is caused by rheumatic fever; permanent heart damage resulting from rheumatic fever is called rheumatic heart disease. Rheumatic fever is brought on by a streptococcal infection commonly known as strep throat or scarlet fever. This disease can affect many body organs but most commonly affects the valves of the heart. The incidence of heart disorders as a result of rheumatic fever is falling dramatically because of advances made in diagnosis, such as the use of throat cultures to detect strep throat.

Treatment Procedures. Advanced medical technology has significantly decreased the lifelong effects of congenital heart disorders. Most congenital heart problems can be corrected surgically, so that students with heart disorders can live normal lives. There are some students, however, who must live with the effects of their condition.

Students with rheumatic fever usually re-

[3]The Epilepsy Foundation of America has a program entitled "School Alert" that presents a basic educational program for classroom teachers, school nurses, and others in recognizing epilepsy and techniques of management in the school and classroom (Epilepsy Foundation of America, 1828 L. St. NW, Washington, DC 20036).

turn to normal school activities after a period of hospitalization and home bed rest. Not all attacks of rheumatic fever result in a heart disorder, but if there is a residual effect, it most often involves the heart. Frequent follow-up medical evaluations for these students are mandatory. Often the student must receive prophylactic penicillin or other preventive antibiotics indefinitely to prevent a recurrence of strep throat, which might result in rheumatic fever.

Educational Implications. The degree of involvement for students with heart disorders is different in each situation, and therefore it is difficult to provide specific recommendations for every student. There are, however, some general principles or guidelines that should be considered. Probably the most important consideration is close communication between teachers and the student's parents. The parents can provide very specific information concerning appropriate expectations and precautions. The student's health records should also be consulted to obtain more complete information. Occasionally the records note that the student's heart condition is self-limiting, which means that the student is able to pace himself and may do without teacher reminders. If there is an indication that the student's activity should be limited, the student's physician would give specific information as to which physical activities may or may not be appropriate.

Generally, the student should not engage in competitive athletics unless the physician specifically approves. Some students may require a shortened school day combined with home instruction, special rest periods, a modified physical education program, or a special diet. Teachers can play an important role in assisting parents to avoid overprotectiveness (an understandable reaction on the part of parents) by encouraging the student to participate in as many activities as possible. Good communication and a strong relationship between the student's parents and teacher cannot be overemphasized.

Hemophilia

Nature of Condition. Hemophilia (also known as bleeder's disease) results from a hereditary deficiency in certain coagulation factors within the blood. It very rarely occurs in girls. It is transmitted from mother to son in a sex-linked passive pattern. It is generally recognized in boys in the first three or four years of life when they seem to bruise easily, bleed easily from minor cuts and scrapes, or bleed in the joints, or during surgery. There may also be bleeding under the skin without a cut or scrape, which destroys surrounding tissues. If the bleeding occurs in the joints, it eventually causes immobility through destruction of the lining of the joint and may result in permanent degeneration of the joints.

Treatment Procedures. In the early years of care for hemophiliacs, massive and frequent blood transfusions of whole blood were routinely provided. Today, because of advanced medical technology and the isolation of the clotting factor, a treatment for controlling and preventing the bleeding tendency is available. Home therapy programs, in which parents and the child are taught intravenous self-administration to replace the deficient blood factor, are now widely practiced. They are also taught to recognize the early signs of bleeding, and the child may be placed on a prophylactic program. Routine administration of the blood factor two or three times a week has significantly contributed to positive benefits for hemophiliacs.

Educational Implications. As with other health impairments, the key to successful programming is close communication among teachers, the student's parents, and medical personnel. The student and his teachers must be aware of limitations for his activity. Naturally, the student should not be involved with any contact sports, but he should be encouraged to participate in other activities that allow him to exercise joints and maintain good exercise and health practices. Swimming is an ideal, non-weight-bearing, lifelong activity that can provide the needed daily exercise.

Although home therapy programs have dramatically reduced frequent absences from school, absences must still be anticipated. School adjustment for students with hemophilia can be difficult because of the discontinuity of programming caused by frequent attacks, changes in physical ability and interests, and fear of injury associated with the active games of boys. Hemophiliac students may want to participate in active games, but they realize the consequences of an injury. As a result of this dilemma, they may withdraw, become self-protective, and shy. Some adolescent boys may rebel against their overprotected life-style by indulging in alcohol or drug abuse, which may have an adverse effect on medication. The student with hemophilia needs considerable emotional support and understanding—a great deal of this support can be provided by an informed and empathetic teacher.

Sickle-Cell Anemia

Nature of Condition. Sickle-cell anemia is an inherited disorder characterized by sickle-shaped red blood cells. The irregularly shaped blood cells become blocked in blood vessels, and this blockage may result in decreased blood supply to some tissues, causing pain in the arms, legs, and abdomen. In addition to the severe pain, other effects are swollen joints, fatigue, and dehydration. This hereditary disorder is more prevalent among the black population.

The condition is characterized by periods of remission and periods of crisis that involve pain. Children under the age of 10 may have as many as 8–10 crises a year, with the number decreasing during adulthood (Kleinberg, 1982). Life expectancy for individuals with sickle-cell anemia is shortened—with an average mortality age of 40.

Treatment Procedures. Treatment during periods of crisis involves bed rest, antibiotics to prevent infections, pain relievers, and high fluid intake. During a serious crisis blood transfusions may be necessary.

Educational Implications. Although learning problems are not associated with sickle-cell anemia, frequent absence from school may result in significant educational delay. These students require frequent hospitalization and extensive convalescence. Close communication among the parents, hospital teachers, homebound teachers, and the regular teacher is essential to reduce the serious educational gaps and delays that may result from this chronic health impairment. Special consideration must also be given to the concomitant psychosocial problems that may result from absences, growth problems (the student may be smaller than age mates and puberty may be delayed), and the conflict between overprotection and independence.

Students with sickle-cell anemia should be allowed to participate in physical education classes and other motor activities as much as possible unless the physician recommends otherwise. Lack of physical stamina prohibits these students from participation in most athletic events, and therefore they should be encouraged to participate in extra school activities that do not require physical activity. Teachers should be aware that sickle-cell anemia causes a need for frequent urination, and the student should be allowed to go to the restroom as necessary. Teachers should also be watchful for changes in vision and should educate themselves as much as possible about this condition.

As with any chronic health impairment, it is essential that the teacher be aware of the social limitations imposed by the condition and attempt to provide the necessary support to the student and his parents. Close communication among parents, teachers, and medical personnel is of the utmost importance.

Cystic Fibrosis

Nature of Condition. Cystic fibrosis is the most common lethal hereditary disease. It is a recessive genetic disorder that results from an inborn error of metabolism. It is a generalized disorder affecting the exocrine glands (outward-secreting glands of the body), often causing severe respiratory and digestive problems. The mucus normally produced by these glands is thin, slippery, and clear; however, in children with cystic fibrosis, the mucus is thick and sticky. This thick mucus clogs the bronchial tubes and if not removed can lead to recurrent lung infections, lung damage, digestive difficulty, and occasionally cirrhosis of the liver. As the condition progresses, more mucus remains and areas of the lungs become blocked.

Treatment Procedures. Inhalation treatments, use of a mist tent, and postural drainage (patting the back in certain areas to loosen the thick mucus) are used to ease the breathing of the child with cystic fibrosis. Parents and therapist employ postural-drainage techniques several times a day.

In the past children with cystic fibrosis often did not survive beyond the primary grades. Today, because of advanced medical-treatment procedures, many may live normal adult lives (Mangos, 1983; Schwartz, 1984).

Educational Implications. Teachers should consider several factors if they have a student with cystic fibrosis in their classrooms:

1. Students may cough frequently. Cystic fibrosis is *not* contagious; therefore there is no need to keep the other students

away during a coughing episode. In fact, students with cystic fibrosis should be encouraged not to try to hide the cough, because coughing clears the mucus from the lungs.
2. They may need to go to the restroom more frequently than other students and should be allowed to do so.
3. They may need to take medication during school hours, and as a result a flexible schedule and arrangements with the school nurse may be helpful.
4. Physical stamina may be impaired because of lung involvement, but students with cystic fibrosis should be encouraged to participate in all activities as fully as possible. It may be necessary to prevent them attempting to hide their condition and going beyond their limit. It may also be advisable to watch them during hot weather because they may perspire excessively and may need added salt.
5. Students with cystic fibrosis may have an increased appetite. Some students with cystic fibrosis may be on a low- or modified-fat diet, and if so the teacher may encourage adherence to the diet.
6. Because frequent absences may be common for the student with cystic fibrosis, teachers must work diligently with hospital and homebound personnel to ensure the best possible education.

Perhaps the most important consideration is that the teacher should assume responsibility for knowing exactly what the student can and cannot do. This is best accomplished by close communication among parents, resource personnel, and the regular teacher.

Acquired Immune Deficiency Syndrome (AIDS)

Nature of Condition. Acquired Immune Deficiency Syndrome is a condition wherein a microscopic-size virus is introduced into the body and attached to the helper T cell, which is the coordinator of the body's immune system. By inserting itself into the chromosomes of the cell, the virus then begins to direct the cell to produce more of the AIDS viruses. The invaded cell swells and dies, releasing many new viruses to continue the attack on other helper T cells. As this process repeats itself, the body's immune system is deprived of the critical helper T cells and is unable to fight off diseases as a healthy body can do. Various diseases then invade the body producing a variety of symptoms, each of which makes the individual more ill. Gradually the body is disease ridden and succumbs to some specific disease or the cumulative effect of many diseases.

Adults are the primary target of the AIDS virus; however, there are children with the disease. Children of school age who have AIDS have generally contracted it at birth from infected mothers or from blood transfusions that contained the virus. Blood for transfusion is now more carefully tested since it is known that the virus may be transmitted in this manner, and blood donors are more carefully screened.

Because of the national publicity regarding AIDS and the issue of whether children with AIDS should be allowed to attend school, questions regarding their right to an education have been asked. N. Jones (1986) suggests that students with AIDS are clearly included under the rules and regulations of PL 94-142 (see chapter 2), and that by using the Individual Educational Program, school personnel may design a program for the student while protecting both the student's rights and those of other students.

Educational Implications. Aquired immune deficiency syndrome, in and of itself, does not preclude regular class work, and therefore requires no modifications in expectations or assignments. The larger issue is whether the student should be allowed to attend school, and this is an administrative/political decision.

The National Educational Association (NEA) issued suggested guidelines for dealing with AIDS in the school (National Education Association, 1986). The NEA guidelines refer to "infected" persons as those who are "asymptomatic carriers" (those infected by the AIDS virus and possibly able to transmit it but who have not developed symptoms) and those who have been diagnosed as having AIDS. Relevant guidelines include the following:

1. Infected students who display behaviors such as biting, who lack control of bodily secretions, or who have uncoverable, oozing lesions shall not be permitted to attend school.

2. If not permitted to attend classes, every reasonable effort must be made to provide the infected student with an adequate alternative education. Teachers who provide the alternative education, if it involves personal contact, must volunteer.

3. Infected students who do not meet Guideline 1 must be reviewed on an individual basis by a team composed of the student's physician, student's parents or guardian(s), public health personnel, and appropriate school personnel including the student's main teacher(s). The focus of the team's review shall be (a) the physical condition, the behavior, and the neurological development of the student; (b) the type of interaction with others in the school; and (c) the impact on both the infected student and others in the school. After a complete review, the team will make a decision as to whether or not that student will be allowed to attend classes.

4. Teachers should not be required to teach infected students unless the student is allowed to attend school according to Guideline 3.

5. Teachers who will have personal contact with the student must be informed of his or her identity by the school employer and provided relevant medical information regarding the student.

At this time it would seem that if students are permitted to attend school, no modifications in teaching are necessary. If a student is not permitted to attend school, accommodations must be made similar to those for any other student requiring home instruction.

ADAPTING PHYSICAL EDUCATION

The student with a crippling condition or health impairment can often successfully participate in nearly all curricular areas. One area, however, that presents special problems is physcial education. If the physical educator has had previous experience or special preparation in this area, he often makes the necessary adjustments to accommodate these students with little difficulty. If the physical educator has not had previous experience or preparation, a student with lim-

ited ambulation or a health impairment may present a special problem. As mentioned previously, activity is essential for these students, perhaps even more so than for students without a disability. Nonhandicapped students routinely get the necessary activity, whereas students with physical problems may be overprotected and not afforded the opportunity to be active. In general, there are at least four ways that physical education activities can be changed to allow greater participation for these students.

1. Change the way all students participate.
2. Change the way one player of each team participates.
3. Modify the equipment.
4. Make special allowances for the handicapped student.

The following suggestions are not intended as a comprehensive or detailed pro-

Creative teachers can find a variety of ways to adapt physical education activities.

gram but should be considered when attempting to modify or adapt programs for students with crippling conditions or health impairments:

1. Consider minor rule modifications of the game or contest.
2. Ask the students how to adapt a game or activity. Some physical educators have had considerable success in asking all of the students to identify ways to modify or adapt an activity.
3. Schedule opportunities for rest. Fatigue may be a factor for the handicapped student. The number of points required to win a game can be reduced, quarters may be shortened, or required distances may be reduced.
4. Use larger balls, larger pieces of equipment, or change equipment—lighter balls, lighter racquets, lower baskets, etc.
5. Use more players on a team, reducing the individual responsibility and activity.
6. Change the way the entire class plays the game—all players on knees, sitting on the floor, using only one hand, or using scooter boards.
7. Have one person on each team assume a functional disability—using a wheelchair, crutches, etc.
8. Create a special role for the handicapped student and one other student on the other team—hand out a baton at the end of a relay, catch a basketball after a goal is made and return it to the shooter.
9. Plan a backup activity in the event that the primary activity does not work.
10. Use as many activities as possible that the handicapped student can do.

We are not advocating that activities be modified every day; this may seriously limit the needed activity of the nonhandicapped students. We are suggesting, however, that

consideration be given to these suggestions and that attempts be made to meet the unique needs of *all* students.

Participation in a regular physical education program can have many benefits and should be encouraged as much as possible. Regular physical education, however, should not preclude the need for physical therapy provided by a physical therapist or for special individualized or adapted physical education provided by a specialist. The regular physical educator is also strongly encouraged to consult with the adaptive specialist or the special education resource or itinerant teacher for additional suggestions.

PURPOSE, CARE, AND MAINTENANCE OF BRACES, CRUTCHES, AND WHEELCHAIRS

Many students with cerebral palsy, spina bifida, muscular dystrophy, and other orthopedic impairments need braces, crutches, or wheelchairs; therefore, the regular teacher should be acquainted with the purpose, care, and maintenance of this equipment. Braces are classified into three general types: (1) corrective, (2) control, and (3) supportive. Corrective braces are used for prevention and correction of a deformity during the student's rapid-growth period. Often during this period the tendons (cords that attach muscles to bones) do not keep pace with the growth of the long bones. When this happens the heel cords may tighten, and surgery may be required to lengthen them to keep up with the long-bone growth. Corrective braces may prevent or delay this surgery. Control braces are used to prevent or eliminate purposeless movement of the type found in athetoid cerebral palsy or to allow movement in only one or two desired directions. Support braces are used to provide the needed support for the child who needs assistance in standing. Often students in a wheelchair do not have the adequate muscle strength or control to support themselves. In this instance, a body brace may be used to support the spine and prevent serious scoliosis. Some students wear braces for only a short time, whereas others need them for many years and perhaps for their entire lives.

It is not the primary responsibility of the regular classroom teacher to maintain this equipment. The teacher is assisted by the therapists, resource or itinerant teacher, and the student's parents; however, he or she may have more contact with the student than the others and may be able to spot-check equipment periodically. For example, the teacher should be watchful for torn or worn leather pieces and should check to see that the brace is not rubbing against the body and causing pressure sores to develop. The teacher may also want to check periodically for loose or missing screws and the general condition of buckles, locks, and joints.

Crutches are used to stabilize the trunk and to provide needed support while standing and walking. Generally, crutches do not call for much care or maintenance, but they should be checked periodically for loose screws, worn rubber tips, and proper height adjustments.

Wheelchairs are most commonly used by students with severe crippling conditions, but it is possible that some students who attend regular classes may need a wheelchair for part or all of their school day. This may be necessary because of slowness, fatigue, or lack of independent travel skills. Wheelchairs must also be checked periodically for worn or broken parts, and the teacher should be aware of posture, fit, and comfort of the child. If the teacher notices any equipment in need of repair, she should immediately report it to the child's therapist, resource or itinerant teacher, or parents.

In the preceding pages we have discussed the most common orthopedic and health impairments that may be found in regular classrooms and that may require modifications and adaptations of curriculum or materials. We have not discussed all the possible conditions because many require no modification. If students with a different type of impairment attend a regular classroom, teachers must assume responsibility by determining precisely what they should and should not do.

SPECIAL EQUIPMENT

The extent and type of special equipment necessary in the regular classroom depend on the age of the student, the severity of the student's condition, and the primary use of the classroom. Younger children may need more specialized equipment since they have not developed the independent living skills or modes of ambulation developed by older students. The severity of the condition most likely dictates the amount and type of specialized equipment needed; logically, the more severe the impairment, the greater the need for adaptive equipment. The third factor, primary classroom use, relates to the general purpose of the classroom itself; if the student is expected to move about frequently (e.g., in a chemistry laboratory), some modification may be necessary. If, on the other hand, the classroom is used primarily for lecture and note taking, the modifications would be very minimal.

The paragraphs that follow review some of the special equipment that may be necessary to accommodate students with orthopedic and health impairments.

General Classroom Furniture and Arrangement

Students in wheelchairs often need an adapted writing or work area (Figure 7–5). Adjustable tables that can be raised or lowered to different heights permit greater flexibility. A pedestal-base table also allows the student in a wheelchair greater maneu-

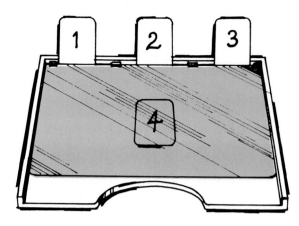

FIGURE 7–5. A cutout lapboard or desktop may be fitted over wheelchairs to provide a work area for students who need one.

verability and freedom than a table with legs. Cut-out desk tops attached to the existing surface or portable lap boards are beneficial for students in wheelchairs. Traditional classroom arrangements of rows of desks are generally inconvenient unless some provision is made for wider aisles.

Chalkboards and bulletin boards may be lowered to be more accessible to the wheelchair student. Relocating classroom items such as coat hooks, alarms, light switches, some doorknobs, plumbing fixtures, and pencil sharpeners, may be advisable in some situations. The practicality of these modifications should be considered in view of cost and necessity.

Many schools built more recently follow designs incorporating modifications to reduce barriers for handicapped students. Modifications incorporated include

1. floors with nonskid surfaces, such as carpeting
2. doors with automatic door checks that allow the door to remain open for wheelchairs and crutch walkers (at the very least, doors should have a grasping bar rather than doorknobs)
3. lowered chalkboards (about 24 inches from the floor)
4. classrooms with two doors, one near the front and another near the back
5. sinks accessible from three sides
6. faucets that self-close
7. toilet facilities near classrooms
8. facilities for students who need additional rest
9. sliding doors on storage spaces
10. a variety of equipment such as standing tables, adjustable seats, and desks

These modifications are not prerequisites for successful mainstreaming of orthopedically impaired students; however, they may facilitate accessibility.

When exit plans for fire drills or other emergencies are routinely developed, care should be taken to make certain that students in wheelchairs or using crutches or braces are not left unattended or without assistance (if necessary).

Communication Devices

Some students who possess average or above-average intellectual ability and are otherwise capable of attending a regular classroom may not have the necessary communication skills to do well in a regular class. For example, many students with cerebral palsy may have well-developed receptive language skills but lack the fine motor coordination needed to express themselves using traditional methods of expression such as writing or typewriting. Other students may have a speech impairment severe enough to seriously limit their functional oral language.

In years past these students were often relegated to an educational program that seriously limited their academic, social, and emotional growth. Today, because of technological advances and alternative communica-

FIGURE 7–6. Student with cerebral palsy using head-pointer and communication board.

commonly used to assist nonverbal students express themselves and answer questions (Figures 7–6 and 7–7). When using a manual communication board, the student points to the numbers, letters, words, or phrases. Other types employ a scanning procedure in which the student operates a moving light to indicate the word selected. The board may require changes as the student's vocabulary develops or new areas of study are pursued. Electronic communication boards are available from several sources. AutoCom[4] displays the student's comments and responses on a television screen, enabling the teacher to include the student in classroom discussions (Figure 7–8). HandiVoice[5] provides a voice output from self- contained vocabulary of over 400 words (Figure 7–9). Express[6] is a microprocessor-based communication aid offering meaningful written and optional speech output (Figure 7–10). Entire thoughts may be programmed into its memory with a single or minimal number of selections.

These are only a few examples from the array of devices available. It is exciting to think about continued technological advances that may greatly enhance the communication process for individuals with expressive or upper extremity motor-control difficulties.

Additional Classroom Aids

Students with orthopedic impairments, because of their difficulty with movement, may use a number of learning aids not typically found in regular classrooms. The aids may be very simple modifications such as clay-wrapped pencils to assist with grasping and

tion systems and devices, students with severe motor or communication problems are allowed greater participation in regular classrooms.

There are many different types of communication systems, ranging from a direct-selection communication board with the letters of the alphabet to highly sophisticated microcomputers. Communication boards are

---

[4]Prentke Romich Co., 8769 Township Rd. #513, Shreve, OH 44676.
[5]Phonic Ear, Inc., 250 Camino Alto, Mill Valley, CA 94941.
[6]Prentke Romich Co., 8769 Township Rd. #513, Shreve, OH 44676.

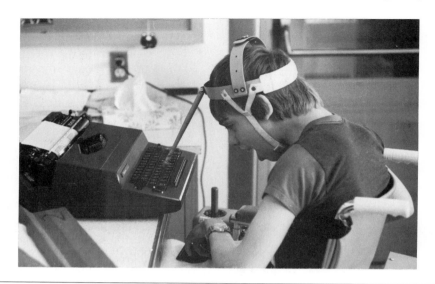

FIGURE 7—7. This multiply handicapped student must use a head-pointer because he cannot hold a pencil or other handwriting tools. He requires a motorized wheelchair and other adapted equipment to be able to function effectively.

FIGURE 7—8. Auto-Com, a portable, microprocessor-based communication system, is operated by moving a magnetic handpiece across surface of board to make word, phrase, or sentence selections that may be read on display or print-out.

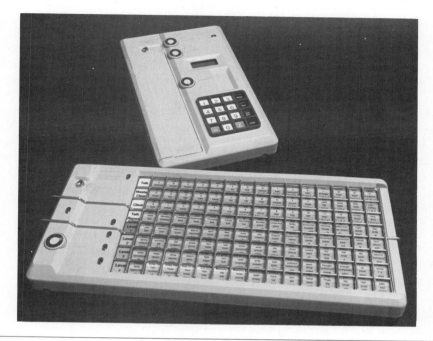

FIGURE 7–9. Two models of Phonic Ear HandiVoice, a portable electronic voice synthesizer that enables the nonvocal individual to communicate.

FIGURE 7–10. Express 3, a communication device used by nonspeaking or severely physically disabled individuals.

holding, four-fingered scissors, or clipboards or elastic tape to hold the paper on the writing surface. Page turners are useful for students with limited arm use; wrist or hand weights may assist the student with limited control. Teaching machines such as magnetic-card machines are often used if they do not require complex motor movements. Conventional and modified typewriters are used extensively. Students who have difficulty with movement may use head wands to strike the keys. Light-operated typewriting machines are operated by fixing a light source to the student's hand or head so that a light spot can be projected on the control panel.

Talking books, previously only available for the blind, are now available for individuals with impairments that prevent them from handling books comfortably. Talking books and talking book machines are distributed by the Library of Congress at no cost to the user.

Resource or itinerant specialists in consultation with the physical and occupational therapist may recommend other ways to modify materials. They can observe the student in the regular classroom and offer suggestions or ways to modify and adapt equipment and materials. Part of their responsibility is to keep abreast of current technological advances and new materials and equipment and share their recommendations with the regular teacher.

SUMMARY

This chapter considers many different, specific conditions and/or disabilities. The students whose needs are described in this chapter do not really fit into a "classification" in the same sense as the hearing impaired or the mentally retarded. But they are grouped together for practical purposes, and there are some logical reasons to do so. There are similarities with respect to some conditions; for example, close medical supervision may be required for students with asthma, arthritis, or epilepsy. (However, for some students, only very minimal supervision may be required.) There are also similarities in that many students with physical disabilities have quite normal learning abilities, if we can modify/arrange the environment so that they can use those abilities. Because it is difficult to predict when any teacher may have need for the information presented in this chapter, all teachers are encouraged to consider and think through the suggestions provided, regardless of their apparent, immediate applicability.

As is the case with other handicapping conditions, effective communication may be the key to a successful mainstream experience for the student with an orthopedic or health impairment. The regular classroom teacher may be the crucial element in communication among the parents, therapists, medical personnel, and resource personnel. The teacher should try to better understand the problems encountered by families of disabled students and try to provide the needed support and assistance. They should recognize that there is a delicate balance among proper care of the condition, overprotection, and the student's need for independence.

The teacher also may be in the best position to observe the effects of therapy, medication, diet, and activity and their influence on the student's behavior and growth. Often the teacher has the opportunity to observe the student in a different setting and for a longer period of time than parents or medical personnel, and if a change in behavior is noted, it should be communicated to the parents.

It is critical that the teacher obtain as complete information as possible about the student's impairment and, after independent study, observation, and consultation, know as precisely as possible what the student should and should not do.

The modifications and adaptations for a student with an orthopedic or health impairment who attends a regular classroom may be minimal. Perhaps the most important factor for the regular classroom teacher to understand is the influence of her attitude on the attitudes of handicapped and nondisabled students alike. The following adage indicates the need for an objective and sensitive attitude:

> What you think of me,
> I will think of me.
> What I think of me,
> Will be me.

When those who daily interact with any individual perceive that individual in a negative way, that perception may be internalized as "fact." If others in the immediate environment—teachers, parents, siblings, and friends—see the individual in a positive light, the individual will probably see himself in this way. Our goal for the disabled is that they should see themselves first and foremost as individuals with many valued abilities and only incidentally as persons with disabilities.

Teaching Students Who Have Speech or Language Disorders

THE DEVELOPMENT OF NORMAL SPEECH AND LANGUAGE

IDENTIFICATION OF SPEECH PROBLEMS

IDENTIFICATION OF LANGUAGE DISORDERS

SUGGESTIONS FOR THE REGULAR CLASSROOM TEACHER

ROLE OF THE SPEECH-LANGUAGE PATHOLOGIST

☐ Why are good speech and language considered a "miracle" by some speech and language authorities?

☐ What must the teacher know about "pragmatics" to be able to effectively assist a student with communication problems?

☐ How different must a student's speech be to be considered a handicap?

☐ Why has the major focus of speech specialists shifted away from articulation disorders?

☐ What is the most common "speech flow disorder" and why has it held such historic interest for speech-language professionals?

☐ What speech or voice disorder is of such potential seriousness that it requires **immediate** referral?

This chapter is about the regular classroom teacher's role in assisting students with speech and language disorders. However, from the beginning, we want to emphasize that our major concerns are with the relationships between speech, language, and communication.

We are often told that the great intelligence of humans is what permits the many advances in, for example, technology and medicine. For many of us, these discoveries and developments are almost beyond our ability to conceptualize. But we must recognize that in spite of our intelligence, without speech, language, and communication, these advances would not have taken place. It follows then, that individuals with impaired speech, language, and communicative abilities will not likely function effectively in a world so dependent on fast, accurate communication.

Our first concern will be to define the abilities that make possible the process we call *communication*. This process involves two or more individuals, with transmission of thoughts or ideas taking place between them. In the simplest form, this involves individual *A* transmitting a thought or idea to individual *B*. To do this, individual *A* must convert his thought/idea/message into some type of symbol system. This is often referred to as *encoding*. Individual *B*, after receiving the message, must *decode* it, or convert the symbols back into the thought/idea/message. The

four major elements of language and their normal relationship in the communication process may be illustrated as in Figure 8–1. The output/expressive skills most used by humans are speaking and writing. The input/receptive skills are listening and reading. The process through which communication takes place may be called an integrative process.

In this chapter, we will start our consideration of communication with speech, one aspect of the complex language system. However, before defining speech, we will note that despite all of the technological advances involving computers and sound-production equipment, we cannot produce really natural-sounding human speech. This marvelous technology, through which we can shop, pay bills, cook meals, fly aircraft, and correct both grammar and spelling when typing, cannot be programmed to produce a version of the English language that includes the richness and variation of speech that is developed simply and naturally by a four-year-old child. What, then, is speech? According to Bernstein and Tiegerman (1985) "Speech is verbal communication. It involves the precise coordination of oral neuromuscular actions to form linguistic units. In addition to speech sounds, rate of speech and rhythm and intensity of sound also contribute to the speech process" (p. 6). Language, according to the same authors, "is the system of rules governing sounds, words, meaning,

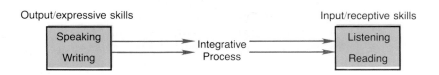

FIGURE 8–1. Integrative process
*Speaking and writing are the major expressive skills. Gestures (especially as in sign language used by the hearing impaired) and facial expressions are among the other expressive modes important in communication.

and use. These rules underlie both linguistic comprehension (the understanding of language) and linguistic production (the formulation of language). While children give evidence of 'knowing' many of the rules of language at quite an early age, precisely how this 'rule learning' occurs is still being researched by investigators" (p. 6). Two further statements, from an American Speech-Language-Hearing Association (ASHA) committee report, will add further meaning to the Bernstein and Tiegerman description. The first, the core definition provided by the ASHA Committee on Language, is "Language is a complex and dynamic system of conventional symbols that is used in various modes for thought and communication" (ASHA Committee on Language, 1983, p. 44). The second, one of the statements made in expansion of this core definition, is "Effective use of language for communication requires a broad understanding of human interaction including such associated factors as nonverbal cues, motivation, and sociocultural roles" (p. 44). Language, then, involves much more than speech and is used both in communication and *thought*. It is the fundamental ability that unquestionably separates humans from other members of the animal kingdom. It is complex, it is not fully understood, and impairments in language will almost certainly lead to impairments in the learning process.

THE DEVELOPMENT OF NORMAL SPEECH AND LANGUAGE

In this chapter we will be concerned with impairments in either speech or language that interfere with effective communication. To aid us in the understanding of some of the disabilities in this arena, we will provide an overview of how normal speech and language develop. Perhaps the automatic, apparently effortless nature of speech and language development is the reason many

educators are poorly informed about a process so basic to academic success. But such knowledge is essential when dealing with those students who are not making normal progress in the areas of speech and language.

A very generalized explanation of how a child learns language skills is that they are acquired through listening and imitation. Such imitation is apparently encouraged when a child learns that language is of value to get what he or she wants, be it attention, adult approval, toys, or food. This general theory is supported by the fact that deaf children have serious problems with language, presumably because they cannot hear and thus cannot imitate.

Despite the many mysteries surrounding the acquisition of speech and language, certain matters are known. Among those things we do know is that speech and language are learned behaviors and that they seem to follow the laws that apply to other types of learned behavior in lower animals and humans. We know that although similarities exist among the more than one thousand languages spoken by humans, there are highly significant differences; there is little apparent logic as to why each race or culture has its specific language patterns. We also know, by observation, that these patterns are perpetuated as children learn the language spoken around them to communicate their needs and desires.

If a child is to speak normally and thus develop language, certain abilities must be present. The child must have the ability to hear, have normal or near normal speech mechanisms, and have adequate (normal or near normal) brain and central nervous system functioning. If he cannot hear or has impaired hearing, he does not receive accurate auditory input to imitate; this results in slow speech development, faulty articulation, or both. If he does not have normal or near normal speech organs, he may be unable to articulate in a manner that is acceptably imitative of others. If his central nervous system is to some degree dysfunctional, he may not be able to receive the proper sensory input, make the necessary associations, or coordinate the muscles of articulation. If the child is mentally retarded, his speech and language development may not follow normal patterns of development. The type of neural dysfunction and the degree of mental retardation have significant effects on the type and degree of speech and language disorders.

If a child has normal abilities, normal environmental stimulation, and opportunity to learn, the development of speech follows a predictable developmental pattern. For most children the first sounds uttered following birth are those accompanying the first exhalation. Very soon, crying begins, and develops into the characteristic crying that parents learn to interpret in terms of specific wants and needs. This may be considered primary communication, but it is not speech. At least three distinctive types of crying seem to be common to all very young babies: a cry that says, "I'm not comfortable!" (wet or too warm, for example), a cry that says, "I'm in pain!" and a cry that says, "I'm hungry—feed me."

These first primitive attempts at communication may appear to be primarily one-way (from the child to anyone who may hear), but in fact they are preliminary to other meaningful sounds to which most parents respond, thus triggering more sounds from the child. This is the start of meaningful two-way communication and provides the base for later speech.

Babbling, beginning as early as 6 weeks or as late as 10–12 weeks, consists of the child combining syllables in some type of random and—as far as we can tell—meaningless order. It is regarded as a milestone in prespeech vocalization, and it is important

that the parent babble or talk back to the child. In addition to the reinforcement the child receives from the parents' returned babbling, there is an obvious element of pleasure that all children seem to derive from hearing their own babbling. If the child cannot hear his own babbling because of hearing impairment, he is not reinforced to continue and thus begins a series of events that may result in severe retardation in speech and language development.

It is likely that many children will actually say their first word by the time they are 1 year old, however, the exact time at which the first word is spoken is less important than giving the child every opportunity to proceed through the requisite developmental steps with the necessary environmental support. This support includes, but is not limited to, (1) a maximum of personal interaction with the child—not "smothering" the child but including her in a maximum of activities and settings consistent with her other physical needs and limitations, (2) providing good adult role models, and (3) a concerted effort to *talk* to the child, using a variety of words, facial expressions, and voice inflections at a level at which the child may be maximally stimulated. This includes deliberate inclusion of the child in conversations when small groups of individuals are together in the presence of the child. If these steps are followed and the child receives a maximum of love and care, she has been given the best possible chance to develop normal speech in later childhood.

After the child develops the ability to say single words, the use of a two-, three-, or four-word sentence may be encouraged if other adults in the environment respond with expansions like "Yes, that is Daddy's hat" or simply with "Daddy's hat."

The exact process whereby the child selects from the vast array of words in his environment the words he first chooses to use is unknown. It appears that the names of food, clothing, animals, and toys, along with *mommy* and *daddy,* are among the earliest words for most children. Words describing actions, such as *give, bye-bye,* and *down,* which may also be demand words, are commonly learned at an early age. Whatever the words, the suggestions given previously relating to maximizing personal interaction, providing a good model, and talking to the child are, if adjusted to the child's level, of value throughout the preschool years. It may be tempting at times to shut the child off because he seems to be talking ceaselessly, but if speech can be directed and encouraged, the payoff will be better language development and at least slightly increased odds of success in the areas of reading and language arts after the child enrolls in school.

It is almost certain that during the preschool years, children exhibit speech characteristics that would be viewed as speech problems requiring correction if they were in existence several years later. Articulation problems abound with almost all young children. These are simply a reflection of partially developed speech production and a partially trained ear for sounds and words. Nonfluencies undoubtedly develop, some of which could be interpreted as stuttering, but most vanish if parents accept them for what they are—a part of the developmental process of most children. The existence of certain normal nonfluencies is emphasized because the efforts of some parents and teachers to correct nonfluencies appear to be an important causal factor in stuttering. Too much reaction to normal nonfluencies by parents and well-intentioned but uninformed

A variety of games and activities assist language development.

teachers may promote rather than reduce stuttering.

This brief consideration of how speech and language normally develop does not attempt to consider some of the theoretical debates among language experts as to what mechanism in the human brain permits the individual to expand his vocabulary from 200–250 words at two years to 2500 words or more at six years. We simply accept this vocabulary development as fact. Other language mysteries are equally puzzling but have at least been analyzed and labeled, so that they may be discussed and given further attention through a variety of ongoing research. For example, we know that the young child develops an understanding of how words are built from sounds, and then arranged into phrases and sentences. As children grow older, they learn to use words differently with, for example, a four year old, from how they would with another teenager or adult. These various language skills, or components of language, are described by the American Speech-Language-Hearing Association (ASHA Committee on Language, 1983) as phonology, morphology, syntax, semantics, and pragmatics. All are rule governed and are essential to an understanding of normal language development. They provide an important part of the basis for analysis of disorders and plans for remediation. We will briefly define and discuss examples of disorders of each of these components.

Phonology is the sound system of oral language. The English language consists of 46 sounds, or phonemes, which are either vowels or consonants. These basic units are combined into meaningful sequences. For example, the sounds of *j, a,* and *m* combined form the *jam.* In this case, each letter stands for a single phoneme; however, in the word *this, th* is pronounced as one sound and is a phoneme. Errors may occur through mispronunciations, omissions, or substitutions.

Morphology refers to the smallest units of language that represent meaning. In general terms, morphology relates to the structure of words to stems and the suffixes or prefixes that modify the meaning of a stem in some fashion. Morphemes can be words that stand alone, like *took, was,* or *that,* or be parts of words like *un,* which, added to, for example, the word *able,* changes the meaning. Similarly, the *s* in *chairs* and the *es* in *dishes* modify the meaning of the stems. Errors may be related to incorrect usage of morphemes, for instance, *goed* and *mostest.*

Syntax refers to the relative subordination of words and clauses. In English, these are often determined by word order. There are a variety of rules governing word order that, if not followed, will result in either a string of words with no meaning or doubt about the meaning of the sentence. The sentence, "The boy bit the dog," has a significant change in meaning if just two words are transposed, namely, "The dog bit the boy." Examples of syntactic errors (violation of rules) include "My teacher gave a talk on the moon," and "The paper said he died last week due to a reporting error." The rules governing morphology and syntax combined make up the rules of grammar.

Semantics encompasses the meanings assigned to words, groups of words, and sentences. *Phonology, morphology,* and *syntax* form the structures of the language system, while *semantics* refers to the meaning of those structures. Knowledge of semantics is reflected in vocabulary usage, concepts that are developed, and the association of words. For example, in the group of words, *man, in, lives, the, house,* and *white,* each word has some element of meaning. By grouping the words *the man lives* and *in the white house,* a greater degree of meaning is reflected. And finally, by putting the words together in a sentence, *The man lives in the white house,* additional meaning is attached. Understanding either the lesser meaning attached to the string of words or the more involved meaning of the sentence depends upon receivers' understanding of the individual words, appropriate word order, and the concept conveyed in the sentence. Semantic errors may be as simple as misunderstanding the meaning of a word (for example, confusing the noun *judge* in isolation, with the verb) or as serious as complete misinterpretation of sentences.

Pragmatics refers to the use of language of communication in varying situations. This would include modifying the choice of words based on the information level of the receiver, on the setting, or on the purpose of communication. For example, simple words might be used with a 3 or 4 year old, while more enriched vocabulary would be appropriate for a 14 year old. At the college level, more complex vocabulary and sentence structure might be appropriate for a presentation to a class and more informal language would be used in the cafeteria. Pragmatics also includes the intention of the speaker, whether it be to provide information, gather information, share an observation or something else. The speaker must be aware of the listener's characteristics including such aspects as level of understanding, interest, ability to respond, and so on.

In summary, *pragmatics* refers to ability of the speaker to conform to the rules of communication that involve modifying language according to the situation, the listener's characteristics, the intent of communication, or some combination of these. Examples of errors include, in our culture, asking personal questions upon just being introduced to a person or using incomplete and/or incoherent sentences when giving an oral presentation.

The components just reviewed as separate entities are very interrelated. Effective communicators have a command of all components even though they may not be able to verbalize many of the rules governing them. Individuals with disabilities in this area are at a disadvantage in communicating their thoughts and ideas effectively. When speech and language are underdeveloped or defective, academic problems almost always result, especially in reading. In the case of more serious problems, there is an apparent correlation with problems in thinking, because it appears that for the most part, humans think in words.

IDENTIFICATION OF SPEECH PROBLEMS

One of the questions asked most often about speech disorders (or suspected disorders) is "How different must a child's speech be to be considered a disorder or handicap?" The answer given by most authorities is that unusual speech is a handicap if it (1) interferes with communication, (2) causes the speaker to be maladjusted, or (3) calls undue attention to itself at the expense of what the speaker is saying. This answer focuses on the effects of the speech rather than on the physiology of speech production. The speech-language pathologist is concerned with helping the student to produce speech in the most normal manner possible and to use it effectively in normal communication in such a manner that the speaker can concentrate on what the student is saying, not how he or she is saying it. This generalization also applies to language disorders, which are often, although not always, related to speech problems.

Speech disorders may be classified in three broad categories: articulation, stuttering, and voice disorders. Articulation disorders are most common; however, stuttering may have more severe ramifications. Voice problems (inappropriate pitch, loudness, or quality) must be considered primarily from the point of view of recognition and understanding. Awareness of voice problems may be, in some respects, even more important than, for example, articulation problems, because there is some possibility of an immediate need for medical attention. Thus the teacher must be able to recognize voice problems to make an appropriate referral. With each of these types of speech problems, it is important to understand and refer students for additional help to avoid becoming engaged in counterproductive efforts or wasting valuable time in relation to the student's overall progress in the area of language development.

Speech, language, and hearing problems are interrelated and may affect learning. This interrelationship is illustrated in Figure 8–2 and explains why the regular classroom teacher may be working with one or more of

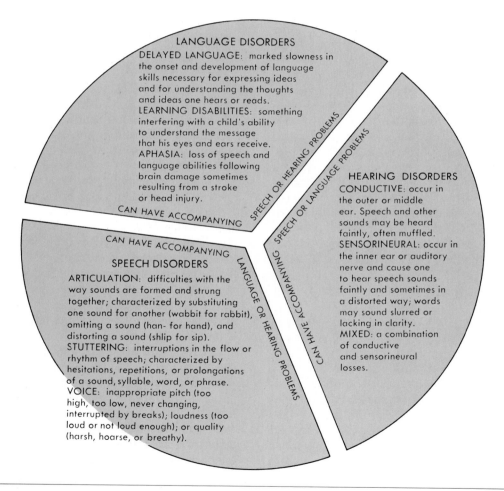

FIGURE 8–2. Disorders of speech, language, and hearing and how they interrelate

Note. From public information materials of the American Speech and Hearing Association; reproduced with permission.

three special education specialists in some cases. These specialists—in the areas of speech, learning disabilities, and hearing impairment—should make the final decision as to who is primarily responsible for providing suggestions and classroom assistance, and that responsibility should be specifically spelled out in the individualized program for the student involved.

Articulation Disorders

Articulation errors were once the major focus of speech-language pathologists, but that focus has shifted because of two major factors: (1) it was increasingly recognized that many young children outgrew minor articulation problems with no specialized assistance, and (2) it became obvious that some of the more serious speech disorders required more time and effort from specialists. This focus shift does not mean that teachers should not refer students if the only obvious difficulty is an articulation problem. Nor does it mean that speech-language pathologists never serve young children who have only articulation problems. In many cases, a combination of evaluation by the speech-language pathologist followed by management suggestions implemented by the regular classroom teacher and the parent proves most effective. The need for the regular classroom teacher to understand and properly play this partnership role is a main theme of this chapter.

Articulation errors are those involving omissions, substitutions, distortions, or additions when pronouncing (articulating) words. The following are examples of articulation errors:

Substitution: wun for *run, dat* for *that, wabbit* for *rabbit, thum* for *some*
Omission: pay for *play, cool* for *school, ift* for *lift, day* for *daddy*
Distortion: shled for *sled*
Additions: buhrown for *brown, cuhow* for *cow, puhlease* for *please, sawr* for *saw*

Certain generalizations applicable in nearly all cases of articulation-error therapy may be used as guidelines for remedial efforts. First, *the student must hear the error.* In most cases the letter or letters are pointed out to him in writing or print so that there can be no question as to what letter or letters are in question; then the student must learn to hear the sound as properly articulated by the teacher or speech-language pathologist. Often the student must learn to listen for the sound in initial, medial, and final positions; then he must learn to differentiate between the sound properly articulated and the sound as he articulates it. This may be done with a tape recorder. The teacher may deliberately mispronounce the sound, and on the playback the student may learn to discriminate the error sound from the correctly produced sound in varying phonetic contexts. After this stage, recordings of both the student and the teacher may be made to assist in recognizing the varying sounds. Other methods or materials may be used; however, learning to *hear* errors is an absolute prerequisite to any further work with articulation problems. This is sometimes called *auditory training.*

When absolutely certain that the student can hear the difference between accurate and inaccurate articulation of the sounds in question, it is necessary that the child learn to produce the correct sound. This may be accomplished through games, exercises, behavior shaping (using approximations of the right sound production and slowly approaching the correct articulation), or any method that seems appropriate to the age and interests of the child. Many young children see little reason to change their speech patterns; this is true with all speech correction but perhaps most often with articulation problems. They seem to get by, and unless they are embarrassed by the reactions of others, they may not care. In some instances we must make them care enough to hear articulatory differences and then motivate them to learn to make the correct sound. Reward systems may be of considerable value in accomplishing this step.

A third step is to have the student incorporate the newly learned, accurately articulated sound in familiar words. Even though the student learns to hear the difference between accurate and inaccurate articulation and to produce the required sound, until it is regularly used in language he or she has not overcome the problem. When an individual has had months or years of practice in saying the sound incorrectly, it takes a fair amount of repetition to develop new speech habits and patterns. Here again, motivation is highly important; with young children, games are often valuable.

In addition to the preceding overall rules for remediation, one general rule must be carefully observed by the regular classroom teacher. If the student is being seen by a speech-language pathologist, the teacher should consult with the specialist to be certain that any special efforts in the classroom are complementary, not contradictory, to efforts of the speech clinician.

Stuttering and Other Speech-Flow Disorders

Most speech authorities agree that stuttering has been and remains the most elusive of the speech disorders. This is true in terms of both cause and treatment, and although new theories and treatments are advocated with some regularity, our review of the pertinent literature leads us to believe that there is no clearly best theory or best treatment.

Stuttering is just one type of a disorder that may be described as a breakdown in the normal flow of speech. Other types receive much less attention, and all can be described as relating to difficulties in one or more of the five generally recognized dimensions of speech flow. Those dimensions are (1) *sequence,* or the order of sounds (for example, the word *cavalry* is often pronounced as *calvary*); (2) *duration,* or the length of time any

phonetic element is produced (a duration problem may lead to confusion through decreased intelligibility and is usually just one part of a more complex problem); (3) *rate,* or the speed of articulation of speech sounds, syllables, or words (like duration, rate is not often a problem except as combined with other speech problems); (4) *rhythm,* or the pattern of phonetic elements (when rhythm is faulty, intelligibility and thus comprehension of speech are endangered); and (5) *fluency,* or the smoothness of articulation of sounds (the extreme example of disfluency is stuttering; other types of disfluency, as in some regional speech-flow patterns, are accepted as normal in some parts of the nation and are at least acceptable in others).

Stuttering, the most highly recognized of the speech-flow disorders, has been explained by speech experts through various theories or hypotheses about its causes. There are many such theories, falling into two major groups: *organic* and *behavioral.* Organic theories propose a variety of neurological causes for stuttering, ranging from older theories involving a lack of cerebral dominance to those that liken stuttering to epileptic seizures. In many of these theories the fact that stutterers do not always stutter is accounted for by postulating a constitutional weakness that tends to "give" under pressure.

Nonorganic theories about the cause of stuttering may be grouped according to three major points of view, each dictating a somewhat different treatment, as may be seen from the accounts that follow. Each of these descriptions is a generalization of two or three closely related theories.

1. Stuttering is a result of the fact that important individuals in the student's early life label normal disfluencies "stuttering." In response, the child focuses on these disfluencies, attempting to eliminate them. Overreaction, fear, tension, and anxiety lead to these disfluencies being

maintained long beyond the time when they would normally be abandoned, thus they become actual stuttering.

2. Stuttering is the result of an unusual need of the child to be understood. When the child tries to maintain listeners' attention, normal disfluencies that might otherwise be overlooked by both speaker and listener lead to more and more frustration. As the speaker struggles (because of internal drives, not outside influence) to become more fluent, tension and frustration lead to continued disfluency.

3. Stuttering is the result of a need to satisfy anal or oral desires, infantile tendencies, or high levels of hostility. These in turn are the result of inadequate or unsatisfactory relationships with parents; various psychoanalytic theories of child-parent conflict explain these conflicts.

Various combinations of these theories have been constructed to form additional theories, but for the nonspecialist, these three are the thrust of stuttering theories. Although various authorities may insist that their approach is based on a specific theory and think that recognition of the cause is highly important, in practice all therapies are notable for their high rate of failure.

Fortunately for the student and the teacher who wants to help the student, certain recommendations are generally applicable to stuttering. These should be followed unless the speech specialist specifically dictates other recommendations. These four relatively simple recommendations involve an *attitude* that the teacher and others who deal with the stutterer should adopt:

1. Do not mention the stuttering; try to reduce the student's awareness of this problem.
2. Minimize those settings and situations that appear to cause increased stuttering.
3. Minimize conflict of all types as much as possible.
4. Encourage speaking when all is going

well, and immediately minimize demands to communicate when stuttering becomes more pronounced.

Primary, or beginning, stutterers may overcome the problem if those around them have accurate information and the right attitude. For secondary or confirmed stutterers, major goals may include acceptance of stuttering as a part of the language pattern and learning to stutter more easily or gracefully.

Though the lack of agreement among speech authorities about stuttering has been emphasized, there is general agreement on a number of "facts" about stuttering that help provide a better total perspective on this complex disorder. Ten such observations follow:

1. Stutterers rarely if ever stutter while singing.
2. Stutterers rarely stutter while speaking in unison or in synchronization with a rhythmic beat.
3. Stutterers rarely stutter while alone or while swearing.
4. Stuttering cannot always be induced, even in those who otherwise stutter regularly.
5. Stutterers tend to stutter on the same words when reading and rereading the same passage. They may *not* stutter on these same words in other sentences.
6. Stutterers tend to be able to predict their stuttering.
7. Time pressure seems to be a factor in causing or increasing stuttering.
8. Stutterers cannot be shown to be biologically different from nonstutterers.
9. Stutterers can learn to hear how their speech flows and understand what normal fluency means; they just cannot *attain* such fluency.
10. Many cases of stuttering (more than 75% by some estimates) simply disappear without any identifiable, provable reason.

Given these facts and the four attitudinal recommendations, the regular classroom teacher should be able to manage the stutterer until the results of evaluation are received. At that point the speech-language pathologist should offer specific recommendations that should be followed. Teachers should make every attempt to obtain prompt assistance with students who stutter and should resist the temptation to try out the various "quick cures" that regularly appear in news magazines and Sunday newspapers.

Voice Disorders

Voice disorders are not nearly as common as articulation disorders (Berko Gleason, 1985), however, they require immediate attention by the regular classroom teacher. That is, the teacher must make a prompt referral to the speech-language pathologist if voice disorders are suspected. If a speech-language pathologist is not available, referral to the school nurse and to the parent is in order.

Voice disorders are generally considered to include disorders of *pitch, intensity, quality,* and *flexibility.* For the most part, these problems do not have the same kind of direct effect on the learning of basic skills as, for example, serious articulation problems may have. In fact, unless they are very different from the norm, they are often accepted as part of the uniqueness of the individual. The following descriptions of these four types of voice disorders are presented so that the teacher may have an overall view of voice disorders and a base from which to consider the need for referral, either to the speech-language pathologist or, through the parents, to the physician.

Pitch problems seldom cause any serious difficulty for the speaker, with the exception of the high falsetto voice in the upper-teenage or adult male. For girls and women, various levels of pitch are accepted, low voices being often regarded as "sexy" and high ones as "feminine." For men, the prob-

lem may be different. Despite a number of recent societal changes in concepts of masculinity and femininity, there is a stubborn persistence of the belief that men should have a voice that is of low or medium pitch. Therefore, a boy with a high-pitched voice that apparently is continuing into his upper-teenage years may benefit from therapy to help him lower the pitch. Sometimes pitch can be lowered, and sometimes it cannot; the matter is usually a sensitive one, but if assistance can be provided, it may help greatly in the social arena.

Voice *intensity,* too loud or too soft, is not often a problem in and of itself, but very loud speech may mean that the individual does not hear his or her own voice distinctly and should serve as a cue to recheck the possibility of a hearing problem. The teacher should also note that if a child speaks indistinctly (as opposed to too softly) and is asked to *speak up,* the result may be even more unsatisfactory than before. In speaking up, many students with indistinct speech give voice to very loud vowel sounds, which even further drowns out the weaker consonant sounds. Therefore the teacher or speech-language pathologist must work on more precise consonant production.

Voice *quality* is the most common voice disorder of the four major types. Three types of voice-quality problems are breathiness, harshness, and nasality. Harshness or breathiness may be caused by vocal abuse (such as occurs at a hard-fought football game) or may be the result of infection or inflammation of the vocal cords. These temporary problems usually go away after a few days of vocal rest. A more serious problem is that which occurs as a result of continued vocal abuse, causing growths to develop on the vocal cords. Such benign growths are fairly common among singers and, to some extent, among those who do a great deal of public speaking. These too may go away with vocal rest or with therapy to assist in more normal voice production. Such growths may be malignant; thus the advice to seek prompt medical attention mentioned earlier is applicable to older students and of course to adults. Malignant growths cause the same type of voice quality problem as benign growths; the only way to check out this possibility is through referral to a qualified specialist. The teacher should be alert for voice disorders and should be particularly alert for rapid changes in voice quality, especially hoarseness or breathiness. If the teacher is in doubt, an immediate referral to the speech specialist or physician is in order.

The fourth type of voice problem is a *flexibility* disorder. The most common flexibility problem is exhibited by the monotone speaker. This problem may result from many different causes, such as physical tiredness, emotional difficulties, voice pitch too near the top or the bottom of the vocal range, or a hearing problem. If the voice is very unpleasant because of a flexibility disorder and the problem persists, referral to the speech-language pathologist is the proper course of action. Seldom does the regular classroom teacher possesss the technical knowledge and skill to assess and attempt to remediate this type of problem on his or her own.

In summary, most voice problems may be of a minor nature and may be properly overlooked. An exception is the case of unusual voice *changes,* particularly those typified by hoarseness, harshness, or breathiness. If these persist, even for a few weeks, referral is recommended.

Other Speech Problems and What to Do

Three other types of speech problems with three specific causes deserve mention: (1) speech problems directly related to *cerebral palsy,* (2) speech problems related to *hearing loss,* and (3) speech problems related to *cleft lip* or *cleft palate.*

Cerebral palsy–related speech problems can run the gamut from mild to very severe. They may in some few cases result in speech that is almost unintelligible, although perhaps as many as one-third of all cerebral palsied individuals have essentially no speech problem. The best general rule to follow with a student whose cerebral palsy leads to speech problems is to provide sufficient time for the student to respond to questions or participate in class discussion and to make every attempt to learn to "decode" his speech. When a cerebral palsied student is assigned to a new teacher, a few short one-to-one sessions between student and teacher can help much toward early understanding of the student's speech. Practical communication is the goal, and speech therapy must be left to the speech-language pathologist except as the specialist provides very specific instructions for assistance in the regular classroom.

Hearing loss–related problems may lead to a variety of speech difficulties depending on various factors, but the major determining factor is the time of onset of the hearing loss. Some speech problems and some language problems are to be expected with hearing impaired students, but with proper assistance they can be minimized. These problems are discussed in chapter 5 and are not further discussed here except to reemphasize that when a student has continued speech and/or language problems, the possibility of a hearing impairment must be fully investigated. In a somewhat similar manner (although for different reasons), mentally handicapped students usually have some difficulties with language and vocabulary development. They may or may not show evidence of difficulties that might be viewed as speech disorders.

Cleft lip and *cleft palate* problems vary in their effect on speech, depending on the depth of the cleft and the success of surgical procedures. Since mid-century most children born with a facial cleft of any severity have been treated surgically during the first few months of life. A cleft lip after surgical treatment seldom causes any serious problem, but a cleft palate is often not completely corrected surgically. The effects of cleft palate commonly include articulation errors and problems with nasality. The correction of these physiologically based speech problems should be left to the speech clinician. As a result of all of the related problems, students with a cleft palate may tend to avoid speaking and may eventually become retarded in vocabulary and overall language development.

Other less common problems include those related to faulty dentition or abnormal laryngeal structure. In many instances such students can be helped, but medical assistance and the best efforts of the speech-language pathologist are required for maximum improvement. It is obvious that the regular classroom teacher will play a significant role in the implementation of the speech program for such students.

IDENTIFICATION OF LANGUAGE DISORDERS

The speech-language pathologist will assess the student to determine whether or not her syntactic and semantic production and comprehension is similar to that of peers. This may be accomplished through the use of standardized tests. An analysis of the students' spontaneous language provides additional information regarding pragmatic production and communicative comprehension. This type of analysis of strengths and weaknesses in language may lead to the discovery of disorders broadly classified as (1) delayed language (including impairment of language development), (2) impairment of acquired language (aphasia), and (3) nonstandard language—in this case, nonstandard English (Berko Gleason, 1985; Bernstein & Tiegerman, 1985).

Delayed Language

Delayed language (also called *delayed speech*) means simply that the individual is unable to use language in the manner normally expected of that age. This inability may be apparently related to some other known disability, for example, a hearing impairment, learning disability, or mental retardation. In such cases there is usually some agreement as to how to proceed, and a joint effort is required among all professionals of different disciplines working with the child and parents.

One of the more common causes of delayed language may be a lack of need for the child to talk, as occurs in a bilingual home or when the student has a twin with whom she is used to communicating more without speech. If parents attempt to anticipate a child's every need, so that speech is not required for basic need fulfillment, these attempts may delay language development. Or if parents literally believe that children should be seen and not heard, this practice may delay speech and language. Fortunately, such children usually play with other children in the neighborhood and thus have the opportunity and the need to speak to be a successful part of the group. The term *delayed speech* is often used to refer to the speech patterns of hearing impaired and mentally handicapped children, but this condition is not the same as delayed speech or delayed language in children who have adequate hearing and normal or above-normal mental ability. Parents who might become overly concerned with the fact that their young child seldom speaks and wonder if something is basically wrong should consider the case of Albert Einstein, who did not speak until after his third birthday. The situation is somewhat different, however, if the child comes to school at the age of five years and still has seriously delayed language. This condition may require special attention, and planning should start with a complete physical checkup to eliminate the possibility of physiological defects. If there are no such disabilities and the child's intellectual level appears to be at least normal, then the environmental background should be reviewed.

Impairment of Acquired Language

Impairment of acquired language (aphasia) is more often associated with adults and is known to follow head injuries, stroke, or the existence of known brain lesions. Thus aphasia is thought to be a matter of a brain injury that leads to a loss of previously functional ability to speak or comprehend the spoken word. *Childhood aphasia* is a general term used for a language dysfunction in children that many authorities believe is caused by a brain dysfunction in the auditory mechanism for processing speech (Berko Gleason, 1985; Owens, 1984). Most authorities describe several specific types of aphasia, but as is the case with stuttering, there is considerable disagreement among these authorities as to the causes and in some cases the treatment. What the teacher is likely to observe is a child who appears to be trying very desperately to find the language to respond to a question, to participate in a discussion, or to ask a question.

Nonstandard Language

Nonstandard language (often thought of as substandard language) is a matter of concern in the United States, primarily with children from lower socioeconomic groups (the majority of whom are blacks) or with bilingual children whose English is difficult for others to understand and is obviously impoverished. Language differences have been a topic of debate in recent years; educators have recognized, for example, that some nonstandard language, although abnormal by middle-class standards, is quite normal in its home setting. At this time no

one can safely predict what direction this particular issue will take. According to the definitions of speech problems, language problems should be considered significant if they interfere with communication, if they cause the speaker to be maladjusted, or if they cause problems for the listener. Outside lower socioeconomic neighborhoods, extremes of nonstandard language may well cause problems for a listener who simply does not understand much of what the speaker is saying. This, in turn, causes problems for the speaker. This problem and that of teaching bilingual (for example, Spanish-speaking) students to communicate in standard English involve issues other than simply "how-to" problems. There are questions of preservation of culture, individual rights, and school district policy. We cannot make pronouncements that apply in all settings, but we must comment that these are real problems and that teachers should use all their available influence (through teacher organizations and legislative influence, for example) to encourage local schools to take an official position and to make some provision for the specialized programs and curriculum adjustments required by students with these unique needs. There is little question about the potential effects of nonstandard English on the lives of most students for whom it is now a problem. It will have detrimental effects in many potential employment settings, particularly when clear written language is required (in written reports, for example). It may also have negative social consequences in some settings but could have positive consequences in others (such as when remaining within one's cultural and ethnic group). One major question—beyond the intended purpose and function of this text—remains: How can we improve standard English language facility and not damage or disrupt attempts to preserve cultural or ethnic heritage?

SUGGESTIONS FOR THE REGULAR CLASSROOM TEACHER

The teacher must remain alert to make referrals of students who may need special assistance in the area of speech or language, and, as discussed earlier, should be particularly alert to possible voice disorders. Often when arithmetic or reading skills are obviously quite low, teachers feel more secure in making referrals, for these are areas in which they feel confident and in which they may have had considerable training. Many teachers have not had similar training with speech and language problems, and therefore the following guidelines may be of value. They may require revision to conform with local practices, but in principle they are generally applicable.

1. For the new teacher who is not experienced in evaluating potential speech problems, overreferral may be the best practice. With experience, the number of referrals may be reduced without the risk of overlooking students who require assistance.

2. If the speech specialist is available for conferences with teachers (and he should be, on either an informal or a formal scheduled basis), teachers should confer with him to learn more about what type of information is needed and who should or should not be referred. Such conferences usually turn out to be informal in-service training sessions and as such are of great value. The number of such conferences can be reduced as the teacher gains experience.

3. When it appears that the speech or language difficulty might be related to other problems such as a hearing impairment or mental retardation, the teacher should check all records and talk with previous teachers (when possible) to determine if these possibilities have been investigated. Any recent audiological evaluation should receive particular attention in a case of possible hearing impairment.

4. In settings in which the speech specialist is overloaded with cases (a common situation), the teacher may expedite matters by describing the type and extent of the problem in detail. It is not enough to say that the child lisps. Many other factors can be considered, such as how consistently the problem occurs, whether it occurs mainly under pressure or when the child is tired, whether it is noticed by other children, and so on.

If the teacher's referral leads to a speech evaluation and the speech specialist begins to provide assistance to the student, usually the specialist also provides specific suggestions to the teacher. The teacher's role depends on the type and extent of the problem. The specialist will have both positive and negative suggestions as to how the teacher may help support the specialist's efforts. Some general as well as specific suggestions follow.

Teachers must remember that children develop language as an imitative function, so teachers have a special reason to provide a good model of correct articulation and broad language usage. How the teacher speaks has a dramatic effect on the students for whom she is responsible; the teacher should be constantly aware of this effect.

Regular classroom teachers are most likely to become involved with speech and speech problems through both regular efforts to promote speech improvement for all students in the class and individualized efforts to assist specific students with known articulation problems. The regular class teacher might read stories (whatever the age level) to model accurate articulation, phrasing, and so on. Listening to tapes may also help broaden the vocabulary and widen the language experience of students. Rhyming or sentence-building exercises may be of value, depending on the age of the student. Certain television programs may provide language enrichment.

In conjunction with the speech-language pathologist and consistent with the particular objectives for the student, structured naturalistic activities may be developed to provide opportunities for using the skills learned in therapy. Such activities for younger children may center around recess, or involve role playing or puppetry. For older students, activities may be based on food preparation, clothing or grooming, or such prevocational tasks as assembling or sorting materials, interviewing, or sequencing tasks.

Many of the activities described in chapter 10, such as cognitive-rehearsal strategies to organize thoughts before speaking, and various written language activities, may enhance the students' abilities with language. For some students, combining and decombining sentences in oral or written form provides linguistic awareness. Using language-experience approaches in the beginning-to-read stage will allow for expansions of the students' vocabulary as well as assist them to see the relationship between spoken and written language.

Providing instruction or oral directions in shorter, less complex sentences with longer pauses and restatements of important information not only provides an appropriate model but also enables the student to understand the instruction. This, of course, is the goal of communication.

Discussing with the student the speech/language activities and what he or she has learned may help reduce any negative feelings about therapy. Responding to a student's efforts at communication in a positive manner will encourage the student and model acceptance for others.

Oral communication may be encouraged through activities like expression of feelings, oral reports, and problem solving. However, the teacher must be sensitive to situations that might be threatening to the student (Morsink, 1984).

Seating arrangements may facilitate opportunities for the student to use oral language in the classroom. Having the student near the teacher tends to restrict rather than enhance interactions (Lewis & Doorlag, 1987). Rather, the student should be surrounded by good speech models.

Discussing pronunciation and the meaning of new words and providing opportunities for the students to use the new words orally and in written form will enrich the language of the student. A structured format for teaching vocabulary includes demonstrating appropriate and inappropriate examples, asking for examples from the students, providing examples by which students can assess their own performance, and providing definitions for the student to identify (Schloss & Sedlak, 1986).

Students lacking conversational skills may be taught the pragmatics of conversation which, according to Schloss and Sedlak (1986) include

1. taking turns
2. initiating
3. clarifying a point
4. following the sequential organization
5. making coherent contributions
6. maintaining a reasonable social distance (p. 237)

In content areas requiring more specific vocabulary (for example, science), quizzes may help ensure understanding of the basic concepts that will enhance comprehension of lectures or explanations. Explanations of the derivations of words may assist some students to comprehend more fully the meaning of a variety of words. For example, if a student learns the meaning of *inter,* as between or among, she may be able to infer the meaning of *intercolonial, intercultural, intercellular, interdependent,* and others.

Students enjoy using the Language Master.

Role playing in appropriate situations provides for practicing skills in effective communication. An example that is applicable in almost any content area is to have a student teach a particular concept or lesson. This requires preplanning what will be taught and how it will be taught. A student might explain the concept of osmosis with the aid of a chart, or the correct positioning of the body when holding a bat, using stick figures. The oral presentation might be rehearsed to ensure clarity.

Encouraging active participation in class may be of great value, especially if a student with some particular problem has advance notice. For example, the teacher might say, "Tomorrow I am going to ask you to comment on the basic differences between communism and democracy. Let's see if you can challenge the thinking of the rest of the class."

The Language Master, a machine providing visual and auditory information, may be a useful tool. This system uses cards with visual representations (words, pictures, or short phrases) on the top and a magnetic tape near the bottom. As the card is inserted in the machine, a verbal message (which the teacher has prerecorded) is played. The student receives simultaneous auditory and visual stimuli. The Language Master will record the verbal response of the student, allowing for playback. The student may, for example, see a picture of teeth and hear the auditory stimulus "The plural of tooth is ———?" The student's response "teeth," is recorded. On the prerecorded message the teacher may have left space for the student's response and provided the correct response so that the student receives corrective feedback or immediate verification of a correct answer. The Language Master also provides practice in a variety of other grammatical aspects, vocabulary, and reading-enrichment exercises.

To combine oral language and sequencing, the teacher may ask students to provide oral directions for certain activities. For example, the teacher might have the student direct the class as they construct a collage for the bulletin board or perform a specific dance. Ask students, in order to practice verbal skills, to interview another student for specific information, such as his favorite sports or least favorite subject and the reasons for the choice. It is important for students to phrase their questions in ways that require more than one-word responses.

When specific targeted skills are being practiced, a tape recorder may be used, and the student allowed time to evaluate his performance. An example (when the use of adjectives is the targeted skill) would be to provide an opportunity for the student to prepare and record a short presentation about a topic of interest. After recording, the student would then evaluate his use of adjectives in the presentation. Videotaping conversations between two students will also allow students to replay the videotape and determine how well they used specific targeted skills.

Teachers at all grade levels must attend to the manner in which they recognize language usage. This attention requires careful planning, but with practice such planning becomes second nature and has positive spin-off effects with all students in the class. The key concepts in such planning and teaching are exposure, encouragement, variety, opportunity, and innovation. The students' interest must be stimulated and main-

tained. A reward system must be established, be it through grades, praise, or privileges, that encourages students to maintain effort. McCormick (1986) suggests that students with speech or language deficits are more alike than different from their peers in that they "need and can benefit from a range and variety of learning experiences; . . . are interested in and want to talk about the same general objects, events and relationships; and . . . seek the same control over their environment" (p. 124).

These ideas and suggestions are samples of what may be done. They may be modified to provide parallel/similar activities and thus provide a wide variety of options for the teacher.

ROLE OF THE SPEECH-LANGUAGE PATHOLOGIST

The speech-language pathologist is the orchestrator of school speech and language services. As such she provides direct services to students with severe or difficult problems while providing advice to teachers who serve students with milder problems. Effective speech programs involve indentification, evaluation, and remediation and depend highly on cooperative working relationships between speech specialists and regular classroom teachers. The American Speech-Language-Hearing Association and others recommend that speech and language programs be organized along a continuum extending from a communicative-development component to a communicative-disorders component (Bernstein & Tiegerman, 1985; Healey, 1974).

In respect to communicative *development* (Figure 8–3, *left*) the speech-language pathologist must make teachers and parents more aware of factors that help students develop good communicative skills, especially those factors that can be a part of the regular classroom or home environment.

*Communication between the speech-language pathologist and the classroom
teacher is essential.*

Many of the suggestions provided in this chapter would be a part of any such program, along with efforts to construct a total curriculum ensuring experiences that will promote maximum communicative skills in all children. This program is primarily developmental and preventive in nature, and, except for orienting teachers newly employed in a given school, the speech specialist has minimum visibility once the program is well established.

Communicative *deviations* (Figure 8–3, *middle*) are those mild to moderate speech and language problems that require some assistance from the speech-language pathologist but with the regular classroom teacher providing much of the direct effort. Instructions, including original instructions and ongoing assistance, are provided by the specialist, and if classroom efforts are not successful, the specialist intervenes more directly, as required in individual cases.

Communicative *disorders* (Figure 8–3, *right*) include the disorders that obviously require specialized help because of their severity and the need to provide specific, one-to-one assistance on an ongoing basis. Even here, much cooperation between the regular classroom teacher and the specialist is necessary, but this type of service requires a much greater time involvement on the part of the speech-language pathologist.

The speech-language pathologist must assist the teacher to "tune in" to situations in the regular classroom in which various class proceedings, including certain standardized academic tests, are greatly affected by a lack of speech or language ability. The speech-language pathologist must determine the most effective ways to improve the student's speech or language and must involve the teacher in such remediation, providing assistance in required carryover activities in the classroom.

Communicative development	Communicative deviations	Communicative disorders
Development and/or preventive programs carried out in class

Speech specialist is involved in total curriculum to emphasize the value of attention to speech and language development

Specialist serves as consultant and also provides some direct teacher training but essentially no *direct* service to students. | Mild to moderate problems (articulation, etc.)

Specialist evaluates and provides instructions to regular class teacher, who implements major elements of program.

Specialist monitors regularly and intervenes more directly as required. | Severe problems that require more intensive one-to-one service by specialist.

Regular class teacher's efforts are quite important here, but most direct service comes from the specialist. |

Service provided by regular class teacher

Service provided by speech specialist

FIGURE 8–3. The comprehensive speech and language program continuum

Speech-language pathologists serve in a variety of settings in public schools throughout the nation. The majority serve in the regular school setting; our focus has been on these efforts. However, they may be a part of a special program for physically handicapped, cerebral palsied, or multi-handicapped students, in which their day-to-day efforts are a much more integral part of the classroom than has been described in this chapter. In this case one or two speech-language pathologists may be assigned to a single building; however, the more typical pattern is that of an itinerant assigned to several buildings. In this typical, regular school assignment situation, the speech-language pathologist is more likely to have a caseload of 40–50 students, although in some areas the load may be considerably higher. As the types of services provided by speech-language pathologists have moved to the right side of the speech-service continuum (Figure 8–3) maximum caseloads have been reduced through state reimbursement regulations, meaning that the regular classroom teacher *must* deal with many of the milder cases. When the speech-language pathologist and the regular classroom teacher develop a system through which cooperative efforts on behalf of individual students are possible, the program is successful and students are the major beneficiaries.

SUMMARY

Services for students with speech disorders have been a generally accepted part of the school program on a national basis for many years. Special assistance to such students remains one of the highly accepted, major programs for handicapped/disabled students in the public schools. Speech/language services range from developmental and preventive programs provided primarily by the regular classroom teacher, through services for mild-to-moderately speech impaired students, to services provided primarily by speech-language pathologists for students with severe speech-language disorders.

This chapter includes a discussion of articulation, stuttering, and voice and language problems, plus some mention of other speech problems related to causes such as faulty dentition. Of these various problems, articulation disorders are the most common and permit the most fruitful assistance in the regular classroom. A highly important rule in the correction of articulation problems and all other remedial efforts carried out by the regular classroom teacher is that if the child is being seen by a speech specialist, the teacher should consult with the specialist to make certain that classroom efforts are consistent with and complementary to the specialized efforts provided in therapy.

Specific assistance to students who stutter should be left to the specialist, but the teacher may follow certain guidelines that seem to reduce the severity of the problem and seldom conflict with specific programs being implemented by the specialist.

Most voice problems require therapy or, in some cases, medical intervention. The classroom teacher should refer students with suspected voice problems to the speech-language pathologist. If a student is undergoing a very rapid voice change (such as unusual harshness or breathiness) and a speech-language pathologist cannot be obtained quickly, the parent should be urged to take the student to see the family doctor or a medical doctor specializing in such problems.

Language problems are the most difficult of the speech and language disorders to diagnose with certainty. Though the regular classroom teacher should become involved with language improvement programs, if a significant language disorder is suspected, referral to the speech-language pathologist is the only acceptable procedure. Language development efforts with the mentally retarded and the hearing impaired are most important and must be carefully coordinated with all other factors of the student's programs. In the remediation of most language problems, the careful planning of enriched language experiences and the employment of all possible motivational techniques are the usual best starting points.

Speech and language problems are manifested through all of an individual's waking hours, and remedial and developmental efforts should be directed toward this total need. With coordinated efforts among the speech-language pathologist, the regular classroom teacher, and parents, maximum benefit may be derived. Without such total cooperative efforts, we may easily fall short of otherwise attainable goals.

Teaching Students Who Are Mentally Retarded

A DEFINITION OF MENTAL RETARDATION

THE NATURE OF MENTAL RETARDATION

CHARACTERISTICS OF MENTAL RETARDATION

RESPONSIBILITIES OF SPECIAL EDUCATION PERSONNEL

CAREER EDUCATION EMPHASIS

SUGGESTIONS FOR THE REGULAR CLASSROOM TEACHER

SECONDARY SCHOOL PROGRAMS

☐ What factors are major determinants in the success or failure of mentally retarded individuals?

☐ What is adaptive behavior? Why is it so difficult to measure with preciseness?

☐ How should we replace biased tests so that we can still identify and assist mentally retarded students?

☐ What effect may deprived living conditions have on intellectual development?

☐ How does career education differ from vocational education? Why is it so important to students who are mentally retarded?

☐ Which mildly mentally retarded students should be admitted to vocational programs?

☐ Can a teacher cause a permanent negative effect on a student by referring him for evaluation for suspected mental retardation?

When asked "What is mental retardation?" a cross section of college students will give a variety of answers and comments. But what are the facts? What do we know about mental retardation and persons who are mentally retarded?

First, we must recognize that many mildly retarded students may "disappear" into the mainstream of adult society after completion of their formal educational program. If an appropriate program is provided, the percentage who will become self-supporting, responsible citizens will increase, and all society will benefit. As for the moderately mentally retarded, truly normal participation in society is unlikely, but many can become partially self-supporting. However, this goal will be achieved only if we provide the right opportunities during their formative years, and sheltered and/or monitored work and living environments for their adult years. It must also be noted that some students who were throught to be moderately retarded may prove to be more capable and thus perform at a higher level than was earlier believed possible.

Because of the closing of many large residential facilities, more and more students who are severely or profoundly mentally retarded will be a part of public school programs, though they will not be "mainstreamed" in the same manner as the mildly retarded and some moderately mentally retarded. We will not focus on the severe and profound levels of mental retardation in this chapter, although regular classroom teachers may have varying degrees of contact with such students, depending on the program philosophy in the local school district.

Finally, as we have previously noted, some hearing impaired and culturally or ethnically different students have been inaccurately identified as *mentally retarded*. Educators must be aware of this possibility and consider the classification of *any* student as possibly inaccurate. We are not indicating that

mental retardation is "curable" but rather that some students who have been classified as *mentally retarded* will, with proper educational opportunities and stimulation, prove the classification wrong.

Since the early 1970s there have been significant changes in public school programming for the mentally retarded. Most of the moderately mentally retarded now attend public schools, and although not all attend classes along with nonhandicapped students, many are in classrooms in a regular elementary or secondary school. Just how this integration will further evolve remains to be seen, but the social benefits of such integration seem to warrant this practice. Our emphasis in this chapter, however, is on the mildly mentally retarded. Although separate special classes remain, it is now generally accepted that mentally retarded students can and should be integrated for at least part of the school day. A slightly different situation exists at the secondary level, as will be discussed.

The main reason for abandoning special class programs for the retarded was that investigators could not prove that separate special classes were superior to regular classes (L. Dunn, 1968; Goldstein, Moss, & Jordan, 1965). This fact, along with concerns about stigma and social development, played a significant role in the advent of mainstreaming. On the other hand, research evidence favoring placement in regular classes (indicating, for example, higher academic achievement or better social adjustment) is not clear-cut. Semmel reviewed the research on this topic and found few, if any, meaningful differences (Semmel, Gottlieb, & Robinson, 1979). We can conclude that while all of the necessary evidence is not yet available, at this point much of the daily educational program for students classified as *mildly mentally retarded* is provided in the regular classroom. The continuation of this trend may be related less to the proven effectiveness of these classes and more to such factors as concerns about improper diagnosis and the time, effort, and funds required to fight lawsuits concerning special classes. But for whatever reasons, students classified as *mildly mentally retarded* are now usually assigned to regular classroom teachers for much of the school day.

A DEFINITION OF MENTAL RETARDATION

Until the mid-1970s, students were often identified as *mentally retarded* (or *mentally handicapped*) solely through the use of an IQ score. These students were, in most instances, referred on the basis of educational and/or academic performance suggesting the possibility of mental retardation, and there is little doubt that this IQ-only identification led to inaccurate classification in some cases. In 1973, the American Association on Mental Deficiency (AAMD) provided the following definition: "*Mental retardation* refers to significantly subaverage general intellectual functioning existing concurrently with deficits in adaptive behavior and manifested during the developmental period."

This definition, developed and accepted by the AAMD (Grossman, 1973), was reaffirmed in the AAMD's seventh manual on classification (Grossman, 1977) and again in its *Classification in Mental Retardation* (Grossman, 1983). The AAMD definition, supported by PL 94-142 and its accompanying regulations, requires substantial agreement between at least two measures before a diagnosis of mental retardation may be made. In the AAMD guidelines, significantly subaverage intellectual functioning is suggested to be *approximately* 70 IQ or below. The 1983 manual notes that considering the IQ with some "flexibility" permits the provision of special education programs for persons with IQs higher than 70 in unusual circumstances. It is important to note that both the results of an IQ test and corroborating evidence on a measure of adaptive behavior are necessary for the diagnosis of mental retardation. If either indicates a higher level of functioning, the student may not be considered mentally retarded.

A conceptual definition of *mental retardation* may be inferred from the cognitive-developmental theories of Jean Piaget. Piaget, whose work has so profoundly influenced education for many decades, provided a way to view the cognitive development of children that may be applied to the mentally retarded. Inhelder (1968) interpreted Piaget's theories and their implications for the mentally retarded and provided comparisons between Piaget's stages and three levels of retardation, plus a fourth level that Inhelder called *borderline intelligence* (see Table 9–1).

Inhelder suggested that retarded persons do not attain the stage of formal operations, and that mildly retarded persons do not usually reach the stage of concrete operations, until midadolescence. This concept is valuable in planning educational programs for mentally retarded students but is not well suited to classification in mental retardation, as required by most state regulations for eligibility for special education services.

Mental age is one term associated with the concept of IQ and is in use to varying degrees among educators and psychologists. The term became popular with the intelli-

TABLE 9–1. Mental retardation and Piaget's stages of childhood development

Levels of Retardation	Piaget's Stages
borderline intelligence	formal operations
mild mental retardation	concrete operations
moderate mental retardation	preoperational thought
severe mental retardation	sensorimotor

gence-testing movement early in the 20th century and is still used to some extent today. Mental age (MA) is a measure intended to indicate the level of an individual's mental ability. It is expressed in terms of the average chronological age (CA) of others who answered correctly the same number of items on a test of mental ability. Thus a student with a mental age of 12 would theoretically be able to answer correctly the same number of questions on a test of mental ability as the majority of 12-year-old students. Mental age was originally associated almost exclusively with the formula that was part of the original concept of IQ, that is, $MA/CA \times 100 = IQ$.

Today, MA data, when used, may be derived in a variety of ways depending on the test(s) used. But however used, it refers to predicted ability to correctly respond to items on a test purporting to measure mental ability.

Classification—Levels of Mental Retardation

When a student is classified as *learning disabled* or *behaviorally disordered,* there may be some indication of severity of handicap or disability; but there is no nationally recognized "level of handicap" designation. In the case of mental retardation, level (severity) of handicap is part of the classification, and two systems are recognized nationally. Grossman's AAMD manual, *Classification in Mental Retardation* (1983) suggests levels and IQ ranges for classification purposes. Although the labeling of mental retardation requires the establishment of subaverage intellectual functioning (low IQ) and deficits in adaptive behavior existing concurrently, levels of mental retardation are almost always given in terms of IQ alone. The levels suggested by Grossman are given in Table 9–2.

Another system is often used by school districts. According to Polloway, Payne, Patton, and Payne (1985), these guidelines ordi-

TABLE 9–2. Levels of mental retardation and IQ (first system)

Level of Handicap	IQ
mild	50–55 to 70
moderate	35–40 to 50–55
severe	20–25 to 35–40
profound	below 20–25

narily specify three levels, educable, trainable, and severe/profound. Though there are no national guidelines for these levels (each state may establish its own) our experience suggests the patterns in Table 9–3, with more national variation in the educable-range guidelines than in the others.

For many years public schools used guidelines and regulations allowing any student who scored below some specific IQ level on an individual test of intelligence to be eligible for a program for the mentally retarded or mentally handicapped. The two most commonly used tests were the Stanford-Binet (Teman & Merrill, 1973) and the Wechsler Intelligence scales (WISC-R) (Wechsler, 1974) (see Chap. 12). In most states parents were consulted, or at least informed before the tests were given, but in some cases they were neither consulted nor informed. Now both federal and state regulations require that parents or guardians give permission before such testing can be initiated.

Until the mid-1970s, the most common upper limit for placement in a program for the mentally handicapped was an IQ below 75 or 80. A few states even had an upper

TABLE 9–3. Levels of mental retardation and IQ (second system)

Level of Handicap	IQ
educable	50–55 to 70–75
trainable	25–30 to 50–55
severe/profound	below 25–30

limit of 85. Some states included in guidelines some mention of evaluation of adaptive behavior (the way an individual functions in social settings, also sometimes called *street behavior*); but before the mid-1970s this was an exception rather than the rule. PL 94-142 and its accompanying regulations required at least two measures for a diagnosis of mental retardation: results of an individual IQ test and corroborating evidence on a measure of adaptive behavior. In addition, school functioning in both academic and social areas should confirm these measures.

Though there are various concerns about the validity and reliability of tests of intelligence, level of adaptive behavior is even more difficult to determine and measures of adaptive behavior are much less precise.

Adaptive Behavior

Most public school students classified as *mentally retarded* were referred for further evaluation due to significant problems in academic areas. The various intelligence tests and the IQ scores they generated correlate highly with academic performance and apparent ability to perform academically. But what about social ability and behavior? One of the recognized characteristics of most mentally retarded students is social behavior below that normally expected for students their age. The AAMD has historically referred to "personal independence and social responsibility" when discussing adaptive behavior. Chinn, Drew, and Logan (1979) discuss differing adaptive behavior expectations at various age levels, reminding us that deficits in adaptive behavior vary by age. Their list of areas of deficits by developmental stages includes the following:

1. deficits during infancy and early childhood
   a. sensory and motor skills
   b. speech and language
   c. self-help skills
   d. socialization

2. deficits during childhood and early adolescence
   a. basic academic skills when applied in practical, daily activities
   b. reasoning and judgment when applied in everyday activities
   c. social skills in group activities and interpersonal relationships
3. deficits during late adolescence and adult life
   a. vocational ability
   b. general social skills (both group and interpersonal)

Perhaps the most widely recognized measure of adaptive behavior is that developed by the American Association on Mental Deficiency (AAMD) and revised as a public school version in 1981. This Adaptive Behavior Scale—School Edition (ABS—SE) includes the following domains and subdomains (Lambert, Windmiller, Tharinger, & Cole, 1981):

Domain 1. independent functioning
  eating
  toilet use
  cleanliness
  appearance
  care of clothing
  dressing and undressing
  travel
  other independent functioning
Domain 2. physical development
  sensory development
  motor development
Domain 3. economic activity
  money handling and budgeting
  shopping skills
Domain 4. language development
  expression
  comprehension
  social language development
Domain 5. numbers and time
Domain 6. prevocational activity
Domain 7. self-direction
  initiative
  perseverance
  leisure time
Domain 8. responsibility

Domain 9. socialization
Domain 10. aggressiveness
Domain 11. antisocial vs. social behavior
Domain 12. rebelliousness
Domain 13. trustworthiness
Domain 14. withdrawal vs. involvement
Domain 15. mannerisms
Domain 16. interpersonal manners
Domain 17. acceptability of vocal habits
Domain 18. acceptability of habits
Domain 19. activity level
Domain 20. symptomatic behavior
Domain 21. use of medications

Patton, Payne, and Beirne-Smith (1986) provide an excellent discussion of the AAMD scale and several others. They also provide a valuable review of major issues relating to the use of adaptive behavior measures in the identification/placement of students in programs for the mentally retarded. They con-

clude that "although mandated by professional guidelines and by law, the use of adaptive behavior as a criterion for determining mental retardation is clouded by confusion" (p. 155).

What then, may we conclude about adaptive behavior and its importance as a concept in mental retardation? Polloway et al. (1985) note that historically there was an emphasis on social concerns, both in défining and understanding mental retardation. However, "throughout the middle of the 20th century the emphasis moved toward intellectual and academic factors. The increased reliance on intelligence in defining retardation is an example of how the initial concept of social incompetence was replaced by one of intellectual subnormality" (p.365). They do not suggest a shift to some exclusive personal-social focus but remind teachers that "a total

Knowledge of performance in the home setting is necessary to evaluate adaptive behavior.

emphasis on academics can lead to isolated teaching of the 3 Rs with no relevance for the real world" (pp. 365–366). We believe this point of view to be of great importance. Personal-social skills alone have limited value. Academic skills alone have limited value. Mentally retarded students require both if they are to function with maximum effectiveness as adults. Students who are mentally retarded will not learn personal-social skills as readily as other students; thus they require specific instruction. This instruction, however, must be individualized, just as academic instruction must be individualized. Fortunately, the past decade has witnessed a resurgence in interest in the teaching of personal-social skills, and special education resource personnel should be able to provide specific suggestions for specific needs and age levels. Polloway et al. (1985) provide a description of 16 commercial programs of value in developing various social skills. Teachers with specific interest may wish to consult this source for further information (pp. 384–385).

THE NATURE OF MENTAL RETARDATION

We have considered mental retardation from the point of view of an acceptable definition, classification systems, and one specific aspect of mental retardation, namely personal-social skills (adaptive behavior). Before proceeding further, it may be of value to attempt to develop a more complete gestalt; we will call this broad, overview concept the *nature of mental retardation.*

One of the best and most succinct introductions to the nature of mental retardation resulted from the efforts of a group of experts in mental retardation asked to prepare a report to guide the Steering Committee of the National Institute of Child Health and Development (NICHD) in developing a five-year research plan for the area of mental re-

tardation. The members of this study group included top experts in the nation on mental retardation. These were the introductory remarks in their report:

Evidence today indicates that the causes of mental retardation are biological, psychological, and social in origin and that they occur frequently in combination in a single individual. Genetic factors, metabolic disorders, and prematurity or other disturbances during pregnancy are a few of its biological determinants, but infection or injury at birth or in early childhood may also underlie mental retardation. In addition, lack of stimulation, inadequate educational opportunities, and generally deprived living conditions may be causal or contributory factors. Whether such factors modify normal developmental processes or cause aberrant neurogenetic programs is not at all clear. The moderate and more severe conditions of retardation most frequently result from disorders or insults that can usually be traced to faulty genes, infections, accidents, diseases, and disorders that cause brain damage. Knowledge is needed from almost every branch of science in order to understand the interaction of these elements in the development and behavior of children and adults.

Mental retardation is identified clinically by the presence of several signs that include, but are not limited to, a significant impairment of intelligence and a concurrent deficit in adaptive behavior. Typically these impairments occur before age 18. The identification of mental retardation through the years has reflected with varying degrees of emphasis a mix of two factors. Before the beginning of the mental testing movement, the primary behavioral characteristic of those who were referred to as mentally retarded was inadequate social adaptation. With the rise of the mental testing movement, specifically with regard to intelligence testing, a greater reliance has been placed on measured intelligence as the primary characteristic in defining mental retardation. The term *intelligence* was used to refer to the ability of the individual to master verbal, visual, and mathematical symbol systems, and the concept of intelligence itself became defined by the instruments that purported to measure it. . . . Social systems, such as diagnostic clinics, public schools, and other service agencies, have created standards of definition that vary on the basis of different perceptions of individual and societal needs. (Purpura, Gallagher, & Tjossem, 1981, pp. 1–2)

With this excellent conceptualization of the nature of mental retardation as a base, we would like to add our beliefs about mental retardation, focusing on the educable mentally retarded (EMR) and programs for them in the public schools.

Our beliefs about the mentally handicapped or retarded include the following:

1. Some students who have been identified as mentally retarded have been mislabeled on the basis of inappropriate or biased tests, insufficient data, or both.
2. Some students who might be viewed as mildly mentally retarded can be assisted to develop intellectually and cognitively to approach the level of normal mental ability.
3. There are "true" educable mentally retarded children (just as there are more severely mentally retarded children—a fact few deny), and they exist in all races, ethnic groups, and socioeconomic levels.
4. EMR students should be identified by multiple criteria, including (a) level of functioning in social situations, (b) level of language development, (c) functioning on an individual test of intelligence (full-scale or global IQ, plus consideration of patterns of subtest scores), (d) emotional maturity, and (e) academic achievement. Ethnic, cultural, social, and economic background must be considered.
5. Many EMR students can be effectively educated in the regular class for the major part of the day if the teacher receives assistance with materials and specific methods.
6. Students who score at the lower end of the range that is often used to describe the EMR (those who have a measured IQ of 50 to 60, with other indicators support-

ing this measure) may require a special class program for a major part of the school day.
7. EMR students will benefit greatly from a program in which career awareness and information is emphasized, starting in the elementary grades. Such a career education program must be much more than "vocational preparation."
8. Most secondary school EMR students will benefit from a special work-experience program coordinated with a life-skills, career education curriculum emphasis.

CHARACTERISTICS OF MENTAL RETARDATION

We will here describe characteristics commonly seen in individuals already classified *mentally retarded,* emphasizing characteristics common to the *mildly* mentally retarded and how these characteristics are manifested. These same characteristics apply also to moderate and severe levels, although at lower levels of mental retardation these characteristics are much more obvious. In fact, usually the moderately and severely mentally retarded are identified long before entering school because their characteristics in total are that obvious. In contrast, the EMR student may *not* be identified until after several years in school. Identification is made latest with those students near the upper end of the range of educable mental retardation, particularly if they have had very good preschool experiences or if they live and attend school in a primarily lower socioeconomic area. This occurs because they are less "different" from other students in their classes.

With the concept of the least restrictive environment, *if* a student is functioning in such a manner that he can remain within the regular classroom with no additional support services, there is no reason to identify him or her as mentally retarded. In fact, if he is functioning satisfactorily in the regular class, his adaptive behavior is most likely within the normal range; therefore, he is *not* mentally retarded even if he has an IQ within the range of mild mental retardation.

Personal-Social Skill Deficits

If accepted definitions of mental retardation are applied as intended, a student cannot be classified as mentally retarded unless there are deficits in adaptive behavior (personal-social skills). For the upper borderline, the mildly mentally retarded, such deficits may not be so great as to be evident every moment of the day; but they are evident and show up in various circumstances. For example, the student may not be able to deal with emotions as well as might be expected considering age and experience. There may be problems with self-directed activities and initiative. Behavior may lead to a general conclusion—usually based on multiple criteria—that the student is "immature." The mildly mentally retarded may be slow in interpreting social signals (for example, of acceptance or nonacceptance) and may have difficulty in getting along with peers, especially when any sort of dissension occurs. Mildly mentally retarded students may have a tendency to socialize with younger children and, when interacting with age peers, may often permit themselves to be blamed for behaviors that are really group-initiated. They may have unusual difficulty in understanding that others see and interpret situations differently than they do. In summary, their personal-social skills are more like those of a child several years younger.

It must be noted that such personal-social deficits may also be seen in the learning disabled and the behaviorally disordered; but with the mentally retarded, it is the combination of this deficit in adaptive behavior and an IQ below some established cut-off point that leads to the classification of mental retardation. Also, as compared to the learning disabled, there is more likelihood that the mentally retarded will have lower personal-social skills in general, whereas the learning disabled student may more likely have some fairly normal personal-social skills, with deficits in only certain areas. The learning disabled may also have totally normal personal-social skills.

General Academic Retardation

The student who is later determined to be educable mentally retarded is usually referred for evaluation because of a lack of progress in academic areas and an inability to learn when taught in the same manner as other students in the class. In primary grades this characteristic is more often first recognized because of poor progress in reading but usually involves *general* academic retardation; that is, the student is having difficulty in all academic areas of the school program.

A rule that generally but not necessarily always applies is that if a student is far behind the rest of the class and has serious academic difficulty in only one area (for example, reading), but is normal or above normal in achievement in another major area (for example, arithmetic), he probably is not mentally retarded. Some students may appear to be making satisfactory progress in first grade, and at that level this rule is somewhat less applicable. But if a third- or fourth-grade student is doing very well in either reading or arithmetic, he is likely not mentally retarded. The degree of symbolic and abstract thinking required for success at the third- or fourth-grade level (assuming the student is the appropriate age for that level) is simply not consistent with mental retardation as it is viewed today.

More will be said later about the fact that academic retardation is also a characteristic of other handicapping conditions (for example, learning disabilities and hearing impairment); the fact that a student is academically retarded does *not* indicate mental retardation. But it is a major characteristic of the educable mentally retarded.

Memory Deficits

The processes involved in memory have been researched by a variety of individuals, and it is one area in which many and varied research efforts continue. Many of these researchers are not directly connected with the field of mental retardation or even special education. Rather, they are scientists who are interested in and intrigued by this complex process (or these complex processes). But regardless of the process, all authorities agree that the mentally retarded have difficulties with memory; and many seem to agree that in teaching the mentally retarded, educators must give attention to assisting them to originally learn and store information. The use of concrete examples and the tactic of presenting information in a variety of contexts (as opposed to many repetitions of the same fact) are suggested by authors such as Polloway et al. (1985) and others. Some research seems to suggest that the long-term memory of the retarded is about the same as that of normal learners; that is, the retarded are no more likely to forget what they have learned than the nonretarded. However, this is true only when what is learned is consistent with their mental abilities (Polloway et al., 1985). Nonetheless, any hard and fast conclusions about memory processes in the retarded—other than that they do have difficulties with memory—must be regarded as tentative.

Below-Average Language Ability

Although language ability that is below average might indicate a hearing impairment, learning disability, lack of opportunity to develop language, or other causal factors, the EMR student almost always has below-average (for age) language ability. The only exception that we have seen to this generalization has been with upper borderline students in situations in which well-informed, highly motivated parents have invested un-

usual efforts at the preschool level. In such cases these children may enter school with normal language ability. Usually it slowly becomes lower than that of the normal peer group, as other children have opportunity to grow in this area.

Below-Average Ability to Generalize and Conceptualize

Below-average ability to generalize and conceptualize is at least partially measured by most individual tests of intelligence and thus is to be expected in most EMR students, since intelligence tests results are a significant part of the base of determining mild mental retardation. It is useful for the classroom teacher to think in terms of the student's abilities in these areas, but care should be taken to avoid confusion between ability to generalize or conceptualize relating to what is read and ability to generalize or conceptualize in other settings. A learning disabled student with a serious reading problem, for example, may appear to be unable to conceptualize if reading is the base for conceptualization. However, he may be able to conceptualize quite well if initial information is provided verbally. In contrast, the EMR student has a tendency to have difficulty with generalization and conceptualization in a variety of settings.

A number of additional characteristics are listed by various authors in texts for introductory courses in education of the mentally retarded, but these five—personal-social skill deficits, general academic retardation, memory deficits, below-average language ability, and below-average ability to generalize and conceptualize—are almost certain to be found in the mentally retarded.

Characteristics in Total

A characteristic is a distinguishing feature or quality, but in the case of the mentally retarded, no single characteristic alone is distinguishing. Rather, it is the total of characteristics that distinguishes retarded from

Students often make great academic and social gains when surrounded by appropriate models.

nonretarded students. The preceding characteristics may be of value to the reader in that they help describe the nature of mental retardation. They are of value to the classroom teacher as clues that may indicate the *possibility* that a given student may be mentally retarded. They are further of value in indicating possible teaching methods or techniques. But according to state and federal definitions and identification guidelines, a student may be identified as mentally retarded only if the results of *both* an individual test of intelligence and adaptive behavior measures indicate he or she is mentally retarded. Even then, if the results are anywhere near borderline or there are any conflicting data, the identification should be questioned.

RESPONSIBILITIES OF SPECIAL EDUCATION PERSONNEL

The responsibilities of special education personnel vary widely in respect to degrees of their students' mental retardation and the existence of other handicapping conditions. In many states the trainable mentally retarded are in an essentially self-contained class for all or at least most of the day. Special education personnel should provide specific guidance to regular classroom teachers as to how the trainable retarded student may best be served in the regular class. How such integration is implemented and the focus of regular class activities when TMR students are integrated will vary widely. Here we will consider "educational programming" for the educable mentally retarded, which involves joint efforts of the regular classroom teacher and the special educator. A variety of special education services should be available, although in reality this variety is *not* available in every community. The following discussion assumes the existence of at least a moderate range of services but not necessarily the extremely broad range available in some of the larger, more comprehensive programs.

SUSAN AND MARIANN: TWO 16-YEAR-OLD STUDENTS

Susan

Age: 16 years

Program: first year in senior high special program
   with limited enrollment in adapted regular classes

Years in school: 11

Physical health: good

Full Scale WISC-R IQ: 65

MariAnn

Age: 16 years

Program: first year in senior high special program
   with limited enrollment in adapted regular classes

Years in school: 11

Physical health: good

Full Scale WISC-R IQ: 66

Based on these data, Susan and MariAnn might be expected to be relatively similar in school performance. Each was referred as a result of "significant academic problems" near the close of the third year in school (second grade). At that time, Susan's IQ was recorded as 62, MariAnn's as 68. Measures of adaptive behavior supported identification of both girls as educable mentally retarded. Each was placed in a special program at the start of third grade. During their elementary school years, each spent approximately two hours each day in a special resource room and the remainder of the day in the regular class.

Susan and MariAnn have lived in the same city throughout their 11 years of school attendance and have been in the same school and same resource room program since they moved to middle school. Other information indicates that the program quality in the two different elementary schools that they attended was essentially the same.

There are no known serious family problems in either family, and parents have been generally cooperative with school officials through the years. Both girls are from white, middle-class families.

But here the similarity ends.

Susan is reading at the upper fourth-grade level, according to standardized achievement tests. She can recognize the words included in the special program reading curriculum (relating to employment, voting, family responsibility, and practical, daily living skills), and next year will move into phase one of the work-experience program with excellent preparation. She is quite successful in the adapted vocational education program taught by a regular class teacher and is as skilled as most other students in her school, including nonhandicapped students, in interpersonal relations. She has learned that she will be rejected or ignored by some students but does not make an issue of their behavior. Susan's speaking vocabulary is somewhat below that of other students her age but not notably so in most normal social situations. (This discrepancy would be noticeable if she were enrolled in some of the advanced classes in her school, but she is not.) In most respects, in the large school Susan attends, she does not stand out as being "different."

MariAnn is reading at the middle second-grade level, according to standardized achievement tests. She has difficulty in reading approximately 50% of the words included in the special program reading curriculum, and she will not likely be ready for phase one for the work-experience program for at least 2 years. MariAnn experiences her greatest difficulty in the adapted vocational education program, where the teacher says, "She has difficulty reading our low vocabulary materials, but her biggest problem is understanding the concepts involved." MariAnn socializes with a few students in the special program but is not well accepted, even by many of the special program students. She has essentially no acceptance by nonhandicapped students. MariAnn's speaking vocabulary is very limited, and she has often attempted to become part of a conversation only to be rejected because her comments make her stand out as "different." Even with very specific suggestions from her teacher, she cannot seem to anticipate such situations.

Perhaps the most important understanding to be gained from the comparison of Susan and MariAnn is that students classified as EMR may perform very differently in regard to both academic achievement and social competence, regardless of similarity of test scores or other variables generally recognized as important. As such students progress through their educational program, projections of educational and social ability and success may become more reliable; but at ages 6, 7, and 8, predictions of future success may be very inaccurate. Certain generalizations may be made based on valid test results and environmental and sociological data, but these are *only* generalizations. Variations in performance are undoubtedly just as great among students diagnosed as EMR as they are among the so-called normal student population.

In the first and second grades, the provision of teaching suggestions and special materials may permit the student to remain full-time in the regular classroom. If the handicap is greater (such as lower level of intelligence, other handcapping conditions, or very inadequate experiental background), part-time placement in a resource room may be an essential part of the total educational plan. In the resource room the student receives much more individual help in developing basic reading and numbers skills, and the special teacher attempts to determine the approaches that best provide maximum growth when the student is in the regular class. Many of these students are later able to come back to the regular class on a full-time basis; however, some need to move into a part-time special class program if the resource room setting proves to be insufficient to provide for unique educational needs. A few students may continue in a part-time special program throughout their school years, but every effort should be made to assist the student to be able to function successfully in the regular class.

When EMR students continue to have significant academic difficulties, there is a cumulative effect that leads to a growing discrepancy between their level of achievement and that of their age peers. The use of high-interest, low-vocabulary materials permits the teaching of many essential concepts; but some curriculum modification becomes inevitable if education is to remain meaningful. If a student receives the benefit of several years of special programming that assists others to return to the regular class but is of much less help to him, by age 12 or 13 a more special program must be considered. Such a program should focus on learning social skills, habits, attitudes, and understandings that will maximize his ability to obtain and retain employment. In conjunction with this emphasis on employability, special efforts to assist him to become a knowledge-

able consumer and a responsible parent and citizen must be initiated. Such programs are often called prevocational at the junior high level and vocational, work-study, or work experience at the senior high level. These students still have some involvement with the regular class program, with emphasis on such classes as driver education, typing, metalwork, body and fender work, and various semiskilled trades as deemed individually appropriate. Personnel from the state rehabilitation services agency can assist in a number of ways, including arrangements for special vocational school training, payment of employers for training functions, and others as seem advisable. In high school a work-study coordinator should be employed to assist in arranging and supervising off-campus work activities.

For the educable mentally retarded for whom initial special programming does not lead to nearly complete reintegration into the regular class, the amount of special programming required may increase as the student progresses through school.

Special educators who work with the educable mentally retarded always hope that there may be a remedial effect to permit return to the regular classroom. This is not, however, very likely if the initial identification of the EMR student was accurate. The hope that this remedial effect might be achieved was fueled by factors in the mid- to late 1970s that exist to a lesser extent now. At that time, when many students from EMR classes were being moved to a more normal, less restrictive environment, there were a significant number of students in such classes who had been placed in EMR classes inappropriately. Some were minority students who were not actually mentally retarded, others were emotionally disturbed, and still others were learning disabled. A few were students who needed a good remedial program, but provision of special education services was less expensive for local districts because they received state funds for special education but not for remedial programs. Thus there were once many such students in EMR classes who with other educational adaptations could function without special education assistance.

During this same time period, the upper IQ limits of mental retardation were lowered and the borderline range was eliminated, and for identification as mentally retarded a measure of adaptive behavior was added to the requirement of subaverage IQ. These changes resulted in a decrease in the number of students identified, since both of these changes led to a more restricted concept of mental retardation.

It is therefore now *less likely* that educators will inaccurately identify students as mentally retarded, and since the upper limits of mental retardation have been lowered, it is now more likely that those students identified as EMR need specialized assistance in addition to what is provided by the regular class teacher.

Commenting on this phenomenon, MacMillan and Borthwick note that "mainstreaming is feasible for only a very small percentage of the mentally retarded population when a restrictive definition is employed, such as is the case in California today" (1980, p. 158). Very little has happened since 1980 to lead to any less restrictive guidelines. The restrictiveness of the definition of EMR presently varies greatly from state to state, and any discussion of mainstreaming of the mentally retarded must be undertaken with the understanding that this variation exists.

Although the purpose of this text is to assist the regular classroom teacher in doing his or her part in this process and to promote the concept of the appropriate, least restrictive environment, we urge the teacher to be aware of the need for special assistance and to demand such specialized assistance as part of the approved individualized educational program (IEP) required by PL 94-142

and state regulations. To do less would contradict both the spirit and the letter of PL 94-142 and everything known about the needs of handicapped students.

CAREER EDUCATION EMPHASIS

Polloway et al. (1985) point out that mildly handicapped individuals must be introduced in a systematic, programmed way to the realities of the responsibilities they will face after completion of their formal schooling. Career education means more than vocational-occupational orientation and training. According to the Council for Exceptional Children (1978), "*Career education* is the totality of experiences through which one learns to live a meaningful, satisfying work life . . ., providing the opportunity to learn, in the least restrictive environment possible, the academic, daily living, personal-social, and occupational knowledge and skills necessary for attaining their highest levels of economic, personal and social fulfillment. This can be obtained through work (both paid and unpaid) and in a variety of other societal roles and personal life styles."

Brolin, a leading national advocate for career education, adds, "Career education is not intended to replace traditional education, but rather, to redirect it to be more relevant and meaningful for the student and to result in the acquisition of attitudes, knowledge, and skills one needs for successful community living and working. It is not meant to be the only education students receive, but it should be a substantial part of the curriculum" (1982, p. 3).

Career education is not "for mentally retarded alone" but is important for all students, particularly those with handicapping conditions. However, the mentally retarded do have a very special need for career education emphasis and may need a comprehensive, full-spectrum emphasis more than most other students, due to the nature of mental retardation. With that in mind, we will review one particular career education approach, as representative of what should be done in this arena.

Donn Brolin has been associated with the concept of career education for handicapped students, with a variety of publications and other contributions in this field, since the early 1970s. His life-centered career education (LCCE) model includes three major areas: daily-living skills, personal-social skills, and occupational guidance and preparation (Brolin, 1978, 1982). Developed as a competency-based approach, this model specifies competencies as follows:

1. managing family finances
2. selecting, managing, and maintaining a home
3. caring for personal needs
4. raising children—family living
5. buying and preparing food
6. buying and caring for clothes
7. engaging in civic activities
8. utilizing recreation and leisure time
9. getting around the community
10. achieving self-awareness
11. acquiring self-confidence
12. developing socially responsible behavior
13. maintaining adequate interpersonal skills
14. achieving independence
15. achieving problem-solving skills
16. communicating adequately with others
17. knowing and exploring occupational possibilities
18. selecting and planning occupational choices
19. exhibiting appropriate work habits and behaviors
20. exhibiting sufficient physical-manual skills
21. obtaining a specific occupational skill
22. seeking, securing, and maintaining employment (Kokaska & Brolin, 1985)

The LCCE model is among the most widely used in career education, and its provision of very specific competencies and subcompetencies makes it unusually valuable in practical application. Brolin points out that an effective program requires close cooperation between the family, the school, and the community. To be most effective, it requires awareness and involvement from the elementary school level upward. Brolin speaks of "four distinct stages of career development: career awareness, career exploration, career preparation, and career placement/follow-up/continuing education" (1982, p. 9).

The LCCE curriculum approach provides guidelines for establishing the curriculum, involving all required participants, and making certain that all essential elements are included in the K–12 school program. It does not specify starting at a given elementary grade level but provides competencies that may be integrated with existing curriculum goals, beginning at various grade levels, depending on the existing program and other factors that vary among school districts.

For more specific details see *Life-Centered Career Education: A Competency-Based Approach* (Brolin, 1978), and for specific suggestions on teaching the 103 subcompetencies, see chapters 3, 4, and 5 of *Career Education for Handicapped Individuals,* 2nd ed. (Kokaska & Brolin, 1985). This type of educational emphasis, however provided, is essential to the final success of programs for the educable mentally retarded.

SUGGESTIONS FOR THE REGULAR CLASSROOM TEACHER

It is important that the regular classroom teacher understand the types of learning problems often experienced by mentally handicapped students; but it is equally important to know that not all mentally handicapped students experience all of these different problems. All students, including the mentally handicapped, have unique capabilities. It is altogether too easy to classify students on the basis of their IQ and the disabilities or academic difficulties supposedly automatically generated as a result of this IQ. About all that can be assumed is that the student has some difficulty with cognitive and academic learning and that some curricular adjustments and adaptations are necessary. This discussion of necessity considers a number of generalized approaches that may be of value with EMR students. But one must remember that each EMR student must be considered individually.

Before making certain specific suggestions, we should also note that a number of the teaching suggestions that work with learning disabled students also work with the mentally retarded. Although the definitions of these two types of handicap are written so that they are separate for purposes of identification and state reimbursement, they in fact may overlap to a considerable extent. Therefore one should also consider the suggestions for teaching the learning disabled (pp. 286 to 302).

Concrete objects may be helpful in the learning process.

The following are general suggestions applicable across subject and skill areas:

Build Motivation to Learn in All Possible Ways. Two major possibilities are (1) using specific reward systems (as with behavior modification techniques) and (2) relating learning situations to the students' known areas of interest. Attempt to discover what things are really important to the student and involve these in teaching whenever possible.

Be Aware of Skills, Information, and Concepts That Are Prerequisites to New Learning Tasks and Do Not Attempt New Tasks Until These Prerequisites Are a Part of the Student's Repertoire. With EMR students it is likely that there will be gaps in skills or basic information not present with nonhandicapped students. These areas must be identified and when possible developed before initiating new learning tasks. In some cases when such prerequisite learning cannot be accomplished in a reasonable amount of time, substitute assignments and modified goals must be established. In any event, just as learning long division in the traditional manner requires an understanding of subtraction, so are there prerequisites in other subject and skill areas. In some cases the prerequisite is a specific skill, in others it is information, and in some it is a concept. This may be particularly important in science and social studies because there are many concepts in these two areas that most students learn incidentally in the course of daily living but for which EMR students may require specific teaching. It is important that the teacher be aware of this possibility and alert to its possible consequences.

Use Concrete (Rather Than Abstract) Examples Whenever Possible. For example, in teaching that 4 plus 3 equals 7, it would be better to ask, "How many pieces of fruit would I have if I had four oranges in this hand and three apples in this hand?" This approach assists the student to visualize the situation and the adding process, making it easier to visualize the answer. The student might have much more difficulty with the question in the abstract, but after learning the process with concrete objects it may then be easier to learn on the more abstract level. Making learning concrete also includes the principle of relating new learning to familiar experiences. This practice should be followed to some extent with all students, but the EMR student may require more of this new-to-familiar emphasis than other students.

Be Aware of a Variety of Possible Readiness and Ability Levels, Both Across and Within Subject Areas. Modify Assignments as Necessary in Recognition of These Variations.   The use of multiple reading groups at the elementary level is common, and most elementary teachers have learned to manage this instructional practice. EMR students may require adjustments for some aspects of reading instruction beyond the traditional three groups but may be able to participate in many reading group activities if other facets of their reading assignments are modified. Similar modifications may be necessary in other subject or skill areas; the nature of such modifications varies among individual students. The teacher must be alert to the likelihood that EMR students may benefit from the content of group reading (what they hear other students reading) and group discussion even if their own reading ability does not permit fluent reading of this material.

At the secondary level, particularly in senior high, it is more likely that EMR students will be in specially scheduled class groupings, but for those classes in which there is no special grouping, the same principle applies. In some schools, simplified versions of reading materials (similar concepts and content, but written in simplified form) are used. In other instances it is a matter of maximizing the learning that can take place through group work. In all cases, if the student can learn *without* modifications and adaptations, this approach is most desirable, but if such learning is possible in many areas of the school curriculum, it is likely that the student is not actually an EMR student.

Make Maximum Use of Group Experiences as a Vehicle for Learning.   This suggestion is included in the preceding discussion of the need to modify reading assignments but should also be followed in all areas of the school curriculum. Very good readers may sometimes learn more efficiently when left alone to read new material, but the EMR is more likely to benefit from oral input when learning new concepts or basic information. This does *not* mean that individualized planning and individual efforts in respect to learning basic skills may be overlooked or short-changed. It does mean that the teacher must involve the EMR student in group experiences whenever possible, especially as a means of learning basic information or new concepts.

Create Opportunities for Verbal Expression.   The EMR student is often less adept at self-expression than nonhandicapped students. The effects of below-average learning ability are cumulative and are readily seen when attempts are made to elicit broad verbal expression. Some teachers may be concerned about a negative effect on the student's self-concept or may perhaps simply become discouraged and thus avoid attempts to encourage the student to engage in further self-expression. This is precisely the wrong approach. Teachers must use both structured, individually planned experiences and any incidental opportunities to encourage the student to improve language development.

Language development requires *experience,* and EMR students require *more* experience with language to develop a given level of language ability than students with average or above-average intellectual ability. A final complicating factor is that if earlier school experiences and provisions have been inconsistent with the child's level of readiness, he may be even more retarded in language development than his intellectual level would indicate. A further complication is the effect of bilingual or bicultural influences. Teachers must be alert to provide all possible opportunities for verbal expression and general language development and to make these opportunities interesting and appropriate to the student's present level of development. Such opportunities are important at both the elementary and the secondary level.

Be Alert to Special Needs in the Abilities to Generalize and Conceptualize. Two abilities, generalization and conceptualization, are among the more significant factors in learning as measured by an individual test of intelligence. Therefore, the EMR student—by definition—has lower-than-average ability in these two important areas. A young student may recognize the plus sign in a mathematical equation but have difficulty understanding that the word *and* (as in "6 and 7 equals 13") has the same meaning as the plus sign. He may understand and follow the rules governing behavior in the cafeteria line but have difficulty relating the same rules to another situation, such as the recess line.

The teacher must specifically point out to the student how one principle may apply in other academic or social situations. Through actual practice with generalization and conceptual skills, the student acquires a repertoire of experiences that provide for maximum development of these abilities. This ability to generalize and conceptualize is critically important as the basis for skills related to successful employment and participation in the adult world, but such skills are regularly overlooked or underemphasized in favor of specific facts or improvement in basic skills such as reading. It is very doubtful whether, for example, an increase of 1 year in the student's basic reading level will be as important to the student as development of the ability to generalize in social situations or conceptualize the requirements of various job-related tasks. It is difficult to demonstrate that any one specific area of learning is more important than any other, but this ability is certainly among the most important for the student with below-average intellectual ability.

Use a Variety of Techniques to Support or Simplify the Learning Task, in Consideration of the EMR's General Learning Characteristics:

1. Reduce distractions in the learning environment whenever possible.
2. Provide for more frequent review.
3. Simplify instructions.
4. Introduce new vocabulary words *before* initiating new assignments (experience indicates which words may more likely cause difficulty—there is no rule or list of difficult words applicable to all students).
5. Assign problems in smaller clusters.
6. When practical, use peer tutors (the viability of peer tutors varies considerably from subject to subject, grade to grade, and student to student).
7. Whenever possible, use filmstrips or films to introduce broad new concepts such as "the tropics" or "the polar regions" or to introduce topics such as a novel or classic that is to be a topic of discussion in the class for a considerable period of time.
8. Provide an outline of important points of reading assignments.
9. Use color coding when appropriate.
10. Use pictures, arrows, and so forth on direction sheets or other written assignments.

11. Avoid true-false tests that require an understanding of language that the EMR may not have (otherwise, his test results may reflect his language level rather than his answers to the actual questions).

These general suggestions provide a brief sample of ideas that have worked with some EMR students. The resource room specialist should be able to provide many more, including ideas that have developed out of the more individualized work taking place in the resource room and the teacher's experience with other students. In many instances alternate approaches are a part of the IEP or the extended ideas that grow out of the IEP. In many instances, especially in the lower grades, activities used with other students in the regular class work also with the EMR student with only minimal modifications.

All of the preceding suggestions are applicable at the elementary level, and many are applicable at the secondary level, but educating the EMR student in the regular classroom at the secondary level remains the more difficult task. This greater difficulty may occur because educational retardation is cumulative, as students fall farther and farther behind their peers as they go through their school program, or because secondary curriculum planners tend to assume basic reading, language, and mathematics skills when they plan course goals and content. In any event, it is likely that the planned secondary curriculum for the EMR is more separate than is the case with most other handicapping conditions. The following section considers the possible content of such a special program, given that it varies in actual implementation throughout the nation.

SECONDARY SCHOOL PROGRAMS

It is quite possible for some EMR students to complete an adapted version of the secondary school program with minimal assistance from special education personnel. When a student can achieve at least modest success with such programming, it may well be the best possible alternative. It certainly is consistent with the concept of education in the least restrictive environment. On the other hand, as long as the student is having educational difficulties and is classified as a student with a handicapping condition, programming decisions must be made by the IEP committee; and social, educational, and career goals must be carefully considered.

In our experience, most students who were formerly a part of an elementary, middle, or junior high EMR program either are apparently ready for a more normal school program by age 14 or 15 or obviously need a more specialized program. If they are ready for a more normal school program, it still may be necessary for them to be enrolled in one or two special class sections taught by the special education teacher; but determination of the best or more appropriate program is strictly an individual matter. Sometimes in larger high schools there may be class sections (taught by nonspecial educators) that are for students who are academically less ready than other students. Such classes may include some students who are considered part of the special education program and some who are not. The major common characteristic of students in such classes may be, for example, reading competency at the third- or fourth-grade level. Therefore, adapted materials may be used with the entire class.

We have observed other programs in which there were central, vocational-training facilities in which EMR students were enrolled. Usually, the large majority of students in such vocational programs are average or above average in mental ability, and the EMR students are fully integrated in vocational classes. In some such programs there is a special education coordinator whose task is to help prepare students through advanced assistance for specialized or technical vocabulary, reading assignments that may be too difficult, and other similar efforts. This coordinator also usually provides assistance to students with learning disabilities or hearing impairments and others who are the responsibility of the school district's special education staff.

When adaptations of existing programs do not meet the needs of handicapped students, more specialized programs must be provided. Hallahan and Kauffman reported (1978) that at that time, the work-study program was the most commonly used program in such cases. Morsink (1984) suggests that work-study or work-experience programs are "an excellent way to provide a transition for the student from the sheltered school environment to the competitive world of work" (p.336). For many EMR students, complete self-support (as adults) is possible if appropriate work training is provided. The work-study approach was originally outlined by Kolstoe and Frey in 1965, and has been used in various forms ever since that time.

The regular classroom teacher may play a role in secondary programs primarily oriented to work-study through providing instruction in areas such as typing, automobile mechanics, home economics, driver education, and other practical secondary school subjects. Assignment to these classes is ordinarily determined on an individual basis, though all EMR students probably take the driver-education course. The special education teacher tries to ensure the student's maximum readiness for certain programs. She needs help and guidance from the regular classroom teacher who receives the student for these classes.

A work-study coordinator, often working in conjunction with vocational rehabilitation counselors, finds employment sites and supervises students on the job. With guidance from the work-study coordinator, the teacher may play a significant role in remedying difficulties the students have experienced in the workplace (Morsink, 1984).

The five major phases of a typical work-study program, as described by Mercer and Payne (1975), are (1) vocational exploration, (2) vocational evaluation, (3) vocational training, (4) vocational placement, and (5) follow-up.

In this sequence students (1) become familiar with the nature of various occupations and the required skills, (2) are provided guided experience with job skills, thus permitting instructors to determine abilities and preferences, (3) receive broad training in a wide variety of vocational areas, (4) are assisted with placement in an actual job, and (5) are assisted with any on-the-job difficulties that may arise. Vocational rehabilitation personnel, employed by rehabilitation services agencies, play a considerable role in this process, especially in the last two steps.

Work-study programs vary widely, but the goal is the same in all instances. The role of the regular classroom teacher varies with the ability level of the students and the availability of special education and rehabilitation personnel; but for the most part, the teachers who teach vocationally related subjects are most involved. Although special educators and rehabilitation personnel retain primary responsibility for these programs, regular classroom teachers may have increasing contact with EMR students in the secondary schools.

SUMMARY

Mental retardation has been recognized for many centuries, but the mentally retarded have been served in the public schools for less than a century. The primary method of serving such students until the past 20 to 25 years was a segregated special class taught by a specially trained teacher. By the 1950s most school systems provided some type of special program for the educable mentally retarded, but many did not accept responsibility for the trainable or the severely handicapped until the coming of PL 94-142 and various court decisions requiring that all handicapped students had the right to an appropriate educational program.

Since the late 1960s, several changes have had a profound effect on how and where mentally retarded students are educated and who provides the basic instructional program. Whereas in 1960 nearly all retarded students were taught in segregated special classes, by the 1980s many were being taught at least part of the day by regular classroom teachers.

A second change is related to the educational and intellectual level of students in the program. In the mid-1970s, *mental retardation* was redefined in a manner that lowered the upper-IQ-level cutoff. The IQ level below which a student might be considered mentally retarded was changed from one standard deviation below the mean to two standard deviations below the mean. In addition, it was agreed that to be classified *mentally retarded,* an individual must demonstrate retardation through subaverage intellectual ability and adaptive behavior. The net result of this change in definition was that many students who had formerly been considered educable mentally retarded were no longer so considered. The average ability level at which students were identified as educable mentally retarded was significantly lowered. At the same time, the trainable mentally retarded were being enrolled in public schools in rapidly growing numbers. Some came from private programs; others came from institutional settings. Thus the schools had an essentially new population of students with much lower mental ability than they had ever dealt with before. In many cases, this meant

a reconceptualization of the nature of education.

Because the major concern in this text is the education of mainstreamed exceptional students, this chapter emphasizes the educable mentally retarded. EMR students tend to have certain unique characteristics, but only three are present in every EMR student: (1) significantly below-average IQ, (2) significantly below-average adaptive behavior, and (3) educational and academic retardation. Other characteristics often observed include coordination problems, low frustration tolerance, poor self-concept, short attention span, poor general language ability, below-average ability to generalize and conceptualize, and play interests below those of age peers. These characteristics are overlapping and interrelated.

This chapter considered the nature of mental retardation, the responsibilities of special education personnel, and a number of educational methods and ideas that may be of value as the regular classroom teacher adapts and modifies the standard curriculum to provide a more appropriate program for the EMR. We offered general suggestions and discussed the more specialized work-study program often used in the secondary schools.

Throughout this chapter, we have indicated that although regular classroom teachers can and should be a major part of educational programming for the mentally retarded, they should also expect support and assistance from the special education specialist.

Regular classroom teachers have made progress in learning to adapt and modify educational methods, and in so doing they have taught EMR students with great success. One of the major benefits of mainstreaming the educable mentally retarded has been that teachers have developed for themselves many new skills and abilities that help all students in their classrooms.

Teaching Students with Learning Disabilities

- [ ] To what extent are learning disabilities and neurologically impaired synonymous terms?

- [ ] Why was the condition called learning disabilities "discovered" so much later in history than mental retardation?

- [ ] Why have learning disabilities been sometimes characterized as the "suburban version of mental retardation"?

- [ ] If learning disabilities typically do not "appear" until the child enrolls in school, are they caused by the school?

- [ ] Is a diagnosis of learning disabilities a permanent (nonremediable) one?

- [ ] How can we differentiate between learning disabilities and behavior disorders when a student's behavior is common to both diagnoses?

- [ ] What are the possible effects on academic learning of impulsive cognitive styles? Of reflective cognitive styles?

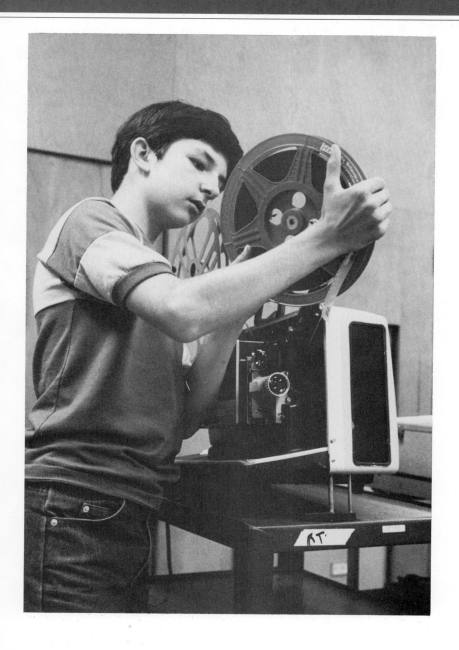

10

When something is more than 20 years old, it is somewhat difficult to consider it "new." However, learning disabilities is the newest of the handicapping conditions. This is especially true in regard to formal recognition in public awareness and in public schools. In terms of their actual existence, however, learning disabilities are probably no "newer" than mental retardation or speech problems. Learning disabilities were not widely recognized until the 1960s, and their nature is such that they are not likely to be recognized even today in more primitive societies. This fact is true for two major reasons: (1) learning disability symptoms become more obvious when the individual attempts to learn to read and to develop mathematical skills and various of the higher cognitive abilities, and (2) unless the condition is well understood, it is likely to be confused with mental retardation. This latter factor is particularly true in those parts of the world where the average educational level is low and measures of mental ability are poorly standardized and infrequently employed.

Our major concern here with learning disabled students is to understand better how the regular classroom teacher may play a cooperative and supportive role, along with the learning disability specialist, in providing the best possible educational program. Although a few learning disabled students may be in separate, self-contained programs, most are in the regular class for most of the school day. The following discussion of the nature of learning disabilities is therefore important, as is also a consideration of the definition of learning disabilities, which is in and of itself a problem in much of the nation.

LEARNING DISABILITIES: DEFINITION AND DISCUSSION

The definition of learning disabilities can best be understood as an umbrella definition—a broad, general definition that includes a number of conditions or disabilities once considered to be separate and distinct (Gallagher, 1986). It is true that various states use somewhat different terms to describe the learning disabled, but it is obvious that they are speaking of the same population.

Most other handicapping conditions are named in relation to the cause of the learning difficulty experienced by those identified as having that handicap or disability. As we learn more about each condition, we become aware of the wide array of difficulties that may result from the handicap. We also learn that these learning difficulties may vary from individual to individual, but there is a degree of security in speaking, for example, of the visually impaired or hearing impaired, for we presume that we know what is causing the problem. Many of us are more comfortable in dealing with something if we think we know its cause. Labels such as *hearing impaired* and *visually impaired* can be called *causally oriented* labels, and their definitions are related to the degree of the handicapping condition. In a similar way, the term *mental retardation* indicates that the cause is lower-than-normal (for age) mental ability and is primarily a causally oriented label. In contrast, the label *learning disability* describes the result rather than the cause of the learning difficulty. Therefore, the condition we call a learning disability is defined in terms of the student's difficulties—what he can and cannot do—and focuses primarily on academic performance.

The label *learning disabled* indicates that a student is having unusual learning difficulties and involves speculation as to possible causes, but it specifically indicates that the *primary* cause cannot be a condition such as mental retardation, hearing or visual impairment, and so on. Therefore it is often called a definition of exclusion.

The following definition was developed at the federal level as a result of the passage of PL 94-142. It is used, with variations and attempts to make the degree of educational discrepancy more specific, in all 50 states. The definition and criteria for determining that a student is in fact learning disabled are as follows:

The Federal Learning Disability Definition

Specific learning disability means a disorder in one or more of the basic psychological processes involved in understanding or in using language, spoken or written, which may manifest itself in an imperfect ability to listen, think, speak, read, write, spell, or to do mathematical calculations. The term includes such conditions as perceptual handicaps, brain injury, minimal brain disfunction, dyslexia, and developmental aphasia. The term does not include children who have learning problems which are primarily the result of visual, hearing, or motor handicaps, of mental retardation, of emotional disturbance, or of environmental, cultural, or economic disadvantage.

Criteria for Determining the Existence of a Specific Learning Disability

(a) A team may determine that a child has a specific learning disability if:
  (1) The child does not achieve commensurate with his or her age and ability levels in one or more of the areas listed in paragraph (a) (2) of this section, when provided with learning experiences appropriate for the child's age and ability levels; and
  (2) The team finds that a child has a severe discrepancy between achievement and intellectual ability in one or more of the following areas:
    (i)   Oral expression;
    (ii) Listening comprehension;
    (iii) Written expression;
    (iv) Basic reading skill;
    (v)   Reading comprehension;
    (vi) Mathematics calculation; or
    (vii) Mathematics reasoning.
(b) The team may not identify a child as having a specific learning disability if the severe discrepancy between ability and achievement is primarily the result of:

(1) A visual, hearing, or motor handicap;
(2) Mental retardation;
(3) Emotional disturbance; or
(4) Environmental, cultural, or economic disadvantage.[1]

In addition to this federal definition, another has been proposed by a committee of representatives of the six national organizations that constitute the National Joint Committee for Learning Disabilities (NJCLD). This definition was proposed in 1981 and reads as follows:

Learning disabilities is a generic term that refers to a heterogeneous group of disorders manifested by significant difficulties in the acquisition and use of listening, speaking, reading, writing, reasoning and mathematical abilities. These disorders are intrinsic to the individual and presumed to be due to central nervous system dysfunction. Even though a learning disability may occur concomitantly with other handicapping conditions (e.g., sensory impairment, mental retardation, social and emotional disturbance) or environmental influences (e.g., cultural differences, insufficient/inappropriate instruction, psychogenic factors), it is not the result of those conditions or influences.

The board of directors of the Association for Children and Adults with Learning Disabilities (ACLD) did not approve of the NJCLD definition and in 1984 proposed a revision and a rationale. They wanted to emphasize how the interference of learning disabilities is *selective*. They noted that it affects some abilities but not others, is variable in its severity and manifestations, and can influence the individual in *life skills* (not just cause difficulty in school or academic areas). In addition, their efforts were directed at describing a condition rather than a group of people.

A number of problems result from these and most other suggested definitions of learning disabilities. Perhaps the most sig-

---

[1] From the *Federal Register* (vol. 42, no. 250, Dec. 29, 1977, p. 65083).

nificant problem is that the definition provides little guidance about the *degree* of educational discrepancy required to identify any individual student as learning disabled. Various attempts have been made to correct this problem either by indicating a percentage of education lag or deficit (e.g., 40% or 50%) or by indicating, for example, that a fifth-grade student must score below the 2.5-grade-equivalent level in one of the academic areas if the student is to be considered learning disabled. In some instances the primary purpose of such regulations or guidelines has been to provide more specific guidance and to reduce confusion; in others, it has been to reduce an unusually high percentage of children identified as learning disabled in a particular state. Whatever the reason, this specification appears to be the major form of state-imposed addition to the federal definition.

It would clearly be much better if we could here provide the reader with a precise, completely unambiguous definition of learning disabilities and offer clear-cut, step-by-step directions for teaching learning disabled students, but this is simply not possible. The federal definition and identification criteria plus the description of characteristics exhibited by some learning disabled students (provided in the following section) should provide a basis for a beginning understanding of learning disabilities. The discussion of how regular teachers refer students for assessment related to learning disabilities should further clarify this issue. The principles for providing educational assistance indicate how regular educators may teach the learning disabled and some of the reasons for the various approaches in use today. Because of the diverse nature of this condition, it may always be necessary to use some exploratory teaching (trying out various approaches that seem to fit the assessment data and available information about a given student), but with better understanding, we can at least explore alternatives that are potentially viable.

CHARACTERISTICS OF LEARNING DISABLED STUDENTS

Significant Discrepancy

The discrepancy between learning potential and actual level of learning is one of two characteristics that are found in *all* learning disabled students. At first glance this might seem easy to verify, but in fact it is confounded by several factors: (1) opportunity to learn (sometimes referred to as amount of meaningful "exposure" to education), (2) level of intellectual potential (IQ), and (3) motivation to learn and other factors. These are in turn related to racial and ethnic language considerations, economic considerations, and a host of other less obvious influences. Therefore, although the significant discrepancy is an accepted requirement for identification as learning disabled, this is not as simple to verify as it might at first seem.

Deficient Learning Processes

Deficiencies or developmental delay in some of the mental processes through which most individuals learn is the second characteristic found in all learning disabled students. This characteristic overlaps with or includes many of the other characteristics discussed in the following sections and is related to some very complex concepts about which leading authorities do not fully agree. According to DeRuiter and Wansart (1982, p. 15), available research indicates that "the study of learning processes in the learning disabled can be organized under five major areas: attention, perception, memory, cognition, and encoding." They further note that a deficiency in any one of these areas "may be involved in the development of inaccurate or incomplete mental structures in the learning disabled." The end result is that the learning disabled

Students with academic problems relating to learning disabilities may be gifted in other areas.

student may be described by the teacher as not able to think as other children do. The teacher may further indicate that the kind of explanations that work with other students do not work with the learning disabled or that the kind of "logic" that other children of the same age exhibit is not seen in the learning disabled student.

In fact, the learning disabled student may not assimilate new information in the same manner as his age peers because his thinking abilities have evolved differently, with adaptations related to his partially inaccurate perceptions, memory, and so on. Or, at the very least, "their learning is less efficient and apparently developmentally delayed" (Reid & Hreska, 1981, p. 51). In some ways a given 10-year-old learning disabled student may think like a typical 10-year-old and in some ways like a typical 6-year-old.

Other Indicators

A number of other indicators are evident with above-average frequency in learning disabled students. No one of these other characteristics is seen in *all* learning disabled students, but each is seen more often in learning disabled students than in the population as a whole. Therefore, although they are useful clues to the possible existance of a learning disability, their presence does not necessarily mean that a given student is learning disabled. These characteristics are discussed in alphabetical order and are included to provide a sample of characteristics often associated with learning disabilities.

Hyperactivity. There are many theories about the *why* of hyperactivity and some debate as to how much activity constitutes hyperactivity, but most authorities agree that the condition often exists in learning disabled students. There is also much debate regarding the existence of a causal relationship between hyperactivity and learning disabilities. In a review of major investigations conducted in the area of hyperactivity, Johnson (1981, p. 353) concludes that present research efforts indicate that "genetic studies are inconclusive, that the relation of organic factors to hyperactivity has not yet been established, that social interaction studies need further investigation, and that the examination of radiation stress effects is still undeveloped." She notes that there is some support for the idea that food additives and lead poisoning may produce hyperactivelike effects in some children but that these causes are a very small part of the total problem.

The controversy about causation is likely to continue for some time, but regardless of the cause, the student who is truly hyperactive is at a distinct disadvantage in the traditional learning situation. It is important, however, to note that the label *hyperactive* has been much overused and should not be applied unless the degree and nature of activity is such that it directly interferes with the learning process.

Incoordination. Below-average (for age) coordination is another characteristic very commonly mentioned by many authorities in the field of learning disabilities. Some highly coordinated students may have learning difficulties, but by and large those students who are identified as learning disabled according to multiple criteria are below average in coordination for their age. The student with learning disabilities is often slower to develop the ability to throw and catch a ball, to skip, or to run, is likely to have difficulty in writing and other fine motor skills; may be generally clumsy; may stumble or fall frequently. (As the field of learning disabilities was evolving, some authorities referred to the "clumsy child syndrome" (Siegel & Gold, 1982). Some coordination problems are related to an inability to assess position in space properly, to problems with balance, or to both. Other coordination problems may be related to a physical or medical condition, but such problems would be discovered during the physical examination required as a part of the assessment process.

Memory Disorders. Memory disorders include those related primarily to short-term memory or long-term memory. They may include either auditory or visual memory. Memory is a complex process that is not fully understood, although various individuals have established theories that seem to explain most of the observable facets of memory. Case-study reports describe individuals who cannot remember where their window is or on which side of the room their bed is placed, even though it has been there for months. Other reports describe students who cannot repeat a simple sequence of three words immediately after hearing them. These types of memory deficits seriously affect the learning process.

Overattention or Attention Fixation. A student who cannot shift his focus of attention in a normal manner has just as much difficulty in learning as one who cannot focus on any object or activity long enough to learn new material. Such a student may regularly focus on some object in the room or outside the window and literally be unable to respond to the teacher's attempts to attract his attention. He shuts out other sensory signals, even those that call attention to something he would very much like to do. It is a matter not of *choosing* to shut out other signals but rather of involuntary overattention. This problem and the problems inherent with hyperactivity (because these two conditions often overlap) may be more difficult to handle in open-concept classrooms. Modifying the classroom setting to deal with these problems or assigning the student to another classroom may be necessary.

Perceptual Disorders. Perceptual disorders include disorders of visual, auditory, tactile, or kinesthetic perception. The student with visual perceptual problems may not be able to copy letters correctly or perceive the difference between a hexagon and an octagon. He may reverse letters or produce mirror writing. The student with auditory perceptual problems may not perceive the difference between different consonant blends or between the doorbell and the ring of the telephone. Because of these perceptual problems the student may at first seem to be lacking in sensory acuity (that is, seem to have a visual loss or be hard of hearing), but when acuity checks out as normal, the possibility of perceptual disorder must be considered.

There are generally accepted theories as to how perceptual abilities developed through the normal developmental paths of learning, but there is much less consensus on what happens—or what to do about it—when perception is not developing normally. There is, however, adequate evidence to suggest that significantly below-average perceptual ability often results in educational retardation.

Poor Self-Concept. It is not at all difficult to see why a child who repeatedly fails develops a poor self-concept. Often these two factors, failure and poor self-concept, become part of a vicious cycle from which the only real escape is improvement in school achievement or some compensatory tactic (often disruptive, acting-out behavior) as a substitute method of building status and self-concept.

Another View of Indicators

A somewhat more systematic way to look at characteristics of students with learning dis-

abilities is to look at those factors referenced in screening devices. The following outline reflects the types of difficulties often observed in learning disabled students:

1. significantly different classroom behaviors
   a. difficulty in beginning or finishing tasks
   b. difficulty in organizing
   c. inconsistent in behavior
   d. difficulty in peer relationships
2. significantly below-average performance in auditory comprehension and listening
   a. difficulty in following directions
   b. difficulty in comprehending or following class discussions
   c. inability to retain information received aurally
   d. difficulty in understanding or comprehending word meanings
3. significantly below-average performance in spoken language
   a. use of incomplete sentences or unusual number of grammatical errors
   b. use of immature or improper vocabulary or very limited vocabulary
   c. difficulty in recalling words for use in self-expression
   d. difficulty relating isolated facts; scattered ideas
   e. difficulty in relating ideas in logical sequence
4. significant academic problems
   a. difficulty in reading fluency
   b. difficulty in associating numbers with symbols
   c. incorrect ordering of letters in spelling
   d. confusion of manuscript and cursive writing
   e. avoidance of reading
   f. confusion of math concepts—addition, multiplication
5. orientation difficulties
   a. poor time concept, no grasp of meaning of time

b. difficulty in "navigating" around building or school grounds

c. poor understanding of relationships (*big, little, far, close, under, on, near*)

d. inability to learn directions (right, left, north, south)

6. motor disabilities or significant under-development for age

a. poor coordination, clumsiness

b. very poor balance

c. awkward, poorly developed manipulative or manual dexterity

d. lack of rhythm in movements

This list of difficulties provides an appropriate conclusion to a discussion of characteristics of the learning disabled, showing that although there are observable behaviors that lead the teacher to suspect problems, that these behaviors do not actually identify the student as learning disabled.

CLARIFYING THE DIFFERENCES BETWEEN LEARNING DISABILITIES AND OTHER DISABILITIES OR HANDICAPPING CONDITIONS

When actual screening instruments are examined by teachers, many note (or protest) that many of the same characteristics are exhibited by hearing impaired or mentally handicapped students. They further note that bilingual children who do not have a complete command of the English language may also exhibit some of these characteristics. Of course, they're correct. The difficulties related to auditory comprehension and spoken language are often seen in the hearing impaired and the mentally handicapped. In addition, orientation difficulties may be seen in the mentally handicapped. Below-average performance in spoken language may be exhibited by some bilingual children, and any combination of these three areas may be seen in some environmentally deprived or culturally different children. As stated previously, these are only indications of difficulties but should become the triggering mechanism for a referral for further evaluation, *particularly if the student has below-average academic performance.*

Mental retardation and learning disabilities may be confused, though in many ways dissimilar. They are different, for example, in that learning disabilities may remain "hidden" for many years, especially if the student is above average in intelligence. In these cases the student is apparently able to compensate through intact learning channels for a disability that exists in other learning channels. For example, a student might have serious difficulties in accurately gaining information through the auditory channel, but with a high level of intelligence and effective learning through the visual channel he may be able to learn and appear to be "normal" in most respects. In this case, one might be tempted to ask, "Why interfere if the student is learning normally?" Part of the answer is that learning that places a student within the average for his age is not necessarily normal or optimum learning for him.

If a student's ability is such that he should be in the top 5% of the class, then achievement at the 50th percentile is not normal. The teacher may be tempted to leave well enough alone, but a 12-year-old student with an IQ of 140 may quite possibly be a learning disabled student if he is doing only as well as 12-year-olds with average intelligence. With proper assistance the student may well improve his achievement dramatically. Of course, he may *not* be learning disabled. The student may have adequately developed learning abilities and simply be unmotivated or may have well-balanced basic abilities that are severely underdeveloped because of very poor educational opportunities. As noted at the start of this section, this type of learning disability may often remain hidden; the student may remain unidentified and unserved.

JIM AND MARK: A STUDY OF SIMILARITIES AND DIFFERENCES

Jim	Mark
Age: 9 years	Age: 9 years
Grade: 3	Grade: 3
Years in school: 4½	Years in school: 4½
Reading achievement: 1.6 (grade equivalent)	Reading achievement: 1.6 (grade equivalent)
Group IQ score: 75	Group IQ score: 75

The preceding descriptions of Jim and Mark are obviously identical until the IQ as indicated by an *individual* test of intelligence is considered:

Full-scale WISC IQ: 68	Full-scale WISC IQ: 102

Through the individual test of intelligence, it is found that Jim is very likely a borderline EMR youngster, whereas Mark is probably a learning disabled student. Additional data are then gathered:

Arithmetic: 1.8 (grade equivalent)	Arithmetic: 3.2 (grade equivalent)

Generally, the EMR student has basic skills in mathematics that are at about the same level as his reading skills, although sometimes they are higher if they mainly involve rote memory. In contrast, many learning disabled students who have severe problems in reading may do near grade-level work in mathematics as long as reading is not required. The reverse may also be true of the learning disabled student; he may do satisfactory work in reading but have significant problems in mathematics. It is the inconsistency in performance among various academic areas and various types of activities that characterizes the learning disabled student. Additional information about the boys' abilities in classroom interaction, apparent ability to learn from peers, and ability to conceptualize follows:

In classroom interaction regarding relationships of planets and the sun, Jim had real difficulty in following the idea of relative movement. Jim can follow class discussion as long as concepts are simple but has difficulty in making generalizations. Jim's speaking vocabulary is better than his reading vocabulary, but it is still far below the class average.

In classroom interaction regarding relationships of planets and the sun, Mark was one of the first in the class really to understand. In most topics related to science, if no classroom reading is involved, Mark does very well. On a verbal level, he conceptualizes and generalizes well. Mark's reading vocabulary (words he can recognize in print) is no better than Jim's; however, his spoken vocabulary is up to the class average in all respects and is above average in science areas.

Often the learning disabled student has a performance profile (in such areas as reading achievement, arithmetic achievement, vocabulary, ability to generalize, and ability to conceptualize) that is characterized by many ups and downs. He sometimes (or in some academic areas) seems quite average or perhaps above average, but in some areas he may be even less able than some EMR students. It is possible for a learning disabled student to be low in *all* areas of achievement and class interaction, but this is unusual. In contrast, the performance profile of the EMR student is usually relatively flat.

The comparison of Jim and Mark, two 9-year-old boys whose educational difficulties at first seem the same, may help clarify the differences between the mentally handicapped and the learning disabled. This is just one example of differences that may be found through a more complete evaluation of students' learning problems.

THE TEACHER'S RESPONSIBILITY TO MAKE REFERRALS

It is the responsibility of the regular classroom teacher to be alert for the possibility that students may be learning disabled and to refer such students for help when it seems appropriate.

Referrals based on a day-to-day experience and observation of any specific student may be the most common way in which children are considered for learning disabilities services, but another way is through some established screening procedure. Screening devices are a preliminary step that may lead to identification but that do not, in and of themselves, identify children. They are useful tools to guide the teacher's observations of students in the class and are an aid in objectifying observations about any particular student. We know teachers who have used screening tools to gain additional insight regarding a student they were planning to refer and who, after completing the scale, realized that the student was essentially normal except for some acting-out behavior that the teacher found particularly troublesome. Thus such scales can be used as actual screening devices (that is, applied to an entire class) or as a tool through which the teacher may more systematically and objectively analyze and summarize a particular student's strengths and weaknesses.

Students who are learning disabled may receive special assistance in the public schools in a variety of ways. In mild cases the regular classroom teacher may be able to provide meaningful and stimulating opportunities for learning with suggestions from a resource or itinerant teacher. In other cases some assistance in a specialized setting may be essential. A student must be officially identified as learning disabled to be eligible for placement in a program for such students.

Formal Identification of the Learning Disabled

We have already discussed the reasons why it is sometimes quite difficult to establish beyond any shadow of doubt the existence of learning disabilities in a specific case. Such identification is probably the most subjective identification procedure involved in special education, except perhaps for the identification of children with behavior disorders. With both learning disabilities and behavior disorders there are clear-cut cases, but many cases are difficult and perhaps some identification procedures should be called questionable. The criteria for identification promulgated by the federal government may seem relatively clear at first glance, but in fact they are quite ambiguous in many respects. The regular classroom teacher is not often required to play a deciding role in the identification procedure, but information about what the student does in day-to-day activities in the regular class is important for the staffing team that must make this decision.

We believe that identification is justified only if it permits some educational provision and assistance that would not be provided without such identification. It is the personal hope of most special educators whom we know that many students with mild learning disabilities can be served in the regular class without ever needing to attend separate, special-service programs. However, the more severe the learning problem, the more likely it is that help from outside the classroom will be needed. For these students, comprehensive and careful identification procedures are essential.

RESPONSIBILITIES OF SPECIAL EDUCATION PERSONNEL

The learning disabilities specialist with whom the regular classroom teacher works may be called a resource room teacher, an LD teacher, a learning disabilities specialist, or a learning disabilities consultant. In addition to providing direct and indirect instructional services, the specialist may contact other personnel who provide diagnostic or assessment services (psychologists, psychometrists, diagnosticians, assessment specialists) and perhaps speech pathologists or occupational therapists.

It is possible that the learning disabilities specialist may do much of the required assessment (except for the determination of IQ) that must take place before actual placement may be accomplished. Who performs which functions depends on many factors, but the size of the school district may be the major factor, with larger districts tending to have more highly specialized diagnostic and assessment personnel. In some districts, some of the assessment may be done by a private diagnostician on a contractual basis with the district. In others, some assessment may be done by a community agency.

In addition to learning disabled students served through the joint efforts of the regular classroom teacher and the learning disabilities specialist, there are some whose disabilities are so severe that they require self-contained class service. In this case the need for such service is determined after careful assessment and is part of a written educational plan. The use of this more restrictive service mode must be based on evidence that this is the most effective manner in which the student may receive the needed instructional assistance. In most cases, after significant improvement has been achieved, the student returns to a more normal educational setting and spends a major part of his day in the regular class. Then it is a matter of joint planning and service provision by the regular classroom teacher and the learning disabilities specialist. Often the need for a separate program in a self-contained class setting reflects the existence of multiple handicaps.

For most learning disabled students, resource-room service is the standard pattern. A resource room is a school setting organized specifically as a place where students with unique learning needs can receive specialized instructional assistance. If properly organized, it contains materials and equipment appropriate for the students with these needs. Resource rooms may be organized for one or several handicapping conditions. Usually the resource teacher works in the resource room. However, the concept of the resource teacher is wider in many schools. In this wider role, the resource teacher serves as a resource person for the regular classroom teacher regarding methods and materials, usually as such methods or materials are related to specific students in the regular classroom. If this teacher moves about from building to building as a resource person, he may be called an itinerant teacher. In practice, we cannot assume that we know what a person actually does simply by knowing his title. Similarly, we cannot assume that two persons who have quite different titles actually serve different functions. The fact is that most learning disability teachers (whatever they may be called) work in a number of different ways to serve the learning disabled student, and in so doing they provide both direct service to the student and indirect service through assistance provided to the regular classroom teacher.

Although the resource room is the most commonly used service vehicle for programs for the learning disabled, it is becoming the most common method used for other handicapping conditions also. A resource room teacher may teach students who have been diagnosed as learning disabled or mentally handicapped or as having behavior disorders. How such settings are managed varies considerably, but all have a system through which a number of students (perhaps as few as 10 or 12, or as many as 20 to 25) receive part-time learning assistance focused on their individual learning needs. The description that follows of one such resource room (a learning lab) provides a look at how such programs may be managed. This is only one way to provide such service, but it gives a reader who has not seen a resource room in action some concept of how it works.

The learning lab is a diagnostic and prescriptive center designed to meet the individual needs of each student. Assets, deficits, and long-range prescriptions are recorded in individual folders. These assets and deficits have been determined by qualified assessment personnel, and the long-range plans were developed by teachers, assessment personnel, and parents.

As the student enters the learning lab each day, he picks up his "tote tray," which contains his *daily-task folder* and other materials. The prescription centers (reading, language, writing, math, etc.) are identified and the student goes to each center according to the arrangement of the task in his task folder. Once he is in the assigned center, the teacher or aide assists him in getting the appropriate materials, understanding the instructions, and beginning the assigned task. The teacher then leaves the student to work independently and goes to other students in the same manner. "Help, please" signs are available at each center for the student who requires help in a task or who is ready to have his work checked.

Students may work in two or three centers each day. Constant monitoring and individual assistance are paramount considerations in the individualized approach. Incomplete tasks or unfinished center activities are ordinarily assigned for the next class period sequentially throughout the week. At the close of each day, individual daily prescriptions are written for the following day.

The center activities and tasks consist of commercial programmed materials, teacher-made games, laminated task cards, record players, cassette-tape players, books, puppets, and assorted activity folders. Although most of the tasks are individually oriented, there is planned opportunity for social development through games, peer teaching, puppetry, and other group activities.

Approximately 20 students are served in the learning lab on a daily basis by the resource teacher and one aide. Five or six students at a time are served at any one time for a period of 1–1½ hours each day (Monday through Thursday). Friday is designated as a day for individual evaluations and testing, teacher and parent conferences, classroom observations, and follow-up activities in the regular classroom.

Learning disabled students are provided an opportunity to improve their self-concept through success-oriented tasks. Since each student works at his own level, at his own rate, and with materials designed to remedy his specific problems, the program is truly individualized. Teaching the student to work independently in the resource room and to continue to do so in his regular classroom is of prime concern. The ultimate goal is to enable each individual to function well within the regular classroom, thereby phasing the student out of the resource room as soon as the necessary remediation has been completed.

Not all resource room programs are self-paced, as this one is, but self-pacing, the use of contracts, and other such techniques that may make the program seem quite different from the regular class are highly effective. At the very least, they make the program "feel" different for the student, a factor that may be quite important.

Because of the small number of students served, more innovative teaching techniques may be used in the resource room, especially those that require more one-to-one teacher student interaction. But whatever is done, it is highly important that the regular classroom teacher be kept informed and that she use all possible parallel and reinforcing activities.

THE ROLE OF THE REGULAR CLASSROOM TEACHER

The first and foremost responsibility of any teacher is to assist each student in class to achieve the recognized goals of instruction in that class to the fullest extent possible. This responsibility extends equally to the learning disabled student, and much of this student's instruction is little different from that of other students in the class. For decades good teachers have been applying somewhat different methods and techniques for certain students in their class who obviously needed much modified programming. In fact, it appears that some students who might have turned out to be among those considered mildly learning disabled have been successful because they have had a sequence of very good teachers who understood the need for individualization, took the time to provide specialized instruction, and assisted the student to overcome his learning difficulties. Therefore, we might conclude that one thing the teacher *must* do is apply all her teaching skill in the case of students with indications of any type of unusual difficulty in learning, regardless of whether that student has been identified as having a learning disability. We hasten to add that students with more serious, specific learning disabilities are not likely to achieve remediation in this manner.

They are much more likely to require very specialized assistance from a learning disability specialist and coordinated efforts from the regular classroom teacher.

Though it is difficult to generalize to fit all situations, we may say that it is most likely that the regular classroom teacher will proceed as follows in dealing with the learning disabled student in her class. The most important step is to modify the student's program in the manner suggested by the learning disabilities specialist. This often involves just one or two subject or skill areas, and the learning disabilities specialist should provide concrete examples of what may be done, including materials to be used. However, the regular classroom teacher remains responsible for the program in class and should apply suggestions, ideas, and materials as they are possible and practical. The role of the learning disabilities specialist is to suggest and assist, not to dictate to the regular classroom teacher. This principle is important and is supported by administrative staff in most if not all schools. This places the responsibility for management of the classroom squarely where it belongs—with the teacher in charge of that class.

The suggestions of the specialist are usually of value, but since the specialist is not present as the school day progresses and as individual situations arise, a number of modifications are necessary to make them work from hour to hour and day to day, even if the suggestions are unquestionably sound. In such situations, the regular classroom teacher must have some basis for further decision making. He or she must also have a basis for program planning in areas of the curriculum for which the specialist has not provided specific guidance.

The needs of any group of learning disabled students are sufficiently unique to make it impossible to say that all must receive some specific type of instruction or that some established set of instructional goals always apply, but it is possible to outline certain principles as a guide for program planning. This approach to program planning for the learning disabled is necessary because of the wide variety of needs of learning disabled students, and this heterogeneity is ensured by the umbrella definition of learning disabilities. The following principles do not tell *what* to teach but can provide *the basis for deciding what to teach*. They also provide guidance as to *how* to teach, but they must be related to the unique needs of each individual student. Guidelines of this nature may be used by the learning disabilities specialist in making teaching recommendations to the regular classroom teacher. But these same guidelines can also be used by the regular classroom teacher when specific program plans are not provided by a learning disabilities specialist, when conditions change, or when no help is provided in dealing with a learning disabled student. The principles that follow are a basis for decision making, and experience indicates that they may be successfully applied by teachers with a variety of teaching styles. There is, in fact, only one type of teacher who cannot use these principles: the teacher who believes that all children learn in the same way and that he knows the only successful way to teach. When students with learning disabilities are assigned to such a teacher, no set of principles will help.

Basic Principles for Program Planning

If the usual teaching method—that used with most other students in the regular class—will work, then that method should be used. Teachers must not use different methods just to be able to say they are doing something different. But different methods, approaches, and techniques should be initiated when the usual methods are not achieving results commensurate with the student's apparent ability to learn. The principles listed and discussed in the following sections should provide concrete assistance in determining how to modify the student's program, but they must be used in conjunction with specific information about the student's abilities, areas of weakness, past educational experiences, and other pertinent information. For the student diagnosed as learning disabled, this information should be available as part of the summary of assessment results; however, it should be further verified through informal assessment and day-to-day observation.

Principle 1 □ ***There is no single "right" method to use with learning disabled students***

Students are referred for assistance in learning disability programs because they are *not* learning effectively through the approach used in the classroom with the general population of students.

Of course, a teacher who knows he is working with a deaf student would not use an approach that is primarily auditory in teaching word-attack skills, but many regular classroom teachers continue to use methods that rely heavily on hearing sounds accurately with students who do not have the ability to discriminate between the sounds that teacher is using. A student may hear *sound* as well as others but be unable to discriminate between different phonemes that sound somewhat similar. An analogous situation may exist with a student who has good visual acuity but who cannot accurately discriminate between certain letters and thus does not do well with approaches based primarily on visual recognition. Acknowledgement of individual problems is essential and forms a basis for trying a number of alternate approaches. It is a major step in understanding that there is no one right method for dealing with learning disabilities. The idea that there is one right method that works for all children with learning disabilities violates common sense and is an outgrowth of a lack of understanding. We cannot always tell through present assessment techniques exactly how to approach every student with learning disabilities, but we can avoid the error of believing in a single approach and must realize that we may need to try a number of methods in certain difficult cases.

Principle 2 ☐ All other factors being equal, the method "newest" for the student should be used

When gathering data about educational history and background, the teacher should make every attempt to determine which approaches and materials have been used with each student. These may not be significant data in all cases, but they are in many. Analysis of this information can have several applications. If certain approaches have been used with little or no success, this may indicate the inappropriateness of such approaches. This is not always the case, however, for such approaches may have been poorly implemented or the student may not have had certain requisite abilities at an earlier date and may possess them now. Nonetheless, this does provide a starting point for further investigation.

An equally important point, and one too often overlooked, is that many students tend to develop a failure syndrome after trying to accomplish a task only to meet repeated failure. In the case of learning to read, the teacher likely feels it necessary to continue to attempt to assist the student to learn to read, or to read more effectively, but the teacher should make a deliberate attempt to use a method that "looks" and "feels" different to the child. The more severe the learning problem and the longer it has been recognized and felt, the greater the need for this procedure. This principle dictates that when a variety of approaches are possible and all other factors are approximately equal, the approach that is most different from earlier methods is likely to be the most effective.

Principle 3 ☐ Some types of positive reconditioning should be implemented

Pioneers in the learning disabilities field such as Fernald and Gillingham (see Gearheart, 1985, pp. 185–206) recognized the value of this principle, a value that remains today. The "newest possible method" (Principle 2) is a part of this positive reconditioning effort, and additional attempts should be directed toward convincing the student that his inability to develop adequate reading (or arithmetic or language) skills is not the student's fault. Rather, it is caused by the failure of the school and teachers to recognize that the student needed to learn by methods different from those used for other children. The obvious point of this effort is to convince the child that he is OK, to boost the child's self-concept to the point that he will approach the learning task with increased confidence and thus maximize the chances of success. Unfortunately, most schools are organized in such a way that students with learning difficulties are reminded daily, sometimes hourly, that they are failures. There is a scarcity of research on the effects of planned positive reconditioning, but the experience of a number of learning disability teachers with whom we have worked, the historical testimony of Fernald and Gillingham, and common sense indicate that *success must be planned.*

Principle 4 ☐ High motivation is a prerequisite to success; deliberate consideration of the affective domain is essential

Because this is such an obvious principle, it is not always properly emphasized. Attempts to maximize motivation are difficult to measure or monitor and may seem unglamorous, except as related to some unusual type of behavior modification system. Principles 2 and 3 are a part of the overall attempt to maximize motivation, but deliberate efforts beyond these two principles must be planned. In the case of older students who may have developed the basic learning abilities necessary for academic success but developed them several years late, a program to promote higher motivation may be particularly important. The fact that various behavior modification techniques are in common use, many with apparent success, attests to the validity of this principle.

This principle also dictates some sort of planned investigation of the affective domain—a look at how the student feels about himself, both in general (in the world outside the academic boundaries) and in respect to his specific feelings as he attempts to achieve within the school setting. Some learning disabled students have such obvious emotional problems that they can scarcely be overlooked. In this case the best approach is to plan and initiate attempts to counteract, remedy, or in some manner attend to these problems. Many of the other principles have the effect of attending to the problems of low self-esteem, and if academic achievement improves, it automatically has a positive effect. But beyond these positive vectors, it is imperative that the affective components be deliberately considered to maximize the potential of other remedial efforts and to prevent the growth of negative emotional components. This investigation of the affective domain, even when there are no overt behavior problems, must be a part of evaluation and planning for learning disabled students.

Tape recording may enhance interest and promote motivation.

Principle 5 ☐ *The existence of nonspecific or difficult-to-define disabilities, particularly with older students, must be recognized*

A serious educational problem in reading or arithmetic can be defined, but if, for example, a secondary student experienced significant visual perceptual problems at an early age and did not have the visual perceptual skills necessary for success in reading at eight years of age but developed them later, it may be almost impossible to pinpoint the specific disability. Significant educational retardation may exist along with, in most cases, a negative attitude toward school. There may be a need to develop second- or third-grade reading skills in a 15-year-old student who has learned many ways to circumvent his reading problem. Some authorities who describe learning disabilities only in terms of specific disabilities that can be neatly defined might say that this is not a learning disability. Our point of view is that this is a learning disability and that it requires very careful consideration and planning.

Principle 6 ☐ *It is important to be concerned and involved with both process- and task-oriented assistance and remediation*

This principle must be followed for the most effective use of time and effort. Many of the earliest efforts to assist learning disabled students centered on remediation of process skills, and little attention was paid to assisting the student to carry these skills over into the actual task of learning to read or understanding arithmetic. Experience has indicated that most students require help in applying newly developed process abilities in the academic setting. The regular classroom teacher plays an important part in this matter, whether it involves planned coordination with the learning disabilities specialist or a situation in which the regular classroom teacher must provide the total program for the student. If a student cannot discriminate visually between *ab* and *ad,* he must learn to do so; he also needs planned practice in using this newly developed ability in a variety of settings. In a similar manner, if a student cannot aurally tell the difference between the *b* sound and the *d* sound, he must learn to do so and must exercise this newly developed auditory discrimination. If the teacher is aware of this need and is alert for opportunities to provide this practice or exercise, it can be of great value. Many specific activities may be suggested by resource personnel, but the principle can be applied by any teacher with or without specific direction from the specialist.

Principle 7 ☐ *One should attempt to determine how the student approaches cognitive learning and then assist him to develop better learning strategies*

This final principle may in many instances be the most important. We all have certain established ways in which we learn. In essence, we develop a way in which we organize the information at hand so that we may learn in some systematic fashion. Precisely how each individual develops his personal learning system is not known; what is known is that some are much better (more organized, more systematic, more effective learners) than others. It is also known that learning disabled students appear to approach many learning tasks in a manner that can only be described as disorganized. It is certainly not like the way in which many of the more successful students approach the same task. This "organization for learning" applies to all learning: motor learning, basic language learning, and high-level conceptual skills.

This principle dictates that the teacher pay as much attention to *how* as to *what* the student learns. It involves an analysis of how an individual thinks—how he approaches cognitive learning—and an effort to help him improve learning strategies. Applications of this principle include the use of cognitive training and the teaching of specific study skills.

It would be naive and a gross oversimplification to say that these seven principles are the key to success with learning disabled students. They do, however, provide a valuable base, a launching platform, if you will, for meaningful planning.

Certain established methods and approaches have in practice tended to be of value more often than others with the learning disabled. We stand by our belief that these seven principles should be given careful consideration in educational planning and that a series of "cookbook" approaches is not the way to proceed to planning for students who are learning disabled. Nevertheless, some methods may serve to illustrate what has proved of benefit. These ideas are of maximum value only if they are implemented within the framework suggested by the preceding seven principles.

Behavior-Management Approaches

Behavior-management approaches may be well known to some readers and new to others. But it is doubtful that any reader of this text has not *experienced* behavior-management techniques, either as the recipient of such efforts or a user of them, perhaps unknowingly. One often thinks of the terms *operant conditioning, behavior modification,* or *applied behavior analysis* when thinking of this topic; but regardless of the term used, we are talking about changing students' behavior. And although one may first think of *behavior* as acting-out or withdrawing, listening and reading are also behaviors. Alberto and Troutman (1986) point out that these principles "can be used to teach academic subjects as well as manage students' social behavior" (p. vi).

Behavior management involves procedures whereby we specify behavioral goals, establish a procedure to reach these goals (usually through reinforcement of some type), and then attempt to assist the student to maintain whatever desirable changes have taken place. In the area of learning disabilities, behavior management very often involves the teaching of basic skills or at least the learning of new facts and has proved quite successful. Often some type of contract (a written agreement) is involved, and positive reinforcement is most often used; however, at other times the student is unaware that behavior modification (shaping or management) is taking place. Obviously the teacher must establish realistic objectives, consistent with the overall learning program for the student. With careful attention to these two factors, this is a valuable technique to use with learning disabled students.

Because more detail about behavioral approaches is provided in chapter 11 and because many readers may already be well informed about the use of behavioral principles to promote learning, we do not include additional information here. We do want to emphasize, however, that this is a potentially valuable technique; it works well with many learning disabled students. We recommend behavioral approaches as applicable and valuable for use with learning disabled students. First, they can help facilitate cognitive learning through some type of reinforcement. Second, they can help reduce activity levels and increase attention to learning; thus the student can make progress in any of a variety of academic or social arenas.

Hyperactive or Highly Distractible Students

The American Psychiatric Association uses the term *attention-deficit disorder* and specifies the symptoms that must be observed before this classification is applied.

However, since most educators use the term *hyperactive,* we will use it here.

The degree of activity necessary to view a student as hyperactive is debatable, and we will not enter the debate here. Teachers do not classify students as hyperactive, but they need to deal with the symptoms often associated with students who are thus classified. These symptoms include impulsivity, short attention span, perseveration, low frustration tolerance, overreaction to visual, auditory, or tactile stimuli, and others. With each of these characteristics it is a matter of a student exhibiting *more* of this characteristic than others his or her own age. For example, all students have a limit to their attention span, but some have a much, much shorter attention span than others. As well, a sensitivity to visual, auditory, or tactile stimuli is also a characteristic of all human beings, children and adults alike. But some students jump at the slightest touch or look up from working on an arithmetic assignment at the slightest sound, whereas others their age can attend to tasks at hand until the stimulation becomes much more intense. It is a matter of *degree,* or the amount of activity, and also a matter of the *character* of the activity. Many hyperactive students appear to be "driven" by some internal force, and their hyperactive behavior comes at inappropriate times when their age peers are continuing to work at the task underway in the class. Hyperactive students typically continue their unusual level of activity even after there are very obvious negative social consequences and even after the apparent triggering factors are long gone.

In summary, then, hyperactive students overreact as compared to other students, and this overreaction leads to negative social consequences, to interference with the learning of others, and to a great reduction in their ability to develop basic skills or to learn new academic material. Many hyperactive students may require much more than the regular classroom teacher can provide (e.g., medication, a highly specialized setting, etc.), but for some, behavior-management techniques may work, and for others planned changes in the classroom environment may be the answer. This latter possibility is very much within the realm of the teacher, and a number of practical steps may improve the learning situation for both the hyperactive student and others in the class. The following suggestions for improving the environment to reduce hyperactivity have worked for other teachers and work with some students. For other students they may be insufficient, but they deserve consideration.

1. When differentiated assignments are possible, assign activities that involve fewer potential distractions. Be careful in the assignment of group activities for the student, considering the size of the group, other students in the group, and similar factors.
2. Change the student's seating assignment according to possible sources of distraction, or if this change does not provide enough environmental control, assign the student to a study carrel. (For younger students this may be called an "office" and at times may be temporarily constructed out of large packing boxes.)
3. Limit the amount and type of materials at the student's desk through the use of a tote tray or a storage and checkout procedure controlled by the teacher.
4. Use some sort of device, such as a headset, to cover the student's ears (used only at selected times).
5. Move the student to another classroom. This is more likely to be necessary if the classroom is an open setting.

These management suggestions involve controlling the teaching and learning environment and should suggest other related ideas. The final suggestion of moving the student to another classroom requires approval and action by the principal in addition to parental involvement. The other suggestions involve decisions that may be made by the teacher, but in some cases the parent must be fully informed to ensure cooperation and reduce the possibility of misunderstandings. For example, when assigning a student to a study carrel or using a headset to muffle sound, both the student and the parent should understand the reason for the modification. Unless this understanding is achieved, the action might be viewed as a punishment.

These suggestions, along with similar modifications that may be obvious in a given practical situation, represent one way to try to help students who overreact to normal visual or auditory stimulation or who exhibit general hyperactivity or distractability. In some instances these are students already identified as learning disabled, but in many cases they are simply students having difficulty learning. In either case, this approach is worth a try, and, as many other teachers have discovered, it might prove to be effective.

Tactile, Kinesthetic, and Multisensory Approaches

The tactile and kinesthetic senses are too often overlooked by teachers as channels for learning, perhaps because the auditory and visual channels appear more effective. This discussion considers the tactile and kinesthetic senses as channels for effective learning and discusses their use as part of a multisensory, visual-auditory-kinesthetic-tactile approach.

For students who cannot see, the sense of touch—the ability to feel shapes and forms and configurations—provides an effective substitute for sight when applied to developing the ability to read. The tactile and kinesthetic learning channels can also be used in various ways to assist some learning

disabled students to learn to read, including the following:

1. Students may be asked to identify objects placed in a cloth bag so that they cannot see them.
2. Students may be blindfolded and asked to identify objects.
3. Sandpaper letters or numbers may be used to promote tactile and kinesthetic learning of these abstract symbols.

In each of these examples, the major purpose of the activity is to provide tactile and kinesthetic support for visual learning, either to assist in developing skills that have been slow in developing or to attempt to straighten out previously scrambled reception and interpretation of visual signals. In some cases it may be well to have children feel a letter or word while looking at it, thus providing simultaneous signal reception through the visual and tactile senses. In other cases it may prove to be more effective to block the visual signal to be certain that the student is completely accurate in tactile sensing alone, before adding the visual. In all of the preceding activities, the important principle is the use of additional sensory modalities to assist in the development of other modalities. This principle is most commonly used to support or assist the visual sense with the tactile sense.

A somewhat different application of this principle involves the teacher or a helping student tracing out letters or sometimes words on the arm or back of the student who needs help. This approach is significantly different in that the student receives no kinesthetic input, only the tactile. The student may be looking at letter cards on a desk and attempting to find one matching the letter traced out on his back or may keep eyes closed and concentrate on feeling the letter or word. A whole variety of games or activities may be developed using this type of assistance when the evidence indicates that this is in fact a need of the student. This type of activity might be misused or overdone if not carefully monitored.

The preceding activities and approaches are most appropriate with primary-age children who show evidence of developmental or remedial needs in the visual-perceptual abilities required for reading.

The kinesthetic and tactile modalities are currently used in a wide variety of learning activities in kindergarten and first grade. They may not be emphasized as such, but experienced primary-grade teachers regularly verify their use and general acceptance. These two modalities may also be a part of an organized teaching approach more often used for remedial purposes with students having unusual difficulties in learning to read. When used along with the visual and auditory channels, these approaches are sometimes called VAKT (visual-auditory-kinesthetic-tactile) approaches, and sometimes they are simply called *multisensory* approaches. One of the best known of such approaches is that first advocated by Grace Fernald over 50 years ago and still in use today. Fernald provided an account of her methods in 1943, and although many variations of her approach have since been proposed, they retain the basic ideas outlined in her original text. The following review of her work illustrates the basic thrust of this approach.

The Fernald approach has been called a multisensory approach, a tracing approach, or a kinesthetic method. The terms *tracing* and *kinesthetic* have been applied because those are unique features of the approach, but the most accurate name for this method is *simultaneous VAKT,* which differentiates her approach from most other approaches called *multisensory* or VAKT.

Before the remedial program is actually started, the Fernald procedure strongly recommends "positive reconditioning." This recommendation is based on the assumption that almost all students who have experi-

enced school failure have developed a low self-concept, particularly in relation to anything associated with school or with formal education. The following suggestions involve conditions to be avoided.

1. *Avoid calling attention to emotionally loaded situations.* Attempts by either teachers or parents to urge the student to do better generally have negative effects. Reminding the student of the future importance of academic success or telling him how important it is to his family should be avoided. If the student is already a failure and knows it, these admonitions or urgings are at best useless and sometimes result in a nearly complete emotional block.

2. *Avoid using methods that previous experience suggests are likely to be ineffective.* This is important both during remediation and during the time of the student's reentry to the regular classroom. If the student is experiencing success in a temporary, out-of-class remedial setting (after school or for a set time period each day) and then must return to class and to methods by which he was previously unable to learn, the remedial program may be negated. Or, after a period in which the student has been out of class on a full-day basis and has found success in a new method, if he must make an immediate return to the former methods with no planned transition, the student may return to his old inability to learn.

3. *Avoid conditions that may cause embarrassment.* Sometimes a new method used in the new setting is effective and satisfactory, whereas in the old setting, unless some special provisions are made, it may seem childish or silly. For example, the tracing involved in the Fernald approach may seem so unusual in the regular classroom that the student may feel out of place there. The reward, that is, the learn-

ing, may not be worth the feelings of conspicuousness and embarrassment.

4. *Avoid directing attention to what the student cannot do.* This is a special kind of problem that might be related to the first condition.

Regardless of what is required, attempting to bring about positive reconditioning and avoiding emotional reversal after the reconditioning has taken place are of prime importance.

Fernald VAKT approach. The first step in each remedial case in the actual classroom or clinic procedure is to explain to the student that there is a new way of learning words that really works. The student is told that others have had the same problem he is having and have learned easily through this new method.

The second step is to ask the student to select any word he wants to learn, regardless of length, and then to teach him to write and recognize (read) it, using the following method:

1. The word chosen by the student is written for him, usually with a crayon in plain, blackboard-size cursive writing. In most cases, regardless of age, cursive writing is used rather than manuscript because the student then tends to see and "feel" the word as a single entity, rather than a group of separate letters.
2. The student traces the word with his fingers in contact with the paper, saying the word as he traces it. This is repeated as many times as necessary until the student can write the word without looking at the copy.
3. The student writes the word on scrap paper, demonstrating to himself that it is now "his" word. Several words are taught in this manner, taking as much time as necessary to completely master them.

4. When the student has internalized the fact that he can write and recognize words, he is encouraged to start writing stories. The student's stories are whatever the student wishes them to be at first, and the instructor gives the student any words (in addition to those mastered) he needs to complete the story.
5. After the story is written, it is typed and the student reads it in typed form while it is still fresh in his mind. It is important that this be done immediately.
6. After the story is completed and the new word has been used in a meaningful way, the new word is written by the student on a card that the student files alphabetically in his own individual word file. This word file is used as a meaningful way to teach the alphabet without undue emphasis on rote memory.

This procedure is often called the Fernald tracing method because the tracing is an added feature in contrast to the usual methods of teaching reading or word recognition. However, it should be noted that the student is simultaneously *feeling, seeing, saying,* and *hearing* the word. Thus this is truly a multisensory approach.

Several points should be carefully observed and followed for maximum success:

1. The word should be selected by the student.
2. Finger contact is essential, using either one or two fingers.
3. The student should write the word, after tracing it several times, without looking at the copy.
4. In case of error or interruption in writing, the word should be crossed out and a new start made.
5. Words should be used in context.
6. The student must always say the word aloud or to himself while tracing and while writing it.

Although many additional details could be given, these points outline the essence of the Fernald approach. This approach has been used with various students having a variety of problems, including those with problems in the auditory channel. However, it is probably most beneficial for students with visual-channel problems, particularly problems of visual sequential memory or visual imagery.

Cognitive-Training Techniques

During the past 10–15 years, a technique called *cognitive training, metacognition,* or *cognitive behavior modification* (CBM) has gained increasing attention. These techniques involve training students to monitor and modify their own cognitive strategies and are applicable from elementary grades through high school. The premise underlying these approaches is that some students do not produce effective strategies for learning; therefore their learning process is ineffective and disorganized. The strategies that tend to require remediation are the plans, actions, steps, and processes that result in efficient learning or problem solving.

Meichenbaum (1983) suggests that teachers examine their own cognitions before attempting to teach thinking skills to students. His guidelines are as follows:

1. *Try out* target behaviors yourself to determine all the steps. Ask students who perform well, and those who don't, to help analyze the task.
2. *Tune in* to students as they perform tasks. Be especially attuned to hesitation and/or confidence expressed verbally and nonverbally by the student.
3. *Choose as a training task an actual task the student performs* (or something similar), otherwise the student will be unable to generalize.
4. *Ask for students' advice* in devising the training. Use the students' actual words whenever possible.

5. *Train subtasks and metacognitive skills* at the same time. Subtasks are the skills needed to perform the task and metacognitive skills are self-questioning, etc. Otherwise the student may develop separate skills.
6. *Provide specific feedback* indicating how the use of the strategy leads to improvement. The goal is not to use the metacognitive strategy but to improve performance.
7. *Teach generalization* by using the strategy under new circumstances. Use a variety of persons in a variety of settings.
8. *Provide a coping model* by demonstrating for the student what happens when the strategy is not used and how to cope with that failure.
9. *Review the strategy* on a planned basis. Provide for reteaching specific skills.

After thinking through these guidelines, teachers may want to begin to use some of the strategies. Remember above all that changing or modifying thinking processes is a long-term task.

A self-questioning strategy (Wong & Jones, 1982) that may assist students in reading comprehension consists of the following steps:

1. Ask, "Why am I reading this?"
2. Locate main ideas and highlight with marker.
3. Write down a question about each main idea.
4. Think about an answer for each question.
5. Read the passage or chapter.
6. Reexamine the questions and compare the mental answers with the answers in the passage just read.

Lengthy chapters should be divided into sections for this strategy to be effective.

Schumaker, Deshler, Alley, Warner, and Denton (1982) devised "a multipass comprehension strategy." Each of the three "passes" through the reading material recommended in this strategy has specific purposes.

The survey pass requires the student to gain as much information from the chapter as possible using chapter title, illustrations and captions, major subtitles, summary, and so on. Paraphrasing the information gathered then leads to a beginning level of comprehension.

The size-up pass requires the student to collect as much information from the chapter as possible without reading it word for word. Questions at the end of the chapter are used to guide finding of dates or italicized words. Cues such as italics, colors, bold print, and so on are changed into questions. For example, if the word *ecosystems* is in bold print, the student may ask, "What does *ecosystem* mean?" or "How is ecosystem related to environment?" The student then skims the section around the word and paraphrases an answer.

The sort-out pass enables the student to evaluate his or her own knowledge of the material. The student tries to answer questions at the close of the chapter or a study guide. A mark is placed by any question the student can answer immediately. If the student is unsure of the answer, he or she locates the answer by skimming the appropriate section of the chapter, then places a mark by that question until all questions are marked.

A number of teachers have found that many students who have difficulty with academic tasks tend to respond impulsively (for example, with wild guessing) to problem-solving situations, virtually ignoring various clues or cues that more reflective students use to good advantage. Since cognitive style is apparently learned, and these impulsive students have not learned to employ their cognitive processes effectively, it seems logical that we should attempt to provide assistance through specific cognitive training. One training technique provided by Meichen-

baum and Goodman (1971) includes teaching specific verbalizations in the following modeling and rehearsal sequence:

1. The teacher models the task to be learned, talking aloud while the student watches and listens.
2. The student performs the task, verbalizing (self-instructing) in a manner similar to that demonstrated by the teacher in step 1. The teacher assists as needed.
3. The student performs the task, self-instructing as in step 2 but with no assistance from the teacher.
4. The student performs the task, self-instructing in a whisper.
5. The student performs the task, thinking the self-instruction that was formerly verbalized.

This self-instructional cognitive training may involve self-instructions such as "I have to try very hard to do it right" or "What must I look at before I decide the answer?" In addition, the student may be trained to supply self-reinforcement by verbalizing statements such as "That was good—I got the right answer."

It is apparent that a variety of cognitive strategies are available. Wallace and Kauffman (1986) indicate that *the* way to enable students to become better thinkers or problem solvers has not yet been discovered; however progress is being made.

Teaching Study Strategies

The direct teaching of study strategies is closely related to cognitive training and may be approached in a number of ways. Direct, systematic teaching of essential study strategies has been recommended by a number of authorities (Alley & Deshler, 1979; Mercer & Mercer, 1985). What is involved is directly teaching the student to improve specific study skills, and the use of this method with the learning disabled is suggested by the fact

Tom Morton

Most students with learning disabilities are in a regular class most of the day.

that many such students appear to have very poor study skills.

Those who advocate the teaching of specific study skills believe that there are specific "techniques, principles or rules that will facilitate the acquisition, manipulation, integration, storage, and retrieval of information across settings and situations" (Alley & Deshler, 1979, p. 13). The focus is on teaching students how to study and learn, not on specific content. Specific techniques or skills are taught that will assist the student in the learning process in content areas as diverse as literature and mathematics.

The rationale for teaching study skills is that, once fully learned, a particular skill may be generalized and used in a variety of content areas (Alley & Deshler, 1979; Deshler & Schumaker, 1986). For example, if a student is taught the skill of note taking, this skill may then be used in history, literature, physics, and so on. For some students, learning study skills may facilitate retention of material in the regular classroom and permit them to be as successful as many of their nonhandicapped peers.

Various authors outline this process differently and there may be some variation in targeted study strategies; but those emphasized by Sheinker and Sheinker (1982) are recognized as among the more essential. They emphasize four major study skills or strategies useful in improving recall, understanding, and generalization of materials learned. These skills are

1. skimming—the ability to determine what is more important without becoming distracted or overinvolved with irrelevant details
2. summarizing—the ability to condense material read into a few key sentences that highlight the relationship between facts and concepts
3. note taking—the ability to write notes about basic information in a meaningful sequence that shows the essential order of facts or events
4. outlining—a more advanced set of abilities requiring a degree of mastery of Skills 1 through 3 above and leading to organization of information and concepts according to their relative value (particularly valuable as a basis for review and study)

Many teachers already teach study skills to some extent, but some apparently do not do so in any organized manner. Even when such skills are taught, students with learning problems often do not learn them as quickly as other students. Sheinker and Sheinker comment about the need for direct, systematic teaching of study skills (1982, p. 1):

Have you ever wondered what happens to all the bits and pieces of information that a student is required to learn, organize, and retrieve? In order to effectively utilize the information to which s/he has been exposed, the successful student must be able to distinguish essential from nonessential information in content material and to discriminate, synthesize, sequence, and organize it. The development of effective study skills helps students learn more about how they learn, and how to take greater responsibility for their own learning.

Sheinker and Sheinker's four workbooks on skimming, summarizing, note taking, and outlining as well as other comparable guides to teaching study strategies provide a valuable resource for teaching all students and are particularly applicable to students with learning problems.

A broad-based approach suggested by Deshler and Schumaker (1986) stresses the importance of appropriate diagnosis of the skills students do not use consistently or efficiently and also those skills they *do* use effectively. The teacher then can examine the various content areas to determine what skills the student must have to function effectively in each area. With the knowledge of what the student already knows and uses and of what demands will be made on him, the teacher may design a specific curriculum for that student. The required skills are then taught in a structured, systematic fashion. They are taught across a variety of content areas, so as to promote generalization.

If long-range goals are developed as to which of the skills a student may need first or which are required before more complex skills are taught, the teacher will be able to follow an organized plan that should maximize progress. Deshler and Schumaker (1986) suggest that a goal of "three to four learning strategies per year" is appropriate (p. 587).

Ideas for Reading and Language Development

The Fernald multisensory approach presented earlier is a fairly complete approach. This section considers ideas for teaching reading and promoting language development that are not a part of any system or approach but are simply good ideas for these purposes. They are a sample of hundreds of similar ideas that may work with some learning disabled students. They should be considered for use *only* as they fit the individual needs of a given student.

1. Have the student trace letters with templates and stencils.
2. Use dry gelatin powder, shaving cream, or finger paint for a base and have the student copy letters or words he usually reverses or write letters or words as you dictate them.
3. Have the student cut letters or shapes out of paper. This helps in discrimination of letters and can provide practice in coordination.
4. Present partially completed letters and have the student complete them.
5. Suggest a mnemonic device for the student who reverses letters; for example, for a right-handed student, "the ball part of the b always points to the hand you write with. If it does not, then the letter is d."
6. Provide the student with pictures that have missing parts and ask him or her to draw them in.
7. When teaching the names of states, capitals, industry, or products, have the student trace them first, then draw them from memory and compare results. The comparison is especially effective if the drawing paper is transparent and is laid over the original or if both are held up against the window.
8. Tape the student's favorite record with vocal and instrumental background. Have the student listen to the tape and transcribe the lyric. Earphones prevent distracting, and being distracted by, other students, and a tape recording allows the student to stop when necessary to take time to write.
9. Provide the student with one or two paragraphs that have all the nouns, adjectives, or verbs omitted. The student can then fill in the missing words. For an alternate activity, have the student fill in the missing words to make the paragraph humorous.
10. On field trips point out objects and simultaneously name them. Using simple sentences, explain the functions of objects or relationships. Have the student repeat important words and functions or relationships. Repetition helps focus attention.
11. After a field trip, show pictures of objects and have the student name them and tell about their function. Have him describe similarities or differences between the picture and the object.
12. Put each step for a recipe on individual cards. Directions for building a model, playing a well-known game, or any other step-by-step directions can be used. Have the student put them in the proper sequence. If the student has difficulty with this, ask him to "talk through" the procedure or, if possible, allow the student to attempt to determine the error.
13. Using newspaper clippings, list questions that are answered either in the article or in captions. To provide practice in skimming, time the student. For practice in critical thinking, have the student seek possible bias or opinion; for practice in synthesizing, have the student read the article and either tape or write a one-paragraph summary.
14. Cut comic strips or books apart and cover the captions (use simple ones if the student finds this difficult). Have the student write her own caption. Sometimes she can compare her captions with the original.
15. Establish a list of the student's assignments. Use a timer and provide the student with a time limit during which the student is to complete each assignment. If the student completes the work during the specified time, provide him with

a reward (five minutes to listen to a record, three minutes to watch a filmstrip, etc.).

16. Teach common punctuation marks, such as the comma, question mark, quotation marks, and exclamation mark. Explain that they constitute a symbol system that aids the communication process in writing and reading. For example, have a student demonstrate what he would say if he saw a building on fire or saw someone fall off a bridge and then how he would write these exclamations ("Fire!" "Help!" etc.). Arrange other hypothetical situations. Provide the student with many opportunities to observe how these punctuation marks translate into our daily speech.

17. Prepare tapes of stories or selections. Have students read with the tape. Good readers can prepare the tapes.

18. To assist the student in note taking, divide five-by-eight-inch cards into three spaces as in the diagram. Space 1 is for major ideas and topics, Space 2 is supporting information, and Space 3 is for summary or questions.

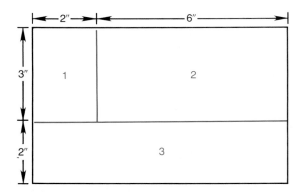

19. Teach map legends as a separate symbol system. Flashcards with the symbol on one side and the definition on the other can be used either individually or in groups.

20. Teach the student the "capitalization overall punctuation spelling" (COPS) method of monitoring errors in writing (Deshler, 1983). The student is taught to ask the following questions after completing a written assignment: (1) Are all first words and names *capitalized?* (2) Does it look good *overall?* Indentation, spacing, legibility, and so on are examined by the student (a checklist of what to look for may be posted on the bulletin board). (3) Are *punctuation* marks used appropriately? (4) Are all words *spelled* correctly? Hint: When teaching this method, have students use different colored pen or pencils to indicate that they have "COPSed" the paper (It is easier to do this if only every other line is used.)

21. Teach the student about words that indicate chronology and sequential or causal relationships. History books usually provide practice in chronological arrangement, science or math books frequently illustrate step-by-step (sequential) arrangements, and in newspaper articles cue words such as "when. . . then. . . ." or "because of. . . therefore. . . ." may be seen.

22. Teach the organization of textbooks as you would any other task. Teach about table of contents, glossary, appendix, index, and so on. Provide enough practice and test the students' ability to use the text efficiently and quickly.

Ideas Related to Arithmetic Skills

Like the reading and language-arts ideas in the preceding section, the arithmetic ideas in this section can be considered a sample of good ideas that may help any student who has difficulty with arithmetic, regardless of whether he is identified as learning disabled. With some inventiveness and ingenuity, many parallel ideas can be developed.

1. Provide the student with many experiences of putting together and taking apart concrete objects to familiarize him with the concepts of addition and subtraction before introducing him to the symbols for plus and minus. Teach the words *plus* and *minus* as part of a separate mathematical language.

2. Teach multiplication as a faster, more efficient way of adding. Provide the student with opportunities to add, time him and then demonstrate how multiplication shortens the time required to solve the problem. This process has to be repeated many times with some learning disabled students.

3. Encourage students to use objects or materials when completing computation assignments. Usually when students are ready to proceed without manipulative materials, they will stop using them.

4. Using a piece of masking tape, make a number line by marking even spaces and numbering (much like a ruler with only inch marks) and place it on the student's desk for referral when he works on computation tasks.

5. Allow students to verbalize what they are writing as they complete arithmetic assignments if they find it helpful. Often, hearing themselves assists them in understanding the task.

6. When a student has made errors in computation, especially when the concept is relatively new, ask the student to explain what he did. The explanation often provides added insight in regard to errors made.

7. Use ordinary playing cards to match numbers or to practice addition and subtraction. (The jack, queen, and king can be zero or wild, or the student can decide each time what numerical value they have.)

8. To reinforce the association between numbers and sets, have the student put clothespins on a hanger as he counts, or have the student close his eyes and count the taps on a drum or piano. More able students can work with those having difficulty.

9. Have students compile daily time lines of the day's activities. These can be displayed on an overhead projector and compared for overlapping and for events that run concurrently. Reference can be made to the time line throughout the day, which assists the student in learning time concepts. These can be lengthened to include weekly or monthly activities.

10. On a tiled floor, use each block as a unit of measure (for example, one block equals one foot, one mile, or one city block). Then construct a room, building, town, or whatever. For students with unusual difficulty, it is helpful to begin with the replication of a room so that they can later refer to the room as a model for larger scale projects.

11. Provide the student with scaled diagrams of the school, campus, and so on. Have him follow the map to get to specific locations. After he can do this efficiently, provide the student with directions without the diagram and ask him to tell you where he will be located if he follows them.

12. Arrange hopscotch, climbing ladders, crossing rivers on rocks, or other similar games on the floor. The student can complete the game by adding, multiplying, dividing, or subtracting.

13. Prepare ditto sheets of multiplication tables. Encourage all students to use them when the task is a concept involving multiplication. In this way the student who is having difficulty memorizing the multiplication tables is not penalized in learning other concepts.

14. Prepare charts that visually represent the relationship of fractions to the

whole. Allow students to use these until they no longer need them.

15. Use a large manipulable clock and provide the students with individual clocks by which to plan the activities of the day. Change the time as activities change. Call attention to the time that has elapsed since the last activity; for example, "It is now 9:40, or 20 minutes until 10. When we began the reading lesson, it was 9 o'clock. Forty minutes have gone by." This assists students in their conceptualization of short time periods and associates the concept with the clock.

16. Have students bring television schedules to school. Have them look up their favorite programs and arrange the hands of their individual clocks to show the times these programs are on. Bus, plane, or train schedules can be used in the same manner.

17. Provide real money or the closest possible replications and set up a store, amusement park, or other business and have the students buy items and receive change. Older students can shop from advertisements in the newspaper. They can prepare budgets, plan meals, purchase foods, and buy clothes. They can also compute the savings from advertisements for "30% off" or "half-price" sales (Table 10–1). Provide experience that will clarify the difference between 25% off and $ .25 off or 30% reduction and $ .30 reduction in price (see Table 10–2).

New Teaching Ideas—How to Use Them

It is important to remember that we must take great care in implementing new instructional methods or ideas so that we do not lose further ground with students who are already behind their age peers in academic achievement. When we try out new ideas with students who are learning normally and those ideas do not prove effective, we may contribute to a slight slowdown in academic progress, but usually there are few side effects. Fortunately, most students simply dismiss any lack of success and move ahead. With learning disabled students, however, time is more critical, and the student's academic ego may be much more fragile. The need for a positive self-image as noted by Fernald has been reported by a number of other authorities, and each setback may further convince the student that he cannot be successful in the academic arena. In addition, the further a student is retarded academically, the more important it is that we make efficient use of every available minute of instructional time. No method or set of ideas is guaranteed, and teachers must also be able to face failure (lack of learning) on the part of learning disabled students, but we do have a responsibility to think through any new approach being used to try to make certain that it is appropriate and that the student is as ready as possible to benefit from this approach.

The teaching ideas previously presented have been used with success with learning

TABLE 10–1.

Item	Price	Reduction	Actual Cost
Potato chips	1.69	30%	
Sugar	2.49	10%	
Paper towels	.78	15%	

TABLE 10–2.

Item	Price	Reduction	Actual Cost
Frozen pies	1.90	30%	
Frozen pies	1.90	$ .30	
Milk	1.40	25%	
Milk	1.40	$ .25	

disabled students and, for that matter, with students who had not been identified as having any specific handicapping condition. But when they are used, they must be used with care and should be appropriate to what is known about the student in question. Behavior-managment approaches, for example, have been known to fail because the reinforcement or reward was entirely inappropriate or because—when a contracting procedure was used—the contract was unclear. If we are to use behavior-management techniques, we must know what we are doing and must have the time, materials, physical setting, approvals (if needed), and all other necessary components to make the plan work.

Ideas involving the use of tactile or kinesthetic channels to support or reinforce visual or auditory learning modalities can for the most part be integrated with other instructional techniques. However, particularly with older students, one should be aware of an element of self-consciousness about any procedure that is too different from what other students are doing. It is also important, if a total multisensory approach is to be used, that the teacher should be certain that she has enough time for the individual monitoring required. Some approaches that may be quite effective in the learning disabilities resource room do not work in the regular classroom because of the very different teacher-pupil ratio.

The preceding sections on ideas for reading, language development, and arithmetic skill development are simply collections of ideas and do not in any way constitute a systematic approach. For the most part, they are ideas that might be found in school curriculum guides for nonhandicapped students. We have seen teachers using them to good advantage with students who have been identified as learning disabled; we include them here as samples of relatively ordinary teaching ideas that may prove to be effective.

We conclude this discussion as we started it, with a reminder to do everything possible to use instructional ideas that are appropriate to the student in question. The concept of readiness for learning (and there are many types of readiness) is important for all children and is particularly important for the learning disabled. The seven principles outlined previously remain better ways whereby the teacher may verify her own perceptions about whether to use any given approach or idea, and these should be considered when there is any question or doubt.

Secondary School Programs for Students with Learning Disabilities

Secondary school programs for the learning disabled are likely to be considerably different from elementary school programs. This difference should hardly come as a surprise, given the knowledge that secondary school programs for the nonhandicapped are also considerably different from elementary school programs. Despite the apparent logic of this difference, many early high school programs for learning disabled students were carbon copies of elementary programs, and they were not particularly effective, for the most part.

Learning disability programs at the elementary level are primarily remedial in nature and tend to focus on building the basic academic skills of reading and arithmetic. In the upper elementary grades, the focus may shift slightly to that of assisting the learner to synthesize, generalize, and conceptualize, but there is usually a continued emphasis on the basic skills. If such elementary programs are successful, it is possible that formerly learning disabled students will no longer require any type of special programming. For these formerly learning disabled students, the only evidence that they had earlier been considered to be learning disabled may be some slightly unusual learning or memory techniques that they may continue to use at the secondary level and perhaps throughout life.

But there are many students who need special assistance at the secondary level, including those who have learning disabilities not recognized until they were older and those for whom earlier efforts were not sufficient. These students may be assisted in a number of ways, and the regular classroom teacher plays an important role in some of the approaches.

Accommodation and Compensatory Teaching. The emphasis or approach most likely to involve regular classroom teachers is that which involves accommodation or compensatory teaching. The following description may clarify the change in emphasis characteristic of accommodation and compensatory teaching, in comparison to remedial teaching (Marsh, Gearheart, & Gearheart, 1978, p. 85):

Accommodation and compensatory teaching refer to a process whereby the learning environment of the student, either some of the elements or the total environment, is modified to promote learning. The focus is on changing the learning environment or the academic requirements so that the student

may learn in spite of a fundamental weakness or deficiency. This may involve the use of modified instructional techniques, more flexible administrative practices, modified academic requirements, or any compensatory activity that emphasizes the use of stronger, more intact capabilities or that provides modified or alternative educational processes and/or goals.

Remediation or remedial teaching refers to those activities, techniques, and practices that are directed primarily at strengthening or eliminating the basic source(s) of a weakness or deficiency that interferes with learning. The focus is on changing the learner in some way so that he or she may more effectively relate to the educational program as it is provided and administered for all students. The presumption is made that there is something wrong with the learner that can be identified and corrected.

Accommodation, adaptation, and the various approaches that may be called compensatory have the same basic goal as the more remedial orientation at the elementary level, but in the secondary school it is more practical and efficient to emphasize the learning of content as opposed to an emphasis on further direct improvement of basic skills. Remedial efforts and the further development of reading or arithmetic skills remain an important goal, but they may often become secondary to the acquisition of important understandings and concepts. Modifications may take a variety of forms, including modifications of course content, of how the information is presented to the student, of how the student is required to respond, and others. The following list of accommodative and adaptive efforts illustrates this principle and provides a starting point for planning by teachers who are attempting to assist learning disabled students in the secondary schools.

1. For students who can express themselves orally but are unable to prepare orderly, well-conceived written reports, a carefully taped response to an assignment might be permitted. Such a response would

then be evaluated for content, thus avoiding a situation in which inability to express oneself in writing masks information and knowledge.

2. If taped reports cannot be accepted, the teacher could agree to address the content of reports without regard to mechanics. Some sort of grading or evaluation system may be devised that, in effect, does not lead to failure because of mechanics but is based on the student's understanding of subject content. Students and their parents must understand and agree to such an arrangement and be told—preferably in writing—that the writing skills that the student does *not* have are deliberately not being evaluated. This should help prevent later claims by the student or parent that the student was not provided an effective education.

3. Peer tutors may be used in many ways and in a wide variety of subject areas.

4. Study-skill classes or sessions may be organized to help the student explore alternate ways to identify, analyze, categorize, and recall information.[2] Since some students have been exposed to only one major method of learning, and since the learning disabled student is likely to require different learning styles and techniques, this method may pay big dividends. Although in some instances this is best accomplished through special class sessions taught by the learning disabilities specialist, in other cases regular classroom teachers have found time to assist students in their classes to learn to develop alternate study skills. This regular classroom effort may have positive effects on other students.

5. Although by the secondary level it may be too late to spend much time on teaching new basic reading skills (word-attack skills and the like), it is not too late to teach students the need for different reading rates for different types of materials. This is another skill that is potentially valuable to other nonhandicapped students.

6. Other skills, such as how to prepare for tests, how to take notes, and how to outline, may be emphasized (see Sheinker & Sheinker, 1982). In some instances, the teacher may agree to provide a student in advance with an outline of material to be learned as a framework within which to organize study.

7. The teacher can provide the student and the resource room teacher in advance with lists of critical new vocabulary words so that the student may study them before presentation in class.

8. The teacher can notify the learning disabilities resource teacher of areas in which the student is falling behind, particularly those that will be essential in future learning (sequential or cumulative skills and information areas).

Adaptive, accommodative, and compensatory approaches are of value for many learning disabled students, and involvement in programs that are as near normal or mainstream in nature as possible is particularly important for students who plan to continue their education beyond high school. A small percentage may go on to a four-year college program (some may continue beyond that point), and a somewhat larger percentage may go into one- or two-year technical or vocational training programs. These training programs are often provided through community or junior colleges, and for many learning disabled students they provide a viable occupational goal. Another group of students will not go beyond high school but will enter the work world immediately after graduating. For these students different types of work-experience programs are being devel-

---

[2]A number of very practical ideas on teaching these skills are presented in four teacher handbooks by Sheinker and Sheinker (1982).

oped that are similar to the programs first used for the mentally handicapped (see chapter 9). The following incident reveals the need for such programs.

A few years ago, in a school district with which we are familiar, a mother who had two sons receiving special education services came to see the director of special education to make certain that her younger son (identified as learning disabled) could participate in the same high school program as her older son (identified as educable mentally retarded). The program was a work-experience program. She was told that the program was only for the educable mentally retarded. In fact, this was a common point of view not too many years ago. This mother knew from information received in staffings that the younger boy had a somewhat higher measured IQ, and asked if that was the basic reason he could not be in the work-experience program. After hedging a bit, the director had to admit that if his IQ were lower, he could have been in the program. The mother then asked if there was some way to make it lower on the records—she was concerned not about labels but about an appropriate program. That particular school district now has a work-experience program for the learning disabled.

In practice, it appears that learning disabled students can successfully manage job assignments that require a higher-than-EMR level of general mental ability but that these students often have just as much need to learn to work with others, to follow directions, to adjust to different job requirements, and to use all their positive attributes and abilities as EMR students. They need to learn which of their disabilities or academic deficits may cause problems and how to circumvent these problems. If problems and failure can be experienced in a supervised setting without dire consequences, students may learn from the problems. This situation is much better than being fired from a job without an opportunity to benefit from the experience.

In addition to participation in planned work-experience programs, a small percentage of secondary level learning disabled students may be enrolled in alternative school programs of various types. We have observed some learning disabled students who achieve considerable success in vocational and technical high school programs, when they have the required aptitude and there is a coordinating staff member (learning disabilities trained specialist) who can assist in finding the right individual classes and teachers and can help the student through special preparation related to specialized terms and perhaps to mathematical understandings essential to the vocational or technical field of interest.

The situation in the secondary school is, in some respects, not very different from that which exists in the elementary school. If individual planning precedes program implementation, if the student is assigned to the right teacher and the right class, and if there is a specialist avilable to provide assistance when required, the learning disabled student often finds success.

SUMMARY

Learning disabilities is the newest of those subdisciplines now recognized as a part of special education. The definition of learning disabilities is an umbrella definition; it includes a number of previously identified, more specific conditions. The definition is somewhat controversial, and there are variations among the states as to certain details; but the existence of the disability is accepted. One of the greatest sources of controversy about the definition is the question of *how much* academic and learning retardation is evidenced before an individual should be identified as learning disabled.

Knowlege of the characteristics of learning

disabled students is one basis for teacher referral. Although some of the commonly recognized characteristics seem contradictory, in composite they are a significant part of the basis for referral or the decision that no referral is needed. Many of the characteristics of the learning disabled are also characteristics of the mentally handicapped, the hearing impaired, or children who are environmentally deprived or culturally different.

The learning disabilities specialist should provide specific guidance about what the regular classroom teacher can do to assist a specific student; but when such suggestions or recommendations are lacking or do not apply, the teacher should proceed on the basis of some established frame of reference. The seven principles outlined in this chapter provide one frame of reference, and there are in addition certain specific approaches and techniques recognized as often effective.

These include, but are not limited to, the use of behavior-management or other behavioral approaches, multisensory approaches, cognitive-training approaches, and, at the secondary level, accommodation and compensatory approaches or work-experience programs.

Because of the unique needs of the learning disabled, teachers are challenged to develop and use unique teaching approaches. Teachers must remain open to new teaching ideas and carefully observe each child's individual learning patterns and, thus, individual needs. Until more specific, verified methods for teaching the learning disabled are developed, teachers must work to better understand the nature of learning, must develop a varied arsenal of teaching methods and techniques, and must learn to match these methods and techniques to the needs of children who are not finding success in the classroom.

Teaching Students with Behavior Disorders

DEFINITIONS

REFERRAL FOR SPECIAL ASSISTANCE

RESPONSIBILITIES OF SPECIAL EDUCATION PERSONNEL

COOPERATION AMONG TEACHERS

TEACHING STRATEGIES RELATED TO MAJOR THEORETICAL APPROACHES

UNIQUE PROBLEMS OF ADOLESCENTS

CHILD ABUSE AND NEGLECT

BEHAVIOR PROBLEMS AND STRESS

SUGGESTIONS FOR THE REGULAR CLASSROOM TEACHER

- [ ] How and why might students be considered behaviorally disordered in one school but not in another?
- [ ] Are behavioral disorders curable?
- [ ] Why is there such a variety of approaches to the treatment of behavioral disorders?
- [ ] If ecological approaches sometimes work, what may be inferred about the permanence of some behavior disorders?
- [ ] What are the distinctions between normal adolescent behavior and behavioral disorders?
- [ ] Are logical consequences and punishment similar, different, or unrelated?
- [ ] What relationships may exist between child abuse and behavior disorders?

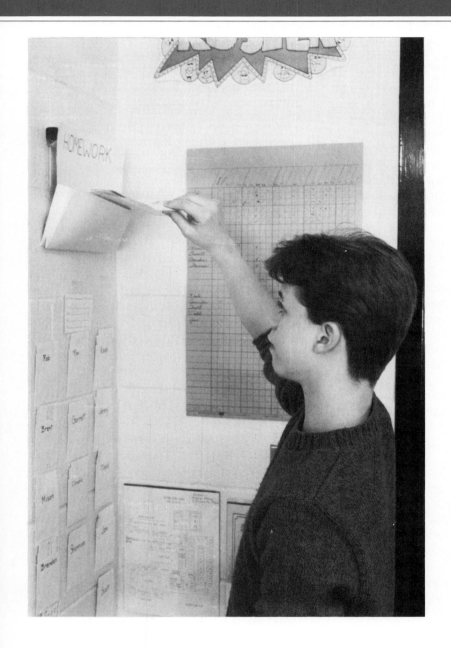

11

"I won't do this," "But he hit me first," "Why do I have to?" "But you said..." "I wasn't talking," "You didn't make *her*," "You are always picking on me," "I hate you" are all comments teachers who have taught more than a few months have heard. Students who more frequently use these statements may be called *aggressive, emotionally disturbed, behaviorally disordered, hyperactive, delinquent,* or *disruptive.* Students who are less outspoken regarding the discomfort they feel may be called *autistic, withdrawn, maladjusted, shy, immature.* Regardless of the terminology, such students find schools less than satisfactory, and good teachers search for more effective ways to assist these students and make school more satisfactory.

Unlike many other disabilities, the field of behavioral disorders is subject to a variety of controversies, including even the name. The federal definition uses the term *seriously emotionally disturbed.* However, professional organizations prefer *behavioral disorders* (Huntze, 1984). We will use the term *behavioral disorders* but the reader should keep in mind that the literature in this arena may use a variety of terminology.

DEFINITIONS

Definitions of *behavioral disorders* are numerous but not universally agreed upon. Bowers and Lambert (1976) suggest that a behaviorally disordered student is one who has a "moderate to marked reduction in behavioral freedom, which in turn, reduces his ability to function efficiently in learning or working with others" (p. 95).

Kauffman (1977) includes in his definition the concept of remediation or correction of the difficulties of the student. Students with behavior disorders "are those who chronically and markedly respond to their environment in socially unacceptable and/or personally unsatisfying ways but who can be taught

more socially acceptable and personally gratifying behavior" (p. 23).

The federal rules and regulations governing the implementation of PL 94-142 define the term *seriously emotionally disturbed* as follows:

The term means a condition exhibiting one or more of the following characteristics over a long period of time and to a marked extent, which adversely affects educational performance:

An inability to learn which cannot be explained by intellectual, sensory, or health factors;

An inability to build or maintain satisfactory relationships with peers and teachers;

Inappropriate types of behavior or feelings under normal circumstances;

A general pervasive mood of unhappiness or depression;

Or a tendency to develop physical symptoms or fears associated with personal or school problems.

The term includes children who are schizophrenic or autistic. The term does not include children who are socially maladjusted unless it is determined that they are seriously emotionally disturbed.[1]

These definitions, together with those indicated in Table 11–1, demonstrate the variety of current definitions. Various authorities describe inclusion and exclusion aspects as well as the strengths and weaknesses of each definition (Hallahan & Kauffman, 1982; Kauffman, 1985; Shea & Bauer, 1987). Although there is little agreement concerning a definition (Apter, 1982; Erickson, 1987; Kirk & Gallagher, 1986; Rich, 1982), "the teacher responsible for teaching a group of children has little difficulty identifying the student with emotional problems" (McDowell, Adamson, & Wood 1982, p. 3). Rather than at-

---

[1]From the Federal Register, 1977, p. 42478. The U.S. Department of Education decided in 1981 that autistic children are to be included in the category of Other Health Impaired.

tempting to find a universally acceptable definition of behavioral disorders, it is more positive to focus on the student as a learner. Teachers do not need precise definitions or labels but rather solutions to the student's learning difficulties.

Normal behavior is often considered a range of behaviors along a continuum. The limits of normal or acceptable behavior are somewhat subjective and are based on cultural, situational, and environmental factors. The teacher observes varying degrees of normal behavior in the classroom each day; therefore, it is not difficult to note when a particular student's behavior exceeds these limits.

On the other hand, of course, teachers do not determine whether a student has a behavior disorder based on arbitrary or capricious factors. The behavior must be present over a period of time, be of sufficient intensity (clearly different from normal), and occur frequently. All students experience emotional crises of various types that may be minor or severe; however, they are usually transitory. The frequency of occurrence, duration, and degree of severity form the guidelines for teachers in determining which students may be referred for special assistance.

REFERRAL FOR SPECIAL ASSISTANCE

When a teacher is aware of behavior that is sufficiently different from normal and occurs frequently and over a period of time, a request for assistance or referral may be made.

Many school districts hold a meeting to discuss the problems of the student before an actual referral is made. This conference usually includes the classroom teachers, special education teacher, principal, counselor (if available), and perhaps the parents. The purpose of this conference is to examine possible factors having a bearing on the student's behavior (such as a death in the family, separation of parents, possible sexual abuse, or other traumatic events) and what techniques or methods have been tried by the teacher and with what success. At this conference the decision may be made to try other management techniques, in which case the meeting is adjourned with the understanding to wait a period of time to provide ample opportunity for a change in the student's behavior. The decision may be made to initiate a referral, in which case the teacher completes a referral form according to the practice of the school district, which is forwarded to the appropriate personnel.

The specialist who teaches students with behavior disorders may, depending on state and local requirements, observe the student in the regular classroom to complete a checklist or rating scale to evaluate the student's classroom interactions. (Figure 11–1) or may ask the regular classroom teacher to complete a checklist (Figure 11–2). More formal checklists may also be used, such as the *Walker Problem Behavior Identification Checklist* (Walker, 1983), which lists observable behaviors; *Burk's Behavior Rating Scale* (Burks, 1977), which requires ratings by the teacher; the *Behavior Rating Profile* (Brown & Hammil, 1983), for which teachers, peers, and the parents provide ratings; the *Hahneman High School Behavior Scale* (Spivak & Swift, 1972), which measures the student's ability to cope with the pressures of the secondary school system; the *Woodcock-Johnson Scales of Independent Behavior* (Woodcock & Johnson, 1983), which measure independent and adaptive behavior in social and communication skills, personal-living skills, and community-living skills.

When the special teacher of the behaviorally disordered observes the student in the regular classroom or asks the teacher to complete a checklist or rating scale, this pro-

Behavior disorders may be expressed as disruptive or withdrawn behavior.

cess must be perceived not as checking up on the teacher or as an evaluation of teaching practices but rather as a preliminary means of objectifying or quantifying the student's behaviors.

The school psychologist (or psychiatrist, as required in some states) assesses the intellectual ability (IQ) of the student as well as personality factors. The IQ measurement is required because by federal definition the inability to learn must not be the result of intellectual factors (Federal Register, 1977, p. 42478). Intelligence tests such as the *Wechsler Intelligence Scale for Children–Revised* (WISC–R) (Wechsler, 1974) or the *Stanford-Binet Intelligence Scale* (Thorndike, Hagen & Sattler, 1986) may be administered.

Emotional, motivational, interpersonal, and attitudinal characteristics are measured by various personality tests; specific tests are chosen according to state or local guidelines or by the psychologist or psychiatrist. These assessment tools were designed to present a relatively unstructured stimulus with the intent of examining the manner in which the student perceives and interprets the test material. Examples are the *Thematic Apperception Test* (Murray, 1938) and the *Rorschach Inkblot Test* (Rorschach, 1942). Presumably this measurement reflects underlying aspects of the student's psychological functioning (Anastasi, 1982). Other evaluation tools used by the psychologist or psychiatrist may include a diagnostic interview, play, questioning, observation, or paper-and-pencil tasks. Whatever devices are used, the major purpose is to gain insight into the personality of the student.

In addition to these types of evaluation, various academic achievement tests are administered by either the psychologist or the teacher of the behaviorally disordered. The nurse may screen the student for vision or hearing impairments, and the social worker considers the student's developmental history.

After all the information is gathered, a conference is convened that includes all the personnel involved in testing the student as well as the classroom teacher, parents, and others (see chapter 2 for a list of persons required by law to attend). At this conference involving input from all members the most appropriate plan is developed for providing assistance to the student. An individual educational program may be written and a placement designated.

For some students with behavior disorders, the least restrictive alternative may be a special class or even a residential school. This type of placement may be necessary when the student is self-injurious, suicidal, completely out of touch with reality, or injurious to others. Most students remain in the regular class with support from the special education teacher.

Behaviors	Date	Length of observation	Mark each time behavior occurs	Comments
Student uses profanity.				
Student must be told more than once to begin work.				
Student destroys property.				
Student talks out inappropriately.				
Student makes inappropriate noises.				
Student moves around aimlessly.				
Student is out of seat.				
Student does not follow teacher directions.				
Student interrupts others.				
Student is verbally abusive to others.				
Student becomes angry with little provocation.				

FIGURE 11–1. Sample items from a specialist's behavior-disorder checklist

Student's name: _____ Date: _____
Birth Date: _____ School: _____
Please check the areas that are applicable. If you wish to make comments, please do so.

Behavior	Frequency			Under what circumstances does the behavior occur?	Comments
	Daily	Weekly	Monthly		
Needs close supervision.					
Destroys property.					
Throws temper tantrums.					
Erratic, unpredictable behavior.					
Indicates poor self-concept.					
Appears angry or hostile.					
Isolates self.					
Appears out of touch with reality.					
Does not achieve at expected academic level.					
Seeks inordinate amount of attention.					
Interferes with learning of others.					
Makes inappropriate noises.					
Threatens to injure self or others.					
Does injure self or others.					
Verbally assaults others.					
Physically assaults others.					
Avoids eye contact.					
Cries inappropriately.					
Refuses to talk with teacher.					
Refuses to talk with others.					
Seems to daydream.					

FIGURE 11–2. Sample items from a regular classroom teacher's behavior-disorder checklist

RESPONSIBILITIES OF SPECIAL EDUCATION PERSONNEL

As noted previously, various individuals may play a role in the assessment and diagnostic evaluation of the student and in resulting conferences. Depending on the decisions made, the major responsibility for the student's education may then reside with the teacher of behaviorally disordered students, or it may be shared by the regular classroom teacher and the specialist. In some cases the psychologist, psychiatrist, or counselor may provide therapy for the student on a regular basis.

When the student remains in the regular class for any portion of the day, it is of utmost importance that the teacher of the behaviorally disordered communicate to the classroom teacher the theoretical orientation being implemented in the resource room and provide continual suggestions for regular classroom strategies to assist the student in his adjustment. Perhaps no other handicapping condition requires as much consistency and communication between regular class teacher and the special educator as behavioral disorders.

The nature of the disruptive behavior of the student may necessitate a mutual support system between the teacher of the behaviorally disordered and the regular classroom teacher. By sharing their frustrations, disappointments, and successes, both teachers can return to the challenge of teaching with renewed vigor.

COOPERATION AMONG TEACHERS

It is essential that the teacher of the regular class and the specialist discuss what methods are to be used with the student. Because there is such a variation in theories about the causes of behavioral disorders and, therefore, a wide variation in treatments, the teachers involved with the student must agree theoretically and personally how best to proceed. Students with behavior disorders are often very manipulative and use any ambiguities on the part of the teachers to their fullest advantage. For example, if the teacher of the behaviorally disordered believes that the student's difficulties are caused by internal hostility and pent-up anger and thinks the way to deal with them is to provide a warm, accepting environment and to allow acting out or aggression so that the student can work through them, then treatment is based on this premise. If, on the other hand, the regular classroom teacher because of his or her personality cannot allow such acting out in the classroom or cannot tolerate barrages of obscene language, the two different approaches will lead to a situation of ambiguity or dissension of which the student can, and will be delighted to, take full advantage.

A second example involves a behaviorally oriented specialist who believes in counting and observing every behavior. The specialist also believes that the student has learned inappropriate behaviors and therefore must learn new behaviors to function successfully in the regular class. This philosophy is reflected in the specialist's plans for treatment. However, in this scenario, the regular classroom teacher believes in allowing students to express themselves freely and personally believes that she must "flow with the students," allowing them many choices in what and how to study. Again, both teachers will be frustrated and the student will take full advantage of the situation.

The regular class teacher and the specialist must arrive at some general agreement, and each must be somewhat comfortable with the other's approach to the treatment. Few teachers are able to teach consistently in manners inconsistent with their personalities. For example, teachers who are extremely creative, take almost all their cues from the students, and plan on a minute-by-minute basis are not usually very comfortable with a structured, precise behavior modification approach. This is not to say that either approach is better or more effective but only that they are different. Both teachers must recognize and acknowledge their unique teaching styles and know how they teach most comfortably and effectively. Then, during the writing of the IEP, each teacher's unique style must be considered when developing the best educational plan for the student. This cooperation requires discussion and compromise, but it is at this point—the writing of the IEP—that various potential conflicts must be resolved.

TEACHING STRATEGIES RELATED TO MAJOR THEORETICAL APPROACHES

There are several major theoretical approaches to teaching students with behav-

ioral disorders. As noted in the discussion of definitions, there is disagreement as to both causes and treatment of behavioral disorders. Table 11–1 and the following discussion describe the key aspects of the major approaches and provide some insight as to how they may be modified and adapted for use in the regular classroom.

Before beginning this section it is necessary to clarify terminology regarding the first theoretic approach. In the early 1960s, the term *behavior modification* was introduced (and later the same decade, the term *applied behavior analysis* was used) to emphasize the application of behaviorist principles to real-life settings. Usually, the term applied behavior analysis refers to a more stringent relationship between the behavior changed and the intervention (Alberto & Troutman, 1986). Applied behavior analysts use the principles of collecting specific data, reinforcement,

TABLE 11–1. Theoretical approaches to behavioral disorders

Approach or Conceptual Model	Causes of Behaviorial Disorders	Treatment Indicated
Biophysical	Internal causes such as chemical imbalances, genetic deficiencies, poor nutrition, disrupted sleep patterns, brain injury.	Use medication like tranquilizers, stimulants, or antidepressants and/or behavior modification.
Behavioral	External causes such as inappropriate behavior learned, reinforced, and maintained by others in environment.	Remove reinforcers that maintain inappropriate behavior, reinforce appropriate behavior, teach acceptable behavior.
Psychodynamic	Internal causes such as unsuccessful negotiation of psychological stages, internal conflicts, guilt feelings.	Allow free expression of feelings, provide accepting warm environment, avoid too many demands.
Sociological	External causes such as society's labeling the student deviant, factors "forcing" rule breaking, lack of social rules that serve as behavior inhibitors.	Modify society, teach alternate behaviors, assist student to establish rules for himself.
Ecological	Internal and external causes, that is, interaction between student's feelings, needs, and desires and society's norms, demands, and responsibilities.	Aid adjustment of either student or environment or both; manipulate either student or environment for the benefit of both.

and observing change in a manner similar to that of behaviorists (Ysseldyke & Algozzine, 1984). In the interest of simplicity we will use the term behavior modification but do want to caution the reader that careful attention to actual behavior change and the interventions used to cause that change is crucial.

As a general rule, when reading journal articles or other books you may assume that behavior modification is defined more generally and applied behavior analysis somewhat more rigorously, but both deal with behavior change.

Behavior Modification

With an acting-out, verbally or physically aggressive student, some variation of behavior modification is ordinarily attempted first. Many educators believe it to be the quickest, most efficient technique to reduce or eliminate inappropriate behaviors (Alberto & Troutman, 1986; Walker & Shea, 1976).

As noted in Table 11–1 the behaviorist assumes that inappropriate behavior has been learned and is being maintained by reinforcement. The key to this approach is to determine the nature of the reinforcement and to eliminate it or to use a more powerful reinforcer to bring about the desired behavior. The teacher becomes a manipulator of the environment of the student and by such manipulation systematically plans changes in the student's behavior.

In practice, this process means that the teacher observes the student, counts the inappropriate behaviors (which have been stated very specifically), and attempts to determine what precedes and follows the behavior. Observing and counting provide the baseline to indicate to the teacher how frequently the behavior occurs, as well as show the seriousness of the behavior. By noting what precedes and follows the behavior, the teacher may gain clues concerning what reinforces the behavior.

After obtaining a baseline and noting possible reinforcers, the teacher carefully selects reinforcers to be applied systematically. They may be provided each time the student exhibits the desired behavior, after a given time period, or after a given number of appropriate responses. For example, with a student who frequently uses obscene language or at the slightest provocation calls other students names, the behavior is defined precisely enough to be observable and countable. The teacher then counts the number of times this occurs during a class period, during a particular time in the day, or during the entire day. This count is usually taken for three to five days to establish the baseline (Figure 11–3). The teacher may also note that after each such occurrence, some or all of the class laughed or that she said something about the name calling to the student. These are possible reinforcers. At this point an intervention is selected, that is, some other reinforcement to be applied. In this example, if the student seems to enjoy the attention and social rewards of having the class and the teacher pay attention to him, the teacher may decide that providing that same attention when the student does not use obscene language may be a powerful reinforcer to the student. This, then, is the intervention. The teacher may decide to praise the student at least three times during every hour. The teacher may then begin to watch for times when the student is working or is paying attention and comment positively on this, making sure that this reinforcement is used at least three times per hour. During this period of intervention, careful records are kept to note whether the obscene language and name calling are decreasing, increasing, or remaining the same (Figure 11–3). If the behavior is decreasing, the reinforcement of the teacher's positive comments may be considered successful. If it is not decreasing, the reinforcer is not powerful enough and

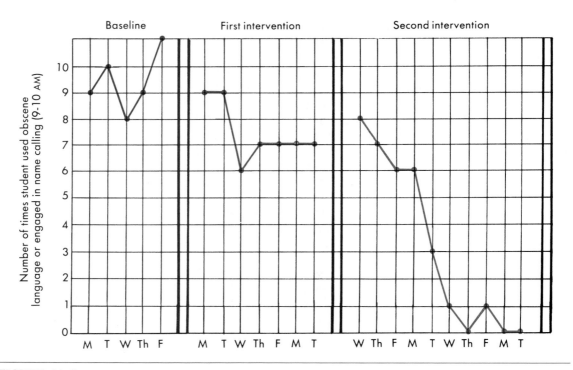

FIGURE 11–3. Sample teacher record of frequency of a student's verbal abuse

Note. The first intervention decreased the behavior but not to an acceptable level, and another was attempted.

another must be selected. This new reinforcer is then tried, records are kept to determine whether the behavior is decreasing, and if necessary still another reinforcer is selected. This process continues until the appropriate reinforcer is found and the behavior is decreased to an acceptable level or eliminated; then the reinforcers are phased out.

In other situations, the teacher's objective may be to increase a desirable behavior. For example, the objective may be to increase the number of times the student volunteers a response during a class discussion. The same principles of obtaining a baseline, attempting an intervention, and noting the results apply, except that in this case the teacher notes whether the behavior is increasing. Comple-

tion of work, time spent on tasks, cooperative efforts with a peer, and effective use of study time are other types of behavior teachers ordinarily want to increase.

Reinforcers. There are a variety of ways to find out what is reinforcing to the student, such as by observing what the student does during free time, asking what he would enjoy doing, or having the entire class make a list of various reinforcers and asking the student to choose from the list.

The reinforcers can be something tangible, a token, an activity, or something social. The type of reinforcer depends on the student, what is acceptable in the school, and what the teacher is comfortable with or may allow.

The goal of the teacher should be to choose the closest approximation to the type of reinforcers that are useful with all students. For example, a teacher should not give cookies to a ninth-grader to eliminate tardiness if providing 10 minutes at the end of the class period to begin homework is sufficient reinforcement to make him come to class on time. If the principal of a school does not allow any students on the playground or in the student lounge except at designated times, then the teacher cannot use free time in such locations as reinforcers. If the teacher has a personal aversion to using food or free time or any other particular reinforcer, these obviously should not be used.

Examples of various types of reinforcers are given in the following list, adapted from Walker and Shea (1976). Types of reinforcers are limited only by the student's and teacher's imagination.

Tangible reinforcers
  cookies
  gum
  peanuts
  soda
  personal grooming aids
  special materials, such as felt pens or colored pencils
  tickets to movies or games
  toys or models
Token reinforcers
  behavior or achievement charts
  checks or points
  happy faces or stars
  individual achievement charts or handbooks
  trading stamps
Reinforcing games and activities
  bean bags
  cards
  checkers
  chess
  crossword puzzles
  dolls, dollhouses, doll clothes
  frisbees
  gliders
  Monopoly

The Dating Game
being excused from a test or assignment
doing a project of own choice
eating lunch at a restaurant
having a soft drink
getting extra recess or time before or after regular recess
getting free time for self-selected activities
going home early
making things, kits, models, and so on
not doing homework
participating in creative drama or dance
playing with puppets or in sand or water
reading a favorite book, magazine, or newspaper
tutoring younger children
using a typewriter
watching a movie on TV
Social reinforcers
being leader or organizer of an event
clapping or cheering by others
demonstrating a skill before the class or to the teacher
getting personal time with teacher, aide, counselor
having work or projects displayed
participating in small-group discussions
receiving verbal praise
Job reinforcers
assisting the custodian
being teacher for a lesson
conducting a class raffle or auction
distributing or collecting materials
feeding fish or other animals
giving a message over the intercom
helping the librarian, teacher, school secretary, nurse, or cooks
operating a slide, filmstrip, or movie machine
picking up litter on school grounds
recording own behavior on a graph or chart
running the ditto machine
taking class roll
serving as secretary for class meetings
watering the plants

Time-Out. Sometimes a student with a behavior disorder requires a period of time during which he must be separated by some physical space in the room. When this separation seems advisable, the teacher can physically move the desk of the student to the front, back, or side of the room to provide a physical space between the student and the rest of the class. The purpose of the removal varies; sometimes it may be to reduce the amount of reinforcement from other students (if the student is in the back of the room or over to one side, his antics are not as visible). Being very near to the teacher often reduces clowning or show-off behaviors and prevents the offending student from annoying others. This method must be used with discretion. When a student is unresponsive to the teacher's requests, he may refuse to move, thereby creating a new problem for the teacher—a test of wills. Or the student may create more commotion as he moves than the move is worth. He may bang his desk against others, knock books off the desk or pencils or papers off other desks, and move very slowly to lengthen the time of the chaos. The teacher must determine whether asking the student to move is advisable.

Another form of time-out is to have a specific place designated as "time-out" and physically marked (for example, bookcases arranged to form an enclosed corner). In this area a rug or pillows might be available along with reading materials or anything else the teacher and students arrange. A class discussion should be held about the purpose of such a time-out space. The teacher may suggest to a student that he should go to the time-out space to have some time to gain control, or the student may choose to go there for the same reason. Care must be taken so that this place is seen not as punishment but rather as a safe haven. The principle is the same as when adults take a walk, go to their bedroom, or ask to be left alone. It is simply a time to reduce tensions that arise from having to deal with a pressing problem.

Regardless of whether the teacher suggests that the student go to the time-out space or he selects it himself, he should come out only when he chooses to. It is im-

portant that the teacher explain in the discussion that using this time-out space does not absolve the student from responsibility for assignments or homework. This explanation should prevent abuses and further misunderstandings. If a student does abuse the privilege, and it is to be expected that behaviorally disordered students may try, the guidelines must be discussed with the offending student—and discussed again and again.

Contracts. No discussion of behavior modification, however brief, should omit the principle of contracting. Contracts are agreements between teacher and student that specify in exact terms what the student must do and what the teacher will do *after* the student has completed his portion of the agreement. This sequence is essential, particularly with students who have behavior or academic problems. The teacher would be in an untenable position if the student were to receive the reward before performing his portion of the contract, an approach analogous to saying, "You can have the ice cream first if you promise to eat your spinach afterward."

Contracts may be informal verbal agreements, simple written statements, or sophisticated writen and witnessed agreements (Figures 11–4 and 11–5). Which is most useful depends primarily on the needs of the student. Secondary students often respond more favorably to more sophisticated written agreements. Sometimes a teacher may want the parents to sign the contract, especially if the task being negotiated is one involving homework. By asking the parents to sign, the teacher is ensuring their awareness of the need to provide a place to do homework that is relatively free of noise and other disturbances. Of course, teachers must realize, particularly with the parents of disruptive students, that the parents' awareness does not ensure follow-through or cooperation.

The following contract guidelines adapted

This contract is between _____ (student)

and _____ (teacher, friend, other)

Date: from _____ to _____
                (this date)   (contract expiration)

Following are the terms of the contract:

_____ (student) will _____

_____

_____

_____ (teacher, friend, other) will _____

_____

_____

When this contract is completed, the contractee will be able to _____

_____

_____

_____

_____

_____

_____   _____

Contractee   Contractor

_____

Witness

This contract may
be terminated by
agreement of parties
signing this contract.
New contract(s) may be
negotiated by the same
parties.

FIGURE 11–4. Sample contract

Note: From *Making It Positively Clear* (p. 23) by P. G. Kaplan and A. G. Hoffman, 1981, Denver: Love. Reprinted by permission.

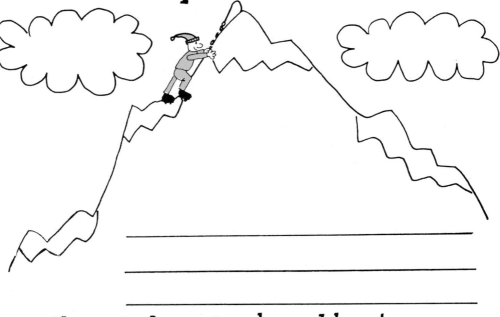

Look At Me

And if that's not enough here is what I plan to do next:

_____

_____

_____

When I do, I'll be able to _____

_____

And I will have it done by _____

| date | student | witness | Teacher |

FIGURE 11–5. Sample contract

Note: From *It's Positively Fun* (p. 27) by F. Kaplan, J. Kohfeldt, and K. Sturla, 1974, Denver: Love.
Reprinted by permission.

from Homme (1970) provide a useful summary of the characteristics of proper contracting:

1. Performance must come before the reward.
2. The reward should immediately follow performance in the beginning.
3. Rewards should be provided frequently and for each approximation.
4. Rewards are provided for accomplishment rather than obedience. The tone of the contract should be "When you do this, you can. . . . "rather than "If you do this, then I will allow you to. . . . "
5. The contract must be fair and honest. The teacher and the student must agree that the reward is appropriate for the task completed. After completion of the task, the teacher must follow through with the reward. If for some unforeseen reason the teacher cannot provide the reward, the student must be allowed to choose another activity or be given the reward at the earliest possible time.
6. The terms of the contract must be clear. A statement like "If you behave during class" is not clear. The teacher may have definite standards in mind in such a case, but the student may interpret "behave" in an entirely different manner.
7. The contract must be positive. This quality is especially important for students who have a long history of conflict with authority figures. A positive statement avoids the threat of punishment and contributes to a positive educational experience.
8. Contracting must be used systematically. The teacher might ask herself what the payoff is for the student as she modifies her behavior. Does she achieve a sense of satisfaction from appropriate behavior, or will she gain satisfaction from being able to have free time? Will this change become the first of a series of small but

ever closer approximations to the desired goal of appropriate behavior in the classroom?

For teachers unfamiliar with negotiating contracts, it may be best to begin with a simple format. The following contract checklist may be helpful in ensuring adherence to all aspects of contracting.

1. Explain contracts and contracting.
2. Show an example of a contract.
3. Discuss possible tasks and list student-suggested and teacher-suggested tasks.
4. Agree on a task.
5. Student and/or teacher suggests reinforcers.
6. Negotiate the ratio of the task to the reinforcer.
7. Identify the time allotted for the task.
8. Identify the criterion or achievement level for a task completion.
9. Agree on the method of evaluation.
10. Negotiate the delivery of the reinforcer.
11. Set the time or date for renegotiation.
12. Teacher and student both sign contract.

Once familiar and comfortable with contracting, the teacher may omit or combine various steps.

Combinations of contracts, point systems, or tokens can also be used. The student and teacher negotiate the items and the possible points or tokens to be earned. The points or tokens can then be traded for free time or other reinforcers (Figure 11–6). By arranging the value of the reinforcers with the students (the three cards alluded to in Figure 11–6) some allowance is made for those students who find it extremely difficult to perform the required tasks. They have a goal for which to strive yet receive something for less successful efforts. There should be a lower limit (145 points in Figure 11–3) below which no reinforcement is given.

There is an element of risk in using this type of contract and point system. If an indi-

5 points possible for each	Mon.	Tues.	Wed.	Thurs.	Fri.	TOTAL
Promptness						
Preparedness (book, paper, pencil)						
Completed homework						
Use of time						
Effort						
Cooperation						
Attitude						
Bonus points for extra effort, extra neat homework						

Name: _____ Date: _____

GRAND TOTAL: _____

175 points or above: Choose from Card 1

160–174 points: Choose from Card 2

145–159 points: Choose from Card 3

FIGURE 11–6. Points or tokens can be traded for reinforcements

vidual student views something on Card 2 as desirable, the student may compute exactly how many points he must have to receive it and thereafter be uncooperative or fail to complete all of the required tasks, knowing he will still receive the reward. If the teacher anticipates this problem, obviously this varying reinforcer system should not be used. If the teacher did not anticipate it, that is, if the student seemed to be discussing the issue in good faith but is now manipulating it to advantage, the teacher should point out this change to the student and use another system of contracting that is more direct.

Modeling.   Research has indicated that children imitate the behavior they observe; how-ever, they are not always discriminating in what they imitate. If the teacher is to use the principle of modeling effectively, appropriate behaviors must be pointed out (for example, "Susie is working quietly" or "I like the way John raises his hand so that I can call on him"). This approach is quite different from calling attention to inappropriate behavior ("Johnny, will you stop talking and raise your hand?"). Some students have yet not learned certain behaviors teachers consider important. In this case the model serves as a demonstration of what is appropriate.

The teacher may want to seat certain students in close proximity to students who will model specific behaviors (such as seating a student behind one who usually does raise his hand and wait to be called on). They are then in a position to observe appropriate behavior and, if necessary, may be unobtrusively reminded that as soon as they raise their hands, they will be called on.

Although modeling may be an effective means of changing behavior, the teacher must keep in mind several elements that may affect the desired results. Some students do not receive sufficient reinforcement merely in the example of a model. There may be a variety of reasons for this lack of reinforcement. The mere fact that a teacher sees a student as a model does not mean the students view him or her in the same manner. The model may be seen as too good, too bright, the teacher's pet, or simply obnoxious. When such is the case, usually the model is subjected to taunts and ridicule outside of class. A more aggressive student may not wait until after class to begin his jeers.

Modeling in its simplest form perhaps works best with younger students. With older students, however, the peer code of conduct is far more powerful than the external selection of a model by the teacher. The student whom the teacher sees as a model may be held in very low esteem by the rest of the class; thus it would be a violation of the peer-group norms to imitate this student in any fashion whatever.

It is generally more productive, at the secondary level, for the teacher to guide students in a discussion of the problems, including (1) assisting them to define the problem precisely (2) establishing appropriate goals, and (3) assisting them in suggesting solutions to the problems. When these goals can be accomplished, peer pressure is often a powerful influence on the behaviorally disordered student.

Much more could be said about behavior modification and its application for behaviorally disordered students. The discussion here is directed toward the basic principles.

One final concern regarding behavior modification must be addressed: the ethical aspect of manipulating another person's behavior. Walker and Shea (1976) have provided the following guidelines for teachers when considering behavior modification:

1. Teachers must consider *why* they want or need to manipulate the behavior of others. Is it to create a positive learning environment for all, or is it some inner need to control the student or exert power?
2. Teachers must attempt to understand the problems of the student. This attempt involves discussion with the student to obtain a clearer understanding of the reasons for what the teacher considers inappropriate behavior. If a teacher learns through this discussion that the student throws his pencil, tears his paper, or whatever every time he is frustrated because that is what his parents do, the teacher can better decide whether or how to use behavior modification.
3. Teachers must determine whether the behavior change will truly assist the student in better understanding himself or his environment. Conformity for the sake of conformity is indefensible.
4. Teachers must be aware that our knowledge of human behavior is in a continuous stage of development. What we believe today may be modified by new information tomorrow. Teachers must keep abreast of developing information in regard to how people behave and why they behave as they do.

There are further questions that teachers must ask themselves as they consider the use of behavior modification:

1. Will my use of these interventions assist this student to be viewed as more normal in this environment?
2. Will it lead to greater acceptance by peers?
3. Is it fair?

4. Does it respect him as an individual?
5. Will he maintain his dignity?

Psychodynamic Approach

Psychodynamic therapy, as a treatment for mental illness, is used in mental-health settings such as hospitals (Rich, 1982). In schools, psychologists and psychiatrists may use it in conjunction with other types of therapy or may adapt it to meet the needs of students. There are certain ethical considerations involving appropriate training and developing expertise with guidance from qualified supervisors that contraindicate use of the psychodynamic approach by teachers, but some variations and adaptations may be of use to the regular classroom teacher. As noted in Table 11–1, the psychodynamic approach involves certain basic assumptions in regard to the cause of the inappropriate behavior. If the teacher believes that the student is extremely angry with himself, peers, the teacher, the school, and the whole world, then allowing the student to express anger in an acceptable manner may serve as a release to the student.

Drawing, painting, or writing may be used as a medium for expression of feelings, as can dance, drama, and role playing. The teacher must decide how and when this method might be used. Often it depends on the age of the student and the structure of the classroom and the school system. In lower grades, because the classrooms are essentially self-contained, the teacher has more latitude in the selection of the time and means of implementation. In the upper grades, when a teacher has a given group of students for only a relatively short time (a 40- to 50-minute period), implementation is much more difficult.

In primarily self-contained rooms, a portion of the room can have an easel, paints, phonograph, or whatever else is necessary for various types of therapy. After the teacher knows the student well enough and thinks that one or more of these expressive media

ums may be helpful, the teacher can discuss with the student when, how, and under what conditions the student may use the materials.

When the school system is departmentalized and students move from room to room, it is usually necessary to make arrangements for this type of activity with the teacher of the behaviorally disordered. In the resource room, the materials may be readily available. Again, it is necessary to determine with the student the guidelines for the use of the materials.

The emphasis with art, music, or dance is not on the production of masterpieces but rather on the student's conveying feelings in a nonverbal manner. Teachers should not be shocked at the pictures or gestures that may result in these therapeutic activities. Sometimes they are motivated by the intent to shock, and on other occasions they may be vivid reflections of the confusion, anger, or guilt of the student.

Puppetry and role playing may also be used to assist students to express their feelings. Puppetry allows for verbal expression without face-to-face contact. Sometimes shy or withdrawn students participate in this form of expression while "hiding" behind the stage. Depending on the age of the students involved, the puppet show may be given to other class members or to younger students. Beginning with nonthreatening materials such as fairy tales usually enables the student to gain sufficient self-confidence to attempt shows that depict situations more true to life.

Role playing, often more successful with older students, is very similar to puppetry. Again, by beginning with less threatening situations, the students gain the motivation they require and can later attempt more threatening forms of dialogue. Generally it is necessary to discuss the feelings that playing a specific role engenders. The use of situations that are part of the student's life can teach the student alternate coping strategies.

For example, in a situation in which a teenager must deal with an alcoholic parent, the student playing the part of the parent gains insight into possible reasons for the alcoholism and during both the role playing and the discussion that follows can learn from the other students new strategies concerning effective ways to handle this problem.

The psychodynamic approach has many variations. It cannot be overemphasized, however, that the teacher must not experiment with the student's emotions. It is a wise policy to discuss with the school psychologist, psychiatrist, or specialist what is best for the student before implementing these techniques in the classroom.

Biophysical Approach

As noted in Table 11–1, the biophysical approach assumes the cause of the student's behavior problems to be internal, that is, genetic, chemical, a brain injury, nutritional deficits, and so on. Obviously the diagnosis of these causes of behavioral disorders is out of the realm of education; therefore, a physician is involved. The medical doctor may prescribe certain medications, and if so, the doctor or the parents may ask the teacher to monitor the student's behavior. This task is not to be taken lightly. At the present time, because the best method of prescribing the exact dosage of these types of medication involves trial and error, reports to the parents or physician are extremely important. With too much medication the student may be lethargic, sleepy, and generally "dopey"; with too little medication, there is no effect. Reports from teachers and parents are the physician's guide for adjusting the dosage to modify the student's behavior (Barkley, 1981). The teacher must be aware of what medication the student is receiving, its possible side effects, and what type of behavior change to expect.

The medical role is dominant in the biophysical approach to behavioral disorders.

Parents and teachers must work in cooperation with the medical professionals to ensure the best possible results for the student.

Sociological and Ecological Approaches

From a sociological and ecological perspective, behavioral disorders are a result of rule breaking, social disapproval, and lack of harmonious interaction between the individual and environment. Regular classroom teachers must be aware of the various backgrounds of all their students and of the powerful influence each has on the student. This awareness is even more important with behaviorally disordered students.

The unacceptable behavior of a student may be the result of the socialization process taking place in the home. When youngsters are taught by their elders that stealing is not wrong but getting caught is, they may demonstrate this belief in school. It is not surprising to discover such youngsters stealing coats, books, assignments, lunches, and so on and having learned their lessons well, doing it with extraordinary finesse. The teacher certainly cannot allow stealing; however, knowledge about what is taught in the home provides insight into the problem.

Students with behavior disorders are frequently in conflict with school, home, neighborhood, and various other social environments. In school, they may conflict with teachers, the principal, cafeteria workers, and others. It is possible that a major part of the conflict is due to a mismatch between the student and one particular environment in the school. For example, the lack of structure plus noise level plus "horseplay" with other students may lead to conflict in the cafeteria. A careful analysis of the subenvironments in the school may pinpoint major trouble areas, and through discussion with the student and scheduling adjustments, alleviation of major stress areas may lead to improved behavior.

In the classroom, conflict may result due to a mismatch between the student's skills, the teacher's teaching style, and certain peer relationships in that particular class. Careful analysis of all factors that might possibly be pertinent and adjustment as required (and as possible) may reduce stress and improve behavior. A word of caution is necessary—the solution is not always an adjustment on the part of teachers and the school. The student must develop some coping skills, which will be important not only in the school and during school years, but also for the rest of his or her life. The ecological approach leads to an examination of interaction between the student and the various environments that exist in the school. Whenever possible, this examination should be expanded to include other environments also; but educators must focus first on the school environment. To apply this approach effectively, we must be careful not to place blame but rather to arrive at a solution that will lead to a reduction of conflict.

The sociological approach seeks to provide assistance in all parts of the student's environment. The dynamics of the family may need to be examined and supportive therapy provided. The teacher may be the most effective person for this task, or someone more skilled in counseling techniques may need to intervene in the interactions between a student and the environment with which he is in conflict.

When a student's behavioral problems are sociological or ecological, it is essential that all appropriate personnel (social worker, parole officers, principal, etc.) be involved. Because the sociological and ecological causes of behavior problems involve the values and mores of society and ever changing interrelationships, a wide range of expertise must be involved in seeking behavior changes. The classroom teacher, because of his or her unique role, may be the catalyst, when working with allied professionals, to change and improve the environments of students with behavior disorders.

Other Approaches

Some approaches that may be valuable to the teacher but are not readily categorized under the other major approaches are briefly described here.

Rudolf Dreikurs. Dreikurs and Cassel (1972), noted psychiatrists, identify several student goals that are generally at cross purposes with those of the teacher. Students with behavior disorders often demonstrate behavior associated with one or more of these goals. Dreikurs suggests various methods of counteracting these undesirable behaviors. Table 11–2 indicates these goals, the behavior the student demonstrates in attempting to reach the goals, and possible alternatives for the teacher.

Dreikurs believes that the student in attempting to achieve these goals, is operating with faulty logic. With *attention getting,* the student feels worthwhile only if people pay attention to him; therefore the student extracts that attention at any price. The student must be made to feel worthwhile at times when not seeking attention so as to realize that he is valuable at all times.

With *power,* the faulty logic of the student is "Unless I win or get you to do what I want, I am not worthwhile." Any teacher soon recognizes that students do have power and that if they are determined they can "win." One need teach only a few months to realize that a teacher seldom can force a student to do anything he or she does not want to do. When a student is seeking power, the best, most disarming device is simply to give it. There are many legitimate ways to do this: give the student the power to choose what and when she will study, enlist the student's cooperation (power) in formulating rules, or provide her with leadership positions. One of the most disarming statements a teacher can make is simply "I know I can't *make* you do anything, I know you don't *have* to do anything, but I'm asking you to please do this."

TABLE 11–2. Counteracting student goals associated with behavior disorders

Goal	Behavior Demonstrated	Teacher Alternative
Attention getting	Attempts to get teacher's attention, shows off, asks useless questions, disturbs others.	Ignore misbehavior if possible, do not show annoyance, give much attention for appropriate behavior, select student for "helper."
Power	Contradicts teacher and other students, deliberately disobeys rules, dawdles, lies, has temper tantrum, "tests" the teacher.	Recognize student's power, give power as much as possible, give student choices, do not argue, avoid struggle for power, ask student for help, make contracts with student.
Revenge	Steals, hurts others, acts sullen or defiant, makes others dislike him, retaliates.	Apply natural consequences, persuade student that he is liked, enlist a buddy to befriend the student, do not show the student that you are hurt or disappointed, enable other students to support him.
Display of inadequacy or hopelessness	Demonstrates inferiority complex, will not try, is discouraged before attempting new activity, gives up too easily, refuses to get involved.	Do not support inferiority feelings, be constructive, get class cooperation, praise student, provide ways for student to demonstrate ability.

Often after such a statement the teacher can observe in the student physical changes such as a reduction of tension in the shoulders, a less defiant stance, and so on—all of which indicate a level of cooperativeness. At this time one can make use of the student's willingness and quickly move on to the task at hand; it is *not* the time for the teacher to flaunt his or her power!

To some students the world and all the people in it seem so hurtful that in their faulty logic, the only thing to do is to gain *revenge.* The student feels disliked by all, distrusted by all, and vulnerable and sees the world as unfair. The teacher must attempt to help the student to see that there are persons who can be trusted, that there are places in which one can be safe, that people can care. This process is very difficult to accomplish because the student often views such attempts with suspicion and lack of trust. When a student displays this type of behavior, the teacher must take care that the remainder of the class does not turn against the student, thus confirming his belief in the absence of any goodness. Punishing a student would further entrench his belief that everyone is out to get him. The application of logical consequences can be a valuable procedure with this student. It may at times help if the teacher can encourage a promising friendship between a revengeful student and another student.

Some students become so discouraged that they seem to give up all hope—they no longer attempt to get even. Their faulty logic may lead to *display of inadequacy or hopelessness,* which includes the building of a protective shield of despair. The shield is reinforced by the student's display of ineptitude, so that nothing is expected of him. When confronted with this type of behavior, the teacher may also be tempted to give up. This student is usually not all that disruptive, does not demand anything from the teacher or classmates, and can easily be allowed to "vegetate." But this student perhaps has the greatest need for the teacher's attention. Attempts to achieve in any arena must be encouraged by the teacher; highly motivating activities must be used to entice the attempts. Mistakes must be handled as learning experiences. It is at times helpful for the teacher subtly to admit mistakes that he or she makes in the presence of the entire class, for example by saying "Did you see how I spelled that today? Didn't I spell it differently yesterday?" and then correcting the error. The student who is demonstrating hopeless behavior must receive much praise—but it must be honest praise.

Younger children usually easily reveal their behavior as goal seeking. The older the student, however, the more effective he is in camouflaging his goals. Often these goals are also intermingled with a desire for excitement, behaviors resulting from drug use, or other contaminating factors. In short, it may be fairly difficult for the teacher to sort out just which goal or combination of goals the student is seeking.

Logical Consequences. Since Dreikurs discussed this concept as early as 1964 (Dreikurs & Saltz, 1964), the term *logical consequences* has often been used in suggestions for classroom discipline. This concept involves teacher attitudes more than actual disciplinary measures. The teacher must believe the basic tenets of this philosophy before the method of logical consequences can be made workable in the classroom.

The first of these tenets is that the class-room is a replica of the democratic system that is an essential aspect of U.S. life. A democratic classroom implies that both teacher and students are working toward a common goal and that no one has more power than anyone else. This principle rules out punishment because punishment is meted out by someone in authority. Clearly, the teacher *is* the adult in the classroom, the teacher *does* have various responsibilities to ensure learning, and the teacher is *not* "one of the gang" or just another child or adolescent. However, even though the teacher does have these responsibilities and is not another child, he or she does not have the right to sit continually in judgment, to hand out punishments, or to be a dictator. (The teacher *can* do these things but will pay the price with students who retaliate and will end up presiding over a collection of students with whom very little learning takes place.) The democratic classroom consists of teacher and students who choose rules for the common good and the goals to be pursued. Within this context, the method of natural or logical consequences can become appropriate.

If the natural flow of events is allowed to take its course, natural consequences become the learning tool of the student. For example, if the student forgets his lunch money, the natural flow of events is that with no lunch money he gets no lunch; therefore, the teacher does not rescue the student, does not scold, does not discuss it. The natural consequence of going without lunch will teach the student to remember his lunch money. At times, of course, the safety of the student does not permit the teacher to allow natural consequences to occur.

There are also times when natural consequences simply are not present, in which case the method of logical consequences may be useful. Logical consequences are structured and arranged by the teacher and *must be experienced by the student as logical;*

that is, *the student* must see the relationship between his actions and the consequences. This awareness is absolutely necessary—it is not enough for the teacher alone to see the relationship. Logical consequences can often be arranged through the manner in which the teacher makes a statement. For example, the statement that "when you are finished with your assignment, you may leave for free time," provides for logical consequences. The responsibility is placed on the student. If he does not finish in time, he may miss free time.This approach does not set the teacher up as the authority handing out privileges or punishments, as the student may perceive in the statement, "I will let you go for free time when you finish the assignment." Or in another example, if two students engage in a fight, the teacher can step in to settle the fight or simply say, "We decided in this room that fights are not allowed and that whoever fights will not be able to go to the gym," and then walk away. Of course the teacher cannot allow students to be hurt, but a reminder of the consequences chosen by the group along with the lack of attention given the inappropriate action often defuses the situation. If not, and if the students are in danger of being hurt, the teacher may need to ask the rest of the class what was decided about fighting. When they state the consequences, much of the punitive aspect and imposition of authority by the teacher are removed from the consequences. The teacher may need to step between the students to stop the fight. Again, this action should be performed with as little imposition of authority as possible. When it is time for the class to go to the gym, the students who were fighting are asked, "What are the consequences for fighting?" When they answer, the rest of the class can be taken to the gym.

The purpose of the use of logical consequences is to assist students to be responsible for their own actions with a minimum of conformity for the sake of conformity. The teacher first asks, "What is likely to happen if I don't intervene?" the answer is usually the natural or logical consequences. The teacher then asks, "What consequence would the *student* most likely see as a result of his actions?" That consequence is the one to use.

Dreikurs and Cassel (1972) suggest several reasons for considering the use of logical consequences: they are a learning process, they are related to the inappropriate behavior, they involve what will happen now, they involve distinctions between the student and his deeds, and they reflect the reality of social order rather than the whim of an adult. The teacher must be an educator who is sympathetic and understanding, who is interested in the situation and the outcome, and who is objective and provides the student with a choice of continuing a behavior or experiencing the consequences.

A thorough understanding and acceptance of these principles may provide the imaginative teacher with a variety of methods using logical consequences to promote a cooperative attitude in the classroom. The interested reader may refer to the references to locate many more of Dreikurs' valuable suggestions concerning discipline in the classroom.

William Glasser. William Glasser (1965) developed a type of individual therapy or counseling that with modification may be useful in classrooms. The basic tenet of this therapy is that all persons attempt to fulfill various needs even though it is at times difficult to interpret the need when the behavior appears irrational or inadequate.

The basic needs are to love and to feel worthwhile to others, to be loved. Glasser believes that all races and cultures have these two needs in common and that all people strive to meet them. How an individual behaves is often the key to whether that person elicits from others the love that he seeks.

Being loved by others is the result of appropriate behavior. When an individual acts in a manner that causes discomfort in others, those significant others find it difficult to demonstrate their love.

Glasser suggests that only by taking responsibility for our actions can we be lovable. The key to his therapy therefore is to assist or "force" persons to be responsible for their actions. In other words, the right way is to assist individuals to gain self-respect and the closeness with others by saying in essence, "I care enough about you to force you to act in a better way, a way whereby you will learn through experience to know what I already know" (p. 19).

Glasser is a firm believer in the rightness or wrongness of actions—for instance stealing is always wrong regardless of the reasons for doing it—and this moral value must be taught to the student. Only when students behave "rightly" do they develop self-respect.

Those interested in further information regarding Glasser's concepts of reality therapy as well as specific techniques for classroom meetings and the means to assist students in developing more responsibility for their actions should consult Glasser's text, listed in the references.

Lee and Marlene Canter. In the mid-70's an approach to *assertive discipline* was developed and advocated by Lee and Marlene Canter (1976). The basic premise of the Canters' approach is that students learn more effectively when the teacher is clearly in charge of the classroom and the students clearly understand what is expected of them. The Canters believe that their approach provides the teacher with the effective means of managing inappropriate behavior constructively while providing a warm, caring atmosphere conducive to student growth. The Canters suggest that many teachers labor under several misconceptions regarding discipline, such as the notion that firm control is

stifling rather than liberating, that students neither need nor deserve firm discipline, and that teachers who are assertive are necessarily authoritarian and dogmatic in their approach. It is necessary, according to the Canters, for teachers to believe they have rights, like the right to determine what behaviors are appropriate, to expect those behaviors from students and to provide consequences when the behaviors are not exhibited. These rights provide the teacher with the opportunity to establish the environment most conducive for learning. On the other hand, students have basic rights also. They have the right to a teacher who supports them when their behavior is appropriate, to receive the teacher's assistance in helping them limit and/or control their inappropriate behavior, and to choose their behaviors with full knowledge of the consequences of their choices. These basic needs of the students and teachers are met through the use of assertive discipline. The teacher never violates the needs of the student nor the best interests of the entire class, but does communicate unequivocally the expectations in relation to behavior and consistently follows through with the predetermined consequences.

Teachers following the assertive discipline approach

1. clearly identify expectations; that is, they go over the day and determine the acceptable and unacceptable behaviors related to each activity (for instance, the amount of talking appropriate when small groups are working as differentiated from working at an interest center or the computer). These are discussed with the students more than once. Students *learn* these expectations by repetition and practice just as they learn multiplication or correct letter-writing form.

2. understand the difference between nonassertive, hostile, and assertive responses to

students' behavior. Nonassertive teachers are generally unable or unwilling to place demands on students or if they do, they retreat at the first sign of opposition. In general they usually accept the decisions of the students. This is clearly not a situation conducive to learning.

The hostile teacher usually feels somewhat out of control and resorts to threats and irrational punishments that infringe on the right of students to have teacher assistance in limiting their behavior and to choose their behavior with complete knowledge of the consequences. This situation, like the first, is not conducive to learning.

The assertive teacher, on the other hand, clearly indicates expectations and insists upon compliance. The teacher's words are always backed up by actions, appropriate behaviors are supported, inappropriate behaviors are quickly and efficiently followed by predetermined consequences. Canter and Canter suggest that teachers practice the assertive responses until they come naturally.

Examples of the three types of responses are:

Behavior: Not paying attention
   Nonassertive: "Won't you please listen?"
   Hostile: "Are you ever going to learn to pay attention? I've asked ten times already this morning!"
   Assertive: "Listen to what I say since I won't repeat it."

Behavior: Fighting on the playgound
   Nonassertive: "It would be better if you tried not to fight anymore."
   Hostile: "You always pick on someone. Why don't you grow up!"
   Assertive: "The rule is we don't fight. Stand here until you are ready to obey the rule."

These examples illustrate the teacher's clear disapproval of the action, an unambiguous statement of what consequences follow,

and what behavior is expected of the student. The assertive response delivers to students the expectation that they can and will choose the appropriate behavior. It is essential that the teacher recognize the appropriate behavior in the same assertive manner: "You did listen and now you know what to do" or "You did stand here. Are you ready to join the group and follow the rules?"

Canter and Canter also suggest that teachers make assertiveness plans in much the same manner in which they write lessons plans for reading, history or math. This preplanning is to be accomplished prior to the beginning of the school year and repeated as often as necessary during the school year. The guidelines for assertiveness planning include determining inappropriate behaviors that are occurring or the potential for them; identifying the specific behaviors students are to engage in; determining positive and negative consequences and deciding on implementation of consequences. An aid for this type of planning may be constructed, duplicated, and used for as many activities as necessary (see Figure 11–7). This type of planning requires visual and mental preparation for both appropriate and inappropriate behavior as well as consequence for both (Charles, 1981). Some teachers may wish to rehearse verbally what they will say so that when the need actually arises, the assertive responses will feel natural.

The reader has no doubt noticed that this approach "borrows" from several other approaches. For more information on this and other models of discipline, the Canter and Canter and the Charles references will provide additional insights.

UNIQUE PROBLEMS OF ADOLESCENTS

As with learning disabilities, most programs for adolescent behaviorally disordered students were developed at the elementary level

Activity	Acceptable behaviors	Consequences	Unacceptable behaviors	Consequences
music class (large group)	playing instruments	at least 4 comments per class recognizing good behavior	playing instruments while I'm talking	saying to the student "We don't play when I'm talking, so I'll take the drum sticks" and taking them until I'm finished

FIGURE 11–7. Assertiveness planning chart

and were adapted for the secondary level (Brown, McDowell, & Smith, 1981). Because of a variety of factors, an acceptable definition of what constitutes behavioral disorders in adolescents has been even more elusive than is the case with younger students. One factor in this definition problem is the lack of a clear definition of what is *acceptable* behavior in normal adolescents. It is generally agreed that adolescence is a time of transition (V. Jones, 1980; McDowell, 1981). It involves the passage of an individual from a position of dependence to one of independence. This passage may be initiated at various chronological ages and lasts a varying number of years. The transition involves both physiological and psychological stages.

Physiological changes include the production of hormones that lead to the development of secondary sex characteristics and the ability to reproduce. During these changes the adolescent begins to look more to peers than parents for approval and has an increasing concern for physical appearance. At the same time the adolescent looks at peers for approval, his peers seem to seek some indefinable standard of how one should look, act, and so on. Any deviations are subject to taunting by peers. Being too tall, too short, too thin, or too fat is a relative characteristic,

but for many adolescents these factors have great significance. Rarely is an adolescent satisfied with his physical appearance, but such dissatisfaction does not always lead to any severe crisis.

Psychological changes take place as a result of the expectation by society as well as the individual for new standards of behavior. No longer are childhood manners acceptable; the adolescent must find a separate identity and become increasingly independent. These psychological changes are likely to cause considerable consternation for the adolescent, school personnel, and parents. McDowell (1981) has described several issues related to these new expectations that although discussed here as separate issues, should be viewed as closely interwoven. When a student demonstrates difficulty in any of these areas, it is usually a reflection of problems in several areas rather than just one:

1. *Status.* Status involves how one is perceived by others. For adolescents, how one is perceived by peer groups is far more important than how one is perceived by parents or relatives. This perception by others is closely allied with the adolescent's self-concept. Status may be conferred by others, as in the case of a class

clown who may be designated thus after one or two incidents and who then accepts this role as a way to gain status and continues the role.

2. *Identity.* Identity is generally developed in two areas: (a) identity with a group (gang, club member, basketball team) and (b) self-identity reflected by a knowledge of who one is, what one believes in, and what one represents. The development of an identity usually involves an element of breaking away from family ties.

3. *Independence.* The degree to which an individual is self-sufficient reflects his independence. Striving for independence involves testing of limits, establishing an identity, and redefining relationships. Perhaps one of the most difficult aspects of gaining a sense of independence for the adolescent involves being expected to act as an adult but enjoying few of the privileges of the adult. In attempting to solve the dilemma, the adolescent may disregard authority, resulting in conflicts in school as well as in the home.

4. *Relationships.* Although they vary from interactions with strangers to intimate interactions, relationships are a vital part of life. Early adolescence involves a seeking out of a same-sex best friend or friends; later, this interaction expands to include members of the opposite sex. As the adolescent strives for identity, independence, and status, he gradually grows away from family support systems, which are replaced by other relationships. Unless various other relationships are developed the adolescent suffers from alienation and feelings of aloneness and inadequacy, which will have adverse effects on development in other areas.

5. *Sex.* Although much has been written recently concerning sex-role stereotypes, the development of a sexual identity is a major issue adolescents must resolve. Any interference with the development of a sexual identity may have lifelong effects. Adolescents must learn about the potential functions of their bodies and how to use them. Religious beliefs, parental attitudes, and peer knowledge affect this development in a positive or negative fashion.

6. *Values.* An individual's identity generally reflects his values, which often become the criteria by which he is judged. Adolescents often seem to reject the values of their parents as they strive for independence and an identity. Because they may be unwilling to live by the values taught by their parents, required by religion, or expected of those of a younger age and yet have not developed workable, consistent values of their own, adolescents find themselves in a dilemma. The inconsistency in judgment and behavior of the adolescent often reflects this seemingly unsolvable puzzle.

7. *Decision making.* The ability to examine alternatives, choose among them, and live with the consequences is important for successful adult living. Objectively examining alternatives is often very difficult for the adolescent. As a general rule, adolescents are more concerned with immediate than long-range goals, and this concern often leads to decisions that in hindsight may be seen as not appropriate. Effective, appropriate decision making is a skill that must be developed and, like any other skill, practiced. Often adults significant to the adolescent are impatient with the inability to make effective decisions. Peers, a lack of acceptable models, and the need for independence may influence the adolescent to make poor decisions that will have lifelong effects.

One or any combination of the seven psychological changes to which the adolescent must adjust may cause short-term or lifelong crises. For a variety of reasons, which usually can be determined only on a case-by-case basis if at all, some adolescents experience problems far beyond those considered normal. They may turn to drugs, alcohol, crime, or, in extreme cases, suicide. This is not to say that every adolescent who experiments with drugs, alcohol, sex, or criminal acts is suffering from a behavior disorder. The problem depends on the frequency, the severity, and the dependence of the behavior.

Teachers of adolescents must be aware of the normal behaviors of adolescents to be able to assist students with special needs. Teachers can employ a variety of approaches that enhance the adolescent's opportunities for successfully negotiating this important stage in life:

1. having an open, honest, respectful relationship with their students
2. providing students with challenging, motivating activities
3. providing frequent and positive attention
4. setting fair and firm limits
5. involving the student in setting goals in both academic and behavioral areas
6. accepting the student as an individual while not reinforcing inappropriate or self-defeating behavior
7. establishing learning environments that ensure considerable success

CHILD ABUSE AND NEGLECT

With the passage of federal legislation in 1974 and the growing national concern reflected by the passage of similar laws in every state about child abuse and neglect, it is imperative that teachers be aware of what constitutes abuse or neglect in their particular state as well as the procedures for reporting suspected cases. All 50 states have legislation that requires citizens in general and school personnel in particular to report suspected child abuse. Each state has specific directives regarding both what types of abuse *must* be reported and what *may* be reported as well as the specific procedures for reporting suspected abuse or neglect. Teachers should consult the appropriate school personnel to determine the procedures mandated in their state.

Since a number of the characteristics of children with behavior disorders are similar to those of the abused child, identification of abused children must be carefully made. The two problems are not synonymous, but they are closely related. Assistance required by the abused child is often similar to that for students with behavior disorders. Halperin (1979) has provided the following description

Major behavior changes may be indicative of child abuse.

of characteristics that may indicate a child who has been mistreated:

1. *The aggressive child.* This child is a quarrelsome, bullying child who may have a pattern of behavior learned from parents who express themselves with physical punishment when they are displeased.
2. *The show-off.* The child who shows off is an extreme extrovert identified by his clowning in class and inability to wait, both behaviors masking insecurity and feelings of inferiority. These feelings may be the result of little or no warmth or attention from the parents.
3. *The disobedient child.* This child is an insolent, disrespectful child who never seems to hear directions and who engages in a continuing power struggle with authority. A lack of recognition in the home may lead to the child's extreme attempts at gaining attention. Parental attitudes toward authority, especially school, may also influence the child's attitudes toward teachers.
4. *The child who cheats, lies, or steals.* Infrequent occurrence of such behavior, especially in younger children, is usually not a cause for alarm, but repeated activities of this nature often reflect a deeper hostility toward family or authority. They can also indicate a need for attention or may result from modeling behaviors in the home.
5. *The child nobody likes.* This child is often listless, sometimes destructive, seemingly incapable of forming satisfying relationships. Commonly this student is absent from school frequently or is a high school dropout. The home environment may lack warmth or satisfying relationships. Family members may live isolated lives; therefore, the child has not learned the skills necessary for productive interactions.
6. *The unkempt child.* This child's dirty face, matted hair, and soiled clothing may result from a lack of proper facilities for bathing or laundering clothing but also from carelessness of the parent. These children do not feel valued and feel little or no pride in themselves, and both feelings are reflected in their work.
7. *The shy or fearful child.* Whether a child is fearful or is shy can be determined by becoming aware of what and whom the child fears. The fearful child is usually afraid or fearful of many persons and things; the fear is generalized. The shy child differs in that his fear is related more to contact with people. The shy child usually speaks in a low voice, sits with head lowered to avoid eye contact, and declines participation in group activities. The shy child may be modeling parental behavior or may be the victim of excessively critical parents who expect perfection. Since the child cannot meet this standard, he hesitates to attempt any task.
8. *The careless child.* Messy papers, desk, and often physical appearance are the hallmark. Often the teacher is unable to decipher the work of the child to evaluate it. Other children trip over the books, papers, and boxes strewn around his desk. The child seems to stumble through life. This careless attitude may be the result of parents who place little value on orderliness or organization, or the child may adopt this pattern of behavior because of excessive demands made by the parents.

This list of characteristics is not exhaustive; however, it indicates some of the various personality patterns that may result from maltreatment. The similarities of these characteristics of maltreated children to those of behaviorally disordered children are obvious.

Additional forms of mistreatment may be

observed by the alert teacher (Halperin, 1979), including abandonment, emotional abuse or neglect, physical abuse and neglect, and sexual abuse.

Abandonment occurs not only when children are very small. When older youngsters are simply left behind or left with an adult, and no provisions are made for their continued support, they have been abandoned.

Emotional abuse or neglect often results in an extremely low self-concept and inappropriate attempts to seek attention. Young females may turn to promiscuous behavior in an effort to receive love and attention. The male may turn to vandalism, drugs, or gangs to feel of value to others or himself. Emotional abuse may take the form of ridicule for failing to achieve the goals parents have set. In such cases the normal parent-child relationship of unconditional caring is either absent or destroyed. Some children withdraw from contact with others because their normal family relationships have been so devastating. Others are so convinced that they are worthless that they begin to act out behaviors that confirm their worthlessness.

Emotional neglect is a lack of involvement by the parents. It is a fault of omission rather than commission. The parents may provide the basics of food, clothing, and shelter but seem unable to provide any of the warmth and caring essential for the development of the child.

Physical abuse and neglect are forms of child abuse. Physical neglect occurs when the physical needs of food, clothing, general care, supervision, or shelter are not met. The actions of the child, such as stealing food or articles of clothing, may seem inappropriate, but they may simply be the attempts of the child to meet his basic needs. In cases in which poverty causes the neglect, social agencies are usually available to assist. Yet poverty is not the reason why some parents neglect their children. Some parents are

barely able to meet their own emotional needs and have little time or concern for their offspring.

Physical abuse is the most often reported and most easily recognized form of maltreatment. The various forms of physical abuse can generally be observed by the teacher. Signs of possible physical abuse include (1) abrasions in various stages of healing; (2) burns shaped like objects such as cigarettes or utensils or burns that indicate immersion in hot water or of having had water poured on parts of the body; (3) injuries that suggest an imprint of belts, clothes hangers, hose, hand, teeth, or rope, injuries on parts of the body inconsistent with a fall, injuries of a peculiar size or shape, or injuries around the head; and (4) bruises of different colors indicating they were received over time.

Children are often very reluctant to discuss why or how they received injuries that result from physical abuse. Victims of physical abuse show a fear of adults that is manifested when they protect their head with their hands or use other forms of apparent self-defense when approached suddenly or unexpectedly by adults.

Sexual abuse involves the range from exposure to fondling, to rape, to incest and may occur from infancy through adolescence. Generally it is not a one-time event except in the case of strangers. Because a sexually abused child generally exhibits no physical signs, the abuse is frequently undetected. Sometimes teachers may observe a sudden change of behavior that occurs at the onset of the abuse or when the child becomes aware that such treatment is not normal among peers. Many sexually abused children attempt to hide the mistreatment because they recognize they are participants in activities that are unacceptable in society. They submit to abuse because of fear of punishment or withdrawal of love, because of their desire for some promised reward, or because they are physically forced to submit. At times the burden of undeserved guilt becomes so great that the child turns to a trusted adult. This confidence must not go unheeded. The matter, although extremely personal, must be investigated. Teachers need to be aware of the proper procedures for reporting suspected sexual abuse.

BEHAVIOR PROBLEMS AND STRESS

The regular classroom teacher may easily succumb to feelings of inadequacy, frustration, and even despair when it seems that all attempted interventions are useless. It can be helpful, however, to reflect on the various aspects of the student's behavior that are not under the control of the teacher. Students may be experiencing stress from the normal developmental stages, such as separation from home for the first time, not knowing what to do about bodily changes that are taking place, approaching graduation with its pressure for deciding a career, and so on. Economic stresses, including poor diet, inadequate housing, lack of privacy, and limited opportunity to participate in social activities may also affect the student. Some students experience psychological stress, such as being told they were or are unwanted, that they will be kicked out if they misbehave, or that they are dumb, a troublemaker, or useless. Others live with an abusive or psychotic parent. Still others endure stress that may seem minor to the teacher but is significant to the student, such as a severe case of acne just at the time of an important date, a friend accidentally spilling soda on the English assignment due next period, or a trusted friend telling someone something that was to have been a secret.

Any one of these types of stress can lead to what Long and Fagen (1981) refer to as a stress cycle. The student experiences a stressful situation that leads to a variety of feelings. The student may feel very uncomfortable with these feelings, thinking that they are unacceptable or wrong. Attempting to deal with the feelings, the student engages in some sort of behavior, which may be an honest reflection of the feelings or an attempt to cover these up. A student who verbally attacks the teacher because of an incomplete assignment may have strong feelings of inadequacy or inferiority because of lack of study time or of a place to study or because the student was fighting with a drunk parent when he should have been finishing his homework. The behavior the student demonstrates leads to an environmental reaction. Other students observe the outburst, and it evokes feelings in the teacher. At this point a power struggle may be initiated. The teacher may feel threatened by the student's verbal abuse and react in an authoritarian manner: "You will *not* speak to me that way!" or "Take your things and go to the principal's office immediately!" In such a case there is no winner, but rather both the teacher and student are acting immaturely. The teacher must be the responsible professional and attempt to interpret the student's actions. Long and Fagen (1981) have suggested a series of guidelines for teaching the student how to cope with various kinds of stress:

1. Be attentive to nonverbal communications. Many students learn early that what they say can be held against them and that speaking evokes angry responses from adults, and therefore they may refrain from verbal communication. However, tense muscles, clenching of fists, rapid breathing, body movements, and looks in the eyes can tell the observant teacher much about the anger or frustration the student is experiencing.

2. Attend as much to *how* a student is speaking as to *what* he is saying. The tone or

short, clipped statements may be more important than what is actually said. A *yes* or *no* said through clenched teeth indicates far more than agreement or disagreement.

3. Label and accept the student's feelings. As the teacher "hears" what is really being said through nonverbal and verbal communication, she is in a position to label the feelings for the student: "You are really angry about this, aren't you?" As the teacher reaches out to the student in this way, the first hesitant step toward a relationship is made. For the student, labeling feelings is one matter, but accepting those feelings is far more complex. The teacher must indicate to the student that the feelings are legitimate even though acting them out is not always acceptable: "I know you are angry, but I cannot allow you to hit another student" or "You have a right to be upset about what she said, but you cannot destroy her property." It must be stressed that the process of labeling and accepting feelings while rejecting specific behaviors is very difficult for students to learn. The teacher needs to repeat this process time and time again.

In providing students with a supportive, helping environment, teachers must be certain that the student takes responsibility for changing his behavior. Sometimes teachers can become too sympathetic and actually support or contribute to the student's inappropriate behavior. The student may begin to feel put upon and feel that because of the stress, he has a right to act this way. The teacher's questions or comments should lead the student to examine the behavior that contributed to the problem and what he can do to change the situation.

The teacher must be aware of and support the student's attempts—however feeble or unsuccessful—to change his situation. Most students did not suddenly begin to have

behavioral problems; therefore, changing behavior for the better is also generally a slow, painful process. The teacher who understands this difficulty can provide encouragement as the student develops the skills necessary to change his behavior.

SUGGESTIONS FOR THE REGULAR CLASSROOM TEACHER

Teachers who have behaviorally disordered students in their classes perhaps find this particular type of handicapping condition most difficult to accept. This difficulty certainly is not surprising because by definition this behavior is *not normal.* Other students in the class also find it difficult. Just as there are no causes or solutions accepted in the major theoretical points of view, there are no certain, quick, easy solutions from an eclectic or experiential perspective.

Whenever inappropriate behavior occurs in the classroom, the teacher must decide quickly whether it is an individual problem with one student or a group problem with the entire class. There are times when a problem in the class dynamics such as a lack of unity, low morale, or negative reactions contributes to the behaviorally disordered student's difficulties. It is manadatory for the regular classroom teacher to examine the dynamics of the class as a whole and, if he or she finds problems, take effective steps for correction. However, it is also mandatory that the individual student's problem receive prompt attention. It is a matter of correcting both areas of concern simultaneously, not one first and then the other. Johnson and Bany (1970) have listed a number of observable behaviors that the teacher may use as a guide for determining whether the general atmosphere of the classroom is a factor further compounding the problem of the disruptive student (Table 11–3).

As a former regular classroom teacher and later a teacher of students with behavior

TABLE 11–3. Observable behaviors when the classroom atmosphere compounds students' disruptive behavior

Classroom Problems	Observable Characteristics
Ease of distraction	undue attention to visitors, noises, movements outside windows, etc.; inability easily to return to task when distracted, almost as if looking for diversions; frequent squabbles over books, pencils, chairs, etc.
Lack of cohesion	division into subgroups: boys vs. girls, minorities vs. majority, various cliques; frequent arguments between subgroups over usual competitive aspects of classroom such as grades, games, differentiated assignments
Lack of conformity to normal standards	excessive noise and talk in routine situations, between classes, going to assembly, etc.; more than usual noise in activities such as handing back papers, correcting work, and completing assignments; nonadherence to rules of quiet talk when in small groups, committees, or ability groups
Put-down of individuals	active hostility or aggressiveness toward one or two students; ridiculing, ignoring, criticizing, or refusing to work with certain students, hiding books or papers of disliked students and attempting to trip them or make them appear clumsy, dumb, different
Resistance and hostility toward teacher	slow-downs or work stoppages created by certain groups' "losing" things, asking for assignments to be repeated, or asking obviously irrelevant questions; accusations of other students that are clearly a challenge to the teacher
Rigidity	unusual restlessness, argumentativeness, or disagreeability when schedules are changed, when a substitute is present, or when different types of assignments are given or classroom activities are varied.
Support for misbehavior	encouragement of acting out, talking back, or clowning around; suggesting disruptive activities to individuals; attention to any misbehavior

Note. Adapted from *Classroom Management: Theory and Skill Training* (pp. 46–47) by L. Johnson & M. Bany, 1970, London: Collier-MacMillan.

disorders, one of the authors found it essential to know and understand himself and his teaching style, to think creatively, to borrow ideas from all sources, to adapt, modify, and keep trying. The suggestions that follow are offered in this spirit. Teachers may, according to their teaching style and personality, use these suggestions to create dynamic new beginnings for the behaviorally disordered students in their classes.

Using facial expressions, pantomime, or charades is a nonthreatening form of releasing feelings or emotions (Necco, Wilson, & Scheidemantal, 1982). When students are comfortable with these techniques, original skits, stories, and real-life events, such as what happened on the playground or on a date, may be acted out. A discussion of the emotion, story, or event is held with all members of the class. This provides an opportunity for reflection and careful consideration of all facets of the situation. As the discussion progresses, the teacher may ask for volunteers to take the part of certain characters or to discuss with individuals what they would do. When there are volunteers to play the part of each character, reenactment takes place. As soon as it begins to deteriorate or when the drama has served its purpose, another discussion is held. The entire class participates, emphasizing the critical feelings, solutions, and alternatives demonstrated. Gradually, as the students are able, the teacher guides the discussion in such a

manner that the reenactment can be applied to real-life situations. The purpose is to enable the students to recreate feelings and emotions while exploring a variety of solutions to their own problems in a nonthreatening atmosphere.

A common difficulty with students who have behavior problems is their inability to wait quietly for teacher assistance or to go on to another task when they encounter a problem and the teacher is not able to assist them immediately. Small signs such as those in

FIGURE 11–8. Need-help sign

Note. From *It's Positively Fun* (p. 7) by P. Kaplan, J. Kohfeldt, and K. Sturla, 1974, Denver: Love. Reprinted by permission.

Figure 11–8 can be attached to the top of a pencil or dowel, which may be placed in a spool or a mound of clay. Such a sign serves as a silent signal to the teacher that the student requires assistance. By using such a nondisturbing system the teacher also reinforces the idea that study or independent activity time is a time to be quiet. It would be unrealistic to place a restriction such as being quiet on the student simply because he tends to be more disruptive and not impose it on the entire class.

Certificates of recognition for working cooperatively with another student may positively influence the behavior of a student with behavior problems (Figure 11–9). Providing the opportunity to share a reward may be an incentive for some students (Figure 11–10). "Renting" popular playground balls, bats, gloves, or areas like a basketball court or softball field is also a powerful incentive for some students (Figure 11–11).

Another incentive is the awarding of five minutes of extra recess or lunch hour. This time can be arranged by allowing students who have earned it to go out before the other students or to remain out after the others must come in. Of course, this method must be approved by the principal and supervising personnel on the playground because proper supervision must be maintained (Figure 11–12).

FIGURE 11–9. Certificate of recognition

Note. From *Positive Pitches* (p. 27) by P. G. Kaplan and A.G. Hoffman, 1981, Denver: Love. Reprinted by permission.

FIGURE 11–10. "Rental" card to share

Note. From *It's Positively Fun* (p. 16) by P. Kaplan, J. Kohfeldt, and K. Sturla, 1974, Denver: Love. Reprinted by permission.

FIGURE 11–11. "Rental" card

Note. From *It's Positively Fun* (p. 16) by P. Kaplan, J. Kohfeldt, and K. Sturla, 1974, Denver: Love. Reprinted by permission.

Gaining the cooperation of other members of the class can be a method of reducing the frequency of disruptive behaviors. Certificates such as those in Figure 11–13 may be used to recognize the efforts of other members of the class when they demonstrate cooperative behavior, or they may be given to students who have demonstrated their ability to accommodate the individual characteristics of other students regardless of whether they are handicapped.

Creating stories may serve as an outlet for a variety of feelings and emotions. The emphasis should be on expression rather than grammar, spelling, or punctuation; however, these aspects of communication should be taught and reinforced in other writing activities.

The procedure for creating stories allows the student to explore a range of feelings and to examine alternatives for problem solving. If a student finds the whole blank sheet of paper intimidating, it may be folded in fourths. The first block is for the beginning,

the two middle blocks allow for elaboration, and the final block is for an ending to the story. At times students may need to be prompted, such as by saying "Write a story with a car as the main character" or "Using these words, write a story" or "Using this picture, describe what happened before and what you think will happen next." In writing stories students should be encouraged to use one-word sentences or pictures if their writing skills are insufficient to permit them to do more.

Such stories often repeat similar themes. By creating an atmosphere of openness and acceptance, the teacher can encourage exploration of other, perhaps more sensitive, issues of concern to the student.

After the stories are written, the teacher may discuss them with the student. However, the teacher must allow the student to make the decision regarding this discussion. Some students are reluctant or unable to verbalize the feelings about which they have written.

When students become more secure and proficient in writing such stories, the concept of alternative solutions may be introduced. The student writes the beginning and middle of the story, while two or three of his classmates write endings for the story. When all are completed, the students may discuss the various solutions or outcomes. Gradually students may then generalize to other areas of life the reflective thinking and understanding of choices and consequences that they applied in writing the stories (Dehouske, 1982).

Because students with behavior problems often receive minimal praise, certificates similar to those illustrated in Figures 11–9 to 11–13 can be used to provide significant positive recognition. Some students attempt to moderate their behavior to receive them. Other students do not actually work *for* them but are exceptionally pleased if the teacher surprises them with one after a situation that was particularly trying for the student.

Depending on the parents' reaction to such reinforcement, students may want to take such certificates home for additional

FIGURE 11–13. Certificate for cooperation

Note. From *Positive Pitches* (p. 27) by P.G. Kaplan and A.G. Hoffman, 1981, Denver: Love. Reprinted by permission.

praise. In other situations the student may not take them home but is additionally rewarded if they are placed in a prominent position on a bulletin board or in a "gooddeeds" scrapbook.

Many reinforcements are available to teachers in addition to free time. The type of certificate illustrated in Figures 11–9 to 11–13 can easily be duplicated and used to reward the student.

When playground equipment, other school property, or on occasion the teacher's personal property, such as a book, Polaroid camera, or some such, cannot be given to the student, a rental system may be designed (see Figure 11–11). The student earns the right to "rent" the use of the object. Rental times can be for a few minutes, overnight, a

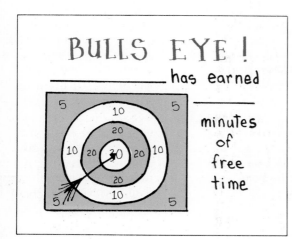

FIGURE 11–12. Extra-time card

Note. From *It's Positively Fun* (p. 18) by P. Kaplan, J. Kohfeldt, and K. Sturla, 1974, Denver: Love. Reprinted by permission.

weekend, or any other amount of time that is negotiated. There is, of course, a risk of damage to the item, but this method also involves an opportunity to teach respect for others' property. The teacher must take care in arranging such rentals so that only those objects that can be replaced are used in this manner and so that the student demonstrates some responsibility for the property of others. Teachers must also recognize that some students are much too destructive to be entrusted with the property of others.

Another incentive that may be extremely motivating with students is to modify assignments based on the teacher's recognition of the feelings of the student. The teacher may say, for example, "I see you are really angry about the fight you had and that you still

Name: _____		Date: _____	
Must do	Should do	Do if there's time	Do not!
reading workbook, p. 37, nos. 1, 3, 5, 7, 8	Use colored pencils to circle the correct answers.	nos. 6 and 9	do nos. 2 and 4 on p. 37
math, pp. 142–143, all even numbers		the odd-numbered ones that have a 4 in them	do numbers that have a 3 in them
Take 10 minutes and listen to your favorite record.	Use the earphones so no one knows you are doing it.		let anyone know you are taking a break
Write 2 paragraphs about your hobby.	Read the rules for a good paragraph before you begin. Write neatly.	Draw a picture that illustrates your hobby.	write more than 2 paragraphs
Work on the mural for social studies.	Take time to think about where you finished last time. Decide what you want to put on it today.	Color what you drew.	do any more than you want
Read pp. 105–110 in your reader.	Read carefully. Watch for the new words. (They are on the chalkboard.) Write down any word that gives you trouble.	Write *your* ending to the story.	read more than 5 pages or write more than 1 sentence for your ending

FIGURE 11–14. Assignment priority schedule

think it wasn't your fault. For now, why don't you write the answers to only these two rows of problems, skip this one, and do the last. As soon as you are finished, you can paint. That will cheer you up, won't it?" In this scenario the teacher is acknowledging the student's feelings and his right to them and at the same time is demonstrating to the student a flexibility in assignments and an alternative for changing the feelings. After an exchange such as this, the student often goes to his desk and begins the assignment. The student hears the lesson about redirecting feelings, but being excused from a part of the assignment provides the needed incentive to complete the task instead of dwelling on the unfairness of the fight and its aftermath.

The method of crossing out five or any other number of problems or exercises is useful for the teacher. When a student is finding it extremely difficult to work, the teacher explains why he or she is making the modification ("I see you are unhappy today") and with a magic marker or red pencil boldly crosses out some portion of the assignment. This technique, used somewhat sparingly of course, surprises or pleases the student so much that he often begins the task immediately. A more complex variation of this principle is illustrated in Figure 11–14. The technique shown there takes considerable preparation by the teacher, but with some students it may pay high dividends.

Some teachers may object to this procedure, arguing that every problem or exercise is necessary. Other teachers argue that not every exercise is essential and that they can determine the competency of the student with fewer exercises. All teachers must decide this matter for themselves.

If daily homework is required or expected in a particular school, allowing one free night as a reward is a powerful reinforcer for some students (Figure 11–15).

Variations of the method of obtaining baseline data for a student, as in the

FIGURE 11–15. No homework permit

Note. From *It's Positively Fun* (p. 17) by P. Kaplan, J. Kohfeldt, K. Sturla, 1974, Denver: Love. Reprinted with permission.

behaviorist approach, can often be useful with disruptive students. Discussing with the student the behaviors that are inappropriate and having him keep a card tally of each time he calls out or engages in the unacceptable behavior often reduces the behavior immediately. He may cheat and not mark the card, but *he* is still aware of his behavior. After class the teacher can discuss with him the number of marks on his card, and at this time the teacher can point out how disruptive the behavior has been, the effect it has on the class, and some possible solutions to the problem.

The same system can be associated with a contract or reward system; the teacher may say, for example, "If there are no more than two marks, you do only the even-numbered math problems." If a reward is contingent on no marks or a certain number of marks, then of course the student must keep an accurate count. In the previous case, in which the student does his own marking, the principle is that he becomes aware of how often he is performing the unacceptable behavior. In the latter case, when the reward or reinforcement is contingent on a specific number of actions, the count must be more accurate, therefore the teacher may want to do the tallying or be sure that the student does in fact mark the card each time the unacceptable behavior occurs.

Disruptive students are commonly unaware of the progress they have made, perhaps because the teacher, after the student has not demonstrated a particular behavior for a time, selects another behavior that is disruptive and begins working on it. The student may feel deprived of the opportunity to enjoy his success. His perception may be that he is always working at something (this may be true in regard to academic areas also) and is not making progress.

To provide an opportunity for the student to note his successes or achievements, a "good-deeds" or "good-work" scrapbook may be kept by the teacher, the student, or both. The scrapbook may be purchased or made of construction paper together with a cover. Achievement certificates awarded to the student may be glued into it along with math, handwriting, or any other academic work sheets. When appropriate, the student may page through and recall the reasons for different awards and note the progress he has made. These books can stimulate a very positive discussion between the teacher and student, which can be rewarding in and of itself. They can also be used at parent-teacher conferences.

Communication with parents is very important when dealing with students with behavior disorders. Telephone calls with good news, made at times when the teacher is less pressured, is an effective way to foster or maintain a good relationship.

Written communication can also be effective with parents. The type of communication illustrated in Figure 11–16 not only communicates the good news to the parent but also provides them with suggestions for assistance at home. The space for parents'

comments or questions demonstrates a desire for true communication; the "bulletin" allows for information or messages from teacher to parent and from parent to teacher.

To allow students the opportunity to identify their own moods or feelings and to indicate them to others, a "feelings board" may be developed with or by the students. The teacher can hold a discussion of the wide variety of emotions, such as being disappointed, shy, happy, tired, excited, hungry, mean, angry, and so on. Students can then make cards with appropriate descriptions on them. Each day as the students come into the classroom, they choose the card that best expresses their feelings and place it on the bulletin board. For some students this choice is quite difficult because they are unaware of their feelings. As frequently as desired by the teacher and/or students, discussions can be held to explore why students feel the way they do, whether these reasons are under their control, and so on.

Sometimes students do not want to publicize their emotions. If so, they can be allowed to place their card on their desk or in their notebook. Some students find that their mood changes during a class period or during the day, in which case they may change their cards to indicate their current mood.

The overall guiding purpose is to assist students to recognize their own feelings and, when appropriate, consider why they feel as they do. When the students recognize the *how* and *why* of their emotions, they can explore alternative solutions to problems and ways to change moods or to gain control over them.

Disruptive and withdrawn students often find it difficult to describe or evaluate their own behavior. The teacher may find it helpful to discuss their behavior with them on a daily basis, usually at the close of the day or the close of a class. Recalling specific circumstances or events one at a time in a factual manner and asking the student to

______ date

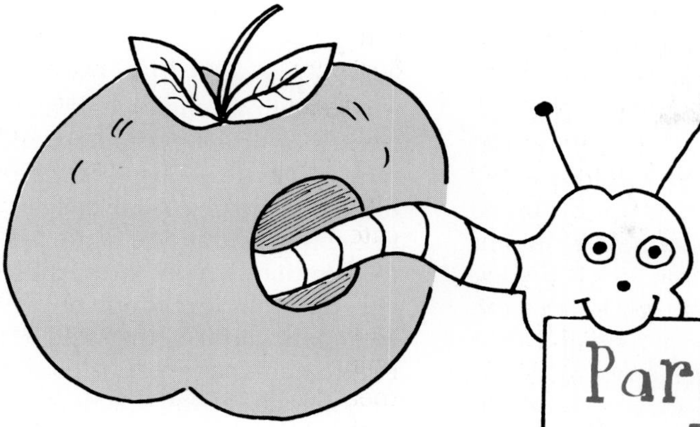

Parent Bulletin

Dear ______

You can be proud of your Child. ______ is working on ______ at School. You can help at home by

______

______

______

If you have any questions or comments please write them and return this form. ______

______

______

______

Thank you very much for your time and effort.

______
signed

FIGURE 11–16. Parent bulletin

Note. From *It's Positively Fun* (p. 35) by P. Kaplan, J. Kohfeldt, and K. Sturla, 1974, Denver: Love. Reprinted by permission.

monitor them are often an effective means of assisting the student. If the student finds this method too threatening, describing the real event in an imaginary setting can objectify it. For example, the teacher may describe an incident this way: "There was a fourth-grade boy who cheated in the ball game. He did not follow the rules of the game, so everyone else got mad and made him get out of the game. He then called them names and they began hitting him. There was a big fight and the teacher had to come over and tell them all to stand by the wall. What really started the fight? Why did the others get so mad? If this boy had played by the rules, how would the story end? If the boy didn't like the rules, what two things could he have done?"

With students who have sufficient writing skills, asking them to write what took place in a particular situation can be helpful. After an angry student has written his account of the event, his anger may be sufficiently diffused and the entire matter can be dropped. At other times his written account can be a matter for discussion. This discussion can be used as a means of teaching alternate behaviors rather than an argument concerning the accuracy of the student's perceptions.

An end-of-the-school-day evaluation that includes clearly positive and some potentially negative aspects is illustrated in Figure 11–17. The student may not be able to make truthful positive statements concerning the first two items; however, the next three are stated in such a way that the student's response is positive. The last space can be used by the teacher to include an item to which the student responds, or it can be filled in with a positive statement of something the teacher observed. This evaluation too may be used for discussion, taken home, or placed in the "good deeds" scrapbook.

Most students with behavior problems need assistance in structuring their day, assignments, activities, and play. The need for structure is indicated by their inability to be-

gin a task or to make the transition from one task to another (for example, reading to math) or from one type of activity to another (recess or time between classes to the beginning of the next class). Some may even have difficulty moving from one type of response to another within the same task (subtraction to addition). With such difficulties experienced in minor portions of the day, it is easy to understand why they find a week or month totally unmanageable.

Generally, if the teacher is organized, it is not difficult to assist students to structure or organize their day. (On the secondary level, this process is accomplished to some extent by the existing organization of the school day.) Simple cards or sheets on which the assignments are written by either the student or the teacher provide a minimum of organization for the student. The use of *started* and *completed* columns allows for a record of what is not yet begun, what is begun but not completed, and what is completed (Figure 11–18). At a glance, both teacher and student know what is left to be completed. The comments column can be used by either the teacher or the student. The teacher may peruse the work and make a comment, or the student may make notes such as "need history book" or "have to ask about this."

In addition to organizing the day or week, the teacher may also call attention to specific goals or qualities that are also to be rated (Figure 11–19). This method is useful only when the student routinely writes or notes the assignments. During the time allotted for completion, the teacher monitors the student's behavior according to the attributes listed. At the end of the period or class the teacher can quickly indicate either a grade or the points received. This record assists the student on a daily basis to note the progress he is making. If he does not make progress, the reasons for his lack of progress may be the basis for a discussion between student and teacher.

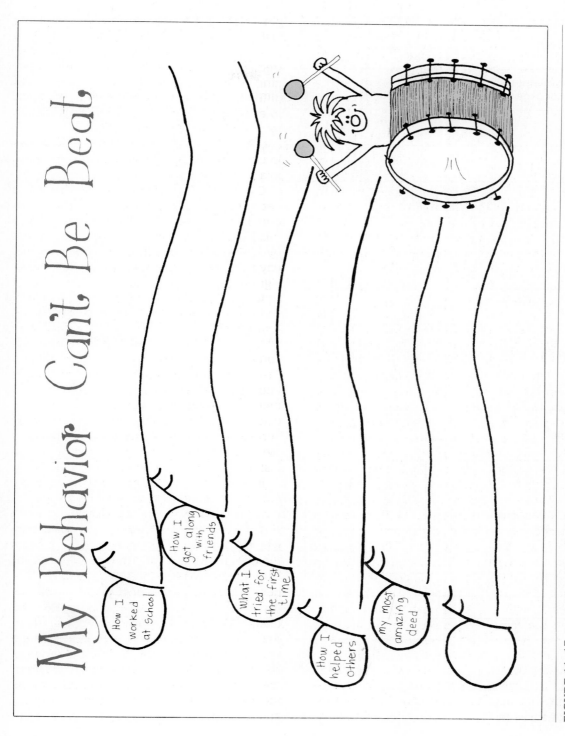

FIGURE 11–17. Behavior self-evaluation

Note. From *It's Positively Fun* (p. 29) by P. Kaplan, J. Kohfeldt, and K. Sturla. 1974. Denver: Love. Reprinted by permission.

Name: _____

Activities, assignments, or page numbers	Started	Completed	Comments

FIGURE 11–18. Format for organizing a student's day

Name: _____ Week: _____

Assignments	Good attitude	Showed effort	Used time wisely	Completed work	Comments
Mon.					
Tues.					
Wed.					
Thurs.					
Fri.					
Teacher's signature: _____					

FIGURE 11–19. Format for rating specific goals or qualities

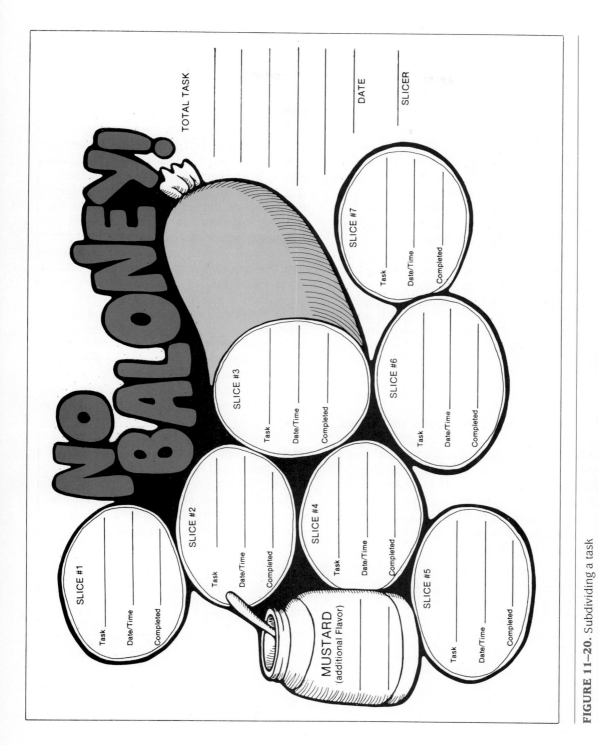

FIGURE 11–20. Subdividing a task.

Note. From *Making It Positively Clear* (p. 40) by P. G. Kaplan and A. G. Hoffman, 1981, Denver: Love. Reprinted by permission.

This type of card or sheet may be useful for either upper-elementary or secondary students. The student uses one card for each class. Some specialists may want to collect the cards so that they too may understand the student's progress.

At times the assignment given to a student may seem overwhelming either because of the task itself or, with some students, because of their lack of organizational skills. Figure 11–20 illustrates one way the task can be subdivided to make it more manageable for the student. It is especially appropriate for assignments like a theme because the various elements of research, outlining, writing, proofreading, and so on can all be "slices." Indicating a date for completion also assists the student in organizing long-term assignments. In addition, an hour period to work on assignments might be sliced into 5- or 10-minute portions, each with its specific task.

SUMMARY

Behavior disorders, like learning disabilities, are difficult to define and subject to some confusion. This is particularly true when mild levels of disorder are considered. On the other hand, there is evidence that most teachers can recognize students whose behavior disorders are of the moderate or severe level, and their major concern is how to manage such students so that they can make progress in the school setting and not cause problems for other students.

Over the years, many theories about behavior disorders, both causes and treatments, have been proposed. Each theory has its staunch proponents; each apparently has some strengths and some weaknesses. The major theories (and the treatments that evolve from them) have been considered in this chapter. In the public schools, it appears that methods derived from the point of view of the behaviorist are more often used, and we gave these primary emphasis.

Because adolescence is a time of rapid and sometimes traumatic change in the life of all students, certain behaviors demonstrated by adolescents may be misunderstood. Stress in the life of the student may produce behavior in the classroom that resembles behavior disorders. The home, parents, peers, and at times even the teacher may contribute to this pressure. In some cases the student may be suffering from abuse at home that produces behavior problems.

Creative teachers will attempt to motivate and challenge students, be understanding and accepting of as wide a variety of behavior as possible (given the best interests of the entire class), and encourage and assist students to change their unacceptable behavior. This is the challenge of teaching.

Teaching Students Who Are Gifted

☐ Are there mentally retarded talented students?

☐ How are giftedness, creativity, and talent different? To what extent do they overlap?

☐ Why was psychomotor ability (including dancing and athletic ability) removed by the U.S. Congress from the federal definition of gifted and talented? Do you support their point of view?

☐ How does "gifted as evidenced by process" differ from "gifted as evidenced by product"?

☐ Under what conditions might you support the establishment of separate special schools for gifted or talented students?

12

The gifted and talented have sometimes been referred to as "the other end of the continuum" of special education. However, this characterization is accurate only as applied to a contrast between the intellectual ability of the gifted as compared to that of the mentally retarded. In fact, there may be gifted blind children, gifted behaviorally disordered children, and so on. Gifted youth and adults are recognized as their giftedness becomes apparent in their productivity, but it is altogether possible that many gifted children are never recognized if their giftedness (and thus "difference" from normal behavior, performance, etc.) leads to teacher criticism or comments they perceive as negative.

Special provision for modified, adapted, or enriched programs for gifted/talented students is made in many school districts, but in others it is almost totally ignored. Since many of these students do better than non-gifted students on the various standardized achievement tests without any special recognition or specialized programming, some educators seem content to ignore their presence. Though there has been some federal recognition of their special needs and their potential as contributors to the nation, that recognition has been backed up by very minimal federal funding; thus the gifted have not received the attention that has come to the handicapped.

Education of gifted students is considered last in this text not because it is less important than, but because it is relatively "different" from, education of the handicapped. It is different in many ways, including the following: (1) It is not really mandated in any state. (A few states have legislation or regulations that might seem, at first reading, to mandate some sort of provision; but in fact, it is often only lip service unless local districts really *want* to provide meaningful, comprehensive service.) (2) There are no significant federal dollars to encourage programs and services. (3) There is no significant litigation dictating special programs for the gifted or talented. (4) Though there are organized parent groups, they do not have the political-advocacy clout, on a national basis, of parent groups organized on behalf of the handicapped. (5) It is difficult to build broad public concern for "poor little gifted children." (6) Though there are a number of talented professional leadership persons working in the area of education of the gifted, there has been some confusion as to whether their efforts should be considered a part of special education or whether it should be some entirely separate entity. This factor, with others, has resulted in a situation in which there has not been the concerted professional power and influence that might have been possible if their role and affiliation had been more clearly defined. (7) The absence of obvious, appropriate special programming does not automatically lead to the kinds of problems that result from the absence of appropriate programs for the handicapped.

Education of the gifted is, in our opinion, critically important. Gifted students are "exceptional," and they deserve special, exceptional educational opportunities every bit as much as exceptional students with handicapping conditions. Ignoring the special needs of students with handicapping conditions may lead to a variety of problems, both personal and societal. Ignoring the special needs of gifted students may lead to problems just as significant, and in fact, may lead to even more severe problems in terms of national leadership, perhaps even national survival. The regular classroom teacher can play a highly important role in assuring the development of more adequate, appropriate programs for the gifted as he or she understands more about the nature of giftedness and the various ways in which teachers may more effectively meet these needs.

PROBLEMS IN DEFINING GIFTEDNESS

We have considered the problems posed by the vagueness and subjectivity of definitions of learning disabilities and behavior disorders. There are similar problems with many definitions of giftedness; however, some states use definitions that may be followed easily but may likely leave out many gifted or potentially gifted students who are culturally different, are from low socioeconomic backgrounds, or are underachievers. Because there is no one definition of giftedness in use in the nation, we will consider several categories of definitions.

IQ-based definitions are relatively popular, because they provide a definite cut-off point for determination of giftedness. Students who score at or above some established point are gifted; those who score below are not. These definitions ignore such things as artistic or creative gifts (unless the student also has a high IQ) and of course tend to discriminate against the poor, those who are culturally different, or those who underachieve for any reason.

Percentage definitions, like IQ-based definitions, may be preferred by some because, on the surface, they provide a definite line of demarcation between the gifted and the nongifted. Percentage-based definitions must be based on some factor or factors, which may be overall academic achievement, intelligence test scores, or scores in one or two academic areas (for example, mathematics or the sciences). The percentage of students considered gifted may vary from 1% to 5% or 10% according to local or state belief. Though percentage-based definitions would seem to be relatively simple to administer, once the scores on which they are based and the percentage considered to be gifted are established, problems may arise. In one school district where it was decided that the top 5%,

based on composite achievement test scores, would be included in programs for the gifted, a considerable controversy quickly developed. When the percentage figure was applied systemwide, some schools (in more affluent areas of the city) had as many as 11% or 12% of their total student population eligible, while others (in low socioeconomic neighborhoods) had less than 1%. So the criteria were interpreted to mean the top 5% of each school. Using this interpretation, there were many students from lower socioeconomic area schools included in the program who had much lower achievement scores and IQs than other students in the school district who were not considered "gifted," according to these guidelines. What had appeared simple and objective when the board of education authorized the program became a public relations nightmare.

Talent-based definitions are those based on demonstrated talent in one or more areas. This might mean talent in music, art, dance, or—in a few cases—unusual talent in science or mathematics. Though this differentiation is not universally accepted, *talented* more often means demonstrated talent for the age of the student under consideration, in one or just a few areas. *Gifted* more often means intellectually gifted. An increasing number of school programs seem to be using *gifted and talented* or *gifted/talented* to describe their programs, thus indicating that both are recognized as important. Talent-based definitions can use achievement test scores if the talent under consideration is in mathematics or science. They must use some type of expert-opinion procedure if the talent under consideration is in an area such as music, dance, or art.

Creativity-based definitions involve attempts to use measures of creativity that, in and of themselves, are subject to much debate. More will be said about creativity later in this chapter.

Finally, we might divide our consideration of definitions of giftedness into two general categories: (1) *after-the-fact*, or *established* giftedness or talent, and (2) indications of *potential* giftedness or talent. Albert Einstein, Michelangelo, or Shakespeare would be internationally recognized as gifted/talented. A 16- or 17-year-old who wins, or even is a runner-up, at Wimbledon would be considered talented. These are established cases of giftedness or talent, but seldom is the matter so clear-cut in the schools. For the most part, school programs must be based on some indication of potential giftedness or talent. And that is the crux of the problem. The questions to be considered include: "To what extent does an IQ of 150 indicate potential intellectual giftedness?" and this might be followed by, "What about an IQ of 135?" In a similar vein, "Is the first violinist in the Children's Symphony Orchestra of New York (age 14) talented?" followed by "What about the fifteen-year-old violinist who barely made the orchestra?"

Giftedness and/or talent, then, is in the eye of the beholder (or of the developer of regulations for any given state or school district). Definitions vary and programs are established to meet the objectives of the accepted definition in any given area. There are, however, at least two definitions that deserve particular attention. One is the definition provided by Marland (1972) and revised very slightly by later congressional action. This is the nearest we may come to a national definition. The other is a definition provided by Renzulli, Reis, and Smith (1981) and Renzulli and Smith (1980) in a discussion of identification of the gifted. These two may be the most-quoted definitions of gifted/talented.

TWO RECOGNIZED DEFINITIONS OF GIFTEDNESS

Marland, as U.S. Commissioner of Education in 1972, provided the following definition of *giftedness*:

Gifted and talented children are those identified by professionally qualified persons who by virtue of outstanding abilities are capable of high performance. These are children who require differentiated educational programs and services beyond those normally provided by the regular school program in order to realize their contribution to self and society.

Children capable of high performance include those with demonstrated achievement and/or potential ability in any of the following areas:

1. General intellectual ability
2. Specific academic aptitude
3. Creative or productive thinking
4. Leadership ability
5. Visual and performing arts
6. Psychomotor ability. (1972, p. 2)

The sixth area, psychomotor ability, was removed by later congressional action (both in PL 93-380 and PL 95-561), with the following rationale: First, artistic psychomotor talents, such as dancing, are included in Area 5, the performing arts. Second, athletic programs for students who have talents in football, baseball, tumbling, and so on are already well served through special programs that have been in existence for years. The purpose of the federal definition was to encourage new programs for students who had not been recognized and served, and it was felt that competitive athletics did not require such encouragement.

The federal definition includes most of the essential elements of a definition of the *gifted/talented*. It specifically mentions "potential ability," thus indicating that the concept is not limited to those who already show such abilities. It recognizes high-level general intellectual ability and specific aptitude in one or more academic areas and it calls attention to creative ability. It also specifically lists leadership ability, and abilities in the visual and performing arts. The definition emphasizes the need for differentiated programs and points out that gifted students may later be able to make significant contributions to society.

Renzulli and Smith (1980) and Renzulli et al. (1981) have provided another definition that takes into account certain factors ignored by the Marland-originated definition. Their belief is that the five categories in the final federal definition are not independent but often overlap to a considerable extent. Further, they believe that there should be a greater emphasis on motivation or task commitment in any definition of giftedness.

Renzulli and Smith (1980) suggest three basic generalizations that can be used to develop what they consider to be an operational definition of giftedness. First, there are three traits common to all truly gifted individuals: (1) above-average general intellectual ability, (2) task commitment, and (3) creativity. From their point of view, based on extensive review of studies of gifted individuals, no *single* trait should be used to identify an individual as gifted. Instead, the *interaction* of these three traits leads to what is now generally recognized as giftedness. The second generalization is that the definition of giftedness should apply to all socially useful performance areas. Giftedness is identifiable only as we find an interaction of ability, task commitment, and creativity and may be found within a wide variety of performance areas. The third generalization is that there is

There is some debate regarding the inclusion of athletic abilities within the classification of gifted/talented.

great need to develop means or measures for assessing a broad range of abilities or potential abilities other than general intellectual ability. Most authors who undertake a discussion of the definition of gifted/talented include this interaction-of-traits definition.

In a summary of a national survey of identification practices in gifted and talented education, Alvino, McDonnel, and Richert (1981) report that although five federal categories of the gifted and talented were recognized (general intellectual, specific academic, creativity, arts, and leadership), there was confusion among these categories, including the regular confusion of "academic" and "general intellectual," with tests being used interchangeably for these two areas. In conclusion Alvino et al. note that

1. identification procedures and practices are in some disarray
2. tests are commonly used in inappropriate ways
3. confusion and/or ignorance of the differences between types of giftedness and/or talent is shown
4. there is a serious lack of formal, validated measures for use with any of the gifted/ talented categories other than intellectual and academic
5. in many respects, the decade since the appearance of the Marland report (1972) has not seen significant progress in correcting the problems of identification cited in that report

This report concluded that intelligence tests were the most frequently cited means used for identification of gifted and talented students.

There is little evidence that practices have changed significantly since that time, and Davis and Rimm (1985), in a summary of identification methods, indicate that "virtually every G/T program is interested in intellectual giftedness" (p. 70). This does not necessarily mean that scores on intelligence tests are used as the sole measure, but if the major interest is in intellectual giftedness, intelligence test scores will tend to receive priority in identification.

Given the fact that high-level intellectual functioning is a major component in the definition of giftedness, and that an individual test of intelligence may be required before a student can participate in a program for gifted students, the fact remains that good teachers will naturally wish to ask questions about the characteristics of gifted students, other than above-average intelligence: "What do gifted students do?" "How do they act?" "How do I know that I should refer a student for possible inclusion in a program for the gifted?" The following section on characteristics of gifted students should help answer such questions.

CHARACTERISTICS OF GIFTED STUDENTS

Characteristics, in reference to exceptional students, means distinguishing traits, qualities, or features. Therefore, when we consider the characteristics of gifted students, we automatically turn to the traits, features, or qualities of students who have already been identified as gifted. The process is really quite circular. Some authors separate characteristics into categories, for instance, intellectual and affective. However, as noted by Davis and Rimm, "the overriding trait— indeed, *the* definition—of very bright students is that they are developmentally advanced in language and thought" (1985, p. 21). Unless we are emphasizing talent (as in music or art), all characteristics are then outgrowths of the concept of a student who is advanced in language and thought. In a given school district or state, the emphasis may be placed on high-level ability in mathematics, the physical sciences, or some such academic area; but in the final analysis gifted students are those doing much better, accomplishing much more, than would normally be expected from students of their age.

The list of characteristics that follows is a composite of lists provided by many authors. Certain characteristics appear in almost every list, sometimes in the same order and the same terminology, and the list here simply provides often mentioned characteristics without comment on their relative merit. This list of common characteristics of gifted, talented, and/or creative students is un-ranked, and in all cases these characteristics are considered relative to what is normal for the student's age.

academically superior
applies systems approaches (often self-devised) to problems
applies abstract principles to concrete situations
careless in handwriting and similar routine tasks
courteous
deliberately underachieves under certain conditions
difficulty conversing with age mates
emotionally stable
extraordinarily verbal
generally curious
gives uncommon responses
has a high energy level, especially in mental and intellectual tasks
has a high vocabulary level
imaginative
intellectually curious
intellectually superior
inquisitive
superior in logical ability
makes individualistic interpretations of new subject matter
obnoxious or rebellious when asked to do repetitive tasks
original (in verbal responses, problem solving, etc.)

outspokenly critical of themselves and others
perceives and indentifies significant factors in complex situations
persistent in achieving goals
has good physical ability
takes pleasure in intellectual pursuits
takes pleasure in pursuing unusually difficult mental tasks
has good power of concentration
recognizes and is uncomfortable with unresolved ambiguity
rebels against conformity
scientifically oriented
seeks older companions
has sense of humor
sensitive to problems of others
skips steps in normal (expected) thinking sequence
socially aware
has strong sense of responsibility
superior in ability to remember details
superior in ability to see relationships
unhappy with most group-participation projects (with normal peers)
unaccepting of routine classroom rules
shows unusual demonstrated talent (in any area)
has an unusually good memory
verbally facile
verbally flexible

Although some characteristics here seem to contradict others, most such contradictions can be explained by (1) the varying definitions and conceptualizations of giftedness, (2) the wide range of possible reactions of different individuals to the same situation (e.g., a given classroom atmosphere), and (3) the effect of radically differing environmental backgrounds of the students in our schools.

Lists of characteristics may be used to assist teachers to nominate students for inclusion in a program for the gifted or to determine which students require modified and/or additional opportunities in the regular classroom when no special programming is available. However, as noted earlier, the basic criterion in many programs for the gifted is above-average intelligence. It is therefore appropriate briefly to discuss the nature of intelligence and how it is measured. Intelligence is a complex matter, but a full understanding of its nature is important in identifying and successfully teaching gifted children and youth.

A major problem in understanding and measuring intelligence is that it has many dimensions. Intelligence is somewhat analogous to physical size; if we ask how big someone is, do we mean how heavy or how tall, or the size of hands, waist, or shoulders, or whether the individual is larger or smaller in some respect than another, or perhaps how the individual compares with norms for his or her age? The possible meanings of this simple question are almost endless, but in comparison the issue of intelligence has many, many more facets. In addition, the measures of various aspects of intelligence are less specific than physical measurements. When we refer to intelligence, we are referring to many factors that we must try to measure in some way, most likely lumped together and referred to as *IQ*. In some ways, this indiscriminate process makes no more sense than reducing a large range of physical characteristics to a single statement of size. Nonetheless, we speak of intelligence in everyday activities, and we think we can recognize those who have greater or lesser degrees of intelligence. Therefore, let us assume that there is some logic to this concept and proceed to examine some of the ways in which intelligence is measured by accepted tests of intelligence.

The Wechsler Intelligence Scale for Children–Revised (WISC–R)

The following description of the *Wechsler Intelligence Scale for Children–Revised* (WISC–R) illustrates one way intelligence is

measured. This is one of the most highly respected individual tests of intelligence and is used for children aged 6 through 16. No one of the 12 subtests alone is accepted as a measure of general intellectual ability, but the composite is considered to reflect overall general intelligence. Therefore, because these subtests are the parts that make up the whole measure, they provide one valuable way to understand the nature of intelligence as we presently view it. In all instances, scores on these measures are compared to age norms for purposes of determining an individual's IQ.

Of the WISC–R's 12 subtests, 6 are part of a Verbal Scale, and 6 are part of a Performance Scale. Normally only five subtests of each part are given, the sixth subtest being provided as an alternate test to substitute if needed for any other subtest in the same scale. Although we will not consider the specifics of test administration, we should note that provisions are made for children who cannot relate readily to the testing situation, that alternate subtests and procedures are provided for children who simply cannot respond to a given subtest, and that in general the individual administration of this test provides for meaningful testing of most children. The following descriptions of the kinds of tasks involved in each of the 12 subtests of the WISC–R are provided to indicate part of what is being tested in a typical individual test of intelligence.

Verbal-Scale Subtests. The *Information Subtest* is essentially a general information test. The child must answer a wide variety of questions of varying difficulty about information that should have been learned through general life experience. The Information Subtest also includes a number of questions closely related to educational experience.

The *Similarities Subtest* measures how well the child can explain the manner in which paired items in varying degrees of difficulty are similar. Success on the Similarities Subtest is believed to reflect knowledge of common elements and may also indicate the individual's level of logical thinking.

The *Arithmetic Subtest* includes a series of practical arithmetic problems. It is designed to avoid dependence on verbal ability and reading skills, but certainly the quality of the individual's school experience in arithmetic may affect his performance.

The *Vocabulary Subtest* includes a master list of words arranged in order of increasing difficulty. With all children this test reflects to some degree the range of language experience and vocabulary usage in the home. It also reflects school experiences, especially with those who have been in school several years.

The *Comprehension Subtest* measures what most would call common sense. Success on this subtest depends on the possession of practical information and an ability to evaluate and apply what has been learned from past experiences.

The *Digit Span Subtest* involves the ability to repeat a series of digits after hearing them only once. The test includes both forward and backward repetition. It is primarily a test of short-term auditory memory but may also reflect attention and concentration.

Performance-Scale Subtests. The *Picture Completion Subtest* requires the student to indicate the missing parts of pictures. Its purpose is to measure the individual's ability to differentiate the essential from the nonessential. To a limited degree it is also a test of visual memory.

The *Picture Arrangement Subtest* requires the child to arrange a series of cartoonlike panels into a sequence that tells a story. Success on the Picture Arrangement Subtest requires the ability to interpret social situations and to comprehend and size up a total situation in relation to its parts.

The *Block Design Subtest* involves the arrangement of sets of red and white blocks to match pictures of designs shown by the examiner. The perception and analysis of forms required in this subtest is thought to reflect ability to analyze and synthesize information.

The *Object Assembly Subtest* requires the assembly of puzzle pieces to complete pictures of commonly known objects. In addition to providing information about visual and motor functions, this test permits the examiner to observe the child's general task approach and reaction to mistakes.

The *Coding Subtest* involves matching numbers and symbols through a code that the individual may keep immediately available for reference. Coding scores are based on speed and accuracy, and motor speed probably is more important than motor coordination.

The *Mazes Subtest* involves tracing a maze on paper. It requires both the ability to follow a visual pattern and general planning capability.

This brief description of the twelve subtests of the WISC–R provides a composite picture of the types of abilities presumed to indicate general intelligence. To the extent that any given student is above average for his age in these tasks, he is considered to be above average in intelligence or possibly intellectually gifted. How *much* above average he must be to be considered gifted depends on state regulations, but regardless of these regulations, students who are to any great extent above their classmates in ability to complete these tasks need special consideration in educational programming to receive maximum benefit from their experiences at school.

As an alternate similar frame of reference for considering whether a student may be intellectually gifted, we suggest in the following section three general types of abilities that most gifted students seem to possess to an above-average degree. This is our own yardstick, but it is consistent with the published beliefs of many learning theorists and to that extent is not wholly original. Teachers are not trained or qualified to administer tests such as the WISC–R but often can measure these three types of abilities.

Areas of Performance Suggesting Above-Average Intelligence

Students *may be* above average in intelligence if they are *significantly above average* in at least two of the following three areas:

1. *Verbal fluency*—includes reading comprehension, verbal reasoning ability, ability to effectively use a broad vocabulary in self-expression, and similar abilities.
2. *Understanding of and ability to manipulate numbers*—includes simple arithmetic computation, ability to quickly apply decimals, percentages, fractions, and so on and to translate from one to the other, ability to estimate answers to number problems and thus to immediately see obvious errors or erroneous number-related conclusions, and ability to apply number concepts in a wide variety of situations.
3. *General reasoning ability*—includes so-called logical thinking, the ability to use inductive or deductive reasoning to arrive at conclusions. This ability might also include the ability to *conceptualize* (classifying, categorizing, generalizing); however, some learning experts view conceptualization as a separate major ability in which general reasoning ability and verbal fluency are combined.

In addition, abilities such as *spatial ability* (ability to perceive spatial or geometric relationships and ability to visualize spatial manipulations or transformations) and overall *perceptual ability and speed* (especially with visual perception) are recognized by a number of authorities as being highly corre-

lated with intellectual ability, but because of their specialized nature, these abilities might be viewed as having secondary importance.

Creativity: What Is It and How Can We Promote It?

Clark (1983) views creativity as the "highest expression of giftedness" (p. 30). She believes that "the most unexplainable part of creativity lies in the fact that, even though few agree on a definition, when we say the word, everyone senses a similar feeling. We may not be able to explain what it is rationally, but we know it just the same. When we are being creative, we are aware of its special excitement" (1983, p. 30). The concept of intelligence and the ability to measure it are much clearer and more precise than the concept of creativity. Torrance (1974), who developed one of the leading measures of creativity (Tests of Creative Thinking), has noted that creativity can be defined in terms of *product* (invention and discovery), *process*, or *characteristics* of the individual who is considered to be creative. His concept of creativity includes many elements that others would ascribe to intelligence but also includes the idea of sensitivity to deficiencies, gaps in knowledge, disharmonies, and the like. A more traditional concept of creativity relates creativity to bringing something new into existence, literally creating something new. This concept recognizes that the individual works with given physical or mental materials but with creativity reshapes or re-generates these materials into something new. Common-use definitions relate creativity to inventiveness and seem to view creativity primarily as the making of a product. Most agree that creativity, like intelligence, is a good thing, but the general population has widely varying concepts of creativity.

If the concept of creativity is limited to creativity resulting in a *product*, there is a fair degree of agreement that the invention of such things as the electric light bulb, the telephone, and the zipper reflects creativity. But could we have predicted that the child who would later become such a creative inventor was creative while still a child? How can we encourage such potential creativity in young children? The answers are not clear-cut, but there are possible indicators of creativity and ways to encourage creativity if in fact the potential is present.

A potentially creative individual might have any of the following characteristics:

1. unusual curiosity
2. unusual persistence
3. unusual imagination
4. originality

A fifth characteristic is sometimes included with these four: restlessness or inattentiveness. This may not be seen until after the child's entrance into school and is usually the result of the teacher requiring meaningless, repetitive tasks that are not challenging to the creative student.

Almost all children show some degree of curiosity, persistence, and imagination. The potentially creative, however, have an unusually high degree of these characteristics compared to age peers. Originality may be the distinguishing characteristic. If we are not alert to the need to watch for originality, we may overlook it, probably because originality in children generally does not produce products with a quality as obvious as with the light bulb, the telephone, and the zipper. Originality in children is related to their age and experience and involves something that would not be expected from an individual of that age or level of experience. For example, a very young child might use a self-constructed lever arrangement to lift something when the child has had no specific experience that would lead to understanding the lever and has not observed someone using a lever. Of course, many people use levers, but most have seen someone else do so or have had a sequence of experiences that led to

understanding the mechanical properties of the lever. Whatever it may be that the child might demonstrate, the question of originality is a matter of whether it is usual or normal for a student of that age and experience to demonstrate that ability, understanding, or insight.

The efforts of J. P. Guilford deserve special mention in any discussion of creativity. In fact, Guilford deserves equal mention for his efforts related to understanding general intelligence, giftedness, and creativity. He developed a three-dimensional conceptual model called the "structure of intellect" with which he predicted the existence of at least 120 distinct types of intellectual ability (Guilford, 1959). This model, which played a major role in triggering debate and research related to "convergent" and "divergent" thinking, has undoubtedly been reproduced in textbooks, dissertations, and scholarly articles more often than any other conceptual model in the history of the study of intelligence. His consideration of divergent thinking, now usually related to creativity, has led to continuing speculation about the true nature of creativity, but unanswered questions still exceed those that have been definitively answered. Guilford's continued personal research and the research of others relating to his concept of the structure of intellect have been essential in the development of interest in the field of creativity.

Getzels and Jackson played a special role in the early development of interest in the existence and measurement of creativity and its relationship to IQ. Getzels and Jackson (1962) compared students with a high IQ (average 150) and low creativity to students with high creativity and IQs averaging 23 points lower. They measured creativity in relation to evidence of divergent (as opposed to convergent) thinking. The academic achievement of these two groups was essentially the same, suggesting that high creativity (divergent thinking) might be as essential as high IQ for school achievement. Other researchers have obtained similar results, but not ail replicative studies have verified their work. There is question today as to whether Getzels and Jackson's results truly mean what Getzels and Jackson argued they meant, but their efforts have been of significant value in promoting additional research involving this elusive quality called creativity. The overlap between giftedness and creativity is generally recognized, but the degree of overlap and the practical importance of differences between students who are creative but not particularly gifted and those who are gifted but not particularly creative remain to be further investigated.

Facilitating the development of creativity is the teacher's responsibility and requires both an accurate general concept of the nature of creativity and some specific ideas and skills. Table 12–1 provides a brief sample of factors and conditions that may facilitate or inhibit creativity. It is probably wise for the teacher who wants to encourage creativity to think in terms of both "what should I do" and "what I should avoid doing," since many schools are organized in such a manner as to encourage the teacher to follow practices that may inhibit creativity. Though there may be disagreement as to how to define *creativity*,

most teachers would undoubtedly indicate an interest in promoting it. With conscious effort to look for creativity and continuing attention to the behavior of individual students, the regular classroom teacher can become a facilitator, rather than an inhibitor, of creative efforts in the classroom.

ECONOMICALLY DISADVANTAGED AND CULTURALLY DIFFERENT GIFTED STUDENTS

Programs may bypass many gifted students through failing to identify them. Depending on which definition of *gifted* we use, these students might more accurately be called *potentially gifted;* but regardless of whether they are called *underachieving gifted, potentially gifted, hard-to-identify gifted,* or some other such label, they should be identified and provided appropriate "services beyond those normally provided by the regular school program" so that they may be able to "realize their contribution to self and society," as recommended in the Marland report (1972, p. 2). The U.S. government has launched many efforts over the past 30 years both to fight poverty and to promote more equitable educational and economic oppor-

TABLE 12–1. Factors/conditions that may facilitate or inhibit creativity

Facilitating	Inhibiting
spontaneous participation and expression	requiring unquestioning obedience to authority
encouragement of many questions; permit divergency from "plan"	no deviation from preestablished lesson plan
unevaluated practice and experimentation	evaluation of all student work, a grade for everything
encouragement of imagination, make-believe, fictional discussion, and writing	discussion only of real, practical ideas
encouragement of problem-solving at all age levels	emphasis on memorizing "correct answers"
a teacher who is open to new ideas and has a strong self-concept, relatively independent of student comment and behaviors	a teacher who "knows he is right" and feels a need for students to recognize this "rightness" regularly

tunities for the culturally different. These programs, in total, have cost hundreds of millions, perhaps billions, of dollars. Such programs have been evaluated by a variety of individuals, and a common conclusion is that these groups need leadership provided by dedicated, motivated individuals from within the group. Such reports do not usually use the term *gifted,* but the inference is clearly there. Society in general needs the leadership of gifted, talented, creative persons, and subgroups such as the culturally different may have even more need.

The various problems related to providing appropriate programs for the economically disadvantaged and culturally different gifted are complex and will require differing solutions in various parts of the nation, and with various subgroups. For example, for the gifted for whom English is a second language, adjustments in identification will be somewhat different than for those for whom English is the first and only language. Programs in which inclusion is based primarily on academic achievement tests will require different provisions from those using multiple criteria. There is no single answer and there are no simple answers, but the first step is widened awareness of the problem. The second step is to accept the principle of flexibility in determining which students should be provided the opportunities available in programs for the gifted.

One way to provide some flexibility and to avoid some of the limitations imposed by percentage figures in state guidelines is the use of a system similar to that advocated by Reis and Renzulli (1982) and Delisle, Reis, and Gubbins (1981). This system is called the "Revolving Door Identification and Programming Model." The model is based on the premise that "a relatively large proportion of persons manifest gifted behaviors at certain times, in certain areas of study, and under certain circumstances" (Delisle, Reis, & Gubbins, 1981, p. 152) and involves selecting a

large (15%–25%) "talent poo level and then providing regularly scheduled enric "designed to capitalize on their ex terests" (Reis & Renzulli, 1982, p. 61✗). Research in Connecticut led to the conclusion that with this approach, those students who scored in the top 5% on standardized tests of intelligence or achievement did no better (in terms of raters' assessment of various abilities) than those who were above average but below this top 5% group.

Until a more precise definition of *giftedness* is developed that permits more accurate identification, the best answer is the use of multiple criteria, along with careful attention to unmotivated students and some administrative arrangement similar to the revolving-door model. While we need to provide for those students who are more readily identifiable as gifted, we also must remain alert to discover gifted or potentially gifted students not presently motivated by the formal educational process and traditional cognitive learning.

Cummins (1984) suggests that in assessment designed to identify gifted students among those of bilingual populations, knowledge of the child's cultural background is a prerequisite for valid interpretation of either observational or test data. He further suggests that until the schools are organized in such a manner that the reward system recognizes culturally specific talents, nondiscriminatory assessment is difficult at best. (In other words, abilities and talents valued in a specific subculture may provide the best basis for determining which students are gifted/talented.) If those completing assessments of bilingual and/or culturally different students are not fully aware of what *giftedness* means in another subculture, teacher observations may be essentially useless in many cases.

Davis and Rimm (1985) believe that "because of cultural bias in test instruments and other identification methods, many typical procedures actually obscure students' giftedness by "proving" these children are *not* gifted" (p. 259). It is of utmost importance that identification be based on potential, rather than present superior performance. Cummins outlines three requirements that must be met if observational procedures are to be used effectively in the identification of gifted/talented minority students. He believes that teachers or psychometricians must

1. have access to the child's linguistic and cultural world outside the school;
2. be knowledgeable about research findings on bilingualism and second language learning;
3. ensure that curricular and extra-curricular activities encourage the display and development of a diverse range of talents. (Cummins, 1984, p. 219)

According to Clark, "our educational system often penalizes children who are raised with significantly different values and attitudes from those found in the dominant culture. Subcultures can create conditions for their members that can be as limiting as those discussed for the disadvantaged" (1983, p. 338). She further notes that "unfavorable socialization experiences, unequal school opportunities, and obvious occupational discrimination all work together to lower the motivation and achievement of black children, especially boys, no matter how gifted they are" (p. 338). Clark provides a chart of "facilitating culturally supported attitudes and abilities" children of subcultures or ethnic groups may bring to the learning situation that may be of interest to those who wish to research this topic further (Clark, 1983, pp. 339–40 and accompanying references).

Actual programs for gifted/talented minority students must often be different from those provided for other gifted/talented students, and the variations and modifications must be specifically tailored for the students under consideration. Our emphasis in this discussion has been on the nature of the problem and especially on the role of the teacher in identification. We believe that this is the place to start, because even if potentially valuable programs are available, if we do not first find those students who should be a part of such programs, the programs are of very limited value. Sensitivity to the problem and a sincere desire to find such students are the responsibility of the regular classroom teacher. We hope this brief consideration will help build such sensitivity and interest.

ORGANIZING SCHOOLS TO TEACH THE GIFTED, TALENTED, AND CREATIVE

The most important factors in establishing and maintaining a good local program for gifted students are (1) appropriate, broad-range identification procedures that identify both the gifted who are presently performing as gifted and the potentially gifted who may not be showing their potential because of various reasons, (2) regular classroom teachers who understand the needs of the gifted sufficiently well to play their essential role, (3) specially trained teachers who are effective with gifted students and who can through cooperative efforts elicit the proper assistance from regular classroom teachers, and (4) administrative interest and support leading to the provision of time, space, materials, and encouragement for the teaching staff to provide a wide variety of appropriate learning opportunities and experiences for gifted students. The regular classroom and specialized teachers are the most important components of this process, but for teachers to provide appropriate learning opportunities and experiences, certain administrative and organizational provisions must be made. The three major administrative and organizational forms are ability grouping, acceleration, and enrichment, discussed in the following sections.

Ability Grouping

Clark (1983) suggests a continuum of ability groupings including the following approaches.

Regular Classroom with Cluster. Although gifted students may be clustered with other bright students, Clark (1983) thinks that this setting is usually inadequate for gifted students because of the set curriculum and group instruction often used, giving similar experiences for everyone.

Regular Classroom with Pullout. Enrollment in the regular class with pullout is better than clustering, since students can experience unique learning opportunities along with other gifted students and can work at their own ability level in their own areas of interest. However, much of the school week may still be inappropriate for the gifted, and too often gifted students may still be required to do all the regular work that they miss when out of their homeroom. To be effective, this provision requires understanding and flexibility from the regular classroom teacher and a good working relationship between teachers.

Individualized Classrooms. In individualized classrooms *all* students are involved in individual, team, and flexible, small-group instruction. In such a setting gifted students can work at their own pace, permitting continuous learning. The potential disadvantage of such a program is that the teacher may not have sufficient resources for 25–30 students and, if not unusually well organized, the class may disintegrate into unstructured chaos. Also, if there are not at least three or four gifted students, there is no opportunity for the gifted student to gain from interaction with peers of the same ability level.

Special Class with Some Integrated Classes. The special class approach with some integrated classes is particularly applicable at grade levels at which the school is organized by subject. Some of the gifted student's classes are with specially trained teachers and other gifted students, and others are regular classes. This approach might also include, at the secondary level, arranging for the student to attend some classes at a local college or university. Another variation is the use of a highly individualized approach in which the student chooses a teacher or advisor who directs independent studies.

This model has much potential because of all its possible variations, but if school officials adopt this model and try to get by with establishing only two or three special class sections and consider them the entire gifted program, the gifted students are cheated. Equally unfortunate is the establishment of such a program and assignment of a teacher who is not well prepared or particularly interested.

Special Class. In this approach gifted students are in a separate special class and have little or no involvement with other students. This may be the most appropriate approach for the *highly* gifted.

Special Schools. The special schools approach takes the special class concept one step further. It is more often used in larger cities with extremely gifted students or students with very special talents (e.g., music, dance, science areas, etc.).

Acceleration

Acceleration is any process that leads to the student's more rapid movement through the regular program of the public schools. It may include early school entrance, grade skipping, planned completion of the three primary grades in two years, early or advanced placement in college, or any other arrangement that leads to a student's completion of the regular school program in less than the normally required time. Gallagher (1975, p. 305) notes that "studies of acceleration and its effects on gifted children are invariably positive, but the concept itself is not well institutionalized or accepted." Clark (1979, p. 44) believes that acceleration should not become the total plan for gifted students but states that "the literature shows very few disadvantages to this provision when used on an individual basis." She further notes that because learning at a faster rate than normal is one of the most commonly found characteristics of gifted students, some provision for acceleration should be available in any program for the gifted.

Enrichment

Enrichment (usually meaning the provision of enriched program components or content within the regular classroom setting) is a part of almost all programs for the gifted. Clark (1983, p. 154) defines enrichment as "the addition of disciplines or areas of learning not normally found in the regular curriculum" and Khatena (1982, p. 257) notes that "acceleration can be thought of in terms of hor-

izontal and vertical enrichment, although, more frequently, it is considered as resulting from enrichment." Enrichment, in its broader sense, means what is provided in the ability grouping and acceleration models. But in popular usage *enrichment* almost always means what the regular classroom teacher provides through a differentiated curriculum within the regular class. Most authorities would agree that for this type of enrichment program to be effective, there must be—at the very least—a supply of special, additional materials, and real (not token) consultative assistance from a specialist in the field of education of the gifted. True enrichment is what programming for the gifted is all about, but claiming to have a program of "enrichment" for gifted/talented students has been a popular way for school districts to avoid providing any significant funds or attention to the needs of the gifted and silencing at least some of the school's critics.

Kirk and Gallagher (1986) believe that "we

Students who are gifted often perform at above-average expectation levels.

can modify the school program for any group of exceptional (gifted) children in three major dimensions: learning environment, skills, and content" (p. 94). Gallagher's concept of "learning environment" is essentially parallel to what Clark calls "organizational patterns" and is reflected in a study published by the National/State Leadership Training Institute (Gallagher, Weiss, Oglesby, & Thomas, 1983). This study provided information regarding the relative popularity of seven methods of changing the learning environment: (1) enrichment classroom, (2) consultant teacher, (3) resource room–pullout, (4) community mentor, (5) independent study, (6) special class, and (7) special schools. This study solicited opinions from teachers, administrators, and parents, and there was substantial agreement among these three groups. The most popular strategy at the elementary school level was the resource room–pullout. At the secondary level, the most popular choice was the special class. (The resource room–pullout was apparently less popular in secondary schools because it didn't fit the secondary school class/subject-area system.) The Gallagher, et al. study did *not* purport to determine which strategy was most effective, only what was most popular. Whatever administrative or organizational option is used, it is important to note that the nature of materials presented and how they are presented remain of critical importance. If only the setting—the environment—is changed, the program is likely to be of minimal value. Which of the administrative structures is best for a given program depends on many factors and varies from location to location. These factors include, among others, the population of the community, the school's location with respect to other schools, the availability of nearby "nonschool" specialized facilities and personnel, the existence of nearby colleges or universities, the school district's funding structure, community biases, and state regulations.

SUGGESTIONS FOR THE REGULAR CLASSROOM TEACHER

As noted at the start of this chapter, education of the gifted/talented is different from education of the handicapped in many dimensions. This is very readily seen in the attempt to teach handicapped students in the most *normal* way possible. Teachers must modify teaching methods to meet individual needs, but if at all practical, students with handicapping conditions should be educated along with nonhandicapped students, using similar methods and techniques. The effort is directed toward making their environment as "normal" as possible.

Gifted/talented students should be educated along with nongifted students, using similar methods and techniques, as long as this achieves the desired results. But if our aim is to stretch and expand the horizons of the gifted and to promote the development of their unusual abilities, teachers should encourage any unusual learning traits, styles, and abilities. With many students with handicapping conditions, teachers may appropriately feel more successful as the student moves toward more normal learning behaviors and normal levels of knowledge and comprehension. With gifted/talented students, when the student becomes *even more different* from her age peers (more advanced, more capable) with respect to, for example, analysis and synthesis skills, then success has been achieved.

There are, however, areas in which our goals for some gifted/talented students would be normal development; for example, that of social skills and competence in interpersonal relationships. But in the targeted areas of giftedness or talent, the goal is to provide opportunities for maximum development, and if educators are effective in achieving this goal, the student is likely to appear "more different" rather than "more normal." It is, however, important to note that programs for the gifted should not be made to look different just for the sake of looking different. They must be *qualitatively different,* they should be much more than a bag of educational tricks.

One of the more comprehensive brief guides to an appropriately designed program for the gifted was provided by Clark (1983). These eight guidelines, organized in a "should-do," "should-not-do" format follow:

The Shoulds and Should-nots of an Appropriately Designed Differentiated Curriculum

1. The curriculum *should* be planned and sequentially organized to include specific expectations for the acquisition of subject matter, mastery of skills, creation of products, and development of attitudes and appreciations related to self, others, and the environment.

   The curriculum *should not* be a potpourri of learning activities that are disjointed and haphazardly selected without reference to specified criteria.

2. The curriculum *should* place emphasis on the interdependence of subject matter, skills, products, and self-understanding within the *same* curricular structure.

   The curriculum *should not* focus on the attainment of cognitive competencies in isolation from the development of affective competencies. Nor should the curriculum focus on affective development without concern for cognitive growth.

3. The curriculum *should* include provisions to meet the need for some type of instructional pacing by any or all of the following means:
   a. Making it possible to accomplish a range of learning experiences in a shorter span of time using a continuous progress curriculum
   b. Assigning students to curricula at levels beyond those expected at the students' age/grade level
   c Eliminating from the curricula what is already learned and substituting curricula more appropriate to student interest, abilities, and needs.

The curriculum *should not* penalize students for being gifted or talented, through restricting their opportunities to learn by ignoring those characteristics that define their giftedness.

4. The curriculum *should* allow for the expression of some aspect of the individual's interests, needs, abilities, and learning preferences. The curriculum *should* be organized to allow for some individualization and self-selection.

   The curriculum *should not* be without defined expectations and clearly expressed opportunities for teacher-directed as well as student-selected learning activities.

5. The curriculum *should* provide opportunities to learn to reconceptualize existing knowledge, to perceive things from various points of view, and to use information for new purposes or in new ways.

   The curriculum *should not* stress the accumulation of knowledge or reinforce mastery without simultaneously encouraging students to be productive thinkers.

6. The curriculum *should* provide learning experiences for students to address the unresolved issues and problems of society and apply personal and social data to analyze, clarify, and respond to such issues and problems.

   The curriculum *should not* focus only on knowledge of the world as it is, but should encourage the development of perceptions of the need to invent in order to restructure the world into what it ideally could be.

7. The curriculum *should* incorporate learning experiences that foster the development of the complex thought processes that encourage the creation of unique products and develop strategies of productive thought. The curriculum *should* teach both fundamental and higher-level thinking skills as integral parts of every learning experience.

   The curriculum *should not* overemphasize mastery of fundamental basic skills, nor should it exonerate gifted/talented students from mastering these. The curriculum *should not* ignore the development of fundamental or basic skills for the mastery of higher-level thinking skills.

8. The curriculum *should* provide opportunities for students to practice leadership and fol-

FIGURE 12–1. Examples of mobiles and displays of Bloom's taxonomy

lowership skills and appropriate and varied forms of communication skills and strategies.

The curriculum *should not* be based on the assumption that gifted/talented students can assume positions of leadership without the development of skills and understandings that promote this end.

While this is a useful guide, you will always need to assess your gifted learners for their particular needs. They are your very best guide to an appropriate curriculum.[1]

[1]From *Growing Up Gifted* (pp. 218–219) by Barbara Clark, 1983, Columbus, OH: Charles E. Merrill. Copyright 1983 by Bell and Howell. Reprinted by permission of the publisher.

Bloom's Taxonomy

One of the most respected conceptualizations of the various levels of learning was provided by Bloom in 1956. Bloom's (1956) taxonomy of cognitive objectives has been applied to curriculum development for all students and has had particular value in use with the gifted. It is of value in understanding the learning characteristics of the gifted and in both individual- and group-curriculum planning. *All* students should be encouraged to develop and exercise higher levels of thinking; but when the regular classroom teacher is working with one or two gifted students, along with a full-size class of more normal learners, it is particularly important to remember to make efforts to provide differentiated opportunities for gifted/talented students. Thinking through the various possibilities and actually providing some additional opportunities may be accomplished through the application of Bloom's taxonomy.

Bloom describes six levels in his taxonomy of cognitive objectives. These levels, from low to high, are *knowledge, comprehension, appli-* *cation, analysis, synthesis,* and *evaluation.* Certain verbs may be associated with each level and are helpful for structuring thinking activities. To encourage the development of higher levels of thinking, teachers may display the levels and related verbs in the classroom. Such displays serve as visual reminders for both students and teachers to use higher levels of thinking. Teachers are urged to use their imagination and creativity in the development of these visual aids. One

TABLE 12–2. Verbs and classroom products related to Bloom's taxonomy

Areas	Definition	Key Verbs	Classroom Products
Knowledge	knowing and remembering facts	match, recognize, identify, list, describe, name, define, show, record, select	Report, worksheet, chart, map
Comprehension	understanding	explain, locate, inquire, demonstrate, discover	Diagram, model, game, picture, teach a lesson, diorama, time line
Application	doing, making use of what is known	model, apply, code, collect, organize, construct, report, experiment, sketch, paint, draw, group, put in order	Survey, diary, mobile, scrapbook, photographs, stitchery, cartoon, model, illustration, sculpture, learning center, construction
Analysis	explaining what is known	categorize, take apart, analyze, separate, dissect, compare, contrast	Graph, survey, report, questionnaire, time line, family tree, commercial, fact file
Synthesis	putting together the known into something new	add to, create, imagine, combine, suppose, predict, role-play, hypothesize, design, what if . . ? invent, infer, improve, adapt, compose, change	Story, poem, play, song, pantomine, news article, invention, radio show, dance, mural, comic strip
Evaluation	judging the outcome	justify, debate, solve, recommend, judge, criticize, prove, dispute	Editorial, survey, panel, self-evaluation, letter, conclusion, recommendation, court trial

Note. From *An Affordable Gifted Program That Works* (p .39) by M. Leiker, 1980, Denver: Coronado Hills School, Adams School District No. 12. Adapted by permission.

such idea is use of a clothesline with "bloomers" representing the six levels. Verbs may be highlighted on the ruffles on the legs. Each level may be a different color, with this color coding consistent throughout learning centers and other areas in the classroom. There are many different ways of displaying the six levels of Bloom's taxonomy; a few examples are shown in Figure 12–1. Table 12–2 lists key verbs that may be used in designing a display of Bloom's taxonomy for the classroom and classroom products that may be developed. The use of Bloom's taxonomy in the classroom is effective in promoting higher level cognitive abilities in gifted students while also encouraging all students to use higher levels of thinking.

Learning Centers. The use of learning centers in the classroom is another means of individualizing instruction to better serve the gifted student. Learning centers may address any subject or topic. A variety of multilevel activities may be developed by the teacher based on student needs and objectives. The learning center may be used to introduce, reinforce, review, or enrich concepts. (Additional ideas and suggestions about learning centers may be found in Chapter 3.)

Bloom's taxonomy may also be used in the development of learning centers. For example, color-coded file folders on specific subjects may be developed that contain a question for each of the six levels of learning. Numerous books on the market offer ideas

---

STORY QUESTIONS RELATED TO BLOOM'S TAXONOMY

Story questions can be developed about any book that students often read. Leiker (1980) created the following questions about Sendak's *Where the Wild Things Are* (1963), a popular book for young readers. Questions may be written on an appropriate figure form (in this case, a monster from *Where the Wild Things Are*) that is laminated and used to develop higher-level cognitive skills. A similar procedure is also of value—if appropriately adjusted for interests and reading level—to learning disabled and mentally handicapped students.

Where the Wild Things Are

Knowledge	Where did Max go?
	What grew in Max's room?
	Where did Max really want to be?
Comprehension	What did Max tame the "wild things" with?
	How did the "wild things" act when they first saw Max?
	What did Max want from his mother?
Application	Show how Max felt when he was sent to his room.
	Draw a picture of the "wild things."
	What could Max have done differently?
Analysis	Why did Mother send Max to his room?
	What probably happened to Max when he was just sent to his room?
	What did Max do to frighten the "wild beasts"?
Synthesis	What would have happened if Max had missed the boat home?
	How would you have changed the story to make it better?
	Create a new monster of your own for the story.
Evaluation	Which ending to the story do you like best?
	Would Max have been happy if he had missed the boat?
	How did the new monster change the story?

Note. Questions from *An Affordable Gifted Program That Works* by M. Leiker, 1980, Denver: Coronado Hills School, Adams School District No. 12. Reprinted by permission.

and patterns for learning centers; however, teachers must exercise their personal creativity and originality in the development of learning centers to meet the needs of specific situations.

Story Questions.   Questions relating to the six levels of Bloom's taxonomy may be written to correspond to specific books, or general questions may be written to correspond to specific books, or general questions may be written to be used with a number of books. The story questions box provides an example of specific questions to accompany a particular book. The activity folders box represents another way to use Bloom's levels for story questioning.

General story questions appropriate to any number of books may also be used. Questions can cover the general categories of humor, adventure, science fiction, animals, distant lands, historical fiction, fantasy, tall tales, biography, folk and fairy tales, and myths. Leiker (1980) lists generic questions corresponding to the six levels of Bloom's taxonomy. The literature questions box (p. 376) provides examples of this type of questioning.

PROGRAM SUGGESTIONS FOR THE SECONDARY SCHOOL

Clark notes that "often those who plan the gifted program in the district concentrate on the elementary school structure and curriculum" (1983, p. 298). There are many reasons for this tendency, but one of the more common is the assumption that the existing structure (advanced classes for students who select solid geometry as opposed to basic mathematics, for example) "takes care of" the needs of gifted/talented high school students. For those who do not understand the nature of giftedness and the needs of gifted/talented students, it might seem logical to believe that the wide variety of classes offered in a large, comprehensive high school

is adequate for gifted/talented students. This simply is not true.

There are, however, at least two types of programs offered at perhaps 20% to 25% of the secondary schools in the nation that are appropriate for many gifted/talented students. These are (1) the advanced placement (AP) program sponsored by the College Entrance Examination Board (CEEB), which may include independent studies, tutorials, or honors classes; and (2) actual college or university classes. The latter is possible, of course, only when there is a college or university nearby and when that college/university is interested in working jointly with the public schools in such a program. Either of these programs may be of value for *some* students, but they are of limited value and even when available, may apply only to students at the senior level. They should not be considered *the* program for gifted/talented; they *can be* a *part* of the program. Other program possibilities include core-curriculum programs for groups of gifted students, seminar programs, interdisciplinary-course programs, exchange-student programs, school-within-a-school programs, community-based internships, independent-study programs, and a variety of acceleration programs. Any and all of these have merit but any one, or two, of these approaches will not provide appropriate programming for all secondary students. An integrated plan, based on some overall concept, is the only really good solution. Such plans may vary from district to district; if carefully thought through (and if based on what gifted students have experienced in the elementary schools previous to entry to the secondary level), they may be quite satisfactory. However, there are a number of established concepts upon which such programs may be based, and it may be advantageous to use some established, verified construct. We will review one such conceptualization, the autonomous learner model, advocated by Betts (1985) and Betts and Knapp (1981).

ACTIVITY FOLDERS USING BLOOM'S TAXONOMY

Learning centers may be developed to encourage the reading and sharing of favorite children's books. Pockets may be attached to the inside of file folders to contain a copy of the book and question-and-activity cards. Folders may then be decorated to make them appealing to students. The following are sample questions to be printed on color-coded "rabbit" cards:

The Velveteen Rabbit (Williams, 1965)

Knowledge:
(red)

1. What toy was the rabbit's friend in the nursery?

Comprehension:
(orange)

2. Give the main idea of the book.

Application:
(yellow)

3. Using the description in the book, draw and color a picture of the velveteen rabbit.

Analysis:
(green)

4. Compare and contrast the ways the various toys treated the velveteen rabbit.

Synthesis:
(blue)

5. Design a new ending to the story.

Evaluation:
(violet)

6. Should the velveteen rabbit have been friends with the unkind toys in the story? Why or why not?

GENERIC LITERATURE QUESTIONS

Science fiction

Knowledge: 1. What is the *setting* of the story? List the main characters.

Comprehension: 2. What was the main idea or theme of the story?

Application: 3. Draw a picture of the *setting* of the story.

Analysis: 4. Compare the environment *(setting)* in this story to your own *setting*. List the things that are the same and different.

Synthesis: 5. Choose one thing from the story that you feel could benefit our world if it existed. Write a short story explaining how you would make it a part of life today.

Evaluation: 6. Anticipate problems. List the major hurdles you would encounter in selling the idea to others.

Adventure

Knowledge: 1. Locate by page number a place in the book that shows *action, conflict, suspense.*

Comprehension: 2. What was the *main bold idea* in the story? What was one exciting event that made you nervous until you knew the ending?

Application: 3. List in order what happened in the story. Put a star next to the most exciting event.

Analysis: 4. In adventure stories, there are *usually two forces* (people or things) *working against each other.* What were they in this story?

Synthesis: 5. Write an adventure story about an event in your life. Be sure to include action, conflict, suspense, and two forces working against each other.

Evaluation: 6. Evaluate your story. Give one point for each of the points in Question 5. How did you score?

Fantasy

Knowledge: 1. Who are the main characters in the story? Where did it take place?

Comprehension: 2. What *extraordinary* thing happened in the story?

Application: 3. In fantasy STRANGE things happen. List 4 things that could never *really* happen.

Analysis: 4. Choose the one thing out of the 4 above that you feel shows the *greatest imagination.*

Synthesis: 5. Write down the thing in your life that you feel is an example of your own imagination at work.

Evaluation: 6. What effect does your imagination have on your life?

Biography

Knowledge: 1. Whose life is the book about? What type of work did the author have to do before writing the book?

Comprehension: 2. *What makes you feel you really know what the person in the book was like?*

Application: 3. Make a diary of the person's life. List only major events.

Analysis: 4. *What emotions did you feel toward the person in the book?* When did you feel these emotions?

Synthesis: 5. How could the author have improved this book? Be specific.

Evaluation: 6. Do you feel biographies are important types of books? Should they be published before or after a main character's death? Why?

Note. An Affordable Gifted Program That Works (p. 63) by M. Leiker, 1980, Denver: Coronado Hills School, Adams School District No. 12. Reprinted by permission.

Autonomous Learner Model

The autonomous learner model, originated for use in the secondary school, is now being advocated and applied at all age/grade levels. This concept is based on the belief that the goal for education of the gifted is for gifted students to become autonomous learners responsible for the development, implementation, and evaluation of their own program. This, of course, is the eventual goal of the program; it is what may be anticipated if the schools provide the appropriate opportunities and activities throughout the school years. The five dimensions of this concept—*orientation, individual development, enrichment activities, seminars,* and *in-depth study*—are illustrated in the autonomous learner model (Figure 12–2). According to Betts,

the Orientation Dimension of the model provides students, teachers, administrators and parents the opportunity to develop a foundation of information concerning the program. Emphasis is placed on understanding the concepts of giftedness, creativity and the development of potential. Students learn more about themselves, their abilities and what the program has to offer. Activities are presented to give students an opportunity to work together as a group, to learn about group process and interaction, and to learn more about the other people in the program.

During the Orientation Dimension of the program, a series of inservices are presented for teachers, administrators, parents and involved community resource people. Again, emphasis is placed on the opportunities possible for students, the responsibilities for students and involved personnel, and information given regarding the overall format of the program.

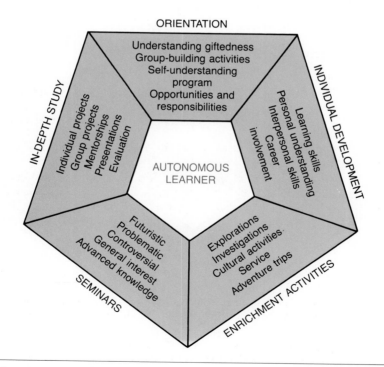

FIGURE 12–2. The autonomous learner model

Note. From *Autonomous Learner Model for the Gifted and Talented* (p. 2) by G. T. Betts, 1985, Greeley, CO: Autonomous Learning Publications & Specialists (ALPS). Copyright 1985 by ALPS. Reprinted by permission.

The Individual Development Dimension of the model [Figure 12–3] provides students with the opportunity to develop the cognitive, emotional and social skills, concepts and attitudes necessary for life-long learning; in other words, to become autonomous in their learning.

The Enrichment Activities Dimension of the model was developed to provide students with opportunities to explore content which is usually not part of the everyday curriculum. Most content in the schools is prescribed. Someone beyond the student is deciding what is to be learned, when it is ito be learned, and how it is to be learned. Within the Enrichment Activities Dimension students are able to begin explorations into their major area(s) of emphasis, related areas of interest, and new and unique areas. Students decide what they want to pursue, how it is going to be arranged, and where and when the learning will take place. Gifted and talented students need responsibility in selecting what they are going to study and how they are going to learn.

The Seminar Dimension of the model is designed to give students, in small groups of three to five, the opportunity to research a topic, present it as a seminar to the rest of the group and other interested people, and to evaluate it by criteria selected and developed by the students. A seminar is essential because it allows students the opportunity to move from the role of a *student* to the role of a *learner*. If students are to become learners, they must have an opportunity for independent individual and group learning, which means having a structure which allows and promotes the development of knowledge by the individuals.

The In-Depth Study Dimension of the model allows learners to pursue areas of interest through the development of a long-term small group or individual in-depth study. The learners determine what will be learned, how it will be presented, what help will be necessary, what the final product will be and how the entire learning process will be evaluated. In-Depth Studies are usually continued

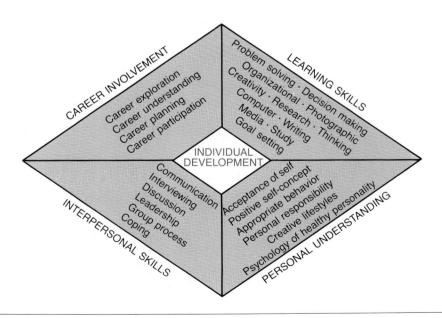

FIGURE 12–3. Individual development dimension

Note. From *Autonomous Learner Model for the Gifted and Talented* (p. 3) by G. T. Betts, 1985, Greeley, CO: Autonomous Learning Publications & Specialists (ALPS). Copyright 1985 by ALPS, Reprinted by permission.

Programs for the gifted should have many dimensions.

for a long period of time. Plans are developed by learners, in cooperation with the teacher/ facilitator, content specialists, and mentors. The plans are then implemented and completed by the learners, with presentations being made at appropriate times until the completion of the project. A final presentation and evaluation is given to all who are involved and interested.[2]

A sample follows of the kinds of activities that may be initiated in such a program. Many more may be found in Betts and Knapp (1981) or in *Autonomous Learner Model for Gifted and Talented* (Betts, 1985).

Service. Activities of benefit to the community are promoted as being a worthwhile component of the gifted and talented program. Students are required to take an active part in working with youth groups, participating in community centers and giving time to various organizations. Such activities are very rewarding for the gifted student.

Adventure Trips. Trips organized, financed, and implemented by students provide a unique opportunity for growth. After research and study of the area, the group experiences San Francisco, the Supai Reservation in the Grand Canyon, or other places that offer intellectual, emotional, and physical challenges.

Being together with other people for days, being responsible for all the decisions made, and learning how to work and live coopera-

[2]From *Autonomous Learner Model for the Gifted and Talented* (pp. 3–4) by G. T. Betts, 1985, Greeley, CO: Autonomous Learning Publications & Specialists (ALPS). Copyright 1985 by ALPS. Reprinted by permission.

tively and to complete a task is an exciting challenge for the students and the teachers. The personal growth that occurs as a result of this experience cannot be duplicated within the traditional environments of learning. The students experience a group closeness that few others ever achieve.

Cross-Age Tutoring.   Since many gifted students are accelerated beyond their age level, they bring a level of expertise to subject areas that others their age may not possess. This knowledge is strengthened and shared by tutoring their fellow students. Tutoring other students, younger or older, proves to be a challenging and worthwhile experience.

Biographical Research.   An understanding of the characteristics, attitudes, needs, and sacrifices made by eminent persons enables the gifted and talented student to better understand his own needs and desires. This understanding is furthered by researching biographies and any autobiography of a person in whom the student is interested or who is prominent in the student's field of interest.

Individual Projects.   Individual projects are "units of learning" designed by the student, aided by the teacher as facilitator. They may take on a variety of forms and be applicable to many areas. For example, a student interested in computers planned and participated in a project to investigate the applications of a computer to the field of art. After learning the techniques of programming, the student created a cartoon using the graphic capabilities of the computer.

On the other hand, a student may earn specific course credit for developing new fields of interest. In this case, the student, the facilitator, and a content-area teacher negotiate a project that fulfills the objectives and requirements for a particular course. The difference here is that the student will go beyond the regular classroom activities and

pursue an interest in depth on his own. As an example, a student was interested in the study of anatomy. After consulting with a biology instuctor, a project was designed in which the student produced a comparative-anatomy study of a shark, a cat, a pig, and a snake. Evolutionary comparisons were made and contrasts were highlighted. The results were presented in a formal paper with a slide presentation to diversified audiences including biologists, college students, and persons in the medical field.

Thus, in both of these projects each student was afforded the opportunity to pursue his individual interests using his own style of learning.

Group Projects.   Group projects differ from individual projects in that two or three students develop the project rather than a single individual. The project is broader in scope but still reflects the interests of each student involved. As an example, three students were interested in working together on a project. One student wrote poetry and short stories; another enjoyed working with lasers and photography; still another was proficient in computer programming. The result of combining these three talents was an original planetarium show, controlled by a computer, and incorporating photographs, poetry, and laser techniques.

Mentorships.   Individual students may find that in order to pursue a particular course of study, it is necessary to engage the help and advice of a consultant. This person is a professional in his field and acts as a guide to the student in developing a course of study. Working with a mentor is a requirement that must be fulfilled by each student sometime during his participation in the program.

As an example, a student interested in creative writing wanted to determine what outlets were available for this skill. After consulting with the teacher, the student decided to investigate the craft of writing short stories. A local author, one who had published several works, was contacted, and together they set out a plan that researched the styles, forms, and publication of short stories. The student explored these topics, discussing each with the mentor. Eventually, the student penned his own short story, had it critiqued by the mentor, edited the story, and submitted it for publication.

The mentorship thus provides the student with contact with a person of authority and a leader in the field. This firsthand experience gives the student invaluable insight into the talent, skills, needs, and frustrations of these persons, and enables the student to make better decisions about his own future. Furthermore, it is an opportunity for extensive use of the community and its varied resources.

Presentations. No matter what avenue of in-depth study the student chooses, a sharing of the learning experience and of the ongoing and final project(s) is essential. This sharing is done in the form of a presentation to an appropriate audience, which may include other students, mentors, and interested professionals in the field. The format of the presentation varies according to the topic and the audience to which it is presented. The presentation could be a formal recital or an art exhibit or the publication of a collection of poetry or the demonstration of a new technique of welding. Included in the presentation is what the student actually experienced, what he learned, and what progress was made. Furthermore, the student describes the personal growth that has occurred and shares this experience with the group. Students compare and contrast their endeavors and share invaluable growth experiences. They are now an integral part of the program. New areas of investigation often result from these sharing experiences.

The needs of secondary school students who are gifted/talented are in many ways similar to those of younger students. However, if the elementary school program has been effective, there will be an even greater gap between secondary gifted students and their normal class peers than was the case, for example, in the second, third, or fourth grade. In the area of social abilities, the gifted student may or may not exhibit advanced development, and this component of his or her development must be carefully considered and monitored. However, one other realm, the affective, also requires careful consideration and planning.

THE AFFECTIVE REALM

There is a real and continuing danger that we may be so impressed with the gifted student's cognitive abilities and our obligation to assist in their development that we overlook the basic need for affective development. Overlooking these needs is not fair to the gifted student and in the long run may have a negative effect on his or her cognitive and academic development and self-awareness.

Whitmore (1980) believes that gifted individuals have the same basic needs as the nongifted; the only difference is in degree. Teaching self-awareness in the classroom helps the student to look for and explore personal strengths and weaknesses, abilities, and goals. The goal of efforts in the affective realm is self-understanding, which may eventually lead to a deeper level of self-awareness, giving the added confidence necessary for success (Betts & Knapp, 1981).

Clark (1983) believes that the gifted may have a number of affective characteristics "different" from nongifted students. These include (1) idealistic tendencies and a sense of justice appearing at an early age, (2) unusual sensitivity to expectations of others, (3) high expectations of self and others, (4) higher level of self-awareness than age peers,

(5) advanced level of moral judgment, and (6) high level of information about emotions that has not been fully integrated. These and other related characteristics may lead to behavior likely to be interpreted (by teachers) as inappropriate and/or insubordinate. Or the gifted student may seem to be insensitive to the affective needs of peers (when he or she is actually oversensitive in many respects). Other children may simply misunderstand the young child who is interested in social concerns, who wants to become involved in what we might call *self-clarification,* or who uses wit to make scathing verbal attacks.

The gifted student's school program should assist affective development in an environment that is nonthreatening to gifted students and their peers. This approach is possible only as teachers understand this need and play an active role in nurturing and developing those characteristics that are necessary to the total development of gifted individuals and to the potential contributions they may make in society.

CRITICAL ISSUES IN EDUCATION OF THE GIFTED/TALENTED

To approach the question of critical issues in education of the gifted/talented, we interviewed Dr. Irving Sato, director of the National/State Leadership Training Institute on the Gifted and Talented (NSLTIGT), a federally sponsored project established in 1972 to provide training programs for the gifted/talented. NSLTIGT provides direct training and information services and has a newly opened Curriculum Development Center to assist educational agencies to deal with critical curriculum issues more effectively.

Our conversations with Dr. Sato, plus materials provided by NSLTIGT, indicates at least three critical issues, each with many components:

1. *Clarity in the definition of gifted/talented and identification methods consistent with definitions.* Sato believes that "whatever definition is used within a given school district, it must be the same throughout the district on all campuses at all grade levels." This then provides greater assurance that children identified at lower grade levels may count on continued, articulated programming as they proceed through the system. Sato suggests that "whatever definition the district develops must accommodate giftedness in areas other than academic." Identification procedures must then be developed out of, and consistent with, the definition adopted by the district or state.

2. *Integrity in program directions.* As used here, *integrity* means both wholeness and honesty. According to Sato, "gifted and talented programs must achieve continuity and articulation as opposed to the fragmented and/or isolated programmatic provisions evident in many school districts throughout our country. This is the essence of wholeness. Honesty in program directions demands that a school district does not claim to the public in official speeches or written documents that it is doing for the gifted/talented what it is not."

3. *Authenticity of teacher in-service education.*

In another dimension, the NSLTIGT began to address issues in curriculum development as it opened its Curriculum Development Center in the fall of 1986. Curriculum issues outlined in Sato, 1986, were (1) curriculum fragmentation, (2) limited availability of appropriate curriculum, and (3) lack of systematic planning to improve curriculum for the gifted/talented. These curriculum issues overlap and interrelate with Critical Issues 2 and 3. In total, these issues represent those which may be the most critical as education for the gifted/talented evolves between now and the year 2000. What we do to resolve these issues successfully will determine the quality of education for the gifted/talented as we enter the 21st century.

SUMMARY

Programs for some gifted/talented students have existed for centuries; but special, differentiated programs for *all* gifted/talented or potentially gifted/talented students is a very recent concept. It is not yet a reality in the nation or even in any one state; however, some states are doing much better than others. Three critical issues, *clarity* in the definition of gifted/talented and identification consistent with the definition, *integrity* in program directions, and *authenticity* of teacher in-service education were outlined. Resolution of these issues would go a long way toward giving education of the gifted/talented the type of priority it deserves.

As for existing programs, they usually involve modifications in both program content and administrative organization, although administrative and organizational changes are of value only insofar as they permit expanded opportunities for the gifted. Special provisions for the gifted may include early entrance to kindergarten, skipping a grade, resource room placement (part-day placement in special setting), special class or special school placement, after-school programs, opportunity to earn college credit while still in secondary school, acceleration in selected subject areas, flexible scheduling, and other similar arrangements. Gifted students may become involved in special internship experiences, independent-study projects, special situations regarding library or computer terminal usage, and other specialized learning experiences. The list is almost endless, but in too many schools the existing programs for the gifted remain highly structured and are limited in value because of this rigidity.

We identified characteristics of gifted/talented students and discussed the regular classroom teacher's responsibility in identification. We discussed creativity and factors that facilitate or inhibit it and reviewed the various problems in identifying economically disadvantaged and culturally different gifted/talented students. These are continuing problems, with many more questions than answers.

We presented various ideas that may be of use with the gifted in the regular classroom. In addition, we presented a summary of what teachers "should do" and "should not do" in such a form as to be of value either for planning a new curriculum or for evaluating an existing curriculum for the gifted.

Valuable progress in educational programming for the gifted/talented has been made in the past 20 years, and if this momentum can be maintained, we will be able to cite the 20th century as one of tremendous impact as regards recognition of, and programming for, gifted/talented students in the public schools. If these advances are to take place, at least three positive conditions must be realized. First, the unique needs of the gifted/talented must become widely recognized by the general public. Second, educators and legislators must agree that additional funds be provided as needed for appropriate, differentiated curriculum offerings. Third, educators and researchers in the field of education of the gifted/talented must make renewed, coordinated, cooperative efforts to determine the most effective ways to provide such differentiated programs.

APPENDIX
BOOKS ABOUT EXCEPTIONAL INDIVIDUALS

The following books, written for children and youth, can be of great value in providing information about exceptional individuals. The following annotated listing is based on areas of exceptionality. Age ranges are provided to assist in determining the approximate reading level; however, some books for older students may still be profitably read to younger students.

VISUALLY IMPAIRED

The Seeing Summer by Jeanette Hyde Eyerly, J. B. Lippincott, 1981.

A ten-year-old is upset when her new neighbor turns out to be blind, but eventually adjusts to the situation. A kidnapping and considerable adventure are wrapped into this fast-paced story. Ages 8–10.

Half the Battle by Lynn Hall, Charles Scribner's Sons, 1982.

A blind 18-year-old and his sighted brother make a grueling, 100-mile trip on horseback that highlights both their conflict and their genuine affection for each other. Ages 11 and up.

"Seeing" in the Dark by Elizabeth Rider Montgomery, Garrard, 1979.

A young blind girl moves to a new home and must adjust to a new teacher and new classmates. This is a mainstreaming success story emphasizing strengths of the blind student and generally helpful attitudes on the part of classmates. Ages 5–7.

My Mother Is Blind by Margaret Reuter, Children's Press, 1979.

This story describes another aspect of disabilities, in this case, the adjustment of the family to a parent's blindness. Ages 5–8.

Blind Outlaw By Glen Harold Rounds, E. P. Dutton, 1981.

A blind horse and a teenager who cannot speak respond to each other and form a lasting bond. Ages 9–12.

The New Boy Is Blind by William E. Thomas, Julian Messner, 1980.

What the blind and the nonhandicapped can learn from each other. Ages 6–10.

The Lake Is on Fire by Maureen Crane Wartski, Westminster, 1981.

An auto accident blinds Ricky and kills his best friend. He is deeply depressed and attempts suicide. This story outlines his "comeback" and includes a good deal of adventure. Ages 10–13.

HEARING IMPAIRED

My Sister's Silent World by Catherine Arthur, Children's Press, 1979.

Heather's eighth birthday as told by her older sister. Heather has a hearing aid and can distinguish sounds but not words. Ages 5–9.

The Waiting Game by Anne Evelyn Bunting, J. P. Lippincott, 1981.

Three high school seniors (one of them deaf) anticipate possible offers of college football scholarships. Ages 10 and up.

Breakaway by Ruth Hallman, Westminster, 1981.

Rob, a 17-year-old, who is almost totally deaf as a result of a diving accident, has many difficulties in attempting to adjust to his situation. His overprotective and domineering mother is one of his major problems. Ages 12 and up.

The Swing by Emily Hanlon, Bradbury Press, 1979.

How two children—one deaf—learn from one another. Their bond is in their mutual love of animals and in the swing that stands between their two houses. Ages 10–12.

Silent Dancer by Bruce Hlibok, Julian Messner, 1981.

A deaf youngster finds pleasure and confidence in her ballet school classes, which have been adapted to accommodate deaf students. Ages 8–11.

Lisa and Her Soundless World by Edna A. Levine, Human Science, 1984.

This book teaches nondeaf children about their deaf peers and also shows deaf children how they can successfully participate in the social environment around them. Ages 8–13.

World of Her Own by Nancy Smiler Levinson, Harvey House, 1981.

A 16-year-old deaf girl is mainstreamed after 9 years in a private school for the deaf. This story includes elements of mystery and romance, along with valuable understandings about deafness. Ages 12 and up.

Words in Our Hands, by Ada Bassett Litchfield, Albert Whitman, 1980.

Three children with normal hearing communicate with their deaf parents. In addition to building understanding of communication with the deaf, there is a good deal of specific information, such as the alphabetic, fingerspelling symbols. Ages 7–9.

Apple Is My Sign by Mary L. Riskind, Houghton Mifflin, 1981.

An interesting, historically pertinent story about a deaf boy at the turn of the century. This story includes a good deal of factual material (see the Foreword) about various sign languages and shows the evolution of sign language. Ages 10–14.

Just Like Everybody Else by Lillian Rosen, Harcourt Brace Jovanovich, 1981.

A first-person story of a teenager who loses her hearing. This book contains a great deal of factual information but also manages to maintain interest and promote understanding of the considerable affective needs of the deaf. Ages 11 and up.

ORTHOPEDIC IMPAIRMENTS OR HEALTH PROBLEMS

Accident by Hila Crayder Colman, William Morrow, 1980.

The first date between two teenagers leads to a tragic motorcycle accident. The story provides a perceptive look at the slow rehabilitation process and, in this case, the related feelings of anger, hopelessness, and guilt. Ages 11 and up.

Darlene by Eloise Greenfield, Methuen, 1980.

A six-year-old girl confined to a wheelchair has problems with attitudes. Ages 5–7.

Alesia by Eloise Greenfield and Alesia Revis, Philomel Books, 1981.

Entries in Alesia's diary provide an intimate look at the daily activities of a teenage girl who overcomes her physical limitations with courage and good spirit. Ages 10–14.

Laura's Gift by Dee Jacobs, Oriel, 1980.

A story about twins and muscular dystrophy. Ages 11 and up.

Angie and Me by Rebecca Castaldi Jones, Macmillan, 1981.

A girl with severe juvenile rheumatoid arthritis has a terminally ill roommate. Ages 9–11.

Little Little by M. E. Kerr, Harper & Row, 1981.

The problems and frustrations of growing up as a dwarf. Ages 11 and up.

Karen by Maria Killilea, Dell, 1983.

We learn about what can be done for a child with spastic cerebral palsy and also come to understand better the emotional trauma involved. Ages 13 and up.

You Can't Catch Diabetes from a Friend by Lynne Kipnis and Susan Adler, Triad, 1979.

A well-done presentation of the problems of juvenile diabetes, emphasizing the problems of the family. Ages 7–12.

Nick Joins In by Joe Lasker, Albert Whitman, 1980.

This story of a 7-year-old in a wheelchair, his fear of school, and the growing ability of his classmates to make him a part of the group provides a hopeful look at successful mainstreaming. Ages 5–8.

It's a Mile from Here to Glory by Robert C. Lee, Little, Brown, 1972.

Early MacLaren, the school's star runner, is temporarily disabled by a freak accident. His struggles and what he learns about being a person versus being a star makes for a valuable book. Ages 9–13.

Mine for Keeps by Jean Little, Little, Brown, 1962.

This classic book, still in print, tells of the return of Sally, a cerebral-palsied girl, from 5 years in a school for the handicapped. The role of others in her adjustment provides an interesting story, with many valuable insights for elementary age students. Ages 9–11.

Only Love by Susan Diana Sallis, Harper & Row, 1980.

This somewhat "heavy" story may be appreciated by some students but has a good deal of sorrow and reality. All does not end on a happy note. It's the first-person narrative of an English girl, a paraplegic who has lived in institutions since she was abandoned as a child. It's a sad love story and may be of value in special circumstances. Ages 12 and up.

Let the Balloon Go by Ivan Southall, Bradbury, 1985.

This book tells of the decision of a boy with spastic cerebral palsy to no longer accept the words *you can't do that.* Ages 9–16.

Marathon Miranda by Elizabeth Winthrop, Holiday House, 1979.

Miranda tells her story and explains some of the problems experienced by children with severe asthma. Ages 9–11.

MENTAL RETARDATION

Love Is Like Peanuts by Betty Bates, Holiday House, 1980.

A 14-year-old girl takes a summer job caring for a brain-damaged, mentally retarded girl with a handsome, 18-year-old brother. This story mixes romance with growing understanding of the condition of mental retardation. Its value is enhanced by perceptive characterizations of the manner in which different persons respond to mental retardation. Ages 11–14.

For Love of Jody by Robbie Branscum, Lothrop, Lee, & Shepard, 1979.

This story, which takes place during the Depression on an Arkansas farm, presents an interesting picture of how Jody, a severely mentally retarded child, changed the life of one family. Ages 9–12.

She's My Sister: Having a Retarded Sister by Jane Claypool Miner, Crestwood House, 1982.

A 16-year-old has great difficulty with the fact that her retarded sister is coming home from her special school and that they will be attending the same public school. Ages 11 and up.

Alice with Golden Hair by Eleanor Means Hull, Atheneum, 1981.

Alice, a nearly 18-year-old, has been in institutions for the mentally retarded since early childhood. This book provides a rare, highly interesting insight into the thinking of the mildly mentally retarded. Ages 11 and up.

Clunie by Robert Newton Peck, Alfred A. Knopf, 1979.

A teenage retarded girl, overweight and poorly accepted by many of her peers, has a variety of difficulties and a generally unhappy life. This story tells a great deal about "how it really is" for many retarded persons. Ages 12 and up.

In My Sister's Eyes by Grace Posner, Beaufort Books, 1980.

The story of a retarded sister, who is at times considered the "skeleton in the closet." Ages 12 and up.

Lester's Turn by Jan Slepian, Macmillan, 1981.

Lester, who has cerebral palsy, determines that he should devote his life to Alfie, his mentally retarded friend whom he believes really needs him. Ages 11–14.

My Brother Is Special by Maureen Crane Wartski, Westminster, 1979.

A teenage girl loves her retarded brother and can't understand people who think of the retarded as "creatures from another planet." Ages 10–13.

My Sister Is Different by Betty Ren Wright, Raintree, 1981.

Carlo has a retarded sister. Sometimes he resents her greatly, sometimes he loves her. A very realistic picture for young readers. Ages 6–9.

LEARNING DISABILITIES

Do Bananas Chew Gum? by Jamie Gilson, Lothrop, Lee, & Shepard, 1980.

A learning disabled boy has repeated failure in school until he is diagnosed as learning disabled and is provided the special help he needs. Ages 9–11.

Will the Real Gertrude Hollings Please Stand Up? by Sheila Greenwald, Little, Brown, 1983.

The story of Gertrude, a teenage girl with learning disabilities, and her cousin Albert, a straight-*A* overachiever. Albert learns a great deal from Gertrude. Ages 11 and up.

Putting Up with Sherwood by Ellen Matthews, Westminster, 1980.

Diane, a fifth grader who feels she has various reasons to feel sorry for herself, is asked to tutor Sherwood, who has a learning disability. Sherwood helps her toward a happier life. Ages 9–11.

Running Scared by Jane Morton, Elsevier/ Nelson Books, 1979.

A straightforward story of a boy's frustration with his inability to achieve in school. Ages 10–14.

Whales To See The by Glendon and Kathryn Swarthout, Doubleday, 1975.

A special class of learning disabled students goes out to sea to watch the semiannual whale migration, and a class of "normal" students happens to be on the same ship. This story provides an interesting view of attitudes. This was written before "mainstreaming" but has some remaining validity. Ages 10 and up.

GIFTED/TALENTED

Daniel's Duck by Clyde Robert Bulla, Harper and Row, 1979.

Daniel, a Tennessee mountain boy of the early 1900s, learns about creative talent, pride, and false pride. Ages 5–8.

No Good in Art by Miriam Cohen, Greenwillow Books, 1980.

Jim, a very talented boy, learns to overcome the negative kindergarten experience that convinced him he was "no good in art." Ages 5–8.

Carol Johnston: The One-armed Gymnast by Pete Donovan, Children's Press, 1982.

The true story of a Canadian gymnast who won All-American honors despite the fact

that she was born with just one arm. This is more a story of talent than the account of a handicap. Ages 8–12.

The Gifted Kids Survival Guide for Ages 10 and Under and *The Gifted Kids Survival Guide for Ages 11–18.* by J. Galbraith, Free Spirit, 1984 and 1983.

These are not "about" exceptional students in the usual sense of the word but are for gifted students to read in order to learn more about themselves. Ages as indicated in titles.

Jemmy by Jon Francis Hassler, Atheneum, 1980.

Jemmy, a half-Chippewa, half-white high school senior is told by her father to quit school in October of her senior year. Initially, she accepts this situation, but through a series of experiences she "discovers" both her native American heritage and great artistic talent. Ages 12 and up.

OTHER BOOKS OF INTEREST

Dibs: In Search of Self by Virginia Axline, Ballantine, 1976.

This is an account of a young "autistic like" child, Dibs, involved in play therapy sessions. Ages 14 and up.

What If You Couldn't . . . ? A Book about Special Needs by Janet Kamien, Charles Scribner's Sons, 1979.

An overview of handicapping conditions, written specifically for elementary school children. Ages 8–12.

The Alfred Summer by Jan Slepian, Macmillan, 1980.

Of four friends, two are not accepted by others because of their personalities and/or circumstances, and two because of their handicaps. This story involves mental retardation, cerebral palsy, epilepsy, and a physically deformed body. Ages 11–13.

Feeling Free by Mary Beth Sullivan, Alan Brightman, and Joseph Blatt, Addison-Wesley, 1979.

The story of five children with handicaps, a follow-up to the television series *Feeling Free*. The theme is that handicapped children are very much the same as all other children. Ages 9 and up.

GLOSSARY

AAMD The American Association on Mental Deficiency. An organization of individuals from many professional disciplines, concerned with mental retardation. The AAMD is, for the most part, an organization of professionals. (Most other groups organized on behalf of the mentally retarded typically include primarily parents of the mentally retarded and laypersons.)

academic planning meeting Group meeting in which the students and the teacher plan the academic program.

acceleration A process leading to a student's accelerated movement through the various grade levels, including early entrance to school, skipping grades, and early or advanced college placement.

acuity Acuteness or keenness, as of hearing or vision.

adaptive behavior Individual's ability to meet standards set by society for his or her cultural group. The American Association on Mental Deficiency considers three areas of performance in assessing adaptive behavior: maturation, learning, and social adjustment.

adaptive physical education Physical education programs designed to meet the specific needs of handicapped students.

Adlerian theory Theory suggesting that schools must become truly democratic, with students playing an active role in the process of their education. One advocate is Rudolph Dreikurs.

ambulation Walking without assistance from others. It may include the use of crutches, a cane, or other mechanical aids.

aphasia Loss or impairment of the ability to use oral language.

articulation problems Most common type of speech problem including addition *(buhrown* for *brown, cuhow* for *cow),* distortion *(shled* for *sled),* omission *(pay* for *play, cool* for *school, ift* for *lift),* substitution *(dat* for *that, wabbit* for *rabbit,* or *thum* for *some).*

assertive discipline An approach to classroom management that encourages the teacher to be in control of the classroom through clear identification of expectations plus an understanding of how to respond to student behavior assertively but without hostility. Lee and Marlene Canter are leading advocates of this approach.

athetoid cerebral palsy A type of cerebral palsy that involves recurring slow wormlike movements of the hands and feet.

audiogram Graph on which results of au-

391

diometric evaluation are charted to indicate the person's ability to hear each tone at each of the presented frequencies.

audiologist   Hearing specialist who administers an audiometric examination.

audiometer   Instrument that produces sounds at varying intensities (loudness) and varying frequencies (pitch) for testing purposes.

audiometric evaluation   A hearing test using a series of carefully calibrated tones that vary in loudness and pitch. This assists in determining the extent and type of hearing loss so that proper remedial or medical steps can be taken to overcome the hearing problem.

aura, epileptic   Subjective sensation that precedes and marks the onset of an epileptic seizure.

autism   Childhood disorder rendering the child noncommunicative and withdrawn.

behavior modification   Techniques offering tools and systematic procedures that teachers may implement to change or modify unacceptable or defiant behavior and encourage more acceptable and appropriate behavior.

cane technique   Use of a cane as an aid to mobility.

career education   The combination of experiences through which one acquires the attitudes, knowledge, and skills required for successful community living and employment. *Career education* is much broader than a series of courses in vocational/occupational areas.

CEC   The Council for Exceptional Children.

central nervous system (CNS)   That part of the nervous system to which the sensory impulses are transmitted and from which motor impulses originate. In vertebrates, the brain and spinal cord.

cerebral palsy   A group of conditions that may seriously limit motor coordination. It is commonly present at birth but may be acquired any time as the result of head injury or infectious disease. It is characterized by varying degrees of disturbance of voluntary movement.

class-action suit   Litigation instigated on behalf of a group of individuals in a common situation (e.g., students with similar handicapping conditions).

classification   Indicating, as a matter of written record, that a committee of professionals has determined that a given student is handicapped (hearing impaired, mentally handicapped, visually impaired, etc.), based on the use of appropriate testing, data gathering, and group consideration and discussion. Traditional classification categories were established by PL 94-142 and reaffirmed in later legislation and regulations; however the various states may use somewhat different classification categories.

cleft lip or palate   Congenital fissure of the palate or lip that can cause articulation errors and problems with nasality. Normally corrected by surgery.

cognition   The process of comprehending and understanding information. The term *cognitive development* is perhaps more often used than cognition and includes efforts (by humans) to learn new facts and develop new understandings and concepts. Most cognitive development is believed to be a result of relating new experiences to previously developed knowledge and understandings.

colostomy   Surgical procedure in which an artificial anal opening is formed in the colon.

conductive hearing loss   Hearing loss caused by interference with the transmission of sound from the outer ear.

congenital   Present in an individual at birth.

continuum of alternative placements   Full spectrum of services that may be tailored to the individual needs of each student at any given time during the student's educational career.

contracture   Condition of muscle characterized by fixed high resistance to passive stretch and generally caused by prolonged immobilization.

control braces   Braces to prevent or eliminate purposeless movement or to allow movement in only one or two directions.

cooperative plan   Plan in which the student is enrolled in a special class but attends a regular classroom for part of the school day. The student's homeroom is a special class.

corrective braces   Braces for prevention and correction of deformity during a child's rapid growth years.

crisis or helping teacher   Teacher who provides temporary support and control to troubled students when they are unable or unwilling to cope with the demands of the regular classroom.

cystic fibrosis   Hereditary disease resulting from a generalized dysfunction of the pancreas.

decibel (dB)   Unit of measurement of the loudness of sound.

defiant behavior   Stubborn or aggressive behavior resulting from forces within the student or within his environment, including his interaction with significant others in his life.

delayed speech   Condition wherein a child does not talk by the time when normal developmental guidelines would indicate that he should be talking.

diabetes   Metabolic disorder wherein the individual's body is unable to utilize and properly store sugar. It is the result of the inability of the pancreas to produce a sufficient amount of the hormone insulin.

diabetic coma   Condition caused by too much sugar (too little insulin) resulting from failure to take insulin, illness, or neglect of proper diet.

diagnosogenic theory   Theory that sees the cause of stuttering as the labeling of normal disfluencies by individuals in a child's early environment.

direction taking   Travel method employed by visually impaired individuals. It involves using an object or sound to establish a course of direction toward or away from an object.

disability   Objective, measurable lack of function; lowered capacity or incapacity.

Down syndrome   A clinical type of mental retardation related to an abnormal arrangement of chromosomes.

Duchenne (childhood) muscular dystrophy   Generally fatal disease characterized by slow deterioration of the voluntary muscles and ending in a state of complete helplessness.

due process   Procedures and policies established to ensure equal educational opportunities for all children. PL 94-142 contains due-process procedures specific to handicapped students.

dyslexia   Severe reading disability accompanied by visual perceptual problems and problems in writing, such as reversals and mirror writing.

educable mentally retarded (EMR) or handicapped   Term used to describe a student who displays the behavior of the mentally handicapped and has an IQ of 50 to 70 and similarly retarded adaptive behavior. The concept of mild or educable mentally handicapped implies that the student can be educated and that with proper educational opportunity, he or she can be a self-supporting, participating member of society.

efficacy studies   Research specifically established to determine the extent to which given educational practices or procedures achieve the desired effects.

electronic mobility devices   Devices to enhance hearing efficiency, detect obstacles, enable an individual to walk in a straight line, or reveal specific location of obstacles in the environment.

environmental factors   Variables such as poverty, racial discrimination, school pressures, and deteriorating families considered when evaluating students.

epilepsy   Not a disease in itself but a sign or symptom of some underlying disorder in the nervous system. Convulsions or seizures are the main symptoms related to this name.

etiology   The study of causes or origins of a disease or condition.

Flanders classroom-interaction analysis   Teacher evaluation tool that takes into consideration the verbal behavior of the teacher and the student. The interaction is analyzed on the basis of categories.

frustration theory   Theory about the cause of stuttering based on the idea that a student may have an unusual need to be listened to, and in the drive to keep the listener's attention, normal disfluencies cause the speaker to become more and more frustrated.

Galloway nonverbal system   Teacher evaluation system that contains a procedure for decoding nonverbal cues associated with six of the seven teacher behaviors of the Flanders category system.

glad notes   Notes given to a student or a student's parents by the teacher for something the student has done to overcome social or academic difficulty.

handicap Subjective or environmental limitation associated with disability.

hearing loss Inability to perceive sounds.

hemophilia Hereditary blood disorder resulting in insufficient clotting.

hertz (Hz) Unit of measurement used to express frequency of sound.

hospital-bound and homebound Terms used for students with chronic conditions requiring long-term treatment in a hospital or at home, who receive special instruction from homebound or itinerant special education personnel.

hostile aggressiveness Behavior characterized by violence toward teachers, peers, and parents, including kicking, hitting, biting, and fighting.

humanistic approach Approach toward troubled students that involves the acceptance of a student's behavior and the reflection of that behavior back to the student. This direct and uncomplicated framework encourages the student to learn, to express, and to better understand his or her feelings in a caring, reflective environment.

hyperactivity Condition characterized by incessant motion or activity that interferes with learning.

hypoglycemia A condition in which there is an unusually low level of circulating glucose in the blood. This may lead to lethargy and learning disabilities.

incontinence Lack of bowel or bladder control.

individualized educational program (IEP) Tool for management of the educational program to assure that each student is provided for individually.

insulin Protein hormone produced by the pancreas and secreted into the blood, where it regulates carbohydrate (sugar) metabolism. Used in treatment and control of diabetes mellitus.

integrate To include/educate in the regular classroom. Implies joint effort on behalf of special and general educators.

itinerant teacher Traveling teacher who works with a given student on a regularly scheduled basis depending on the student's needs at a particular time.

kinesthesis The sense by which movement, weight, position, and so on are perceived.

kyphosis Curvature of the spine; hunchback.

language nonfluency General lack of smoothness in language production.

learning disabled student Student who displays the following characteristics: (1) significant discrepancy between the individual's achievement and his apparent ability to achieve or perform, (2) normal or above-average intelligence, and (3) normal sensory acuity.

learning lab Diagnostic and prescriptive center designed to meet the individual needs of each student.

legally blind Category of visually impaired individuals having central visual acuity of 20/200 or less in the better eye after correction, or visual acuity more than 20/200 if there is a field defect in which the widest diameter of the visual field subtends an angle no greater than 20 degrees.

listening helper or buddy Peer in the classroom who helps the hearing impaired student in such things as turning to the correct page, taking notes, or adjusting to a new class or school.

litigation Carrying on a suit in a court of law.

magic circle Technique used by elementary school teachers to help troubled students dispel the feeling that they are significantly different from those around them. The teacher attempts to foster an atmosphere of warmth and honesty in which each student contributes his thoughts and feelings and listens respectfully to his peers.

mainstreaming Maximum integration of handicapped students into the regular classroom, coupled with concrete assistance for non–special education teachers.

manual communication A method of communication in which fingerspelling and/or sign language is used in place of speech.

mental retardation Significantly subaverage general intellectual functioning existing concurrently with deficits in adaptive behavior and manifested during the developmental period.

misclassification Inaccurate classification (see *classification*). Misclassification of many minority students was a major factor in the litigation against school districts that contributed to the move toward "mainstreaming."

mobility Individual's movement from one point in his or her environment to another.

muscular dystrophy A progressive condition in which the muscles are replaced by fatty tissue.

myelomeningocele Type of spina bifida in which a sac containing part of a malformed spinal cord protrudes from a hole in the spine.

near-point vision Ability to see at close range, as in reading.

neurotic-tendencies theory Theory that portrays stuttering as the outcome of such needs as satisfaction of anal and oral desires, infantile tendencies, and other Freudian-theory regressions.

occupational therapy Therapy directed at upper extremities emphasizing activities of daily living such as tying shoes, eating, or other routine activities.

ophthalmologist Medical doctor specializing in the diagnosis and treatment of diseases of the eye; licensed to prescribe glasses. Also called an *oculist*.

Optacon Device that converts printed material to either a tactile or auditory stimulus.

optician Craftsman who makes glasses and fills the prescriptions of ophthalmologists and optometrists.

optometrist One who specializes in eye problems but does not possess a medical degree. Licensed to measure visual function and prescribe and fit glasses.

oral communication Approach to teaching hearing impaired students in which communication is carried on through spoken language, e.g., speech reading, listening, and writing without sign language or fingerspelling.

orientation Blind individual's use of his remaining senses to establish his position and relationship to objects in his environment.

orthopedic impairments Physical impairments related to disorders of the joints, the skeleton, or the muscles. Students with orthopedic impairments make up one major part of the more general classification *physically handicapped;* the other major part relates to health impairments such as asthma, diabetes, and so on.

orthoptist A nonmedical technician who directs prescribed exercises or training to correct eye-muscle imbalances and generally works under the direction of an ophthalmologist.

osteoarthritis Degenerative arthritis usually confined to one joint.

otologist Medical doctor specializing in diseases of the ear.

overattention Condition in which an individual focuses on one particular object and seems unable to break the focus.

paralysis Loss or impairment of function in a part of the body.

paraplegia Paralysis of the lower limbs or lower section of the body.

partially sighted Category of individuals whose visual acuity is better than 20/200 but is still significantly impaired.

pedagogy The art, science, or profession of teaching.

perceptual disorders Disorders involving visual, auditory, tactile, or kinesthetic perception.

perfectionism Extreme fear of failure or criticism, sometimes seen in troubled students.

perseveration Persistent repetition without apparent purpose.

petit mal seizures Epileptic seizures of short duration (5–20 seconds) that may occur as many as a hundred times a day. The student may become pale and stare into space, his eyelids may twitch, and he may demonstrate jerky movements.

physical therapy Therapy directed at lower extremities emphasizing posture, gait, movements, and the prevention of contractures.

plus factors Additional instruction that visually impaired students might need in nonacademic areas, such as braille, orientation and mobility, and typewriting.

poliomyelitis Acute viral disease characterized by involvement of the central nervous system. Sometimes results in paralysis.

postlingual deafness Deafness occurring after the development of speech and language.

prelingual deafness Deafness that is present at birth or develops in early life before the development of speech and language.

prereferral intervention A system in which special consultive help is requested, with the hope that formal placement within the framework of special education services might never be required. Prereferral intervention is based on the principle of prevention.

pressure theory Theory that views the cause of stuttering as developmental pressures that promote disfluency.

problem-solving meeting Group meeting in which students learn to examine situations, propose solutions, and evaluate the results.

prosthesis Artificial arm or leg to replace an amputated part of the body.

psychoanalytical approach Approach to troubled students in which the teacher provides ways for the students to bring into consciousness their unconscious repressions. All program cueing comes from the student. Used in residential schools and not readily adaptable to a public school setting.

psychomotor or temporal lobe seizures Complex seizures that affect motor systems and mental processes and are manifested by peculiar behavior such as licking or chewing of lips or purposeless activities. May last for a few minutes or several hours.

quadriplegia Paralysis affecting both arms and both legs.

readability level Indication of the difficulty of reading material in terms of the grade level at which it might be expected to be read successfully.

referral In most cases, a formal request for assistance in planning a more meaningful educational program for a given student. This usually means completing a form providing certain basic information on the student "referred," including reason(s) why assistance in required. (See also *prereferral intervention.*)

rehabilitation Restoring to a former capacity. For example, a student may suffer damage to a limb and, through therapy, the limb may be restored to good condition and use. The term is commonly applied to a variety of services designed to assist individuals in overcoming handicaps, especially in preparation for employment. Such services are referred to as *vocational rehabilitation services.*

remediation Correction of a deficiency. Often refers to correction of academic deficits such as problems in reading.

residential or boarding school School established for visually or hearing impaired, emotionally disturbed, or mentally retarded students because local school districts did not offer the needed services; usually provides 24-hour care and treatment.

residual hearing Individual's remaining hearing after some hearing loss.

resource room teacher Teacher who provides supplemental or remedial instruction (usually daily) to a child enrolled in a regular classroom. The assistance is regularly scheduled in a room that has been specifically designated for that purpose.

responsibility-oriented classroom Classroom in which student is responsible for his own behavior, academic success, and his failure. He cannot blame his environment, parents, or peers for his own behavior; he has the ability to choose. The classroom is neither a teacher-dominated nor a student-controlled room but rather is a joint effort to learn, relate, and experience. One advocate is William Glasser.

rheumatoid arthritis Systemic disease characterized by inflammation of the joints and a broad spectrum of other manifestations involving destruction of the joints with resultant deformity.

rubella German measles.

scoliosis Abnormal lateral curvature of the spine (C curve).

seizures Excessive electrical discharges released in some nerve cells of the brain resulting in loss of control over muscles, consciousness, senses, and thoughts.

sensorineural hearing loss Hearing loss associated with damage to the sensory end-organ or a disfunction of the auditory nerve.

sighted-guide technique Technique in which a visually impaired individual grasps a sighted person's arm just above the elbow, enabling him to "read" any movement of the guide's body.

Snellen chart Chart consisting of letters, numbers, or symbols of graduated sizes to be read at a distance of 20 feet to determine field visual acuity. A special Snellen chart to be read at a distance of 14 inches may be used to measure near vision.

sociometry A technique used to measure the social structure of a group or class.

spastic cerebral palsy A condition characterized by jerky or explosive motions when a child initiates a voluntary movement.

special education A subsystem of the total educational system for the provision of specialized or adapted programs and services or for assisting others to provide such services for exceptional youth and children.

special educator One who has had specialized training or preparation for teaching the handicapped and who may also work cooperatively with the regular classroom teacher by sharing unique skills and competencies.

speech handicap A disorder of speech that (1) interferes with communication, (2) causes the speaker to be maladjusted, or (3) calls undue attention to the speech as opposed to what is said.

speechreading A highly important skill for the hearing impared in which the individual learns to observe lip movement, facial gestures, body gestures, and other environmental clues, to supplement whatever degree of residual hearing is present. The term *speechreading* has, for the most part, replaced the term *lipreading,* which emphasized only one part of this skill.

spina bifida Serious birth defect in which the bones of the spine fail to close during the 12th week of fetal development resulting in a cyst or sac in the lower back that is generally surgically treated during the child's first 24–48 hours of life. Varying degrees of paralysis in the lower extremities are generally observed.

tactile Pertaining to the sense of touch.

task analysis Breaking a skill into smaller parts.

taxonomy A classification system.

teacher-move analysis Tool that evaluates interaction between teacher and student by placing teacher behavior into eight categories, called teacher *moves.*

tinnitus Hearing noises within the head.

total communication Total-language approach for the hearing impaired in which there is equal emphasis on speech, auditory training, and a system of visual communication.

trailing To follow lightly over a straight surface with back of fingertips to locate specific objects or to get a parallel line of direction.

visual acuity Measured ability to see.

visual-auditory-kinesthetic-tactile (VAKT) approach Multisensory approach to teaching reading. Designed by Grace Fernald to assist children with severe reading disabilities.

voice problems Disorders of pitch, intensity, quality, or flexibility of the voice.

REFERENCES

Abeson, A., & Zettel, J. (1977). The end of the quiet revolution: The education for all handicapped children act of 1975. *Exceptional Children, 44,* 114–127.

Affleck, J. O., Lowenbraun, S., & Archer, A. (1980). *Teaching the mildly handicapped in the regular classroom* (2d ed.). Columbus, OH: Merrill.

Alberto, P. A., & Troutman, A. C. (1986). *Applied behavior analysis for teachers* (2d ed.). Columbus, OH: Merrill.

Alcorn, P. (1986). *Social issues in technology: A format for investigation.* Englewood Cliffs, NJ: Prentice-Hall.

Allen, V. L. (1976). The helping relationship and socialization of children: Some perspectives on tutoring. In V. L. Allen (Ed.), *Children as teachers: Theory and research on tutoring.* New York: Academic.

Alley, G., & Deshler, D. (1979). *Teaching the learning disabled adolescent: Strategies and methods.* Denver: Love.

Alvino, J., McDonnel, R., & Richert, S. (1981). National survey of identification practices in gifted and talented education. *Exceptional Children, 48,* 124–132.

American Speech-Language-Hearing Association (ASHA), Committee on Language. (1983). *Definition of language.* ASHA, 25, 44.

Anastasi, A. (1982). *Psychological testing* (5th ed.). New York: Macmillan.

Anthony, D. (1971). *Seeing essential English.* Anaheim, CA: Anaheim School District.

Apter, S. (1982). *Troubled children/troubled systems.* New York: Pergamon.

Aronson, E. (1978). *The jigsaw classroom.* Beverly Hills, CA: Sage.

Asher, S. R., & Hymel, S. (1981). Children's social competence in peer relations. In J. D. Wine & M. D. Syme (Eds.), *Sociometric and behavioral assessment.* New York: Guilford.

Asher, S. R., Oden, S. L., & Gottman, J. M. (1981). Children's friendships in school settings. In L. G. Katz (Ed.), *Current topics in early childhood education* (Vol. 1). Norwood, NJ: Albex.

Asher, S. R., & Taylor, A. R. (1982). Social outcomes of mainstreaming: Sociometric assessment and beyond. In Phillip Strain, *Social development of exceptional children.* Rockville: Aspen.

Ballard, J., & Zettel, J. (1977). Public Law 94-142 and section 504: What they say about rights and protections. *Exceptional Children, 44,* 177–185.

Barkley, R. (1981). *Hyperactive children: A handbook for diagnosis and treatment.* New York: Guilford.

Barraga, N. (1983). *Visual handicaps and learning* (Rev. ed.). Austin, TX: Exceptional Resources.

Beez, W. (1970). Influence of biased psychological reports on teacher behavior and pupil performance. In M. Miles & W. Charters, Jr. (Eds.), *Learning and social settings: New readings in the social psychology of education.* Boston: Allyn & Bacon.

Beez, W. V. (1972). Influence of biased psychological reports on teacher behavior and pupil performance. In A. Morrison & D. McIntyre (Eds.), *The social psychology of teaching.* Baltimore, MD: Penguin Books.

Behrman, M. (1984). *Handbook of microcomputers in special education.* San Diego, CA: College-Hill.

Bennett, R. (1982). Applications of microcomputer technology to special education. *Exceptional Children, 49,* 106–113.

Berko Gleason, J. B. (1985). *The development of language.* Columbus, OH: Merrill.

Bernstein, D. K., & Tiegerman, E. (1985). *Language and communication disorders in children.* Columbus, OH: Merrill.

Betts, G. (1985). *Autonomous learner model for the gifted and talented.* Greeley, CO: Autonomous Learning Publications and Specialists.

Betts, G., & Knapp, J. (1981). Autonomous learning and the gifted: A secondary model. In *Secondary programs for the gifted/talented.* Ventura, CA: National/State Leadership Training Institute on the Gifted and Talented.

Bigge, I. L. (1982). *Teaching individuals with physical and multiple disabilities* (2d ed.). Columbus, OH: Merrill.

Bloom, B. (Ed.). (1956). *Taxonomy of educational objectives: The classification of educational goals: Handbook 1: Cognitive domain.* New York: McKay.

Bornstein, H. (1974). Signed English: A manual approach to English language development. *Journal of Speech and Hearing Disorders, 3,* 330–343.

Bowers, E., and Lambert, N. (1976). In-school screening of children with emotional handicaps, in N. Long, W. Morse, and R. Neuman (Eds.), *Conflict in the classroom: The education of emotionally disturbed children.* Belmont, CA: Wadsworth.

Brolin, D. (Ed.). (1978). *Life-centered career education: A competency-based approach.* Reston, VA: Council for Exceptional Children.

Brolin, D. (1982). Life-centered career education for exceptional children. *Focus on Exceptional Children, 14*(7), 1–15.

Brophy, J. E. (1983). Expectations: An update. *Journal of Educational Psychology, 75,* 631–661.

Brophy, J., & Good, T. (1974). *Teacher-student relationships—causes and consequences.* New York: Holt, Rinehart & Winston.

Brown, G., McDowell, R., and Smith, J. (Eds). (1981). *Educating adolescents with behavioral disorders.* Columbus, OH: Merrill.

Brown, L. L., & Hammil, D. (1983). *Behavior Rating Profile.* Austin, TX: Pro-Ed.

Brown, N. (1982). CAMEO: Computer-assisted management of educational objectives. *Exceptional Children, 49,* 151–153.

Bruininks, R., Rynders, J., & Gross, H. (1974). Social acceptance of mildly retarded pupils in resource rooms and regular classes. *American Journal of Mental Deficiency, 78,* 377–383.

Bryan, T. (1974). Peer popularity of learning disabled children. *Journal of Learning Disabilities, 7,* 621–625.

Buell, C. (1950). Motor performance of visually handicapped children. Unpublished doctoral dissertation, University of California, Berkeley.

Burks, H. F. (1977). *Burks Behavior Rating Scales.* Los Angeles: Western Psychological Service.

Canter, L., & Canter, M. (1976). *Assertive discipline: A take-charge approach for today's educator.* Seal Beach, CA: Canter & Associates.

Carbo, M. (1983). Research in reading and learning style: Implications for exceptional children. *Exceptional Children, 49,* 486–494.

Cartledge, G., & Milburn, J. F. (1986). *Teaching social skills to children* (2d ed.). New York: Pergamon.

Cartwright, G. P., Cartwright, C. A., & Ward, M. E. (1984). *Educating special learners.* Belmont, CA: Wadsworth.

Charles, C. M. (1981). *Individualizing instruction.* St. Louis: C. V. Mosby.

Chinn, P., Drew, C., & Logan, D. (1979). *Mental retardation: A life cycle approach.* St. Louis: C. V. Mosby.

Clark, B. (1979). *Growing up gifted.* Columbus, OH: Merrill.

Clark, B. (1983). *Growing up gifted* (2d ed.). Columbus, OH: Merrill.

Cleary, M. E. (1976). Helping children understand the child with special needs. *Children Today, 5,* 24–31.

Coleman, M. C., & Gilliam, J. E. (1983). Disturbing behaviors in the classroom: A survey of teacher attitudes. *Journal of Special Education, 17,* 121–129.

Council for Exceptional Children. (1978). *Position paper on career education.* Reston, VA: author.

Cummins, J. (1984). *Bilingualism and special education: Issues in assessment and pedagogy.* San Diego, CA: College-Hill.

Davis, G., & Rimm, S. (1985). *Education of the gifted and talented.* Englewood Cliffs, NJ: Prentice-Hall.

Dehouske, E. (1982). Story writing as a problem-solving vehicle. *Teaching Exceptional Children, 1*(1), 11–17.

Delisle, J. R., Reis, S. M., & Gubbins, E. J. (1981). The revolving door identification and programming model. *Exceptional Children, 48,* 152–156.

Delquadri, J., Greenwood, C., Whorton, D., Carta, J., & Hall, R. (1986). Classwide peer tutoring. *Exceptional Children, 52,* 535–542.

DeRuiter, J., & Wansart, W. (1982). *Psychology of learning disabilities.* Rockville, MD: Aspen.

Deshler, D. (1983). Intervening with learning disabled adolescents: A learning strategies perspective. Presented at annual Kephart Memorial Symposium, Aspen, CO.

Deshler, D., & Schumaker, J. (1986). Learning strategies: An instructional alternative for low-achieving adolescents. *Exceptional Children, 52,* 583–590.

DeVries, D. L., & Slavin, R. E. (1978). Team games tournament: A research review. *Journal of Research and Development in Education, 12,* 28–38.

Donaldson, J. (1980). Changing attitudes toward handicapped persons: A review and analysis of research. *Exceptional Children, 46,* 504–512.

Dreikurs, R., & Cassel, P. (1972). *Discipline without tears.* New York: Hawthorn Books.

Dreikurs, R., & Saltz, U. (1964). *Children: The challenge.* New York: Hawthorn Books.

Dunn, R. (1983). Learning style and its relation to exceptionality at both ends of the spectrum. *Exceptional Children, 49,* 496–506.

Dunn, R., & Dunn, K. (1978). *Teaching students through their individual learning styles.* Reston, VA: Reston.

Dunn, R., & Price, G. (1980). The learning style characteristics of gifted students. *Gifted Child Quarterly, 24*(1), 33–36.

Dusek, J. B. (1985). *Teacher expectancies.* Hillsdale, NJ: Lawrence Erlbaum.

Dusek, J. B., & Joseph, G. (1983). The basis of teacher expectation: A meta-analysis. *Journal of Educational Psychology, 75,* 326–346.

Dworkin, N. (1979). Changing teachers' negative expectations. *Academic Therapy, 14,* 517–530.

Ehly, S. W., & Larsen, S. C. (1980). *Peer tutoring for individualized instruction.* Boston: Allyn & Bacon.

Epstein, L. (1978). The effects of intraclass peer tutoring on the vocabulary development of learning disabled children. *Journal of Learning Disabilities, 11,* 518–524.

Erickson, M. (1987). *Behavior disorders of children and adolescents.* Englewood Cliffs, NJ: Prentice-Hall.

Esposito, B., & Reed, T. (1986). The effects of contact with handicapped persons on young children's attitudes. *Exceptional Children, 53,* 224–229.

Faye, E. (1976). *Clinical low vision.* Boston: Little, Brown.

Fernald, G. (1943). *Remedial techniques in basic school subjects.* New York: McGraw-Hill.

Fink, A., & Semmel, M. (1971). *Indiana behavior management system 2.* Bloomington, IN: Center for Innovation in Teaching the Handicapped.

Flanagan, J. (1960). *Test of general ability: Technical report.* Chicago: Science Research Associates.

Flanders, N. (1965). *Teacher influences, pupil attitudes, and achievement.* Washington: U.S. Department of Health, Education and Welfare, Office of Education.

Foster, G., Algozzine, B., & Ysseldyke, T. (1980). Classroom teacher and teacher-in-training susceptibility to stereotypical bias. *Personnel and Guidance Journal, 59,* 27–30.

Gallagher, J. (1986). Learning disabilities and special education: A critique. *Journal of Learning Disabilities, 19,* 595–601.

Gallagher, J. J. (1975). *Teaching the gifted child.* Boston: Allyn & Bacon.

Gallagher, J., Weiss, P., Oglesby, K., & Thomas, T. (1983). *The status of gifted/talented education: United States survey needs, practices, and policies.* Los Angeles: National/State Leadership Training Institute on the Gifted and Talented.

Galloway, C. (1968). Nonverbal communication. *Theory into Practice, 7,* 172–175.

Gearheart, B. (1974). *Organization and administration of educational programs for exceptional children.* Springfield, IL: Charles C. Thomas.

Gearheart, B. (1985). *Learning disabilities: Educational strategies* (4th ed.). Columbus, OH: Merrill.

Gearheart, B. R., & Litton, F. (1979). *The trainable retarded: A foundations approach* (2d ed.). St. Louis: C. V. Mosby.

Getzels, J. W., & Jackson, P. W. (1962). *Creativity and intelligence.* New York: John Wiley & Sons.

Glasser, W. (1965). *Reality therapy.* New York: Harper & Row.

Goldstein, H., Moss, J., & Jordan, L. (1965). *The efficacy of special class training on the development of mentally retarded children* (U.S. Office of Education Cooperative Project No. 619). Urbana, IL: University of Illinois.

Goldstein, A., Sprafkin, R., Gershaw, N., & Klein, P. (1980). *Skillstreaming the adolescent: A structured learning approach to teaching prosocial skills.* Champaign, IL: Research.

Good, T. (1970). Which pupils do teachers call on? *Elementary School Journal, 70,* 190–198.

Goodman, H., Gottlieb, J., & Harrison, R. (1972). Social acceptance of EMRs integrated into a nongraded elementary school. *American Journal of Mental Deficiency, 70,* 412–417.

Gottlieb, J., & Budoff, A. (1973). Social acceptability of retarded children in nongraded schools differing in architecture. *American Journal of Mental Deficiency, 78,* 15–19.

Gottlieb, J., Cohen, L., Goldstein, L. (1974). Social contact and personal adjustments as variables relating to attitudes toward educable mentally retarded children. *Training School Bulletin, 71,* 136–148.

Graden, J., Casey, A., and Christenson, S. (1985). Implementing a prereferral intervention system: Part 1. The model. *Exceptional Children, 51,* 377–384.

Gresham, F. M. (1982). Misguided mainstreaming: The case for social skills training with handicapped children. *Exceptional Children, 48,* 422–433.

Gronberg, G. (1983). Attitude responses of nonhandicapped elementary students to specific information and contact with the handicapped. Unpublished doctoral dissertation, University of Northern Colorado.

Grossman, H. (1983). *Classification in mental retardation.* Washington: American Association on Mental Deficiency.

Grossman, H. (Ed.) (1977). *Manual on terminology and classification in mental retardation.* Washington: American Association on Mental Deficiency.

Grossman, H. (Ed.). (1973). *Manual on terminology and classification in mental retardation.* Washington: American Association on Mental Deficiency.

Guilford, J. P. (1959). Three faces of intellect. *American Psychologist, 14,* 469–479.

Gustason, G., Pfetzing, D., Zawolkow, E., & Norris, C. (1972). *Signing exact English.* Rossmore, CA: Modern Science.

Guttman, J., & Bar-Tai, D. (1982). Stereotypic perceptions of teachers. *American Educational Research Journal, 19,* 519–528.

Hagen, D. (1984). *Microcomputer resource book for special education.* Reston, VA: Reston.

Haisley, F. B., Christine, A. T., & Andrews, J. (1981). Peers as tutors in mainstream: Trained "teachers" of handicapped adolescents. *Journal of Learning Disabilities, 14,* 224–226.

Hallahan, D., & Kauffman, J. (1978). *Exceptional children: Introduction to special education.* Englewood Cliffs, NJ: Prentice-Hall.

Hallahan, D., & Kauffman, J. (1982). *Exceptional children: Introduction to special education* (2d ed.). Englewood Cliffs, NJ: Prentice-Hall.

Halperin, M. (1979). *Helping maltreated children:*

School and community involvement. St. Louis: C. V. Mosby.

Hanson, V. (1983). Juvenile rheumatoid arthritis. In J. Umbreit (Ed.), *Physical disabilities and health impairments* (pp. 240–249). Columbus, OH: Merrill.

Harris, J., & Aldridge, J. (1983). Three for me is better than two for you. *Academic Therapy, 18,* 361–365.

Harris, M. J., & Rosenthal, R. (1985). Mediation of interpersonal expectancy effects: Thirty-one meta-analyses. *Psychological Bulletin, 97,* 363–386.

Hatfield, E. M. (1975). Why are they blind? *Sight Saving Review, 45*(1), 3–22.

Healey, W. (1974). *Standards and guidelines for comprehensive language, speech, and hearing programs in the schools.* Washington: American Speech & Hearing Association.

Hersh, R. H., & Walker, H. M. (1983). Great expectations: Making schools effective for all students. *Policy Studies Review, 2,* 147–188.

Homme, L. (1970). *How to use contingency contracting in the classroom.* Champaign, IL: Research.

House Ear Institute. (1985). *So all may hear.* Los Angeles: author.

Huntze, S. (1984). *Council for Children with Behavioral Disorders position paper.* Adopted November 14, 1984. Personal communication with Sharon Huntze.

Iano, R., Ayers, D., Heller, H., McGettigan, J., & Walker, V. (1974). Sociometric status or retarded children in an integrative program. *Exceptional Children, 40,* 267–271.

Idol-Maestas, L. (1981). A teacher training model: The resource/consulting teacher. *Behavioral Disorders, 6,* 108–121.

Inhelder, B. (1968). *The Diagnosis of Reading in the Mentally Retarded.* New York: John Day.

Irwin, R. B. (1955). *As I saw it.* New York: American Foundation for the Blind.

Itard, J. M. G. (1962). *The wild boy of Aveyron.* New York: Appleton-Century-Crofts.

Jackson, G., & Cosca, G. (1974). The inequality of educational opportunity in the Southwest: An observational study of ethnically mixed class-rooms. *American Educational Research Journal, 11,* 219–229.

Jackson, N. F., Jackson, D. A., & Monroe, C. (1983). *Getting along with others—teaching social effectiveness to children.* Champaign, IL: Research.

Johnson, A. (1981). The etiology of hyperactivity. *Exceptional Children, 47,* 348–354.

Johnson, D. W., & Johnson, R. T. (1975). *Learning together and alone; Cooperative, competitive, or individualized.* Englewood Cliffs, NJ: Prentice-Hall.

Johnson, D. W., & Johnson, R. T. (1978). Mainstreaming: Will handicapped students be liked, rejected, or ignored? *Instructor, 87,* 152–154.

Johnson, D. W., Johnson, R. T., Nelson, D., & Read, S. (1978). *Mainstreaming: Development of positive interdependence between handicapped and nonhandicapped students.* Minneapolis: University of Minnesota, National Support System.

Johnson, D., & Myklebust, H. (1967). *Learning disabilities: Educational principles and practices.* New York: Grune & Stratton.

Jones, N. (1986). The education for all handicapped children act: Coverage for children with acquired immune deficiency syndrome (AIDS). *Journal of Law and Education, 15,* 195–206.

Jones, V. (1980). *Adolescents with behavior problems: Strategies for teaching, counseling, and parent involvement.* Boston: Allyn & Bacon.

Jose, J., & Cody, J. (1971). Teacher-pupil interaction as it relates to attempted changes in teacher expectancy of academic ability and achievement. *American Educational Research Journal, 8,* 39–49.

Kanner, L. (1964). *A history of the care and study of the mentally retarded.* Springfield, IL: Charles C. Thomas.

Kauffman, J. M. (1977). *Characteristics of children's behavior disorders.* Columbus, OH: Merrill.

Kauffman, J. M. (1985). *Characteristics of children's behavior disorders* (3d ed.). Columbus, OH: Merrill.

Kester, S., & Letchworth, G. (1972). Communication of teacher expectations and their effects on achievement and attitudes of secondary school students. *Journal of Educational Research, 66,* 51–55.

Khatena, J. (1982). *Educational psychology of the gifted.* New York: John Wiley & Sons.

Kirk, S., & Gallagher, J. (1986). *Educating exceptional children.* Boston: Houghton Mifflin.

Kleinberg, S. (1982). *Education of the chronically ill child.* Rockville, MD: Aspen Systems.

Kokaska, C., & Brolin, D. (1985). *Career education for handicapped individuals* (2d ed.). Columbus, OH: Merrill.

Kolstoe, O. & Frey, R. (1965). *A high school work-study program for the mentally retarded.* Carbondale, IL: Southern Illinois University Press.

Kraemer, M. J., & Bierman, C. W. (1983). Asthma. In J. Umbreit (Ed.), *Physical disabilities and health impairments* (pp. 159–166). Columbus, OH: Merrill.

Kretschmer, R. R., & Kretschmer, L. N. (1978). *Language development and intervention with the hearing impaired.* Baltimore: University Park.

Lambert, N., Windmiller, M., Tharinger, D., and Cole, L. (1981). *AAMD-ABS school edition.* Washington: American Association on Mental Deficiency.

Leacock, E. (1969). *Teaching and learning in city schools.* New York: Basic Books.

Levine, J. (1986, Nov. 3). The toughest virus of all. *Time,* 76–78.

Levine, J. M., & Wang, M. C. (1983). *Teacher and student perceptions: Implications for learning.* Hillsdale, NJ: Lawrence Erlbaum.

Lewis, B. L., & Doorlag, D. (1987). *Teaching special students in the mainstream* (2d ed.). Columbus, OH: Merrill.

Long, N., & Fagen, S.(1981). Therapeutic management: A psychoeducational approach. In G. Brown, R. McDowell, & J. Smith (Eds.), *Educating adolescents with behavior disorders.* Columbus, OH: Merrill.

MacMillan, D., & Borthwick, S. (1980). The new educable mentally retarded population: Can they be mainstreamed? *Mental Retardation, 18*(4), 155–158.

Mangos, J. A. (1983). Cystic fibrosis. In J. Umbreit (Ed.), *Physical disabilities and health impairments* (pp. 206–213). Columbus, OH: Merrill.

Marland, S. (1972). *Education of the gifted and talented: Report to the Congress of the United States by the U.S. Commissioner of Education.* Washington, DC: U.S. Government Printing Office.

Marsh, G., Gearheart, C., & Gearheart, B. (1978). *The learning disabled adolescent: Program alternatives in the secondary school.* St. Louis: C. V. Mosby.

Marsh, G., Price, B. J., & Smith, T. E. (1983). *Teaching mildly handicapped children: Methods and materials.* St. Louis: C. V. Mosby.

McCandless, B. (1973). *Children and youth: Behavior and development.* New York: Dryden.

McCartney, B. (1984). Education for the mainstream. *The Volta Review, 86*(5), 41–52.

McCormick, L. P. (1986). Keeping up with language trends. *Teaching Exceptional Children, 18*(2), 123–129.

McDaniel, T. (1986). A primer on classroom discipline: Principles old and new. *Phi Delta Kappan, 68,* 63–67.

McDowell, R. (1981). Adolescence. In G. Brown, R. McDowell, & J. Smith (Eds.), *Educating adolescents with behavioral disorders.* Columbus, OH: Merrill.

McDowell, R., Adamson, G., & Wood, F. (1982). *Teaching emotionally disturbed children.* Boston: Little, Brown.

McLoughlin, J. A., & Lewis, R. B. (1986). *Assessing special students* (2d ed.). Columbus, OH: Merrill.

Meichenbaum, D. (1983). Teaching thinking: A cognitive behavioral approach. In *Interdisciplinary Voices in Learning Disabilities and Remedial Education.* Austin, TX: Pro-ed.

Meichenbaum, D., & Goodman, J. (1971). Training impulsive children to talk to themselves: A means of developing self-control. *Journal of Abnormal Psychology, 77,* 115–126.

Mendels, G., & Flanders, J. (1973). Teacher expectations and pupil performance. *American Educational Research Journal, 10,* 203–212.

Mercer, C., & Mercer, A. (1985). *Teaching students with learning problems* (2d ed.). Columbus, OH: Merrill.

Mercer, C., & Payne, J. (1975). Programs and services. In J. Kauffman & J. Payne (Eds.), *Mental retardation: Introduction and personal perspectives.* Columbus, OH: Merrill.

Milburn, J., & Cartledge, G. (1976). *Build your own*

social skills curriculum. Unpublished manuscript, Cleveland State University.

Minner, S. (1982). Expectations of vocational teachers for handicapped students. *Exceptional Children, 48,* 451–453.

Morrison, A., & McIntyre, D. (1969). *Teachers and teaching.* Baltimore: Penguin Books.

Morsink, C. (1984). *Teaching special needs students in regular classrooms.* Boston: Little, Brown.

Morsink, C., Soar, R., Soar, R., & Thomas, R. (1986). Research on teaching: Opening the door to special education classrooms. *Exceptional Children, 53,* 32–40.

Murray, H. A. (1938). *Thematic Apperception Test.* Cambridge: Harvard University Press.

National Education Association. (1979). Teacher opinion poll. *Today's Education, 68,* 10.

National Education Association. (1986). Recommended guidelines for dealing with AIDS in the schools. *Journal of School Health, 56,* 129–130.

Necco, E., Wilson, C., & Scheidemantal, J. (1982). Affective learning through drama. *Teaching Exceptional Children, 15*(1), 22–25.

Nihira, K., Foster, R., Shellhaas, M., & Leland, H. (1974). *AAMD adaptive behavior scale,* (rev. ed.). Washington, DC: American Association on Mental Deficiency.

Office of Resources for the Disabled. (1982). *Guidelines for interpreting for the hearing impaired.* Greeley, CO: University of Northern Colorado.

Owens, R. E. (1984). *Language development.* Columbus, OH: Merrill.

Panda, K., & Bartel, N. (1972). Teachers' perception of exceptional children. *Journal of Special Education, 6,* 49–58.

Parents' Campaign for Handicapped Children and Youth (1978, December). Editorial statement on the "least restrictive alternative setting." *Closer Look,* p. 5.

Patton, J., Payne, J., and Beirne-Smith, M. (1986). *Mental retardation* (2nd ed.). Columbus, OH: Merrill.

Payne, J., Polloway, E., Smith, J., & Payne, R. (1981). *Strategies for teaching the mentally retarded* (2d ed.). Columbus, OH: Merrill.

Pfeiffer, S. (1982). The superiority of team decision making. *Exceptional Children, 49,* 68–69.

Polloway, E., Payne, J., Patton, J., & Payne, R. (1985). *Strategies for teaching retarded and special needs learners* (3d ed.). Columbus, OH: Merrill.

Prillaman, D. (1981). Acceptance of learning disabled students in the mainstream environment: A failure to replicate. *Journal of Learning Disabilities, 14,* 344–346.

Pritchard, D. G. (1963). *Education and the handicapped: 1760–1960.* London: Routledge & Kegan Paul.

Public Law 94-142 (Education of the Handicapped Act of 1975). *Federal Register, 42,* 163 (August 23, 1977).

Purpura, D., Gallagher, J., & Tjossem, T. (Eds.). (1981). *Mental retardation: An evaluation and assessment of the state of the science.* Bethesda, MD: National Institute of Child Health and Human Development, U.S. Department of Health and Human Services.

Quigley, S., & Paul, P. (1984). *Language and Deafness.* San Diego, CA: College-Hill.

Reid, D., & Hreska, W. (1981). *A cognitive approach to learning disabilities.* New York: McGraw-Hill.

Reis, S. M., & Renzulli, J. S. (1982). A case for a broadened conception of giftedness. *Phi Delta Kappan, 63,* 619–620.

Renzulli, J., Reis, S., and Smith, L. (1981). *The revolving door identification model.* Mansfield, CT: Creative Learning.

Renzulli, J., & Smith, L. (1980). An alternative approach to identifying and programming for gifted and talented students. *Gifted/Creative/Talented, 15,* 4–11.

Reynolds, M. C., & Birch, J. W. (1982). *Teaching exceptional children in all America's schools* (rev. ed.). Reston, VA: Council for Exceptional Children.

Rich, H. L. (1982). *Disturbed students.* Baltimore: University Park.

Richards, W. (1986). Allergy, asthma, and school problems. *Journal of School Heatlh, 56,* 151–152.

Ritter, C. (1986). *Charity Forrester Ritter: Tomor-*

row may bring the answer. Los Angeles: House Ear Institute.

Rorschach, H. (1942). *Rorschach Inkblot Test.* New York: Grune & Stratton.

Rosenthal, R., & Jacobson, L. (1968). *Pygmalion in the classroom.* New York: Holt, Rinehart & Winston.

Rosenthal, R., & Rubin, D. G. (1978). Interpersonal expectancy efforts: The first 345 studies. *Behavioral & Brain Science, 3,* 377–415.

Rubovits, P., & Maehr (1971). Pygmalion analyzed: Toward an explanation of the Rosenthal-Jacobson findings. *Journal of Personality and Social Psychology, 19,* 197–203.

Salend, S. J. (1984). Factors contributing to the development of successful mainstreaming programs. *Exceptional Children, 50,* 409–416.

Salend, S. J., & Johns, J. (1983). Changing teacher commitment to mainstreaming. *Teaching Exceptional Children, 15,* 82–85.

Samuels, S. J. (1981). Characteristics of exemplary reading programs. In J. Guthrie (Ed.), *Comprehension and teaching: Reviews of research* (pp. 33–49). Newark, DE: International Reading Association.

Sato, I. (1986). NSLTIGT curriculum development center to address critical curricular issues. *Quarterly Bulletin, 13*(3), 1–6.

Scheffers, W. L. (1977). Sighted children learn about blindness. *Journal of Visual Impairment and Blindness, 71,* 258–261.

Schlesinger, H. S. (1985). Deafness, mental health, and language. In F. Powell, T. Finitzo-Hieber, S. Friel-Patti, & D. Henderson (Eds.), *Education of the hearing impaired child.* San Diego: College-Hill.

Schloss, P., & Sedlak, R. (1986). *Instructional Methods for Students with Learning and Behavior Problems.* Newton, MA: Allyn & Bacon.

Schumaker, J., Deshler, D., Alley, G., Warner, M., & Denton, P. (1982). Multipass: A learning strategy for improving reading comprehension. *Learning Disability Quarterly, 5,* 295–304.

Schwartz, L. L. (1984). *Exceptional students in the mainstream.* Belmont, CA: Wadsworth.

Semmel, M., Gottlieb, J., & Robinson, N. (1979). Mainstreaming: Perspectives on educating handicapped children in the public schools. In D. Berliner (Ed.), *Review of research in educa-* *tion* (Vol. 7, pp. 126–130). Washington, DC: American Educational Research Association.

Sharon, S., & Sharon, Y. (1976). *Small-group teaching.* Englewood Cliffs, NJ: Educational Technology.

Shea, T., & Bauer, A. (1987). *Teaching children and youth with behavior disorders.* Englewood Cliffs, NJ: Prentice-Hall.

Sheare, J. (1978). The impact of resource programs upon the self-concept and peer acceptance of learning disabled children. *Psychology in the Schools, 15,* 406–412.

Sheinker, J., & Sheinker, A. (1982). *Study strategies: A metacognitive approach: Skimming, note taking, summarizing, outlining* (four handbooks). Rock Springs, WY: White Mountain.

Sheinker, J., & Sheinker, A. (1983). *Study strategies: A metacognitive approach.* Rock Springs, WY: White Mountain.

Siegel, E., & Gold, R. (1982). *Educating the learning disabled.* New York: Macmillan.

Simpson, R. (1981). Further investigation and interpretation of the expectancy effect generated by disability labels. *Diagnostique, 17,* 101–108.

Siperstein, G., Bopp, M., & Bak, J. (1978). Social status of learning disabled children. *Journal of Learning Disabilities, 11,* 98–102.

Slavin, R. E. (1978). Student teams and comparison among equals: Effects on academic performance and student attitudes. *Journal of Educational Psychology, 70,* 532–538.

Slavin, R. E. (1980). Cooperative learning. *Review of Educational Research, 50,* 315–342.

Smith, M. (1980). Meta-analysis of research on teacher expectation. *Evaluation in Education, 4,* 53–55.

Soar, R., Soar, R., & Ragosta, M. (1971). *The Florida climate and control system.* Gainesville, FL: Institute for Development of Human Resources, College of Education, University of Florida.

Sorenson, A. B., & Hallinan, M. (1984). Effects of race on assignment to ability groups. In P. L. Peterson, L. C. Wilkenson, & M. Hallinan (Eds.), *The social context of instruction.* New York: Academic.

Spivak, G., & Swift, M. (1972). *Hahneman High School Behavior Scale.* Philadelphia: Department of Mental Health Sciences, Hahneman Medical College & Hospital.

Stephens, T. (1978). *Social skills in the classroom.* Columbus, OH: Cedars.

Strain, P. S. (1982). *Social development of exceptional children.* Rockville, MD: Aspen.

Taylor, R., Smiley, L., & Ziegler, E. (1983). The effects of labels and assigned attributes on teacher perceptions of academic and social behaviors. *Education and Training of the Mentally Retarded, 18,* 45–51.

Thorndike, R. L., Hagen, E., & Sattler, J. (1986). *Stanford-Binet Intelligence Scale* (3d ed.) Chicago: Riverside.

Torrance, E. P. (1974). *Torrance tests of creative thinking technical manual.* Lexington, MA: Personnel.

Turnbull, H. (1986). *Free appropriate public education: The law and children with disabilities.* Denver: Love.

Tymitz-Wolf, B. L. (1982). Extending the scope of in-service training for mainstreaming effectiveness. *Teacher Education and Special Education, 5,* 17–23.

Unruh, D., Gilliam, J., & Jogi, A. (1982). Developing concept analysis skills. *Directive Teacher, 4*(2), 26–31.

Vargas, J. (1986). Instructional design flaws in computer-assisted instruction. *Phi Delta Kappan, 67,* 738–744.

Vaughn, B. E., & Langlois, J. (1983). Physical attractiveness as a correlate of peer status and social competence in preschool children. *Developmental Psychology, 19,* 516–567.

Vaughn, D., & Asbury, T. (1977). *General opthamology.* Los Altos, CA: Lange Medical.

Walker, H. M. (1983). *Walker Problem Behavior Identification Checklist* (rev. ed.) Los Angeles: Western Psychological Service.

Walker, J. E., & Shea, T. M. (1976). *Behavior modification: A practical approach for educators.* St. Louis: C. V. Mosby.

Wallace, G., & Kauffman, J. (1986). *Teaching stu-dents with learning and behavior problems* (3d ed.). Columbus, OH: Merrill.

Wechsler, D. (1974). *Wechsler Intelligence Scale for Children–Revised.* Cleveland: Psychological Corporation.

Wechsler, H., Suarez, A., & McFadden, M. (1975). Teachers' attitudes toward the education of physically handicapped children: Implications for implementation of Massachusetts Chapter 766. *Journal of Education, 157,* 134–141.

Whitmore, J. (1980). *Giftedness, conflict, and underachievement.* Boston: Allyn & Bacon.

Wilson, K. (1981). Managing the administrative morass of special needs. *Classroom Computer News, 1*(4), 8–9.

Winter, R. J. (1983). Childhood diabetes mellitus. In J. Umbreit (Ed.), *Physical disabilities and health impairments* (pp. 195–205). Columbus, OH: Merrill.

Wong, B., & Jones, W. (1982). Increasing meta-comprehension in learning disabled and normally achieving students through self-questioning training. *Learning Disability Quarterly, 5,* 228–240.

Woodcock, R. W., & Johnson, M. B. (1983). *Woodcock-Johnson Scales of Independent Behavior.* Allen, TX: DLM Teaching Resources.

Ysseldyke, J. E., & Algozzine, B. (1982). *Critical issues in special and remedial education.* Boston: Houghton-Mifflin.

Ysseldyke, J. E., & Algozzine, B. (1984). *Introduction to special education.* Boston: Houghton-Mifflin.

Ysseldyke, J., Algozzine, B., & Allen, D. (1982). Participation of regular education teachers in special education team decision making. *Exceptional Children, 48,* 365–366.

Zilboorg, G., & Henry, G. W. (1941). *A history of medical psychology.* New York: W. W. Norton.

Zirkel, P. A. (Ed.). (1978). *A digest of Supreme Court decisions affecting education.* Bloomington, IN: Phi Delta Kappa.

NAME INDEX

SUBJECT INDEX